European Union Law

Fourth edition edited by
Robert M MacLean LLB (Hons), Dip LP, LLM, Solicitor

HLT Publications

HLT PUBLICATIONS
200 Greyhound Road, London W14 9RY

First Edition 1990
Reprinted 1991
Second Edition 1992
Reprinted 1992
Reprinted 1993
Third Edition 1994
Fourth Edition 1995

ISBN 1 0 7510 0591 6

British Library Cataloguing-in-Publication.

A CIP Catalogue record for this book is available from the British Library.

Printed and bound in Great Britain.

CONTENTS

ACKNOWLEDGEMENTS

The Author and the Publisher wish to thank the University of London LLB (External) and the University of Glasgow for their kind permission to reproduce and publish problems from past examination papers.

Caveat

The answers given are not approved or sanctioned by either the University of London or the University of Glasgow and are entirely our responsibility. They are not intended to be 'model answers', but rather suggested solutions.

These solutions are designed to perform two fundamental purposes, namely:

a) to provide a detailed example of a suggested solution to an examination question; and

b) to assist students with research into the subject of European Community law and to further their understanding and appreciation of the nature of Community law.

Note

Please note that the solutions to this WorkBook incorporate the law as it stood in June 1995. It has not been able to include European Union/Community legislation or cases reported after this date.

INTRODUCTION

This Revision WorkBook has been designed specifically for those undergraduate students studying European Union law, the subject formerly known as European Community law or simply Community law. Before proceeding to discuss the contents of this WorkBook it is best to explain the relationship between these two apparently distinct subjects.

The Treaty on European Union (TEU) created the European Union, the organisation which succeeded the European Community. The European Community is now a part of the European Union along with the European Coal and Steel Community and Euratom. In addition, the TEU has created new areas of competence for the new organisation in fields which were not covered by the Treaties establishing the European Community, the ECSC or Euratom. For example, the TEU conferred on the European Union competence in areas such as foreign policy, security policy, justice and home affairs. The result is that the European Community continues to exist as a component part of the European Union.

The European Community also remains the most significant component of the European Union and, to date, the EC Treaty is the source of the overwhelming proportion of legal principles which can be attributed to the European Union. When the European Union absorbed the EC Treaty, it absorbed not only the terms of the Treaty but also the whole corpus of legal principles that had been generated in the last 35 years of the operation of that organisation. To a certain extent, therefore, Community law is synonymous with the law of the European Union unless referring to the operations of the new organisation in one of its new areas of competence.

In this WorkBook the term 'European Union' is used in Chapters 1 and 2 because these are the main subjects in which the non-EC dimension of the functioning of the organisation is most important. Thereafter, we shall revert to the term 'European Community law' when describing the relevant substantive legal principles, since these originate from the EC Treaty alone and no other sector of the European Union's activities.

Each individual chapter of the text deals with a particular subject matter found in the curricula of most courses dealing with European Union/Community law. At the same time, coverage has not been restricted to any one particular syllabus but has been designed to embrace all the principal topics which are found in university and college examinations on this subject. The text is best used as a supplement to the recommended reading suggested by course organisers of individual programmes.

Each chapter contains an introduction which explains the scope and general contents of the topic covered. This is followed by detailed 'key points' which advise students on the minimum content of materials with which they must be familiar in order to properly understand the subject. Recent cases and relevant materials are included where appropriate.

The most valuable feature of the Revision WorkBook remains the examination questions themselves which direct the attention of the student to the issues most frequently raised in examination papers. Questions have been selected in order to cover the most popular issues raised in examinations. Each question has a skeleton solution followed by a suggested solution. Although students are not expected to produce a skeleton solution in examinations, it is a useful examination technique which assists to ensure a well structured, balanced and logical answer.

This Revision WorkBook has been prepared by university lecturers experienced in teaching this specific syllabus and the solutions are intended to be illustrations of full answers to problems commonly posed by examiners. They are not 'model answers', for at this level there is almost certainly more than one solution to each problem. Nor are the answers written to the exacting time limits of examinations. They are designed to bring the most salient and important points of law to the attention of the student and to illustrate an appropriate methodology in each case.

The opportunity has been taken, where appropriate, to develop themes, suggest alternatives and to set out additional material to an extent not possible by the student in the examination room. This has been done to provide the student with a full answer from which he or she might select the most relevant points while at the same time benefiting from the variety of the questions.

We believe that, in writing full opinions to each question, we can assist you with your study of Community law and can further your understanding and appreciation of the law of the European Community.

In this 1995 edition the final chapter contains the complete June 1994 University of London LLB (External) European Community Law question paper, followed by suggested solutions to each question. Thus the student will have the opportunity to review a recent examination paper in its entirety, and can, if desired, use this chapter as a mock examination – referring to the suggested solutions only after first having attempted the questions.

HOW TO STUDY
EUROPEAN UNION LAW

The recent recognition of the importance of European Union/Community law in many respects reflects the dramatic transformation which the European Community has undergone throughout the course of the last decade. The institutional changes in the structure of the Community, introduced by the Treaty on European Union (the Maastricht Treaty), which at last have been approved by all 15 Member States, have transformed the Community from an essentially economic organisation into a true European Union. Further, the growing volume of legislation emanating from the Community is itself evidence of the increasingly important role of the European Community as a source of legal principles.

European Community law is a sui generis species of law. It has been created by drawing upon the reservoir of legal principles contained in the legal systems of the Member States. For various reasons, the English legal system has not played a significant role in this evolution. Community law has been fashioned under the influence of the civilian legal systems of continental Europe. For that reason, students with common law backgrounds may not readily identify with some of the concepts and institutions of Community law. Students must therefore exercise patience when studying Community law in order to appreciate the unique nature of Community law.

To understand Community law, a basic comprehension of the fundamental elements of this system must be achieved. This requires intensive consideration of subjects such as the relationship between the Community legal order and the legal systems of the Member States, the different forms of Community legislation and the hierarchy which exists between them, the judicial techniques of the European Court and the fundamental principles of Community law which have been developed in order to allow the Community to function on the basis of the rule of law. These matters form the essential core of the Community legal system, and the edifice of Community law has been erected upon them.

Further, it is also important to acquire a comprehension and overall perception of the subject and to understand how particular topics interrelate. European Community law is characterised by an extensive overlapping of topics. Points which are brought up in one particular section of the syllabus continuously recur in other areas of the subject. An overall general knowledge of each individual topic will ultimately facilitate the acquisition of an extensive and detailed knowledge of the complete subject.

Students should also adopt an appropriate methodology towards answering questions of Community law. Legal authority in Community law is derived primarily through the Community Treaties and secondarily through Community legislation, particularly Regulations and Directives, and the decisions of the European Court. The European Court has been responsible for a considerable number of the fundamental principles of the Community, and cases of important legal significance have been cited throughout the text. Familiarity with these precedents is absolutely essential to the study of Community law.

Once the basic skills and methodology have been acquired in approaching problems involving questions of Community law, the task of identifying and applying the relevant legal principles to the issue becomes increasingly simplified. These skills may best be acquired through a study and appreciation of the techniques involved in answering examination questions. The objective of this text is therefore not primarily to provide students with pro forma answers to questions, but to teach them the skills involved in approaching questions which have European legal implications.

REVISION AND EXAMINATION TECHNIQUE

It is not the purpose of this Revision WorkBook to serve as a substitute for attending lectures, studying the recommended readings or attempting take home essay questions. Engaging in such practices would not only be dangerous because individual lecturers stress different areas of the syllabus, but also because they can never lead to a proper appreciation of the subject. A failure to spend time learning the law will inevitably be exposed. Acquiring legal qualifications is only the beginning of a legal career. In a competitive legal environment, those not thoroughly familiar with the law will be less likely to succeed.

Engaging in such practices also has other limitations. They deprive the student of opportunities to clarify points of difficulty and to expand upon difficult matters during the course of the programme. An exchange of ideas is essential for a complete appreciation of the complexities involved in the application of European Community law, and may provide insight into difficulties which might arise in final examinations. This WorkBook is therefore designed to supplement diligence and effort, the combination which most often leads to success.

An individual syllabus should therefore be supplemented by reference to the various relevant chapters in this WorkBook. Familiarity with the principal issues and the types of question which might arise allows students an opportunity to formulate appropriate responses to possible questions arising during the term. In turn, this should encourage the expansion of ideas and alternative proposals for answering questions at the end of the course.

A number of points are relevant to the study and revision of Community law. A proportional relationship may be established between relevancy and final score. Students should therefore avoid commentary and deviation from the terms of the question. As many relevant points as possible should be included in an answer. Vagueness can be avoided by becoming acquainted with the principal concepts and principles in each individual area of the syllabus. For this purpose, the WorkBook emphasises the most important basic issues in the key point sections of the book.

Further, in law relevancy is almost invariably related to authority. The sounder the legal authority adduced in support of a proposition, the greater the cogency of the argument. Frequently, although a student has correctly answered the problem, the answer will not score highly. This may often be attributed to the lack of authority cited to support the argument. Problems are posed not only for the purpose of testing common sense, but also in order to ascertain a candidate's knowledge of the law.

At the same time, methodology is important. This is the style adopted by a candidate for reaching a particular conclusion to a question. Although methodology is often related to organisation, it is best acquired through practice. While this WorkBook is designed to facilitate the acquisition of an appropriate methodology by proposing suggested solutions, there is no substitute for trial and error prior to the examination.

In European Community law, questions fall into two main categories. On the one hand an examiner may pose an 'essay type' question which will specify a particular topic for discussion. Although at first it might appear that such questions allow an almost infinite discretion for answering, in fact the examiner will undoubtedly have a number of basic points in mind which must be covered in a successful answer. Consequently, essay type questions are best attempted on subjects in which the student has acquired a familiarity with the basic concepts.

On the other hand, an examiner may set a 'problem type' question. In such cases, the student is presented with a set of hypothetical facts and instructed to apply the law. Unless suggested to the contrary, the stated facts require no proof and the student should proceed on the basis that these facts are supported by sufficient evidence. The student should refrain from deducing the existence of facts to the contrary unless such an inference is unavoidable.

Obviously, in order to remain relevant, the student must be able to distinguish between relevant and irrelevant facts, and must be able to apply the law to the relevant facts. Again an examiner will require that a number of basic points are covered to score a reasonable mark. In order to attempt such questions, read the facts carefully, ascertain the most important matters, and sketch out the applicable law prior to attempting the problem itself. Organisation will also ultimately result in a higher score and more often than not less time will be spent answering the question.

Where the law on a certain matter is unsettled, the examiner will be attempting to solicit comment on the nature of the controversies which have created this state of affairs. In addition, the examiner may also be looking for an outline of the opposing view. The candidate need not support one or other opinion, but should refer to which side of the argument is legally most plausible.

Questions may also be divided into a number of parts. Most frequently, all the sections will relate to the same topic, if not the same principles behind a specific area of Community law. The problem may be phrased in such a way that the only plausible answer to another part of the question is to answer the first in a certain manner. If a discrepancy does arise between the answer to the first part, and the answer suggested by the language of the later part, most often this will not be fatal if a cogent, reasoned legal argument has been advanced in the answer to the first part. A student may propose alternative solutions to the later part of the question, although most likely this process will be time consuming.

Finally, there is no substitute for proper preparation before entering the examination room. If a student has to ascertain distinctions and differentiations under examination conditions, not only will the answer be confused, but it will also most likely be insufficient. An appreciation of the major concepts, principles and rules of Community law is best acquired before endeavours are made in the examination room.

TABLE OF CASES

TABLE OF COMMUNITY LEGISLATION

Community Regulations

Community Directives

Community Decisions

TABLE OF UNITED KINGDOM LEGISLATION

1 THE ORIGINS AND NATURE OF THE EUROPEAN UNION

1.1   Introduction

1.2   Key points

1.3   Relevant cases

1.4   Relevant materials

1.5   Analysis of questions

1.6   Questions

1.1 Introduction

The European Community originally consisted of three separate, yet closely related, economic organisations each established by independent international agreements. The first Community was the European Coal and Steel Community (ECSC) formed under the Treaty of Paris signed in 1951. This was followed by two more Treaties, signed in Rome in 1957, namely the European Economic Community (EEC) Treaty and the European Atomic Energy (Euratom) Treaty. Of these, the most important is the EEC Treaty (now known as the European Community Treaty) which covers most economic activities other than those regulated under the two other agreements.

The six original Members of the Community – Belgium, France, Germany, Italy, Luxembourg and the Netherlands – have been joined by an additional six Member States. In 1973, membership of the Community was increased by the admission of the United Kingdom, Ireland and Denmark. These three states were followed by Greece in 1981 and Spain and Portugal in 1986. Since 1 January 1995, membership of the Community has been increased to fifteen Member States following the accession of Austria, Finland and Sweden. Negotiations are presently in hand for the admission of a considerable number of other states from both Eastern Europe and the Mediterranean area.

The European Community also significantly evolved in terms of its own internal structure from the embryonic organisation established under the EC Treaty. First, in 1986, the Single European Act was agreed which changed many of the internal institutional features and processes of the Community. Similarly, the Treaty on European Union 1992 (the Maastricht Agreement) has transformed the European Community from a primarily economic organisation into the European Union.

The European Community has not in fact ceased to exist but has now been subsumed within the broader umbrella of the European Union, an organisation created by the Treaty on European Union (TEU). The TEU has a constitutional structure based on three pillars: (a) Pillar 1, which is the EC Treaty as (substantially) amended; (b) Pillar 2, which comprises provisions relating to common foreign policy and security policy; (c) Pillar 3, which contains provisions for co-operation in the fields of justice and home affairs.

Although the European Union now incorporates the European Community, both the EC Treaty itself and the laws established thereunder remain important in the operation of the European Union for two reasons. First, the EC Treaty is one of the three cornerstones of the new European Union. Second, the law of the European Community has developed over a period of more than 35 years, in contrast to the embryonic legal principles being developed under the two other branches of EU competence.

1.2 Key points

a) *The treaties founding the European Community*

   i) The European Coal and Steel Community (ECSC) Treaty

      The ECSC Treaty was signed in Paris on 18 April 1951 and consists of 100 Articles, three annexes and three protocols, together with a convention relating to transitory provisions. This Treaty established the world's first genuine supranational organisation. The purpose of the ECSC Treaty was to establish a common market for coal and steel products.

      The ECSC Treaty required the Member States to abolish import and export duties and charges having equivalent effect, as well as quantitative restrictions, on the movement of coal and steel products. In addition, measures or practices which discriminated between producers, purchasers or consumers on the basis of nationality were prohibited. Restrictions were also placed on the rights of Member States to grant subsidies or aid in order to promote domestic production.

      The Treaty rationalised coal and steel production throughout the six participating states and reduced levels of protectionism in these industrial sectors. The result was a more efficient industry and a significant increase in the gross national products (GNP) of the participating states.

      Since the negotiation of the EC Treaty, the significance of the ECSC Treaty has declined. In fact the ECSC Treaty is due to expire in 2001 and already the European Commission is exploring the best means of bringing the issues regulated by that agreement within the scope of the EC Treaty.

   ii) The European Economic Community (EC) Treaty

      The EC Treaty was signed in Rome on 25 March 1957 and consists of 248 Articles, four annexes, three protocols and an implementing convention on the association of overseas countries and territories with the Community. Article 2 of the Treaty originally identified four objectives for the common market: (1) the promotion of harmonious economic development throughout the Community; (2) continuous and balanced economic expansion among the Member States; (3) the raising of standards of living among the population of the Community; and (4) the development of closer relations among the Member States.

      In order to construct the common market, Article 3 of the Treaty originally instructed the Member States to pursue the following policy goals:

- the elimination, as between Member States, of customs duties and of quantitative restrictions on the import and export of goods, and of all other measures having equivalent effect;
- the establishment of a common customs tariff and a common commercial policy towards third countries;
- the abolition, as between Member States, of obstacles to the free movement of persons, services and capital;
- the adoption of a common agricultural policy;
- the adoption of a common transport policy;
- the creation of a Community competition policy;
- the approximation of the laws of the Member States to the extent required for the proper functioning of the common market;
- the creation of a European Social Fund to improve employment opportunity for workers;
- the establishment of a European Investment Bank to facilitate the economic expansion of the Community; and
- the association of overseas countries and territories in order to increase trade and promote economic development.

The states participating in the Treaty agreed to consolidate their individual economies into one single, enlarged internal market and to simultaneously form one single entity for the purpose of conducting economic relationships with non-participating states. Authority to administer the economic development of the organisation has been delegated to a centralised body with an institutional structure which functions independently from the influence of one or more Member States. The formation of the European Community involved the transfer of a considerable degree of national sovereignty to create a supranational body capable of regulating its economic affairs.

As we shall see later, the Treaty on European Union significantly amends many of these objectives with a view to establishing a European Union based on the EC Treaty, but supplemented by additional obligations contained in new Treaties and Protocols.

iii) The European Atomic Energy (Euratom) Treaty

The Euratom Treaty was also signed in Rome on 25 March 1957, and contains 225 Articles. The purpose of this agreement is to create a specialist market for atomic energy. Euratom is designed to develop nuclear energy, distribute it within the Community and sell the surplus to non-Community states.

Since the objectives of Euratom differ from those of the ECSC Treaty and the EC Treaty, it is no surprise that the goals of Euratom are also different. Among the main goals of Euratom are the following:

- to promote research and to ensure the dissemination of technical information throughout the Community;
- to establish uniform safety standards to protect workers and the general public from atomic hazards;

- to promote investment in the nuclear energy industry;
- to maintain regular and reliable supplies of ores and nuclear fuels; and
- to make certain that nuclear materials are not diverted for aims other than peaceful purposes.

b) *The structure of the European Community*

The EC Treaty seeks to achieve the creation of the common market by pursuing four fundamental principles:

i)   The free movement of the factors of production – goods, labour, services and capital – within the territory of the Community.

ii) The progressive approximation of economic policies among Member States, including the creation of common Community policies in key economic sectors such as agriculture, competition and transport.

iii) The creation of a Common Customs Tariff (CCT) for the regulation and administration of trade between Community and non-Community countries.

iv) The establishment of a Common Commercial Policy (CCP) for the conduct of economic relations between the Community and the rest of the world.

The first two of these principles are matters which fall within the internal competence of the Community, while the second two concern the external competence of the Community.

Again it should be noted that these fundamental principles have been supplemented by others by virtue of the Treaty on European Union.

c) *The Single European Act*

Progress towards the creation of a common market under the EC Treaty was painfully slow. While the Community was reasonably successful in erecting a Common Customs Tariff and in implementing the Common Commercial Policy, by the early 1980s the Community had failed to achieve the transition toward the free movement of factors of production: see the *Commission Report on Completing the Internal Market* COM (85) 310 Final (1985). This failure led to a re-evaluation of the organisational structure and general goals of the Community, culminating in the adoption of the Single European Act in 1986.

The Single European Act was an international agreement among the Member States of the Community and not a statute of the British Parliament. This agreement made a number of significant changes to the Community Treaties including:

i)   The inauguration of the internal market programme designated for completion by 1992: Article 8A EC Treaty.

ii) The introduction of majority voting in the Council of Ministers for the enactment of certain measures: Article 100A EC Treaty.

iii) The creation of the cooperation procedure for the participation of the European Parliament in the Community legislative process: Articles 7(2), 49, 100A(1) EC Treaty.

iv) Recognition of the European Council as a formal organ of the European Community: Article 2 Single European Act.

v) The grant of authority to the Council of Ministers to create a Court of First Instance: Article 168A EC Treaty.

In addition to these changes, the Single European Act also reaffirmed the political objectives of the Community. It reiterated the commitment expressed in the preamble to the EC Treaty to 'lay the foundations of an ever closer union among the peoples of Europe', by stressing the need to strive for 'concrete progress towards European unity'. Cooperation in both economic and monetary policy was added as an express aim of the Community, as was the preservation, protection and improvement of the environment.

Many of these goals and objectives have now been superseded by the amendments made to the EC Treaty by the Treaty on European Union. Hence, for the most part, the changes brought by the Single European Act are now only of historical significance.

d) *The nature of European Community law*

European Community law is a supranational species of law which prevails over the laws of all Member States, including the law of England. As the European Court has explicitly observed, the Community Treaties have created a new legal order which now interacts to form part of the legal systems of all Member States and constitutes a body of principles which their courts and tribunals are bound to apply: *Costa* v *ENEL* [1964] ECR 585.

This new legal order has a number of characteristic features:

i) Community law is a sui generis form of law which evades the traditional classifications made within English law. It transcends the distinction often drawn between public law and private law and also the distinction between civil and criminal law.

ii) Community law not only provides a defence to legal proceedings, but may also furnish grounds for legal action or for interim injunction.

iii) Principles of Community law cannot be categorised into a distinct group of principles in the same way as the law of tort or contract may be in English law. Community law is capable of pervading any branch of national law, public or private.

iv) Community law – whether in the form of Treaty provisions, Community regulations or unimplemented Community directives – prevails over prior and subsequent inconsistent provisions of national law.

e) *The Treaty on European Union 1992 and the future evolution of the Community*

The European Community is presently undergoing a process of transformation from a primarily economic organisation into a true European Union. This transformation is to be brought about the Treaty on European Union signed in February 1992 at Maastricht. The Treaty has now been ratified by all the Member

States and entered into force in October 1993. Austria, Finland and Sweden acceded to the European Union, not only the European Community, and are therefore full members of both.

The Treaty itself consists of a number of titles dealing with different matters:

Title I: Common Provisions – this deals with the general principles behind the new European Union;

Title II: Provisions amending the EC Treaty (Pillar 1);

Title III: Provisions amending the ECSC Treaty;

Title IV: Provisions amending the Euratom Treaty;

Title V: Provisions on a Common Foreign Policy and Security Policy (Pillar 2);

Title VI: Provisions on Cooperation in the Fields of Justice and Home Affairs (Pillar 3); and

Title VII: Final Provisions.

The Treaty also contains a number of supplementary protocols defining or clarifying certain subjects and authorising derogations including:

i) the Protocol on the derogation of the United Kingdom from the obligations established to further monetary union;

ii) the Agreement on Social Policy concluded between the Members of the European Community with the exception of the United Kingdom.

Titles II, V and VI define the organic and most significant competencies of the European Union and the remaining titles contain provisions designed to ensure that the powers conferred on the European Union under the three main pillars are exercised in an integrated fashion within a unified institutional framework. However, in essence, these three Titles together form the heart of the constitution of the European Union.

Pillar 1: The European Community

The Treaty on European Union significantly amends the EC Treaty but, at the same time, the EC Treaty remains the most important pillar of the European Union at the present time. The main amendments made to the pre-1993 EC Treaty may be summarised as follows:

• redefinition of the institutional and organisational structure of the decision-making processes within the organisation;

• the addition of new areas of competence to the spheres of activity previously occupied by the European Community;

• the creation of new principles to regulate the functioning of the European Union including the principle of subsidiarity;

• the introduction of new provisions to regulate economic policy co-operation;

• the incorporation of new competencies in the field of monetary policy co-operation;

• the creation of the concept of the citizenship of the European Union.

Pillar 2: Common Foreign Policy and Security Policy

Title V of the Treaty on European Union creates this competence, but in fact co-operation in this area has been taking place among the Member States for at least the last decade. Quite clearly, this dimension of political co-operation will become increasingly important in the future but at the moment the principles on which the common foreign policy is to be structured remain vague.

Fundamental objectives of the policy are specified such as the safeguarding of common values and fundamental interests, maintaining the independence of the Union, the promotion of democratic and the perpetuation of the rule of law. Nevertheless, a considerable amount of work is still required to fashion the detailed principles on which the evolution of this policy will be based.

Examples of measures taken under the common foreign policy provisions include the decision approving joint action in preparation for the 1995 Conference on the Treaty of Non-Proliferation (Council Decision 94/509/CFSP (1994)) and the decision on the common position of the Member States in support of the Middle East peace process (Council Decision 94/276/CFSP (1994)).

In the area of security, the TEU envisages a strengthened role for the Western European Union (WEU), an organisation created in 1954 but which has largely remained dormant since its conception. This organisation is specifically identified as the 'defence component' of the European Union.

Pillar 3: Justice and Home Affairs

Co-operation on justice and home affairs is an inter-governmental matter which now falls within the competence of the European Union. The fields which are expressly included within the ambit of this policy include: (a) asylum policy; (b) control of external frontiers; (c) immigration policy; (d) drug enforcement policy; (e) international fraud; (f) co-operation between civil and criminal courts among Member States; (g) customs co-operation; and (h) co-operation among the police forces of the Member States.

To a large extent, this competence has also been constructed on past co-operation in these areas, a phenomenon which evolved as a corollary of the original operations of the European Community. Nevertheless, legal measures may be used to implement policy decisions in each of these areas which will strengthen the effectiveness of actions in these fields.

f) *The amended EC Treaty and the competencies established in relation to political, economic, monetary and fiscal affairs*

Over and above its original objectives and purposes, the Treaty on European Union inserted new competencies in the EC Treaty. The most important of these concern the political dimension, economic and monetary policy co-ordination and a series of new objectives to be pursued through the EC Treaty.

i) The political dimension – citizenship of the Union

Article 8 of the EC Treaty, as amended by the Treaty on European Union, establishes the concept of European citizenship.

Every person holding the nationality of a Member State is to be considered henceforth to be a citizen of the European Union. Citizens of the Union are to enjoy the rights conferred by the EC Treaty and are subject to the duties imposed by that agreement.

Article 8A confers every citizen of the Union with the right to move and reside freely within the territory of the Member States, subject to the limitations and conditions laid down in the EC Treaty and by the measures adopted to give effect to this right.

Each citizen of the Union will have the right to vote and to stand as a candidate in the Member States where he or she resides, regardless of the nationality of that person under Article 8B(1). Council Directive 93/109/EC (1993) lays down the arrangements for allowing citizens of the European Union the right to vote and stand as candidates in elections for the European Parliament in the Member State in which they are resident. Similarly, Council Directive 94/80/EC (1994) creates rights to participate in municipal elections for citizens residing in Member States other than their own.

ii) Economic policy coordination

The development of economic policy within the Community is to be based on the principle of an open market economy, with free competition, and a favouring of an efficient allocation of resources: Article 102A EC Treaty.

The Commission is instructed to submit recommendations for the conduct of the economic policies of the Member States to the Council and the Council in turn is required, acting by a qualified majority vote, to draft broad guidelines on the basis of these recommendations.

The Council, acting on the basis of reports submitted by the Commission, has been given responsibly for monitoring economic developments in each Member States as well as ensuring the consistency of the economic policies of Member States with the broad guidelines referred to above: Article 103(3) EC Treaty, as amended.

The amendments made by the Treaty on European Union to the EC Treaty are less than comprehensive as to the principles to be pursued for the purposes of economic policy coordination. The following are the few express principles stated in the amended Treaty:

- Member States shall avoid excessive government deficits: Article 104C(1);
- Member States are required to maintain budgetary disciplines and the Commission is empowered to monitor the development of the budgetary situation and of the stock of government debt in the Member States; and
- Overdraft facilities or any other type of credit facilities with the European Central bank (ECB) or with the central banks of the Member States in favour of government bodies are generally prohibited; Article 104(1).

iii) Monetary policy coordination

The Treaty on European Union continues the three stage programme towards monetary and fiscal union.

Stage 1:

The first stage, outlined by the Single European Act, was increased cooperation among the Member States within the framework of the European Monetary System. Before 1 January 1994, all Member States were to complete phase one of the programme, namely:

• the elimination of all restrictions on the movement of capital between Member States and between Member States and third countries; and

• the adoption of programmes intended to ensure the lasting convergence necessary for the achievement of economic and monetary union.

This rigorous time-table was upset by the turmoil in the foreign exchange markets in July and August 1993. The move to wide bands within the ERM in particular had a devastating impact on the programme. Therefore, this timetable had to be rescheduled.

Stage 2:

For the second stage of the programme, the European Monetary Institute (EMI) was established which held its inaugural session in January 1994. The statute of the EMI is laid down in a Protocol annexed to the EC Treaty.

The main functions of the EMI are:

• to strengthen cooperation between the national central banks;

• to strengthen coordination of the monetary policies of the Member States with the aim of ensuring price stability;

• to monitor the functioning of the European Monetary System; and

• to hold consultations concerning issues falling within the competence of the national central banks and affecting the stability of financial institutions and markets.

The EMI is also instructed to carry out the preparatory work for the third stage of economic and monetary union. By 31 December 1996, at the latest, the EMI is required to specify the framework for the third stage of the programme, including the functioning of the two central institutions of the third and final stage: the European System of Central Banks and the European Central Bank: Article 109F(3) EC Treaty as amended.

Stage 3:

The third stage of the programme is the creation of a central European banking system for the whole of the Community and the adoption of a single currency. It should be observed that in a separate Protocol to the Treaty on European Union, the United Kingdom reserved its right to notify the Council whether or not it intends to move to the third stage of economic and monetary union.

Article 4A of the EC Treaty, as amended, authorises the establishment of a European System of Central Banks (referred to as the 'ESCB') and a European Central Bank (referred to as the 'ECB').

The powers and functions of the ESCB are regulated by a separate Protocol to be attached to the EC Treaty, known as the Statute of the ESCB.

The ESCB is to be composed of the European Central Bank and the national central banks of the Member States. The primary objective of the ESCB is to be the maintenance of price stability and support for the general economic policies of the Community with a view to contributing to the achievement of the objectives of the Community.

There are some institutional provisions regulating the composition and powers of the European Central Bank in the amended EC Treaty. However, its main functions and powers have still to be defined in detail.

iv) The addition of new policy objectives to the EC Treaty

The Treaty on European Union amends Article 3 of the EC Treaty by adding a significant number of new policy objectives to that provision. Broadly speaking these may be grouped into three categories:

- The development of new common Community policies

  This requires the formulation of common policies in the following fields:

  – encouragement for the establishment and development of trans-European transportation networks;
  – the environment;
  – consumer protection;
  – the attainment of a high level of health protection.

- The formulation of an industrial policy

  This policy is intended to achieve three goals:

  – the strengthening of the competitiveness of Community industry;
  – the promotion of research and technological development;
  – the introduction of measures in the sphere of energy, civil protection and tourism.

- The pursuit of a social and cultural policy

  This is a miscellaneous classification involving the following objectives:

  – the strengthening of economic and social cohesion;
  – formulation of a policy in the sphere of development co-operation;
  – a contribution to education and training of quality and to the flowering of the cultures of the Member States.

g) *The Treaty establishing the European Economic Area*

In addition to the Maastricht Treaty, 1992 also saw the negotiation of another important agreement known as the European Economic Area (EEA) Agreement. This agreement was signed by the European Community and the European Free Trade Association (EFTA).

The purpose of this agreement was to extend many of the basic concepts of

Community law into the laws of the EFTA states, which originally included Austria, Iceland, Finland, Norway, Sweden and Switzerland. The agreement applies many principles of the acquis communautaire to these states, including the four freedoms and competition law. Switzerland subsequently withdrew its participation in the scheme and the Agreement came into effect on 1 January 1994, between the European Community and the EFTA states with the exception of Switzerland and Liechtenstein.

Austria, Finland and Sweden have now acceded to the European Community/Union and therefore as of 1 January 1995 the only important members of the EFTA participating in the agreement are Norway and Iceland. The future function of the EFTA and the institutional edifice which was established to give effect to its terms is therefore uncertain.

1.3 Relevant cases

Costa v *ENEL* [1964] ECR 585: The Community Treaties have established a new legal order stemming from the limitation of sovereignty or a transfer of powers from the Member States to the European Community and have thus created a body of law which binds both their nationals and themselves.

Donckerwolke v *Procureur de la Republique* [1975] ECR 1921: Member States are prohibited from enacting measures of national legislation on matters which fall within the competence of the Community by virtue of the Community Treaties unless express authority to do so has been delegated.

EC Commission v *EC Council* [1971] ECR 263: The Member States no longer have the right, acting individually or even collectively, to enter into international obligations with third states if the subject-matter of such agreements falls within the scope of the Community Treaties.

In *Re ILO Convention 170 on Chemicals at Work* [1993] 3 CMLR 800: Judgment of the ECJ declaring that the competence of the European Community extends to all areas where there are common policies or positive measures.

R v *Secretary of State for Foreign and Commonwealth Affairs, ex parte Rees-Mogg* [1994] 1 All ER 457: Decision from the Queen's Bench confirming the consistency of the statute ratifying the Treaty on European Union with the constitution of the United Kingdom.

1.4 Relevant materials

C Closa, 'Concept of Citizenship in the Treaty on European Union' (1992) CML Rev 1137.

D Curtin, 'Constitutional Structure of the Union' (1993) CML Rev 17.

A Toth, 'Principle of Subsidiarity in the Maastricht Treaty' (1992) CML Rev 1079.

S Norberg, 'Agreement on a European Economic Area' (1992) CML Rev 1171.

H Hahn, 'European Central Bank: Key to European Monetary Union or Target?' (1991) CMLR 783.

1.5 Analysis of questions

Questions relating to the origins and nature of the European Community present complex problems since it is often difficult to ascertain the legal principles that the examiner is trying to elicit. Students attempting questions in this field may be penalised if their answer is vague, even although this particular part of the syllabus is relatively undefined. As yet, questions on the nature of the European Union remain relatively scarce and hence the following questions will concentrate on the traditional notion of the European Community as essentially an economic organisation.

1.6 Questions

QUESTION ONE

'The Community constitutes a new legal order in international law, for whose benefit the States have limited their sovereign rights, albeit within limited fields, and the subjects of which comprise not only the Member States but also their nationals.' Case 26/62 *Van Gend en Loos* v *Netherlands*. Discuss.

University of London LLB Examination
(for External Students) European Community Law 1989 Q1

General Comment

A basic question requiring the student to discuss the unique nature of the European Community in the international society.

Skeleton Solution

• Nature of sovereignty; power to legislate.
• Limits on state sovereignty.
• Scope of Community law.
• Rights of individuals under Community law.

Suggested Solution

The European Community is a supranational organisation. It is neither an international organisation nor a federal state. By merging certain aspects of their sovereignty, the Member States have created a unique legal structure. Further, the law which emanates from this structure also has a supranational character. By creating a Community of unlimited duration which has its own institutions, its own personality, its own legal capacity, a capacity to conduct international relations and real legislative powers stemming from the transfer of sovereignty from the Member States to the Community, the Member States have established a sui generis form of law – European Community law.

Membership of the European Community entails a significant transfer of sovereignty from the Member States to the Community. For example, Member States no longer possess sufficient sovereignty to enact legislation on matters which fall within the competence of the Community: *Donckerwolke* v *Procureur de la Republique* (1975). Equally, Member States can no longer enter international agreements with non-Community states if the subject-matter of such agreements relates to issues within the domain of the Community: *EC Commission* v *EC Council (ERTA)* (1971). However, perhaps the greatest limitation on the sovereignty of Member States is that Community law prevails over inconsistent prior or subsequent national legislation: *R* v *Secretary of State, ex parte Factortame (No 1)* (1990).

The European Community legal system is unlike the international legal system. While the jurisdiction of the International Court of Justice is confined to disputes among sovereign states, the EC Treaty expressly recognises the rights of individuals to challenge acts of the Community institutions in the European Court, and national courts are able to refer disputes involving individuals for consideration by the European Court under the preliminary reference procedure established by Article 177 of the EC Treaty. The European Court has also expanded the application of Community law to individuals by recognising the right of individuals to rely upon Community Treaty provisions, regulations and directives. National courts have greatly assisted in this process by acknowledging that the jurisprudence of the European Court requires that Community rights can be vindicated in national courts and tribunals by individuals.

While the force of Community law resides in the transfer of sovereignty by Member States, at the same time the European Court has recognised that the legal systems of the individual Member States form an integral part of the Community legal system: *Costa* v *ENEL* (1964). Both the European Court and the House of Lords have recognised that rights of individuals under the Community Treaties must be protected by national courts: per Lord Bridge of Harwich in *R* v *Secretary of State, ex parte Factortame (No 3)* (1989). Directly enforceable Community rights are part of the legal heritage of every citizen of the Member States of the Community. Such rights are automatically available and must be given unrestricted retroactive effect. The persons entitled to the enjoyment of such rights are also entitled to direct and immediate protection against possible infringement of them. The duty to provide such protection rests with the national courts.

Recognition by national courts of the rights of individuals under Community law allows individuals to rely on such rights in national courts and tribunals. Therefore, Community law can be used as a defence to a civil action or as a ground for initiating a civil action. Thus, in *Brown* v *Secretary of State for Scotland* (1988), the plaintiff founded upon Community law to establish rights in a civil action concerning the right of foreign nationals to seek state support for further education. Conversely, in *Société Technique Minière* v *Maschinenbau Ulm GmbH* (1966), the defendants relied on Article 85(2) of the EC Treaty as a defence to an action for breach of a contract dealing with exclusive sales rights. Equally, Community law can constitute a ground for a criminal prosecution or may be a defence to such an action. For example, in *Anklagemyndigheden* v *Hausen and Son I/S* (1990), the defendant was charged with violations of Community regulations concerning maximum permitted daily driving periods and compulsory rest periods and fined accordingly. Similarly, in *Pubblico Ministero* v *Ratti* (1979), an accused charged with failure to comply with minimum manufacturing standards relied on an unimplemented Council directive to avoid liability.

A number of corollaries stem from the principle that Community law confers rights on individuals which national courts and tribunals must recognise. First, the European Court will not permit the efficacy of Community rights to vary from one Member

State to another. Community rights must be consistent throughout the Community. Second, Member States cannot maintain national measures which would deny access to such rights: *Factortame* case above. Third, Member States cannot remove the power to enforce Community rights from national courts. Finally, where the legislation of a Member State is declared incompatible with Community law, the legislative bodies of the state are under an obligation to amend or repeal the offending legislation.

QUESTION TWO

'The structure of the EC Treaty suggests that the architects of the Community believed that economic integration was the road to political harmony.'

Discuss.

Question prepared by the Author

General Comment

A question requiring a simple narrative answer based on the functions of the European Community.

Skeleton Solution

• The four fundamental principles of the economic integration within the EC.
• The four freedoms; coordination of economic policy; the CCT and the CCP.
• The failure of the Community to achieve these objectives.
• The amendments made by the Maastricht Agreement.

Suggested Solution

As expressed in the EC Treaty, economic integration between the Member States is to be achieved through adherence to four fundamental principles: (a) the free movement of the factors of production – goods, labour, services and capital – within the territory of the common market; (b) the progressive approximation of economic polices among Member States, including the creation of common Community policies in key economic sectors such as agriculture, fisheries and transport; (c) the creation of a common customs tariff (CCT) for the regulation and administration of trade between the Community and non-Community countries; and (d) the establishment of a common commercial policy (CCP) for the conduct of economic relations between the Community and the rest of the world.

The free movement of factors of production is pursued through the elimination and progressive reduction of four forms of discrimination: (1) between domestic products and products originating from other Member countries as regards commercial transactions; (2) between nationals and other Community citizens in the field of employment; (3) between domestic suppliers of services and Community suppliers of similar services; and (4) between domestic capital and similar forms of investment from Member countries. In particular, the elimination of discrimination requires the abolition of customs duties and quantitative restrictions on intra-Community trade. As a consequence of Community membership, Member States may no longer unilaterally impose tariffs or quotas on goods originating within the Community. Equally, laws and administrative practices which discriminate against workers from Community countries seeking employment in other Member States are contrary to Community law, as are national laws and practices which limit the supply of services or investment from Community countries.

Coordination of economic policy in fields such as agriculture, fishing, transport, competition, regional development and social policy is essential to ensure that these freedoms are promoted, and not gradually eroded or undermined by inconsistent national economic policies. The most successful, and also the most controversial, Community economic policy is the Common Agricultural Policy (CAP) which is designed to increase agricultural productivity, to ensure a fair standard of living among the agricultural community and to stabilise agricultural markets within the Community. Although most of the Community policies were originally specified under the Community Treaties, a number of other policies, including the environment protection policy, the regional assistance policy and the energy policy, have been derived as a consequence of the functions of the Community.

The flow of commodities and products into the Community from foreign states is regulated by the common customs tariff which creates a single customs union from the individual customs territories of the Member States. In essence, the common customs tariff is a comprehensive tariff schedule which applies to goods entering the Community from destinations outside the Community. This system ensures that products entering the Community are liable to the same uniform rates of customs duties regardless of the port of entry in the Community. In addition to specifying applicable rates of duty on non-Community goods, the common customs tariff also regulates reliefs from duty, customs valuation and customs classification.

Functioning in conjunction with the common customs tariff, the common commercial policy serves to regulate the external economic policy of the Community towards non-Community states. In discharging its responsibilities under the common commercial policy, the Community enters into international economic agreements to regulate trading relationships between the Community and third states. The Community, through the agency of the European Commission, undertakes multilateral negotiations within the General Agreement on Tariffs and Trade (GATT) and pursues bilateral economic negotiations with individual states. An extensive network of agreements now exists between the Community and third states regulating economic matters. These agreements may be classified according to form and content into four groups: (a) multilateral trade agreements negotiated within the context of the GATT; (b) bilateral free-trade agreements; (c) association agreements, which are usually concluded with states about to become members of the Community; and (d) development and assistance agreements with developing states.

The original draftsmen of the Community Treaties clearly believed that the pursuit of these four fundamental objectives would ultimately achieve the creation of a comprehensive common market among the Member States of the Community. In reality, progress towards this goal has been painfully slow. This lack of progress was generally attributed to the cumbersome decision-making processes within the Community which obstructed the adoption of measures to eradicate barriers and impediments to the free movement of goods, labour, services and capital. These failures led to a re-evaluation of the organisational structure and general goals of the Community, culminating in the adoption of the Single European Act in 1986.

With the negotiation of the Treaty on European Union, it is clear that the EC Treaty, as amended, acted as a catalyst to closer integration among the peoples of Europe. This integration is no longer merely economic, but also political, social and cultural. The Treaty on European Union reflects this development and marked a significant step towards political harmony among the populations of the 15 Member States.

The Treaty itself recognises that it is a 'new stage in the process of European integration' initially started with the EC Treaty. In order to advance this process of integration, a concept of citizenship of the Union has been introduced as have mechanisms to increase economic, monetary and fiscal co-operation among the Member States.

None of these policy objectives could have been obtained without the foundations laid by the process of economic integration started by the EC Treaty and which developed over the last 35 years. Hence, it is true to say that the architects of the EC Treaty were correct in identifying economic integration as the appropriate vehicle for achieving political harmony among the states of Europe.

QUESTION THREE

Discuss and evaluate the system established by the EC Treaty for enforcing the fulfilment by Member States of their Treaty obligations.

University of London LLB Examination
(for External Students) European Community Law 1989 Q4

General Comment

A problem requiring a narrative description of the techniques used for the enforcement of obligations among the Member States of the Community.

Skeleton Solution

• The rule of law in the European Community.
• Actions between states and actions brought by the Commission.
• Effect of decisions of the Court.
• Enforcement mechanisms.
• Article 171(2) of the EC Treaty as amended by the Treaty on European Union.

Suggested Solution

The European Community is based on the rule of law. Disputes between Member States and disputes between Community institutions and Member States must be settled through the proper procedures, with final recourse to the European Court for adjudication on the merits of the dispute. In order to enforce Community obligations, the EC Treaty provides that actions for infringement of Community law against Member States may be raised by either another Member State or the European Commission acting on behalf of the Community.

One Member State may bring a direct action against another if it considers that the other state has failed to fulfil its obligations under the Community Treaties: Article 170 EC Treaty. The Court exercises exclusive jurisdiction over all disputes between Member States arising out of the subject matter of the Community agreements. Member States are expressly forbidden to resolve such disputes by any other means: Article 219 EC Treaty.

However, the right of a Member State to initiate a direct action against another Member State is subject to certain preconditions. A Member State alleging a violation of Community law must first bring the matter to the attention of the European Commission. The Commission is required to deliver a reasoned opinion on the matter after allowing the parties in dispute to submit arguments. Only after the Commission has delivered this opinion, or has failed to do so within the prescribed period, may the Member State continue. If the Commission indicates that it has no intention of pursuing the action, or if the Commission fails to deliver an opinion within three months of the matter being raised, the complaining state may bring the action itself.

Direct diplomatic confrontation between Member States is avoided if the European Commission pursues the matter in the name and interests of the European Community. A large majority of complaints are settled after the Commission delivers its reasoned opinion on the merits of the case. The remaining cases are often continued by the Commission on behalf of the complaining Member State.

Only one case by one Member State against another has actually proceeded to judgment and this involved proceedings brought by France against the United Kingdom: *France v United Kingdom (Re Fishing Mesh)* (1979). The United Kingdom enacted an Order in Council which regulated the size of the mesh of fishing nets in an attempt to conserve fishing stocks. Fishing policy is a matter within the competence of the Community and the Council of Ministers had earlier passed a resolution allowing Member States to introduce conservation measures, but only on the condition that prior consultations were held with the Commission. The United Kingdom had failed to enter into such consultations prior to enactment of the Order. The master of a French trawler was arrested by British fishery protection officers and convicted of using nets with a smaller mesh than the minimum authorised by the Order in Council.

France complained to the Commission that the Order had been adopted without the prior approval of the Commission and was therefore contrary to Community law. The Commission furnished a reasoned opinion which supported the contentions of the French government, but did not assume responsibility for continuing the action. The French government therefore brought the matter before the European Court in the form of a direct action against the United Kingdom. The European Court held that the British Order in Council had indeed been enacted without the necessary requirements being observed and consequently the United Kingdom was held in breach of Community law.

Although actual inter-state proceedings before the Court have been extremely rare, Member States frequently threaten to take such measures. For example, in 1990, the United Kingdom warned France that a direct action would be raised under the inter-state procedure after the French government threatened to restrict exports of cars to France manufactured in the United Kingdom by Japanese corporations. France claimed that the cars in question failed to satisfy the Community rules of origin and were therefore not Community goods entitled to unrestricted entry into the French market. The French government also averred that Japanese investment in car manufacturing within the United Kingdom was in reality an indirect means of circumventing French quotas on the importation of Japanese cars. In reply, the British government argued that at least 80 per cent of the costs of the cars in question had been incurred in the United Kingdom, a percentage which clearly satisfied the rules of origin adopted under the EC Treaty. As an immediate consequence of the threatened action, the French government eventually agreed to allow the vehicles into France as Community goods.

In contrast to actions between Member States, enforcement actions by the European Commission against Member States are a common occurrence. Under Article 155 of the EC Treaty, the Commission has primary responsibility for ensuring that the Member States uphold their Community obligations. Article 169 of the EC Treaty authorises the Commission to commence proceedings against any Member State suspected of violating its Community obligations. The same provision also specifies a formal pre-litigation procedure which must be exhausted before commencing actual proceedings in the Court.

In practice, even before engaging in this formal procedure, the Commission informally notifies the Member State alleged to have violated its Community obligations and invites comments on the behaviour under investigation. While such communications are often successful, a failure on the part of a Member State to justify its conduct, or a refusal to remedy the behaviour in question, will set the formal pre-litigation procedure in motion.

If informal communications have proved unsuccessful the Commission delivers a reasoned opinion on the matter after giving the Member State concerned an opportunity to submit its observations. Should the Member State fail to comply with the terms of the Commission opinion within the period prescribed, the next stage is to bring the matter to the attention of the Court. Since the purpose of delivering a reasoned opinion is to give the defendant state an opportunity to respect its Community obligations, the Commission must allow a reasonable period for the Member State to comply. A reasonable period is determined in the light of the facts surrounding the case. If the Commission imposes excessively short time limits, the action may be dismissed by the Court: *EC Commission* v *Belgium (Re University Fees)* (1989). In the event that the formal pre-litigation process fails to procure a satisfactory resolution of the issue, the Commission can initiate proceedings before the European Court.

If the Court decides that a Member State has contravened its Community obligations it will only rule that a violation of the obligation has occurred. Thereafter the government of the offending Member State is obliged to 'take the necessary measures' to amend or repeal its laws or practices to conform to the decision of the Court: Article 171(1) EC Treaty. No specific period is specified within which a state must act to comply with the judgment, but prima facie the period for compliance 'should be no longer than the minimum period needed for adopting the remedial measures required': *EC Commission* v *France (Re Tobacco Prices)* (1990).

The Treaty on European Union adds an additional paragraph to Article 171 and introduces a process whereby a Member State can be fined for failing to implement a Court ruling. This involves a three stage process.

Once a decision has been given by the Court and a Member State has not complied with its terms within a reasonable period, the Commission shall deliver a reasoned opinion to the state concerned after having given that state an opportunity to submit its observations on the matter. The reasoned opinion shall specify the points on which, in the opinion of the Commission, the Member State has not complied with the Court's decision.

The second stage involves a second action against the Member State, this time under Article 171(2) itself. In these proceedings, the Commission may specify any penalty which should be paid by the Member State for the failure to act. This penalty may take the form of either a lump sum or a penalty payment, the latter being a sum required to be paid by the Member State at regular intervals until the breach is remedied.

The final stage is for the Court to rule on the issue of whether the Member State has failed to comply with its obligations under Article 171(1). If it has not, the Court may require the Member State to pay the lump sum or penalty payment.

But there is some scepticism as to how this procedure will work in practice and the extent to which this will resolve the problems surrounding the enforcement of Community law against Member States.

First, private individuals cannot raise actions in the European Court against Member States. Accordingly, this is not an avenue open to private individuals, only the European Commission. Private individuals must continue to rely on the remedies available in their national courts against government bodies alleged to have engaged in practices contrary to Community law.

Second, the exact powers of the Commission to specify the amount of the fine is not stated. There is no maximum, or minimum, level of fine which may be proposed by the Commission. It is also not clear whether the European Court is bound to impose the exact fine suggested by the Commission in the event that a Member State is found to have violated this obligation. Can the Court modify the proposed amount in accordance with the terms of its second ruling?

Third, there is no mechanism in the Article to compel a Member State to pay the sum. For example, the penalty cannot expressly be deducted from its budgetary contributions. Therefore, in the event that a Member State persistently refuses to pay the prescribed penalties there is little that can be done to compel it to do so. This is a substantial flaw in the procedure.

Hence, the amendment to Article 171 may not be as successful in ensuring the enforcement of judgments against Member States as it might appear at first sight.

QUESTION FOUR

'Community law is not like national law: it is not like international law; it is a special category of law.' Discuss.

University of Glasgow LLB Examination
1989 Q3

General Comment

A problem which focuses on the nature of European Community law itself and requires a contrast to be drawn with other forms of law.

Skeleton Solution

• Differences between Community law and national law.
• Differences between Community law and international law.
• Characteristics illustrating the unique nature of Community law.

Suggested Solution

Community law is unlike national law for a number of reasons. First, national law is incapable of regulating relationships between sovereign states. Secondly, national laws do not possess the special characteristics of Community law. Principles of Community law may be given direct effect in a number of different legal systems; and these principles prevail over inconsistent provisions of national law. However, unlike national law, Community law does not regulate the whole spectrum of relationships between individuals in a domestic society. Community law is confined to the parameters set by the Community Treaties, although the judicial activism of the European Court has stretched the application of Community law to its fullest.

Nor does Community law have many features in common with international law. International law is the law which regulates the relations between states. The sources of international law are international agreements and international custom, supplemented by general principles recognised by civilised states and the writings of respected jurists: Article 38(1) Statute of the International Court of Justice. While limited mechanisms have been established to confer international rights upon individuals, such as the international human rights agreements, on the whole international law is confined to inter-state relations. In addition, the international law of economic relations is primitive, centring around the General Agreement on Tariffs and Trade (GATT).

Although the Community itself is founded upon three international treaties, as amended, Community law is applicable to both Member States and individuals. Further, Community law has its own independent sources of law. The European Court generally avoids referring to international law as a reservoir of legal principles, mainly because international norms regulating economic relations are underdeveloped.

Nor is the international community as institutionally organised as the Community. While the Community has organs to perform legislative, executive and judicial functions, the counterpart institutions at the international level cannot claim to be as effective in the promulgation of legal measures, the adjudication of disputes or the enforcement of judgments.

European Community law is a supranational species of law which prevails over the laws of all Member States, including the laws of the British Parliament. It transcends the public and private distinction which is frequently drawn in English law. Community law may be invoked in an extensive range of actions, both civil and criminal. Not only does it provide a defence to legal proceedings, but it may also furnish grounds for legal action or for interim injunction: *Argyll Group plc v Distillers Co plc* (1986); and *Holleran v Daniel Thwaites plc* (1989). Principles of Community law cannot be categorised into a distinct group of principles in the same way as the law of tort or contract may be. Consequently, it cannot be stated with certainty that a particular area of British law will remain unaffected, or unlikely to be affected, by Community law.

Matters concerning issues of Community law most frequently arise where there is a cross border element involving another Member State, or where a subject has been regulated by Community measures of harmonisation, or where Community measures are necessary to implement Community policies in sectors such as fishing, agriculture or commerce. Community law now extends into areas inconceivable even a decade ago. It regulates almost all commercial activities including the export and import of goods to and from the United Kingdom to other Member States, manufacturing, commerce, the supply of services, investment, fishing, and farming. Community law also now functions in a number of related areas of law including employment law, social security law, company law, competition law, tax law, consumer protection law, banking law, insurance law and intellectual property law.

Further, the competence of the Community to enact legislation has been considerably expanded as an immediate consequence of the Single European Act, and even more significantly by the coming into force of the Treaty on European Union.

However, political initiatives have not been the only source of impetus for the growth of Community law within national legal systems. The European Court of Justice itself has been a catalyst towards extending the scope of Community law far beyond the terms of the Treaty of Rome. In a number of judgments, the European Court has created fundamental principles of Community law through the process of interpretation. Both the principles of the supremacy of Community law over national law and the direct effect of provisions of Community Treaties and unimplemented Community directives owe their origins to the jurisprudence of the European Court.

The unique nature of Community law also requires the legal systems of each Member State to adapt to its characteristics. Within the United Kingdom, even accepted constitutional doctrines and precepts require modification to facilitate the reception of Community law. For example, the constitutional principle that Acts of Parliament cannot be reviewed in the event of inconsistency with international obligations entered into by the United Kingdom requires modification in light of the three Community Treaties, in particular the European Community Treaty. Indeed, even the House of Lords has been prepared to concede that inroads have been made into the principle of parliamentary sovereignty by accession to the European Community: *R v Secretary of State, ex parte Factortame (No 3)* (1989).

2 THE INSTITUTIONS OF THE EUROPEAN UNION

2.1 Introduction

2.2 Key points

2.3 Relevant cases

2.4 Relevant materials

2.5 Analysis of questions

2.6 Questions

2.1 Introduction

As originally conceived, each of the three separate European Communities possessed a separate Commission and Council but shared the same parliamentary assembly and Court of Justice. The Merger Treaty 1965 consolidated these institutions into one set for all the Communities. This process resulted in four principal organs – the Council of Ministers, the European Commission, the European Parliament and the European Court.

The Single European Act recognised the status of the European Council within the Community framework but did not amend the EC Treaty to give this organ formal institutional status. At the same time, the Act gave the Council of Ministers formal authority to create a second division within the European Court to be known as the Court of First Instance.

The pre-existing institutional structure contained in the amended EC Treaty was not significantly altered by the Treaty on European Union although the Court of Auditors was given formal recognition as an institution of the European Community by an amendment to the EC Treaty to that effect. Hence, the institutional structure of the European Union is composed of these five organs although only the Council of Ministers has changed its name to the Council of the European Union. The European Commission, the European Court of Justice (and the Court of First Instance) and the Court of Auditors remain, at least in name, institutions of the European Community. This is because the majority of the functions of these four organs are performed on the basis of the powers conferred under the EC Treaty, while the Council of Ministers exercises authority under all three pillars of the Treaty on European Union.

2.2 Key points

a) *The European Council*

   i) Composition and structure

      The European Council consists of all the Heads of Government of the Member States and their respective Foreign Ministers, together with the

President of the European Commission who is assisted by another Commissioner. The Treaty on European Union specifies that the European Council shall convene twice each year: Article D.

ii) Competence and powers

The European Council is designed to facilitate the coordination of European Foreign policy. Responsibility for the agenda lies with the Member State which has the Presidency of a separate Community institution – the Council of Ministers.

The Council possesses no formal powers. Rather, it is a forum for discussions, on an informal basis, relating to issues of common Community concern. However, the Treaty on European Union declares that the European Council shall 'provide the Union with the necessary impetus for its development and shall define the general political guidelines thereof'. Through consultations at this level, Member States agree to maximise their combined influence on global affairs through coordination, convergence, joint action, and the development of common principles and objectives.

b) *The Council of Ministers*

i) Composition and structure

The Council of Ministers consists of one national representative from each Member State, the exact composition varying according to the subject of discussions. A distinction is drawn between two types of Council meetings:

- General Council meetings: these are attended by the Foreign Ministers of the Member States.
- Specialised Council meetings: these meetings are attended by the various national Ministers with responsibility for the subjects on the agenda for discussion.

The office of the President of the Council rotates in alphabetical sequence among the Member States in six month periods. The Presidency of the Council of Ministers has been synchronised with the Presidency of the European Council. This ensures that a single Member State is responsible for the general progress of the Community as a whole during its period of tenure.

Since the government Ministers who participate in the Council of Ministers also have national responsibilities and therefore cannot be permanently present in Brussels, a subsidiary organ has been established in order to maintain consistency and continuity in the work of the Council. This organ, called the Committee of Permanent Representatives (known by the French acronym COREPER), has been formed to perform two main functions:

- to provide liaison between national governments and Community institutions for the exchange of informations; and
- to prepare draft Community legislation with the Commission for final submission to the Council itself.

COREPER is composed of the ambassadors of the Member States accredited to the Community, often assisted by national officials from the civil services of their respective Member States. The individual members of COREPER represent the interests of their respective countries and not those of the Community.

ii) Competence and powers under the EC Treaty

The Council of Ministers is the principal decision-making organ of the Community and has competence to deal with the following matters:

- the adoption of Community legislation;
- the formulation of Community policies;
- the finalisation of international agreements with foreign states on matters which fall within the competence of the Community;
- drafting the Community budget in conjunction with the European Parliament;
- taking those decisions required to ensure that the objectives specified in the EC Treaty are achieved.

Article 145 of the EC Treaty allows the Council to delegate authority to the European Commission for the implementation of policies and rules established by the Council.

The most important power of the Council of Ministers is the capacity to enact Community legislation. The Community legislative process is exceedingly complex, particularly after the amendments made by the Single European Act and the Treaty on European Union. As a result of the amendments made by the Single European Act, two legislative procedures existed:

- the original legislative procedure; and
- the 'cooperative procedure';

The European Parliament is more closely involved in the law-making process when the cooperation procedure is required. Cooperation procedure extends to Community legislation regulating the following subjects:

- the elimination of discrimination on the ground of nationality;
- the freedom of movement of workers and the freedoms of providing services and establishment; and
- harmonisation measures relating to the establishment and functioning of the internal market.

The co-operation procedure has been retained in the post-Maastricht legislative structure under Article 189c of the EC Treaty, as amended.

The Treaty on European Union adds a third legislative procedure to this already confusing picture by introducing the 'co-decision procedure'. The co-decision procedure is regulated by new Article 189b of the EC Treaty and follows, in broad terms, the co-operation procedure although it is a more comprehensive legislative process.

Under the co-decision procedure, the Commission retains discretion to submit legislative proposals which are sent to both the Council and the Parliament. The Council, acting by qualified majority, and after obtaining the opinion from the Parliament, is required to adopt a common position on the proposal. This common position is communicated to the Parliament.

After examining the common position of the Council, the Parliament has four options:

- To approve the common position in which case the measure returns to the Council for formal approval;
- To take no action in which case, after a period of three months, the Council may adopt the proposal;
- To suggest amendments to the common position which must be by an absolute majority and these suggested amendments are returned to the Commission and amended before being resubmitted to the Council; or
- To reject the common position, again by an absolute majority, in which case a Conciliation Committee may be established to resolve the impasse.

The new procedure is intended to give the Parliament a greater voice in the legislative process. This is achieved by compelling the Council to act unanimously in the event that it wishes to override the proposed amendments made by the Parliament.

iii) Voting

Article 148 of the EC Treaty stipulates that 'save as otherwise provided, the Council shall act by a majority of its Members'. In reality, most treaty provisions require qualified majorities or unanimity. A common requirement is for the use of a qualified majority. A system of weighted voting has been created for the purpose of determining a qualified majority under Article 148 EC Treaty. According to this scheme, votes are allocated on the following basis:

After the amendments made to Article 148(2) of the EC Treaty by the Treaty of Accession for Austria Finland and Sweden, votes are weighted in the following manner:

10 votes	–	Germany, France, Italy and the United Kingdom
8 votes	–	Spain
5 votes	–	Belgium, Greece, the Netherlands and Portugal
4 votes	–	Austria and Sweden
3 votes	–	Denmark, Ireland and Finland
2 votes	–	Luxembourg

The total number of votes now stands at 87 votes. For the adoption of measures by a qualified majority, there must be at least 62 votes in favour where the EC Treaty requires such acts to be adopted on a proposal from the Commission, and 62 votes in favour, cast by at least ten members, in all other cases. Since the accession of the new Member States in January 1995, a blocking minority has become 26 votes. This number of votes allows a coalition of Member States to prevent the adoption of measures which require a qualified majority.

The use of majority voting in the Council has been more common since the passing of the Single European Act which extended majority voting to a more substantial range of matters than had previously been the case. Similarly, the Treaty on European Union continued this process and enlarged the number of areas subject to majority voting.

iv) The legal basis for enacting measures and legislation

Since the Council of Ministers is the principal decision-making body of the Community, it is responsible for ensuring that the measures which it approves are adopted on the proper legal basis. The legal basis for the adoption of a measure depends on its subject-matter and not the type of measure. Depending on the subject-matter involved, different procedural and voting requirements must be respected.

Failure to comply with these requirements may render a measure open to challenge by the European Commission, the European Parliament, the Member States and, in certain circumstances, private individuals.

For example, in *United Kingdom* v *EC Council (Re Hormones)* [1988] 2 CMLR 453, the UK challenged the legal basis on which the Council adopted a directive prohibiting the use of certain types of hormones. The measure was adopted under Article 43 – which required a qualified majority – but the United Kingdom claimed that the proper legal authority was Article 100 which required unanimity. The Court held that the proper legal basis was Article 43 although the measure was declared void on technical grounds.

c) *The European Commission*

i) Composition and structure

The European Commission is composed of 20 Commissioners – two from each of the five largest Member States together with one from each of the smaller Member States. Commissioners are appointed by agreement between the various Member States and hold office for renewable periods of five years.

The Commission functions as a collegiate body and recognises the principle of collective responsibility. Voting within the Commission is by simple majority and deliberations are private and confidential. In order to ensure efficiency within the Commission, special responsibilities are distributed to each individual Commissioner.

The Commissioners are also assisted by a considerable body of Community civil servants. This Secretariat is organised into 23 departments known as Directorates-General. Each department is presided over by a Director-General who is responsible to the Commissioners whose portfolio includes that particular department. As a matter of policy, the Directors-General are usually of a different nationality from the Commissioners to whom they are responsible.

ii) Competence and powers

The Commission performs four separate functions which are set out in Article 155 of the EC Treaty:

- to ensure respect for the rights and obligations imposed on Member States and Community institutions by both the Community Treaties and measures made under the authority of these agreements;
- to formulate, participate and initiate policy decisions authorised under the Community Treaties;
- to promote the interests of the Community both internally and externally; and
- to exercise the powers delegated to it by the Council for the implementation and administration of Community policy.

The Commission has ultimate responsibility to ensure that the interests of the Community are protected.

The most important power of the Commission is the ability to institute proceedings before the European Court against:

- any Member State suspected of violating its Community obligations (Article 169 EC Treaty); and
- any Community institution considered to have acted outside its power: (Article 173 EC Treaty).

The Commission has also been delegated a considerable range of executive and legislative powers by the Council of Ministers. For example, Article 87(1) EC Treaty authorises the Council to delegate responsibility for the administration of competition policy to the Commission. In the discharge of this function, the Commission has authority, in certain circumstances, to investigate complaints, to impose fines, and to require Member States to take appropriate action to prevent or terminate infringements of competition policy. Often delegated authority also vests power to legislate in the Commission.

d) *The European Parliament*

  i) Composition and structure

Members of the European Parliament were originally appointed by their respective national parliaments according to internal parliamentary procedures. In 1976 the Member States agreed the Act Concerning the Election by Direct Universal Suffrage of Members to the European Parliament which facilitated direct elections to the European Parliament.

A total of 626 members of the European Parliament (MEPs) are elected for terms of five years. Seats are allocated to Member States in approximate proportion to their populations. The distribution of seats, as modified by the Treaty of Accession for Austria, Finland and Sweden, is as follows:

99 representatives – Germany

87 representatives – France, Italy and the United Kingdom

64 representatives – Spain

31 representatives – Netherlands

25 representatives – Belgium, Greece and Portugal

22 representatives – Sweden

21 representatives – Austria

16 representatives – Denmark and Finland

15 representatives – Ireland

6 representatives – Luxembourg

The distribution of seats within the United Kingdom is regulated by the European Parliamentary Elections Act 1978, as amended by the European Parliamentary Elections Act 1993. Constituencies are drawn up by the Boundary Commissioners and 72 seats are allocated to England, eight to Scotland, four to Wales and three to Northern Ireland.

Members of the European Parliament are seated according to their political affiliations and views and not their nationalities. The majority of parties in the European Parliament are coalitions between national parties. In June 1995, the Socialist Party was the largest single party, followed by the European Peoples' Party, and then the European Democrat Party (which is essentially composed of British Conservative MEPs).

ii) Competence and powers

The European Parliament represents the interests of the peoples of Europe. As originally conceived, the European Parliament lacked any real powers other than an essentially advisory competence. The Parliament has, however, gradually acquired a significantly more important role in the functioning of the Community.

Now the Treaty on European Union has been approved, the Parliament's legislative competence has passed through three distinct stages:

Stage 1:　Original legislative role

Stage 2:　The Co-operation procedure

Stage 3:　The Co-decision procedure

In addition to its legislative functions, the Parliament also possesses a considerable number of powers, mainly over the European Commission as opposed to the Council of Ministers. In particular, the Parliament may exercise the following powers:

• The consent of the Parliament is required for the admission of new Members into the Community and for the conclusion of association agreements between the Community and third countries (Articles 237–238 EC).

• The European Commission is obliged to answer questions submitted by Members of the European Parliament (Article 140 EC). Both written and oral questions may be submitted.

• The Commission is required to submit an annual general report to the Parliament on the affairs of the Community which is the subject of an annual parliamentary debate (Article 143 EC).

• The Commission may be collectively dismissed by a motion of censure carried by a two-thirds majority in Parliament (Article 144 EC).

- The Community budget is prepared by the Commission and submitted to the Council of Ministers, but the Parliament may approve or modify the budget depending on the expenditure involved (Article 203 EC, as amended).
- The opinion of the Parliament must be sought during the decision-making processes before the adoption of certain measures (Articles 43, 54, 56 and 87 EC).
- The Treaty on European Union introduces a new petition procedure which entitles any citizen of the Community to petition the Parliament on matters which fall within the scope of the Parliament's competence.

While the European Parliament exercises considerable supervisory control over the Commission, the same cannot be said of its relationship with the Council of Ministers.

iii) Power of the Parliament to compel judicial review of the acts of other institutions

The power of the European Parliament to challenge the validity of acts of other Community institutions and Member States is not as explicitly stated in the EC Treaty as the powers of both the Council of Ministers and the European Commission in this respect: see Article 173 and Article 175 of the Treaty.

Its right to bring actions for failure to act under Article 175 was eventually recognised in *European Parliament* v *EC Council (Re Common Transport Policy)* [1987] ECR 1513, where the Court held that the term 'institutions of the Community' included the European Parliament.

Similarly, its right to initiate proceedings to protect its interests under Article 173 was recognised in *European Parliament* v *EC Council (Re Tchernobyl)* [1992] 1 CMLR 91. In what was a dramatic reversal of its earlier decisions, the Court held that the Parliament could competently bring an action where the complaint was brought to protect the rights of the Parliament under the Community Treaties; see also *European Parliament* v *EC Council (Re Students' Rights)* [1992] 3 CMLR 281.

Both these rights have now been recognised through amendments made to Articles 173 and 175 of the EC Treaty by the Treaty on European Union.

e) *The European Court of Justice*

i) Composition and structure

The Court of Justice, which sits in Luxembourg, now has 15 judges who are assisted by eight Advocate-Generals, although until 6 October 2000 an additional Advocate-General will be appointed due to a political compromise reached during the accession of Austria, Finland and Sweden. Each Member State is entitled to appoint a judge of its own nationality.

Every three years there is a partial replacement of the judges (eight and seven after each three-year period) as well as Advocate-Generals (four on each occasion). Judges are eligible for re-election for another term. The President of the Court is elected by the judges from among their number for a term of three years, although again he or she may be re-elected.

In each case before the Court, an Advocate-General is appointed to deliver an impartial and legally reasoned opinion after the close of the pleadings by the parties, but before the judges sitting on the case render their decision. This opinion is a preliminary to a decision by the Court and the Advocate-General is not given a vote in the actual voting among the judges.

The structure and organisation of the Court is regulated by a separate Protocol to the EC Treaty – Protocol on the Statute of the Court of Justice of the European Economic Community. Matters of procedure are regulated by this Protocol, including the content of oral and written pleadings, rights of production, citation of witnesses, costs and expenses, and periods of limitation. These rules are supplemented by others contained in the Rules of Procedure of the European Court of Justice.

ii) Jurisdiction

The jurisdiction of the European Court of Justice may be classified into three distinct categories:

- Contentious jurisdiction: this refers to the right of the Court to hear direct actions between Member States and Community institutions, as well as actions by individuals against the acts of Community institutions.
- Plenary jurisdiction: this refers to the right of the Court to award damages for unlawful acts committed by Community institutions.
- Preliminary ruling jurisdiction: the European Court has jurisdiction to hear cases referred by the national courts of Member States on matters relating to the interpretation and application of Community law.

The nature of the jurisdiction of the European Court forms the next two chapters of this book.

iii) Advisory opinions

Both the Council of Ministers and the European Commission are authorised to submit legal questions to the European Court for advisory opinions. This power has been used most often by the European Commission to limit the competence of the Council to act, or alternatively to reinforce its own constitutional position: see *EC Commission* v *EC Council (Re ERTA)* [1971] ECR 263.

One of the most significant cases in recent times was Opinion 1/91 *Re the Draft Treaty on a European Economic Area (No 1)* [1992] 1 CMLR 245. This case centred around the question of whether a treaty between the European Community and the European Free Trade Association (EFTA) was compatible with Community law.

f) *The Court of First Instance*

i) Composition and structure

The Single European Act authorised the Council of Ministers to create a Court of First Instance to alleviate the volume of work before the European

Court of Justice. The Court of First Instance was established by Council Decision 88/591 and now consists of 15 judges. Members of the Court are appointed by agreement between the Member States for periods of six years. The members of the Court of First Instance elect a President from among their own number.

No provision has been made in the Council Decision for the appointment of Advocates-General to the Court of First Instance. However, judges of the Court may be called upon to perform the task of an Advocate-General. The actual organisation of the Court is specified in the Rules of Procedure for the Court of First Instance.

The constitutional authority for the functioning and operation of the Court of First Instance has now been incorporated into the EC Treaty by amendments made by the Treaty on European Union. Article 168A of the amended EC Treaty regulates the composition of the Court as well as the extent of its jurisdiction and therefore effectively supersedes the authority vested by the Single European Act.

ii) Jurisdiction

The jurisdiction and powers of the Court of First Instance have been carved from those of the European Court of Justice itself. The Court of First Instance does not extend the jurisdiction of the European Court, but rather, it exercises certain aspects of the Court's functions. In particular, the creation of the new Court does not alter the jurisdictional relationships between the European Court system and the individual national courts and tribunals of the Member States.

This jurisdiction extends to the following classes of actions:

• Actions or proceedings by the staff of Community institutions.

• Actions for annulment and actions for failure to act brought against the Commission by natural or legal persons and concerning the application of Articles 50 and 57–66 of the ECSC Treaty. Such actions relate to Commission decisions concerning levies, production controls, pricing practices, agreements and concentrations.

• Actions for annulment or actions for failure to act brought by natural or legal persons against an institution of the Community relating to the implementation of competition policy.

Where these actions are accompanied by claims for damages, the Court of First Instance has jurisdiction to decide the related claim.

The Court of First Instance cannot hear cases brought by either Member States or Community institutions. Nor may the Court answer questions submitted by national courts through the preliminary ruling procedure which is reserved to the European Court of Justice.

Appeal from the Court of First Instance to the European Court is competent but only on point of law and subject to the appellant demonstrating the existence of one of the grounds of appeal specified in Article 51 of the amended European Court of Justice Statute. Three grounds of appeal have been established:

- Lack of competence on the part of the Court of First Instance, such as an excess of its jurisdiction.
- A breach of procedure before the Court which has had an adverse effect on the interests of the appellant.
- An infringement of Community law by the Court of First Instance, such as an error in the interpretation or application of Community legal principles.

A substantial number of appeals have now been heard by the European Court of Justice under the appeal procedure, the majority of which concern decisions of the CFI on competition matters: see, for example, *Publishers Association* v *EC Commission*, judgment of 17 January 1995, not yet reported. The Court, in particular, has assiduously stood by the principle that it will refuse to consider appeals alleging errors of fact as opposed to errors of law: see *Hilti AG* v *EC Commission (No 2)* [1994] 4 CMLR 614.

2.3 Relevant cases

EC Commission v *EC Council (Re Harmonised Commodity Descriptions)* [1990] 1 CMLR 457: A failure by the Council of Ministers to consult the European Parliament on the adoption of a measure when specified in the Community Treaties renders the putative measure void.

European Parliament v *EC Council (Re Tchernobyl)* [1992] 1 CMLR 91: First successful action by the European Parliament against the Council challenging the legal basis of a measure.

European Parliament v *EC Council (Re Students' Rights)* [1992] 3 CMLR 281: Confirmation of the right of the European Parliament to challenge measures under the authority of the EC Treaty.

Re the Draft Treaty on a European Economic Area (No 1) [1992] 1 CMLR 245: Reference by the European Commission of the constitutionality of the European Economic Area Agreement.

Hilti AG v *EC Commission (No 2)* [1994] 4 CMLR 614: Appeal from the CFI to the European Court restricted to points of law.

2.4 Relevant materials

W Ungerer, 'Institutional Consequences of Broadening and Deepening the Community' (1993) CML Rev 71.

D Wyatt & A Dashwood, *European Community Law* (third edition, 1993), 19–178.

L Brittan, 'Institutional Development of the European Community' (1992) Public Law 567.

U Everling, 'Reflections on the Structure of the European Union' (1992) CML Rev 1053.

B Vesterdorf, 'The Court of First Instance of the European Communities' (1992) CML Rev 897.

2.5 Analysis of questions

Questions dealing with this particular subject-matter most often take the form of narrative essays rather than factual problems. Most often, the student is asked to analyse or examine the relationships between institutions rather than provide a description of the nature of one particular institution. An understanding of the roles and powers of each organ is therefore essential, as is a basic comprehension of their interaction.

2.6 Questions

QUESTION ONE

To what extent is it true to say that the Council is the European Community's legislator?

University of London LLB Examination
(for External Students) European Community Law 1991 Q6

General Comment

A question requiring a narrative, descriptive answer. In order to score well, it is not only necessary to identify the Council's role in the legislative process, but also the influence of the other bodies in the procedure.

Skeleton Solution

• The strength of the Council's position in the legislative procedure.
• The influence of the Commission on the content of measures.
• The increasing influence of the European Parliament.
• The co-operation procedure and the *Tchernobyl* decision.

Suggested Solution

There is little doubt that the Council of Ministers is the principal decision-making organ of the Community. As a body composed of national representatives, it embodies the interests of the Member States of the Community and ensures that each state retains a voice in the formulation of Community policy and legislation. Its position in the hierarchy of institutions is such that virtually all the decisions and legislation passed at the Community level must be approved by the Member States through the medium of the Council.

The only limited exception to this general rule is that occasionally the Commission is authorised to enact regulations in particular sectors by the Council delegating authority to act or by the provisions of the Community Treaties. For example, in the administration of competition policy, the Commission retains considerable discretion as to the application of the relevant rules of competition law.

While the Council exercises virtually unrestrained authority to enact legislative measures, this is not to deny that certain constraints are placed on the ability of the Council to influence the content of these rules. The final say in the enactment of Community legislation certainly resides with the Council, but in the formulation of these rules, both the European Parliament and the European Commission exercise some influence.

The European Commission has responsibility for proposing Community legislation and initiating policy. It is the Commission, in conjunction with the various consultative bodies, that constructs draft legislation. Naturally, in the discharge of this duty, the Commission retains considerable discretion as to the contents of a draft measure. At the same time, the Commission is often acutely aware that proposed measures that are too ambitious will be vetoed in the Council of Ministers. In practice, therefore, draft measures are often continuously passed between the Council and the Commission for revision and modification, a process that dilutes the Commission's influence in the drafting of legislation.

At the same time, the European Parliament has been given a greater role in the legislative process than originally envisaged under the EC Treaty. Before the Single European Act, the function of the Parliament was essentially advisory. Although some provisions of the Treaty required the consent of the Parliament for the adoption of certain measures, on the whole Parliament could only provide advisory opinions and often the Commission was not even obliged to seek such an opinion, although in practice it often did so.

The Single European Act introduced the so-called co-operation legislative procedure. This procedure extends to the adoption of Community legislation in the following matters: the elimination of discrimination on the grounds of nationality; the free movement of workers and the freedom to provide services; and harmonisation of measures designed to implement the single internal market programme.

Under this procedure, the Commission continues to exercise responsibility for the initiation of proposals which are sent to the Parliament for an opinion before being sent to the Council of Ministers. The Council is then required to reach a 'common position' on the proposed measure, acting by qualified majority. A common position is simply a consensus on the basic elements of the proposal.

This common position is referred to the Parliament which provides the Parliament with an opportunity for a second reading of the proposal. The Parliament has three months to consider its position and to arrive at a decision. If the Parliament approves the measure, or cannot agree on a decision, the Council is free to adopt the measure. If the Parliament challenges the proposal, any proposed amendments are sent back to the Commission which revises the measure in the light of these suggestions. The measure is then resubmitted to the Council which can adopt the proposal (by a qualified majority), adopt the Parliament amendments not approved by the Commission (by unanimity), or amend the Commission proposal itself (by unanimity).

Although the co-operation procedure has increased the influence of the Parliament in the legislative process, it has not eroded the ability of the Council to veto proposals to which opposition exists inside the Council. The general effect of this has been to delay the adoption of certain measures upon which there is no consensus.

The position of the European Parliament in the legislative process has also been strengthened by the decision of the European Court in the *Tchernobyl Case* (1990). The Parliament sought to challenge its lack of standing to review acts of the Council under Article 173 of the EC Treaty. This article reserves the right of judicial review over the acts of the Council to Member States and the Commission.

The Court agreed with the contentions of the Parliament that it should have the right to demand the judicial review of Community acts in which it has an interest. This decision alters the constitutional balance of the Community and represents an endorsement on the part of the Court for a greater role for the Parliament in the legislative processes of the Community.

QUESTION TWO

What role does the Commission play in the European Community's legal and institutional structure? What are the principal factors which have influenced the development of its role since 1958?

University of London LLB Examination
(for External Students) European Community Law 1992 Q4

General Comment

This is a straightforward question in which students are required to provide a detailed description of the European Commission's role in the constitutional structure of the Community. Relatively high marks may be scored in the event that the student has a grasp of the basic elements of this part of the syllabus because of the general nature of the question.

Skeleton Solution

• The constitutional position of the Commission in the instructional structure of the Community.
• Powers: supervisory functions, initiation of policy, protection of the interests of the Community, exercise of powers conferred by both treaties and legislation.
• Factors influencing the role of the Commission since 1958.
• Additional powers and functions exercised by the Commission today.

Suggested Solution

The European Commission plays an orchestrating role within the Community in the formulation of Community legislation and policy. While it performs its functions in conjunction with other Community institutions, particularly the Council of Ministers and the European Parliament, the Commission is ultimately responsible for the initiation of policy and legislative proposals.

Without the Commission, no Community legislation would be enacted, no international negotiations entered into with other countries, and there would be considerably fewer instances of Member States being brought before the European Court for infringements of Community law. While the Council of Ministers represents the interests of the Member States and the European Parliament the interests of the peoples of Europe in the running of the Community, the Commission is the embodiment of the Community interests in the process. Ultimately, it is the European Commission that has responsibility to ensure that the interests of the Community are fully protected, particularly as against the Member States.

Originally the Commission was given four functions under Article 155 of the EC Treaty.

First, the Commission is required to ensure respect for the rights and obligations imposed on both Member States and Community institutions by the Community Treaties and Community legislation. Acting under this authority, the Commission regularly institutes proceedings against Member States alleged to have violated Community obligations (Article 169 EC Treaty) and against Community institutions considered to have acted outside the scope of their powers (Article 173 EC Treaty).

Second, the Commission has been given charge of formulating, initiating and participating in the policy making process within the Community. It is this function that gives the Commission much of its power within the legislative process. While the Council of Ministers is the organ which eventually approves legislative proposals, the Commission has considerable discretion as regards the shaping and content of those proposals. It is true that both the Council of Ministers and the European Parliament are able to suggest amendments to proposals but, ultimately, without the drafting of proposed measures no policies would ever be formulated and no legislative measures ever enacted.

Third, it is required to promote the interests of the Community inside and outside the Community with regard to relations with other countries. Thus, the Commission is permitted to conduct negotiations with third parties on matters that fall within the scope of the Community's competence as defined in the constitutional treaties.

Finally, the Commission is instructed to exercise the powers delegated to it by the Council for the implementation and administration of Community policy. For example, the Commission has extensive powers as regards the enforcement of Community competition policy. It can enact decisions requiring private companies and firms to desist from certain anti-competitive practices and can impose fines subject to review by the European Court.

The functions and powers of the Commission were not substantially altered by the Merger Treaty in 1967. This agreement merely consolidated the functions and powers of the Commission in one single source.

The same cannot be said of the Single European Act (SEA) negotiated in 1986 which significantly amended the EC Treaty. This agreement in fact had three separate effects on the powers of the Commission. Firstly, the treaty altered the relationship between the Commission and the European Parliament in the legislative process as far as legislation on certain subjects was concerned. Secondly, the Act gave greater competencies to the Community in certain areas of policy. Since the Commission is in charge of the formulation of policy, any growth in the responsibilities of the Community necessarily entails a greater amount of power in the hands of the Commission. Thirdly, the role of the Commission in the external affairs of the Community was greatly enhanced through recognition of the institutional status of the European Council.

Obviously, any requirements imposed on the Commission to cooperate, consult or discuss proposed measures with another Community organ tend to dilute its power over the shape and contents of the proposed measure. The more influence Parliament acquired in the legislative process, the less dominance the Commission will be able to exercise. This development has required the Commission to change its role in the Community legislative framework in light of its changing function.

At the same time, the Single European Act considerably extended the areas of competence of the Community. Matters which were previously considered outside the remit of the Community were expressly included within its competence after the 1986 amendments. For example, the Community now has new responsibilities in the fields of consumer protection policy, environmental protection policy, economic cooperation, social policy and research and technological development.

The organic growth in responsibilities within the Community directly affects the powers and duties of the Commission. Essentially, the Commission can assert its competence over all matters falling within the scope of the Community Treaties as amended. As the competence of the Community grows so too does the power and influence of the Commission. In the new areas of responsibility added by the SEA, it is the Commission that has the power to influence the shape and content of these policies simply because it drafts proposals in these areas for consideration in conjunction with the other Community institutions.

The next major restructuring of the European Community will occur now the Treaty on European Union, signed at Maastricht in February 1992, has been ratified by all Member States. The influence and authority exercised by the Commission after this change will be assessed in accordance with the principle that as a general proposition, any growth in responsibilities for the Community involves a related growth in the powers of the Commission.

QUESTION THREE

The choice of legal basis is a highly controversial, political matter'. What are the guiding principles governing the choice of legal basis? Illustrate your answer with reference to recent case law.

University of London LLB Examination
(for External Students) European Community Law June 1993 Q1

General Comment

The question requires an examination of the principles behind the selection of the most appropriate basis for adopting Community measures. There is ample case law from the court in this connection which candidates are invited to use to illustrate the relevant principles. The subject of the question is relatively unusual although the number of cases presently being brought before the ECJ on this point has recently significantly increased. Possibly this provides the background to the origin of the question.

Skeleton Solution

- The proper choice of legal basis: voting requirements, consultations and procedure.
- The case law regulating legal principles applicable to the selection of the legal basis.
- The sanctions for exceeding the legitimate basis for adopting measures.
- The growing influence of the European Parliament.

Suggested Solution

All regulations, directives and decisions of the Council, and the Commission for that matter, must state the legal basis on which they were enacted, the reasons why the measures were required and also reference must be made to any proposals or opinions which were required prior to their adoption; Article 190 EC Treaty. But, in any event, all acts of Community institutions must have a legal basis in the EC Treaty and, in the absence of a proper basis, such acts would be ultra vires.

The most important aspect of selecting the proper legal basis for a measure is that this choice determines the necessary procedural requirements including the necessary vote required in the Council of Ministers for the adoption of the measure, the degree of consultations required between the Council and the European Parliament and the decision-making processes which must be followed for the measure to be approved.

Voting requirements vary not according to the nature of the measure – a regulation, a directive or a decision – but rather according to the subject-matter which the measure is intended to regulate. Article 148(1) of the EC Treaty specifies the general rule that, save as otherwise provided, the Council shall act by a majority of its members. But, in fact, the original EC Treaty required a unanimous vote for the adoption of most measures which resulted in a mere trickle of legislation being approved.

The EC Treaty was significantly amended in 1986 by the ratification of the Single European Act which introduced majority voting into many more areas of Community competence. Much of the legislation adopted in pursuit of the single internal market programme, for example, was adopted on the basis of Article 100A of the Treaty which authorises majority voting for harmonising measures designed to complete the internal market.

At the other extreme, many areas still require a unanimous vote. Under Article 235, if action by the Community should prove necessary to the attainment of the objectives set out in the Treaty, but the Treaty has not provided the required powers, the Council may adopt the appropriate measures but only by means of a unanimous vote.

The voting criteria required for the adoption of a measure will, of course, significantly affect the nature and content of the final measure. Where unanimity is required, a single Member State may delay the adoption of a measure indefinitely. This has the effect of frustrating negotiations even when the other 11 Member States are in unison.

The United Kingdom, for example, has blocked the adoption of the proposal for a draft statute for the creation of a new legal persona known as 'the European company'. The UK government argues that the appropriate legal basis of the measure is Article 235 while the other Member States claim that Article 100A is a perfectly adequate legal basis. Article 235 requires unanimity while Article 100A merely requires a qualified majority. The UK has used its own legal interpretation to demand significant amendments to the proposal to limit the rights of workers to participate in the management of this type of company. Further, the United Kingdom has threatened that if the measure is adopted under Article 100A, it will immediately initiate proceedings to have the European Court review the matter.

So, the legal basis and the voting requirements fundamentally shape the final form of the measure adopted quite simply because the minority of Member States have more ability and influence in the content of the final measure when unanimity is required than when a qualified majority is sufficient.

A substantial number of cases have come to the attention of the European Court for judicial review of the legal basis for the adoption of Community acts. While the selection of the appropriate legal basis is partly a political matter, the choice must be based on proper legal grounds. It is therefore inaccurate to claim that this selection is solely a political, and not a legal, matter. In fact, the European Court has built up a considerable reservoir of legal principles to allow the review of this selection.

First, the Council of Ministers cannot change the legal basis of a measure proposed by the Commission without proper justification. Thus, in *EC Commission* v *EC Council (Re Generalised Tariff Preferences)* (1987), the Commission proposed that the adoption of two measures should be based on Article 113 of the EC Treaty which requires a qualified majority. The Council did not state the legal basis on which it finally adopted the measure – opening itself to an additional challenge under Article 190 – but resorted to a unanimous vote which implied that the measure had been adopted under Article 235.

The Commission raised proceedings in the European Court which held that the Council had sufficient authority to adopt the measures under Article 113. Since unanimous voting had been used and not a qualified majority, the defect was not purely formal and therefore the Court declared the measures void.

Second, the choice of the legal basis for the adoption of a measure does not simply depend on the convictions of a Community institution as to the objective being pursued by the measure. The decision to adopt on the basis of a particular provision must be based on 'objective factors' which are amenable to judicial review: *EC Commission* v *EC Council (Re Generalised Tariff Preferences)*, supra.

Third, the previous practice of a Community organ in the adoption of similar measures has no bearing on the future voting practices of that organ. For example, a mere prior practice on the part of the Council cannot justify derogation from the strict requirements of the Treaty as regards legal basis; see *United Kingdom* v *EC Council (Re Hormones)* (1988).

Fourth, where authority to adopt a measure is split among two or more provisions, the institution exercising the power is required to adopt the measure in order to satisfy all the relevant provisions. Hence, for example, where a measure is being adopted on the basis of two provisions, one requiring unanimity and the other a qualified majority, the measure must be adopted unanimously; see *EC Commission* v *EC Council (Re Harmonised Commodity Descriptions)* (1990).

But, the Court will not slavishly nullify a measure simply because a formal defect exists as regards the legal basis. So, for example, the Court will not declare a measure null and void where, although adopted on the incorrect legal basis, the proper legal basis imposes approximately the same procedural requirements.

The second important consequence of the selection of the proper legal basis is that many of the provisions conferring power to adopt measures can only be properly exercised after some form of consultation with the European Parliament. In this respect the Parliament's powers have grown considerably. Initially, Parliament's right to be consulted in the Community legislative and decision-making processes was extremely limited. However, failure to engage in consultations, in those few areas which required consultations, rendered a putative measure void; see *SA Roquette Freres* v *EC Council* (1980).

The influence of the Parliament in this process grew considerably after 1986 once the Single European Act was adopted. Now Parliament is fully involved in the framing of legislative proposals especially under the co-operation procedure. Failure to consult the Parliament properly will render any measure adopted null and void if the omission constitutes an infringement of an essential procedural requirement.

The Parliament is now more actively than ever challenging the legal basis for measures adopted by the Council. First in *European Parliament* v *EC Council (Re Tchernobyl)* (1992), and more recently in *European Parliament* v *EC Council (Re Students' Rights)* (1992), the Parliament has sought judicial review of measures adopted by the Council alleging that the measures in question were enacted by the Council on inappropriate legal grounds.

Finally, the choice of legal basis will also determine the proper internal Community procedure to be followed for the adoption of a particular measure. For example, where a harmonising measure is adopted under Article 100 of the EC Treaty, the non-co-operation procedure is, pending ratification of the Treaty on European Union, applicable and only informal consultations are required with the Council. But, if a measure is adopted under Article 100A the co-operation procedure must be employed. This involves a different series of rights and duties for the Council and the Parliament, but also for the European Commission which has responsibility for drafting the final measure after the Council and the Parliament have had their say.

QUESTION FOUR

What is the role of the European Parliament in the institutional balance of the European Community? How has it developed since the inception of the Community and how might it develop in the future?

University of London LLB Examination
(for External Students) European Community Law June 1993 Q2

General Comment

This question involves a commonly recurring theme in past examination papers. The examiner is seeking to test knowledge of the institutional balance within the Community with special reference to the role of the European Parliament. This requires a statement of the constitutional balance vis-à-vis the European Parliament and the Council on the one hand and the Parliament and the Commission on the other. Essentially the question itself is relatively straightforward and should pose no problems for the well versed candidate.

Skeleton Solution

• Doctrine of the separation of interests and the role of the European Parliament in this process.

• The powers of the Parliament over the Commission.

- The budgetary powers of the Parliament: the main power exercisable over both organs.
- Powers over the Council and the proposed amendments to these powers in the Treaty on European Union.

Suggested Solution

The EC Treaty, as the constitution of the Community, is based on the doctrine of the separation of interests rather than the separation of powers. The Council of Ministers embodies the interests of the Member States while the European Commission represents the fundamental interests of the Community. The role of the European Parliament is to preserve and protect the interests of the peoples of the Community. At present, pending the amendments to the EC Treaty to be made by the Treaty on European Union (Maastricht Treaty), the Parliament is ill-equipped and exercises insufficient authority to carry out this function particularly as regards the Council's activities.

The powers of the European Parliament in the institutional balance of the Community are, paradoxically, aimed at countering the exercise of authority by the European Commission rather than the Council of Ministers. This should not, strictly speaking, be surprising since the EC Treaty was drafted by representatives of the Member States. But, in fact the most constitutional authority within the Community institutional framework is vested in the Council of Ministers. Any further augmentation of powers for the Parliament should therefore be directed against checking the powers of the Council and not the Commission.

At its inception, the European Parliament had a minor role to play in striking the institutional balance within the Community. Its primary authority lay in its power to collectively dismiss the Commission by a motion of censure carried by a two-thirds majority of votes cast if representing a majority of the members of the Parliament; Article 144 EC Treaty.

On occasions motions had been tabled in the Parliament for the censure of the Commission but, to date, none has been successfully carried. In practice this device is considerably less powerful than it might first appear. Individual Commissioners cannot be dismissed by a vote of the Parliament; all the Commissioners must resign. Therefore, such a motion would penalise Commissioners who have not committed any indiscretion. Also, if the whole Commission cabinet was sanctioned, an undesirable vacuum of authority would develop pending the appointment of a new cabinet. The Parliament has no influence in the selection of the new Commissioners who would be selected by the governments of the Member States.

Parliament members are also permitted to put questions to Commission officials which the Commission staff are obliged to answer; Article 140 EC Treaty. Questions may be submitted both orally and in writing. Commission officials may be subject to scrutiny in both the plenary session and committees of the Parliament. This power is part of the watchdog function carried out by the Parliament. Questions may also be asked of the Council, but these have neither the formal authority nor the same degree of compunction as those submitted to the Commission.

In a similar vein, the Commission is also required to submit an annual general report to the Parliament on the subject of the affairs of the Community; Article 143 EC Treaty. This report forms the basis for the annual Parliamentary debate on the affairs of the Community.

One power, which is exercised over the Council as much as the Commission, is the Parliament's role in the budgetary procedure. The Community's budget is, at present, prepared by the Commission and submitted to the Council, but the Parliament may approve or modify the budget depending on the type of expenditure involved; Article 203 of the EC Treaty, as amended.

The Parliament has power to approve all non-compulsory expenditure – administrative and operational expenditure – which accounts for approximately 25–30 per cent of the total budget each year. In other words, the Parliament can modify this aspect of the budget to a considerable degree. But as regards the remainder of the budget – the compulsory expenditure – the power of the Parliament is confined to proposing modifications which are deemed accepted unless the Council rejects these proposals. The vote of the Council in such a matter is by qualified majority.

Ultimately, Parliament has authority to reject the budget as a whole if, acting by a majority of its members and two-thirds of the votes cast, it believes there are 'important reasons' to reject the draft budget; Article 203(8) EC Treaty. In such an event, the Parliament may request that a new budget is submitted to it for approval. In fact, in 1979 the Parliament did reject the draft budget by a vote of 299 votes to 64, with one abstention.

The power to approve the budget is perhaps the main illustration of the Parliament's power to balance the institutional processes within the Community. It is a power that can be equally exercised over the Council and the Commission alike. However, again the power to veto the whole budget is one which the European Parliament must exercise carefully in order not to create havoc within the Community order.

In any event, the Council has constitutional authority to bring the European Parliament before the European Court if it is suspected that the Parliament has itself abused its powers over the budget; see *EC Council* v *European Parliament (Re the Community Budget)* (1986).

As stated earlier, Parliament's influence over the Council is finite and takes two main forms: power to approve the admission of new members and limited participation in the legislative processes.

Under Articles 237 and 238 of the EC Treaty, the consent of the Parliament is required for the admission of new members into the Community and for the conclusion of association agreements between the Community and third states. The negotiation of an association agreement is a preliminary step towards membership of the Community. The Parliament can technically veto the decision of the Council on admission and establishing association agreements which is a significant limitation on the Council's authority in this respect.

But, the historical impotence of the Parliament in restraining the actions of the Council is most evident in the legislative processes carried out within the Community. The legislative competence of the Parliament has progressed through three identifiable stages.

The original legislative role of Parliament was primarily consultative. The Parliament commented on proposals put forward by the Commission before the Council. It had a right to be consulted on certain matters, ie. under Articles 43, 54, 56 and 87 of the EC Treaty, but in practice the Commission frequently consulted the Parliament during the consultative phase of drafting legislation.

This consultative role was circumscribed in two respects. First, the vast majority of measures did not strictly require the views of the Parliament and so the Council could generally ignore its views. Second, unlike the Member States and the Commission, the Parliament was not permitted to bring proceedings in the European Court against the Council under Article 173(1) of the EC Treaty. Hence, Parliament exercised little control over the activities of the Council.

In 1986, the Single European Act altered the constitutional balance of authority in the Community slightly by introducing the co-operation procedure. The use of the co-operation procedure was required to enact legislation in specific subjects and especially the freedom of establishment, working conditions, and certain forms of harmonisation legislation. The co-operation extended the authority of the Parliament over the Council insofar as the Parliament was permitted two opportunities to discuss proposed measures but, as always, ultimate authority to adopt or reject measures resided in the Council of Ministers.

After the passing of the Single European Act, the Parliament was also successful in persuading the European Court to recognise its standing to bring proceedings against the Council. After a series of unsuccessful cases (see *European Parliament* v *EC Council (Re Common Transport Policy)* (1987); and *European Parliament* v *EC Council (Re Comitology)* (1988), the Court eventually recognised the standing of the Parliament to act to safeguard its powers under the Treaty as long as the action was raised solely with that objective; see *European Parliament* v *EC Council (Re Tchernobyl)* (1992).

The Treaty on European Union consolidates both these advances in the Parliament's authority over the Council. First, a new comprehensive legislative process modelled on the co-operation procedure will be introduced applying to all legislation, not just legislation on particular subjects. This process is to be known as the 'co-decision procedure' and is contained in Article 1896 of the amended EC Treaty. Second, Parliament's right to initiate proceedings against the Council of Ministers is formally recognised in an amended Article 173(3) of the EC Treaty.

In the final assessment, while the European Parliament presently exercises considerable supervisory control over the activities of the Commission, the same cannot be said of its relationship with the Council of Ministers. Whether or not the Treaty on European Union will establish the Parliament as an adequate counterweight to the Council can only be assessed once the new provisions in the Treaty on European Union are inserted into the EC Treaty itself.

QUESTION FIVE

Can the European Court of Justice be usefully compared with the United States Supreme Court?

University of Glasgow LLB Examination
1989 Q10

General Comment

A problem requiring the student to compare the function of one particular organ in the Community with comparable institutions in another country.

Skeleton Solution

- The structure of the ECJ and the Supreme Court.
- Constitutional positions.
- Scope and nature of powers.
- Jurisprudence and degree of judicial activism.

Suggested Solution

Comparisons between the European Court of Justice and the US Supreme Court have a limited value because of the different constitutional position of the two judicial bodies and their historical development and evolution. While the US Supreme Court is the highest judicial body within the United States, which is a federal state, the European Court exercises a considerably more restrictive jurisdiction as regards subject-matter. It is a supranational court which functions over an organisation of states which could not be described as even a loose confederation. Other significant differences exist between these bodies. However, from the jurisprudence of the European Court, it is clear that the Court perceives itself as a tribunal which presides over an embryonic federation of states.

Under the American Constitution, the jurisdiction of the US Supreme Court is virtually absolute. This jurisdiction is hierarchical and the Supreme Court is the court of final instance. Disputes concerning individuals and governmental authorities may be adjudicated before the Supreme Court. In contrast, the European Court decides disputes between sovereign states concerning the subject-matter of the Community treaties. Individuals have access to the European Court through both the contentious jurisdiction of the Court and by way of a preliminary reference from national courts. However, disputes concerning matters unrelated to the Community treaties are excluded from the jurisdiction of the European Court. Thus, a dispute between an individual and the national authorities of his Member State will not be heard before the European Court unless the matter relates to an issue of Community concern. This is a significant limitation on the ambit of the Court's jurisdiction.

Both the US Supreme Court and the European Court are courts of final instance, where the matter is an issue of Community concern in the case of the ECJ. After the decision in *Marbury* v *Madison*, the Supreme Court has unquestioned authority to declare a legislative measure – from either a state or the federal government – void when it conflicts with the terms of the American constitution. The European Court has assumed the same power after its decision in *Costa* v *ENEL* (1964). In this case, the European Court held that an Italian statute which was inconsistent with Community law could not prevail in the event of a conflict. Through consistent jurisprudence, the European Court has developed the doctrine of the supremacy of Community law which proclaims that Community law prevails over inconsistent provisions of national law, whether passed before or after the Community treaties (or Treaties of Accession) entered into force. Neither the American Constitution nor the Treaty of Rome expressly confers upon the Supreme Court or the European

Court the power to declare acts of legislation invalid. However, both courts have assumed this power by pursuing a deliberate policy of judicial activism.

Further, the constitutional sources of authority of both courts are radically different. The American constitution is an instrument which establishes the foundation for the administration of justice within a particular state. The Community Treaties – and in particular the Treaty of Rome – are international agreements among sovereign states. The Community Treaties do not establish a framework for the creation of a single state nor do they safeguard the fundamental rights of individuals.

While the European Court has attempted to address the issue of fundamental human rights by asserting that such principles 'form an integral part of the Community system' (*Nold* v *EC Commission* (1974)), in general the Court perceives the rights of individuals in terms of factors of production. In other words, the vast corpus of Community law relating to the individual deals with individuals as workers and concerns their rights under employment law, social security law and the right to further education. On occasion, the European Court has concerned itself with issues such as the right to privacy, the freedom to practise a religion, the right to possess property, the right to lawyer-client privacy, issues of substantive and procedural due process of law, the non-retroactivity of criminal legislation, and the right to refrain from self-incrimination. But, the Court has no explicit mandate to deal with these issues. These matters remain within the scope of the European Convention on Human Rights 1950 and the system of protection established under that agreement. In contrast, these subjects form a considerable part of the volume of cases heard before the US Supreme Court.

The position of the European Court has become even more distinct, from a constitutional perspective, now that the European Community has transformed itself into the European Union. Under the terms of the Treaty on European Union, the role of the European Court is restricted to the interpretation and application of the EC Treaty, the ECSC Treaty and the Euratom Treaty as well as jurisdiction to decide whether a particular matter falls within the scope of these three treaties or within the ambit of the other competences established under the TEU, namely the provisions on common foreign and security policy or the provisions on justice and home affairs.

Since the jurisdiction of the European Court within the European Union is strictly circumscribed, it cannot be said that the ECJ exercises an all-embracing competence over the constitution similar to that enjoyed by the US Supreme Court. The US Supreme Court is not excluded from conducting judicial review of matters as significant as US foreign policy or co-operation in the fields of justice and home affairs. This distinction is a significant point of departure in the respective roles of the two courts.

It would therefore be a dangerous policy on the part of the European Court if it was to imitate the jurisprudence of the US Supreme Court. While both courts have demonstrated a similar degree of judicial activism, the subject matters dealt with by each court remain undoubtedly distinct. Further, the constitutional position of each court is radically different from the other. It would therefore be a more advisable policy for the European Court to fashion principles itself and to continually refer to treaty sources of authority to support its policy of activism.

3 THE CONTENTIOUS JURISDICTION OF THE EUROPEAN COURT OF JUSTICE

3.1 Introduction

The contentious jurisdiction of the European Court of Justice is the power of the Court to hear direct actions brought against Member States and Community institutions. Actions against Member States and institutions may be initiated by other Member States or institutions. Individuals and legal persons cannot bring a direct action against a Member State under the contentious jurisdiction of the European Court. However, they may institute an action under the contentious jurisdiction of the Court against an institution if they can successfully demonstrate that certain conditions have been satisfied.

3.2 Key points

a) *Actions against Member States*

An action relating to an infringement of Community law by a Member State may be raised by either another Member State or the European Commission acting on behalf of the Community.

Under Article 170 of the EC Treaty, one Member State may bring a direct action against another if it considers that the Member State concerned has failed to fulfil its obligations under the Community Treaties. The Court exercises exclusive jurisdiction over all disputes between Member States arising out of the subject matter of the Community Treaties. Member States are expressly forbidden from resolving such disputes by any other means: Article 219 EC Treaty.

A number of procedural preconditions must be satisfied before a Member State can initiate a direct action against another. These are:

i)   The Member State alleging the violation must bring the matter to the attention of the European Commission.

ii) The Commission must deliver a reasoned opinion on the matter after allowing the parties in dispute to submit arguments.

iii) Only after the Commission has delivered this opinion, or has failed to do so within the prescribed period of three months from notification of the matter, can the Member State continue its action.

iv) if the Commission indicates that it has no intention of pursuing the action, the complaining state may bring the action itself.

v) The scope of any subsequent court proceedings under Article 169 is circumscribed by the pre-litigation notification intimated by the Commission to the Member State: see *EC Commission* v *Denmark (Re Taxation of Imported Motor Vehicles)* [1994] 2 CMLR 885.

Under Article 169 of the EC Treaty, the European Commission is authorised to commence proceedings against any Member State suspected of violating its Community obligations. The same provision also specifies a formal pre-litigation procedure which must be exhausted before commencing actual proceedings in the Court:

i) While not strictly required under Article 169, the Commission informally notifies the Member State accused of violating its obligations of the allegations and invites comments on the behaviour under investigation. A failure by a Member State to justify its conduct will set the formal pre-litigation procedure in motion.

ii) The Commission conducts an investigation into the matter and delivers a reasoned opinion on the subject after giving the Member State concerned an opportunity to submit its observations. Member States are under a separate obligation to co-operate with the Commission in its investigation and failure to do is a separate violation of Community law; see *EC Commission* v *Greece (Re Electronic Cash Registers)* [1992] 3 CMLR 117.

iii) If the Member State fails to comply with the terms of this opinion within the prescribed period, the Commission will bring the matter to the attention of the Court. However, the Commission must give the Member State a reasonable time to comply with the reasoned opinion: *EC Commission* v *Belgium (Re University Fees)* [1989] 2 CMLR 527.

Violations of Community law may result from both acts and omissions by Member States. Article 5 of the EC Treaty requires Member States to take all appropriate measures to ensure respect for Community obligations and to 'abstain from any measure which could jeopardise the attainment of the objectives of this Treaty'. Common causes of action against Member States include the existence of incompatible legislation or the introduction of administrative practices which are inconsistent with Community law.

Member States cannot justify their failure to comply with their Community obligations by reference to their constitutional inability to control provincial or regional branches of government: see *EC Commission* v *Belgium (Management of Waste)* [1989] 2 CMLR 797.

If the Court of Justice finds against a Member State, it does not pass a sentence but delivers a purely declaratory judgment which notes the fact that a Member State is in default. Originally, this judgment had no executory force and the

European Commission or the Court were unable to impose sanctions to compel the offending state to redress its behaviour.

The Treaty on European Union introduces a new procedure by amending Article 171 of the EC Treaty. Now the Commission is empowered to recommend that a Member State is fined if it fails to comply with an adverse judgment. Fines are imposed by the Court on the basis of a second action brought at the instance of the Commission.

b) *Actions against Community institutions*

A direct action may also be brought in the European Court to review the acts of Community institutions. The European Court has exclusive jurisdiction to review the legality of acts of Community institutions and has sole competence to declare an act of a Community institution invalid: *Foto-Frost* v *Hauptzollamt Lubeck-Ost* [1988] 3 CMLR 57. The legal consequence of a successful challenge is that the Court will declare the measure null and void.

Community acts and measures which may be challenged include regulations, directives, decisions and all other acts capable of creating legal effects. Measures which have been held not to have such an effect include statements of objection, guidelines and internal procedural matters; see *Les Verts* v *European Parliament* [1989] 2 CMLR 880.

Member States, the European Commission and the Council of Ministers are privileged applicants for the purposes of initiating an action for judicial review of Community acts: *Italy* v *EC Council* [1979] ECR 2575. The standing of these parties in such actions is presumed. The fact that a Member State challenges an act of an institution addressed to another Member State is not a bar to judicial review. See *Italy* v *EC Commission (Re British Telecom)* [1985] ECR 873.

While Article 173(2) of the EC Treaty explicitly recognises the standing of natural and legal persons to bring an action for judicial review directly to the European Court, such individuals must demonstrate that the act being challenged constitutes 'a decision which is of direct and individual concern' to the applicant. Decisions of the Council or the Commission addressed to a particular individual cause few problems in establishing direct and individual concern: see *Tokyo Electric Company plc* v *EC Council* [1989] 1 CMLR 169.

The fact that the act challenged by the individual is in the form of a Community regulation or a decision addressed to another person does not ipso facto exclude the possibility of establishing that the measure is a decision of direct and individual concern to an unrelated individual. In order to succeed, an individual must demonstrate that the regulation or decision addressed to another person is, despite its form or substance, a decision of direct and individual concern. See *ARPOSOL* v *EC Council* [1989] 2 CMLR 508; and *Sociedade Agro-Pecuaria Vincente Nobre Lda* v *EC Council* [1990] 1 CMLR 105.

Private parties who can demonstrate direct and individual concern in a Community measure, and who decline to initiate direct proceedings against the Community institution on this basis, cannot later challenge the validity of the measure by bringing proceedings in a national court. In such circumstances, the European Court will decline to answer a preliminary reference from the national court: *TWD Textilwerke Deggendorf GmbH* v *Germany*, judgment of 9 March 1994, not yet reported.

Three separate grounds have been established by the Community treaties as a basis for judicial review of the acts of Community institutions. These are:

i) Actions to annul an act of a Community institution.

ii) Actions against a Community institution for failure to act.

iii) The plea of illegality.

i) Actions of annulment

Article 173 of the EC Treaty expressly confers on the European Court jurisdiction to review the legality of acts of both the Council of Ministers and the European Commission. Although the provision makes no reference to the acts of the European Parliament, the Court has reviewed such acts on a number of occasions. See for example *EC Council* v *European Parliament* [1986] ECR 1339. The Court is empowered to review all acts of the Community institutions other than recommendations and opinions: Article 173(1) EC Treaty.

An act of a Community institution may be annulled on the basis of one of four separate causes:

• Lack of competence on the part of an institution to adopt a particular measure.

• Infringement of an essential procedural requirement.

• Infringement of a provision of a Community treaty or a rule relating to the application of such provisions.

• Misuse of power by a Community institution.

In practice, these substantive grounds for annulment merge into each other and the jurisprudence of the European Court does not clearly distinguish the application of each cause in particular cases.

According to Article 176 of the EC Treaty, where an act has been declared void by the Court, the institution which is responsible for the adoption of the putative measure is obliged to take the 'necessary measures' to comply with the judgment of the Court.

The limitation period for actions of annulment is two months from either the publication of the measure which is being challenged or from the date of the notification to the applicant: Article 173(3) EC Treaty. This period applies regardless of whether the action is brought by a Member State, another Community institution or an individual. While these time limits are onerous, the Court has been prepared to extend the limitation period in cases where the measure being challenged lacks 'all legal basis in the Community legal system': *EC Commission* v *France* [1969] ECR 523.

ii) Actions for failure to act

If a provision of the Community treaties imposes a duty to act on either the Council of Ministers or the European Commission, and one or other of these organs fails to take the appropriate course of conduct, proceedings may be instituted under Article 175 of the EC Treaty (or the counterpart ECSC Treaty and Euratom Treaty provisions) for failure to act.

As a preliminary requirement to the initiation of an action for failure to act, the alleged omission must be brought to the attention of the institution concerned. Thereafter, the particular organ has two months to define its position. An organ may define its position without adopting a particular measure. For example, where the Commission has explained its position and justified its non-activity in terms which are consistent with its obligations under the Community Treaties, the Court has held an action for failure to act inadmissible: *Alfons Lutticke GmbH* v *EC Commission* [1966] ECR 19. This has created a distinction between a failure to act and a refusal to act. The former constitutes a prima facie ground for review while the latter amounts to a negative determination which must be challenged on grounds other than an action for failure to act.

iii) Plea of illegality

Under Article 184 of the EC Treaty, notwithstanding the expiry of the limitation period established for actions of annulment, any party may, in any proceedings which involve a Council or Commission regulation, invoke a plea of illegality in order to have the regulation declared inapplicable. This plea differs from the other grounds for judicial review in that it does not itself constitute a separate or independent cause of action, but allows a party to plead that a regulation is inapplicable in actions initiated on some other jurisdictional basis. The main purpose of this device is to allow challenges to be made to regulations outside the limitation period specified for actions of annulment: see *Simmenthal SpA* v *EC Commission* [1979] ECR 777.

The fact that Article 184 does not constitute a distinct ground for judicial review was made clear in *Worhrmann* v *EC Commission* [1962] ECR 501 where the Court stated:

'It is clear from the wording and the general scheme of this Article that a declaration of the inapplicability of a regulation is only contemplated in proceedings brought before the Court of Justice itself under some other provision of the Treaty, and then only incidentally and with limited effect.'

In order for a plea of illegality to be successful, the regulation upon which the plea is based must be applicable – directly or indirectly – to the principal issue with which the particular application to the Court is concerned: see *Simmenthal SpA* v *EC Commission* [1979] ECR 777.

c) *Plenary jurisdiction*

The term 'plenary jurisdiction' is one more familiar to continental civilian lawyers than their common law counterparts. It refers to the ability of a Court to hear actions which require the Court to exercise its full powers. The plenary jurisdiction of the European Court extends to two principal forms of actions:

i) Actions for damages based on the non-contractual liability of the Community.

ii) Actions to review penalties imposed by Community institutions.

A third ground of plenary jurisdiction related to cases involving disputes between the Community and its staff (staff cases) under Article 179. The jurisdiction to hear such cases was transferred to the Court of First Instance.

Actions based on the contractual liability of the Community do not fall within the plenary jurisdiction of the European Court because jurisdiction to interpret and enforce contractual obligations is governed by the choice of jurisdiction chosen by the parties to the contract: Article 215(1) EC Treaty. Contractual disputes involving the European Community may therefore be brought before the appropriate national courts. The European Court only exercises jurisdiction over contracts involving the Community if a particular clause in the contract refers disputes to arbitration before the European Court. See *EC Commission* v *Zoubek* [1986] ECR 4057.

i) Actions based on the non-contractual liability of the Community

The European Court has jurisdiction over non-contractual claims against the Community by virtue of Article 178 of the EC Treaty. Non-contractual liability is a residual category which comprises all the liabilities of the Community other than contractual liability. The Court is instructed by Article 215 of the EC Treaty to develop the Community law of non-contractual liability from 'the general principles common to the laws of the Member States' in order to 'make good any damage caused by its institutions or by its servants in the performance of their duties'.

One recent case illustrates the elements required for a successful action based on the (non-contractual) liability of the Community. In *Sociedade Agro-Pecuaria Vincente* v *EC Council* [1990] 1 CMLR 105, the European Court observed that:

'[T]he Court has held in previous decisions that by virtue of Article 215(2) of the [EC] Treaty, the [non-contractual] liability of the Community presupposes the existence of a set of circumstances comprising the unlawfulness of the conduct alleged against the institution, actual damage and the existence of a causal link between the conduct and the alleged damage.'

Three elements are therefore necessary to establish the non-contractual liability of the Community: an unlawful act (or omission) which can be attributed to the Community; injury on the part of the applicant; and a causal connection between the act itself and the commission of the injury.

In certain circumstances, non-contractual liability may be imputed to the Community even although the national authorities of a Member State were actually responsible for the commission of the act which is alleged to give rise to the liability. In *Krohn Import-Export Co* v *EC Commission* [1986] ECR 753, the European Court established the principle that, where a national authority or body is obliged under Community law to comply with the instructions of the European Commission, any claim for compensation based on non-contractual liability should be directed against the Commission and not the national authorities.

ii) Actions to review penalties

The European Court has jurisdiction to review penalties imposed by Community institutions. Article 172 of the EC Treaty authorises the Council of Ministers to enact regulations to regulate this aspect of jurisdiction. However, in the past, the Council of Ministers has tended to grant this authority in specific regulations dealing with particular subjects, rather than to adopt a comprehensive regulation to govern this aspect of the Court's jurisdiction.

A typical illustration of the Council granting such a power of review is contained in Council Regulation 17/62 which concerns the administration of Community competition policy. As regards competition policy, the jurisdiction of the Court is defined in the following terms:

'The Court shall have unlimited jurisdiction within the meaning of Article 172 of the [EC] Treaty to review decisions whereby the Commission has fixed a fine or periodic payment; it may cancel, reduce or increase the fine or periodic payment imposed.'

Unlimited jurisdiction permits the Court to cancel, reduce or increase a penalty imposed on a commercial enterprise by the Commission.

3.3 Relevant cases

France v *United Kingdom (Re Fishing Mesh)* [1979] ECR 2923: The sole illustration of a complaint by one Member State against another proceeding to judgment by the Court.

Star Fruit Co SA v *EC Commission* [1990] 1 CMLR 733: A private individual does not have the right to compel the Commission to institute proceedings against a Member State suspected of violating Community law.

EC Commission v *France (Re Tobacco Prices)* [1990] 1 CMLR 49: Prima facie, the period for complying with an adverse judgment against a Member State should be no longer than the minimum period needed for adopting the required remedial measures.

Foto-Frost v *Hauptzollamt Lubeck-Ost* [1988] 3 CMLR 57: The European Court has exclusive competence to declare an act of a Community institution null and void and this power cannot be exercised by a national court.

Sofrimport SARL v *EC Commission* [1990] 3 CMLR 80: A decision outlining the necessary requirements for an individual to establish standing in an action to review an act of a Community organ.

EC Commission v Greece *(Re Electronic Cash Registers)* [1992] 3 CMLR 117: obligation to co-operate with the Commission in its investigations under Article 169.

EC Commission v *Denmark (Re Taxation of Imported Motor Vehicles)* [1994] 2 CMLR 885: the Commission is limited in any subsequent action under Article 169 to the matters which were brought to the attention of the Member State in the pre-notification procedure.

3.4 Relevant materials

LN Brown, *The Court of Justice of the European Communities* (third edition, 1989).

A Dashwood & R White, 'Enforcement Actions under Articles 169 and 170 EC' (1989) 14 EL Rev 388.

MCEJ Bronckers 'Private Enforcement of 1992' (1989) 26 CMLR 513.

RM Greaves 'Locus Standi under Article 173 when Seeking Annulment of a Regulation' (1986) 11 EL Rev 119.

3.5 Analysis of questions

Questions relating to the contentious jurisdiction of the European Court are particularly popular among examiners. Students must be familiar with the different grounds for the exercise of the contentious jurisdiction of the Court, together with the various causes of action. While this aspect of Community law is particularly complex, it should be pointed out that this subject is a reliable one for preparation for examination purposes.

3.6 Questions

QUESTION ONE

To what extent will Article 171(2) of the draft Treaty on European Union ('Maastricht') and the judgment of the European Court of Justice in *Francovich* resolve the problems surrounding the enforcement of Community law in the Member States by the Commission and for the benefit of individuals?

*University of London LLB Examination
(for External Students) European Community Law June 1993 Q8*

General Comment

This is an essay-type question requiring a narrative answer and concerns the recent constitutional developments within the Community. In order to answer the question properly, it is necessary to be familiar with the background to the changes and to offer a well-reasoned legal opinion on the effects that the changes will bring.

Skeleton Solution

- The problems encountered in the operation of the original Article 171: repetitive actions, non-implementation, delay.
- Outline of the terms of new Article 171(2).
- Shortcomings of the amendments: uncertainty, mechanisms for enforcement.
- Decision of the ECJ in the *Francovich* case and the conditions for establishing liability.
- Contribution of these changes to enforcement of Community law in Member States by the Commission *and* private individuals.

Suggested Solution

The original terms of Article 171 of the EC Treaty merely required Member States found in violation of their Community obligations by the European Court to 'take the necessary measures' to comply with the judgment. No other mechanism was created to enforce judgments against Member States. Nor were any sanctions specified for failure to comply with the terms of an adverse decision.

On the whole, this obligation was sufficient to compel most Member States to amend their laws to comply with the decisions of the Court. However, certain states, in particular Italy, acquired a reputation for ignoring the rulings of the Court. Other states, such as France, refused to obey the decisions of the Court when it ruled against them on particularly sensitive issues. While the record for complying with the decisions of the Court was initially respectable, towards the end of the early 1980s, the position had deteriorated and in 1991 the European Commission reported that over 50 decisions of the Court remained unimplemented.

There are a number of notorious cases where Member States persistently refused to adhere to the decisions of the Court. For example, in 1969 the European Court ruled that an Italian law imposing an export tax on art treasures was contrary to the principle of the free movement of goods: *EC Commission* v *Italy (Re Tax on Art Treasures)* (1985). Italy refused to amend its laws and a subsequent action was brought by the Commission: *EC Commission* v *Italy (Re Failure to Implement Community Obligations)* (1972). Again Italy ignored the ruling and the matter was only eventually served through a political compromise.

Another illustration of a Member State refusing to comply with the decisions of the Court occurred when the Court condemned France for its ban on imports of mutton and lamb from the United Kingdom: *EC Commission* v *France (Re Sheepmeat from the UK)* (1979). Again the Commission was required to bring fresh proceedings against France for violation of Articles 171 and 5 of the EC Treaty.

The increasing willingness of Member States to resist the rulings of the Court has been caused by two primary factors. First, although the Court has powers to grant interim measures in an action by the Commission for enforcement of a Court judgment under Article 186, it has been reluctant to use them to compel a Member State to comply with a ruling. For example, when France imposed the embargo on mutton and lamb products from the United Kingdom, the Court refused to grant the interim measures requested by the Commission because France was already under an obligation to implement the ruling by virtue of Article 171.

Second, Member States have traditionally been allowed a lengthy period to comply with adverse rulings from the Court. Technically this period is restricted to the minimum period needed for the adoption of the necessary remedial measures; *EC Commission* v *France (Re Tobacco Prices)* (1990). In practice, the workloads of the Commission and the Court, combined with the procrastinations of governments, mean that a Member State found in violation has an excessive period within which to act and most do act after a sufficient period. However, the effect of this situation is that there are lengthy delays pending the adoption of amending national laws.

In terms of the original Article 171, the only remedy available to the Commission to enforce a Court ruling was to repeatedly bring proceedings against Member States alleging that, in addition to the original violation, the states had also breached Article 171 by failing to implement the decision. Clearly this was an unsatisfactory situation.

The Treaty on European Union adds an additional paragraph to Article 171 and introduces a process whereby a Member State can be fined for failing to implement a Court ruling. This involves a three stage process.

Once a decision has been given by the Court and a Member State has not complied with its terms within a reasonable period, the Commission shall deliver a reasoned opinion to the state concerned after having given that state an opportunity to submit its observations on the matter. The reasoned opinion shall specify the points on which, in the opinion of the Commission, the Member State is not complying with the Court's decision.

The second stage involves a second action against the Member State, this time under Article 171(2) itself. In these proceedings, the Commission may specify any penalty which should be paid by the Member State for the failure to act. This penalty may take the form of either a lump sum or a penalty payment, the latter being a sum required to be paid by the Member State at regular intervals until the breach is remedied.

The final stage is for the Court to rule on the issue of whether the Member State has failed to comply with its obligations under Article 171(1). If it has not, the Court may require the Member State to pay the lump sum or penalty payment.

There is some scepticism as to how this procedure will work in practice and the extent to which this will resolve the problems surrounding the enforcement of Community law against Member States.

First, private individuals cannot raise actions in the European Court against Member States. Accordingly, this is not an avenue open to private individuals, only the European Commission. Private individuals must continue to rely on the remedies available in their national courts against government bodies alleged to have engaged in practices contrary to Community law.

Second, the exact powers of the Commission to specify the amount of the fine are not stated. There is no maximum, or minimum, level of fine which may be proposed by the Commission. It is also not clear whether the European Court is bound to impose the exact fine suggested by the Commission in the event that a Member State is found to have violated this obligation. Can the Court modify the proposed amount in accordance with the terms of its second ruling?

Third, there is no mechanism in the Article to compel a Member State to pay the sum. For example, the penalty cannot expressly be deducted from its budgetary contributions. Therefore, in the event that a Member State persistently refuses to pay the prescribed penalties there is little that can be done to compel it to do so. This is a substantial flaw in the procedure.

Hence, the amendment to Article 171 may not be as successful in ensuring the enforcement of judgments against Member States as it might appear at first sight.

The European Court's ruling in the *Francovich* case (1993) is, however, a completely different matter. This case established the principle that Member States can be liable to private individuals for failing to comply with Community law if the failure causes injury or damage to those individuals.

The facts of this case may be briefly stated as follows. The plaintiff raised an action in an Italian court claiming damages for loss of salary caused by the failure of the Italian government to establish a fund to pay redundancy payments in the event that an employee is made redundant through the insolvency of his or her employer. The duty to establish such a fund was imposed by a Community directive which Italy had failed to implement.

The Italian court referred the question to the European Court for a preliminary ruling. The European Court replied that, under Community law, states are liable to private individuals for failing to comply with Community law if three conditions are satisfied:

- the purpose of the Community measure which was not respected by the Member State was to create private rights for individuals;
- the nature and content of these rights must be identifiable from the terms of the measure; and
- there must exist a causal link between the failure by the Member State to comply with Community law and the injury sustained by the individual.

In the event that these conditions are fulfilled, the Member State is liable to remedy the consequence of any damage or injury suffered as a result of the denial of Community rights.

However, again there are a number of shortcomings in the operation of this right. Each Member State is responsible for adopting procedures to allow for the vindication of this right. Hence, within the United Kingdom, the national courts are responsible for ensuring that a mechanism exists to bring such actions against the UK government. As yet, the legal basis for such a claim in English law is uncertain: see *Bourgoin* v *Ministry of Agriculture, Fisheries and Food* (1986).

In addition, there is no certainty as to the types of Community measures that may be relied on to establish such rights. In the *Francovich* case itself, the infringement of Community law was a failure to implement the terms of a directive. It is not automatically the case that violations of EC Treaty articles, regulations, decisions or general principles of Community law will also result in this form of liability. This is a matter which the Court has still to resolve.

Also, it is not clear from the case whether or not the European Court must have held the Member State in question in violation of Community law through a direct action under Article 169. In the *Francovich* case, the Court had already found Italy in breach of Community law in an earlier direct action brought by the Commission. It is not apparent from the decision if such a ruling is a prerequisite to a successful action in a national court.

Notwithstanding these shortcomings, the Court's decision in this case is a landmark case establishing that Member States can be liable to private individuals for failing to comply with Community law. Prior to the ruling, this liability had not been definitively established; see *Asteris AE* v *Greece* (1990). The Court has still to elaborate on the exact scope of this right, but there is little doubt that the decision will encourage a rash of cases on this point which will hopefully clarify the position.

But, since the principle of Member State responsibility for violations of Community law can be asserted in national courts, which have powers to enforce their decisions, this is likely to be a more effective remedy for private individuals seeking redress for injury suffered than the mechanisms which are to be introduced by Article 171(2).

QUESTION TWO

Liquidgold plc is one of only four manufacturers in the European Community of a new type of liquid sweetener manufactured from barley. Drinkitdown Ltd, a manufacturer of soft drinks, was so attracted by the economics of using this type of sweetener that it has installed new machinery in its factory suitable for use with the barley sweetener. In January it entered into a contract with Liquidgold to purchase 10,000 tonnes of the sweetener each year for the next five years, this quantity being the amount needed to meet its current production requirements.

Last month, fearing adverse effects on the Community sugar industry, the Council adopted a Regulation imposing production quotas on the barley sweetener. An annex to that Regulation, which expressly refers to the four manufacturers by name, fixed Liquidgold's annual quota at 7,500 tonnes.

Having discovered that the other three manufacturers are already bound by contracts covering the whole of their permitted production, Drinkitdown is faced with a choice between cutting back its production or converting its factory to use sugar at a cost of £500,000.

Advise Drinkitdown as to the remedies available to it with regard to the Council Regulation.

University of London LLB Examination
(for External Students) European Community Law 1990 Q4

General Comment

A typical problem-type question which requires the application of the relevant law to the facts of the question.

Skeleton Solution

• The applicable substantive principles of Community law.
• Standing to challenge a regulation.
• Problem of time bar; plea of illegality.
• Possibility of an indirect challenge through the Article 177 procedure.

Suggested Solution

In order to mount a successful challenge against the Council Regulation which imposes production quotas on the barley sweetener, Drinkitdown must establish the existence of one of four separate causes of action: lack of competence; infringement of an essential procedural requirement; infringement of a provision of a Community Treaty or a rule relating to the application of such provisions; or the misuse of power by a Community institution. From the facts of the case, the only possible cause of action would be on the basis of an infringement of the terms of the Community Treaties or the principles of Community law which have been derived from these treaties.

The Regulation was adopted as a measure to protect the Community sugar industry and would therefore be subject to the Common Agricultural Policy (CAP), the objectives of which are set out in Article 39 of the EC Treaty. This article recognises the general principle of proportionality. This principle requires that measures introduced to regulate a particular activity must be not be disproportionately onerous in relation to their derived benefit. In other words, if the harm caused by the introduction of a regulation outweighs any possible benefit, the measure may be challenged as being contrary to the principle of proportionality which is a recognised rule of Community law: *EC Commission* v *France (Re Imports Restrictions on Milk Substitutes)* (1989). If Drinkitdown could establish that the Council Regulation limiting the production of the sweetener caused more injury than assistance, the Regulation could be challenged on this basis.

Alternatively, Drinkitdown could attempt to demonstrate that the enactment of the Regulation contravenes the principle of legitimate expectation. For example, in *Mulder* v *Minister van Landbouw* (1989), the European Court held that a farmer who had suspended milk production pursuant to a Community scheme could not be subsequently excluded from the allocation of milk quotas after the scheme had been discontinued. The Court held that the farmer had a legitimate expectation that at the end of the programme he would be in a position no less favourable than that which he would have enjoyed had he not acceded to the scheme. Clearly, Drinkitdown could argue that it had a legitimate expectation that its expenditure on plant conversion would not be misspent as a result of a Community measure.

While Drinkitdown may have a legitimate cause of action to challenge the Council Regulation, in order to show standing Article 173(2) requires individuals and legal persons to demonstrate that the act being challenged constitutes a decision which is of 'direct and individual concern' to the applicant. The fact that the act challenged by the individual is in the form of a regulation or a decision addressed to another person does not ipso facto exclude the possibility of establishing the measure is a decision of direct and individual concern. However, an action for judicial review of a regulation or a decision addressed to another person is considerably more onerous than review of a decision explicitly addressed to an individual.

The Council Regulation imposing the production quotas refers to four manufacturers by name, including Liquidgold, but does not refer to Drinkitdown. Drinkitdown must therefore establish that the Regulation is in fact a 'decision' under Article 173(2), in which it has a direct and individual concern. In order to show that the Regulation is a decision, Drinkitdown must prove that, while the measure takes the form of a regulation, it is in fact a series of individual decisions in the form of a regulation. An example of applicants successfully proving that a regulation made by the Commission constituted a decision is *International Fruit Company* v *EC Commission* (1971). In this case, the particular Community regulation challenged established a system of import licences to limit the importation of dessert apples into the Community according to supply and demand in the market. Importers could only receive an import licence if the volume of their proposed imports did not exceed a certain level. The Court held that this regulation was not a generally applicable measure, but a 'conglomeration of individual decisions taken by the Commission under the guise of a regulation'. This determination was made on the basis that applications over a certain quantity were automatically disqualified from the competition for import licences. In the present case, it would be relatively simple to establish that the Regulation is in fact a conglomeration of individual decisions since the Regulation itself is expressly confined to the activities of four businesses.

If Drinkitdown can establish that the Regulation is in fact a decision, it must then be shown that the decision is of direct and individual concern. In order to have direct concern, the effects of the decision must immediately affect the applicant without depending on the exercise of discretion by another body. Thus, in *ARPOSOL* v *EC Council* (1989), the European Court held that the applicants could not establish direct concern because the implementation of the Community measure depended on the intervention of the national authorities of Member States. In another case, the applicant was refused standing because the administration of a Community measure allocating quotas actually depended on distribution by Member States to individuals: *Bock* v *EC Commission* (1971). However, where the national authorities have no discretion in implementing a Community measure, direct concern may be established: see *Sofrimport SARL* v *EC Commission* (1990). The criterion of direct concern may therefore be presumed.

In addition to having a direct concern in the decision being challenged, Drinkitdown must also establish an individual concern. When a decision is not expressly addressed to an individual, in order for the measure to be of individual concern, it must be demonstrated that it affects 'their legal position because of a factual situation which differentiates them individually in the same way as to the person to whom it is addressed': *Sociedade Agro-Pecuaria Vincente Nobre Lda* v *EC Commission* (1990). See also *Dentz und Geldermann* v *EC Council* (1988). The contested measure must affect the applicant by reason of certain peculiar attributes or factual circumstances which differentiate the applicant from all other persons: see *Sofrimport SARL* case, above. The mere ability to ascertain more or less precisely, or even to establish the identity of the persons to whom a measure applies, does not immediately imply that the measure is of individual concern to them: *Cargill and Ors* v *EC Commission* (1990).

Individual concern has been established where a regulation named specific undertakings and applied specific measures to them, where the regulation had as its subject-matter the individual circumstances of three named importers, and where a decision was issued by the Commission in response to the requests of a particular group, even although the final decision was addressed to another person. Conversely, if an act applies to objectively determined situations and entails legal effects for categories of persons generally and in the abstract, it has general application and is incapable of having individual effect: *Cooperativa Veneta Allevatori Equini* v *EC Commission* (1989). Drinkitdown might therefore have difficulty establishing that the Regulation is of individual concern.

If Drinkitdown was successful in challenging the validity of the Regulation, it could also be successful in obtaining compensation from the Community for injury sustained as a result of the unlawful measure. Article 215(2) of the EC Treaty states that, in the case of non-contractual liability, the Community shall, in accordance with the general principles common to the laws of the Member States, make good any damage caused by the institution responsible for the unlawful measure. Article 178 of the EC Treaty confers jurisdiction on the European Court to decide disputes relating to damages on the basis of the non-contractual liability of the Community.

Alternatively, Drinkitdown may indirectly challenge the validity of the Regulation on any legal grounds by means of reference for a preliminary ruling by a national court to the European Court under Article 177 of the EC Treaty. Such a reference may be made where it is relevant to the outcome of pending legislation. Indeed, in *Foto-Frost* v *Hauptzollamt Lubeck-Ost* (1988), the European Court held that such a reference was necessary in a case involving a challenge to a Community measure because only the European Court had the power to render such an act invalid. An Article 177 reference may be made regardless of the locus standi of the applicant and any time limits: see *International Fruit Company*, above.

If the European Court was prepared to declare the Regulation invalid, it would not be applicable to Liquidgold and therefore Drinkitdown could rely on the sales contract negotiated between itself and Liquidgold.

QUESTION THREE

On 1 December 1988 the Commission of the European Communities took a decision instructing the British Customs authorities to stop issuing import licences for textile imports from Guatemala until 31 December 1989. The Commission's decision was taken in accordance with a Council Regulation, approved in July 1985, which established a quota for each of the Member States on such imports and entrusting the Commission with the enforcement of the Regulation.

According to the Commission, the quota assigned to the United Kingdom was reached on 27 November 1977.

On 29 November 1988 Wooltex, a British company, applied to the British Customs authorities for a licence to import 40,000 T-shirts from Guatemala. Wooltex's application was refused on the grounds that it would violate the Commission's decision.

Advise Wooltex as to any remedies which it may have under EC law.

University of London LLB Examination
(for External Students) European Community Law 1989 Q5

General Comment

A problem primarily involving the issue of challenges to measures of Community institutions, but with additional complexities.

Skeleton Solution

• Possible proceedings under Article 173.
• Problem of limitation.
• Claim for compensation based on the non-contractual liability of the Community.

Suggested Solution

An act of a Community institution may be challenged under Article 173 of the EC Treaty on the basis of any one of four separate grounds: lack of competence; infringement of an essential procedural requirement; infringement of a Community Treaty or a rule relating to its application; and misuse of powers. The factual circumstances of this problem indicate that a number of these grounds may have relevance in providing Wooltex with advice as regards possible remedies against the Commission's action.

An act of a Community institution may be annulled on the basis of a lack of competence if the organ acted without appropriate power. If the wrong institution has acted or, alternatively, if the right body has acted but without the appropriate authority, the act in question may be reduced on the grounds of a lack of competence: see *Meroni and Co* v *ECSC High Authority* (1957–58). If Wooltex can prove that the Council Regulation delegating authority upon the Commission to issue such decisions is ultra vires the decision can be successfully challenged. If the Council has no competence to delegate authority to the Commission under the terms of the EC Treaty, the measure itself is null and void. Wooltex may also be able to establish that, by imposing an absolute ban on the importation of textiles, the Commission has exceeded its authority.

Annulment of an act of a Community institution is also possible if, in adopting the measure, the institution was guilty of infringing an essential procedural requirement. The act will only be annulled if the procedural error is substantial or involves an important step in the decision making processes: see *SA Roquette Freres* v *EC Council* (1980). In order to constitute a breach of an essential procedural requirement, the error must significantly compromise the position of the applicant. For example, if a Community measure requires the convening of a hearing to investigate a matter, and no such meeting is held, the omission will normally vitiate any final decision on the matter: *ACF Chemiefarma* v *EC Commission* (1970). Alternatively, where an organ is obliged to set out the reasons for its decision, failure to do so will amount to infringement of an essential procedural requirement: *Control Data Belgium NV* v *EC Commission* (1983). Unfortunately the facts of this case do not suggest these are possible grounds for a valid challenge.

A further complication could be added by the fact that the prescription period for actions of annulment is two months from either the publication of the measure which is being challenged or from the date of notification to the applicant: Article 173(3) EC Treaty. Where the measure has not been published or notified to the applicant, the two months prescription period runs from the date on which knowledge of the measure may be imputed to the applicant. While these time limits are onerous, the Court has been prepared to extend the limitation period in cases where the measure being challenged lacks 'all legal basis in the Community legal system': *EC Commission* v *France* (1969).

In the event that Wooltex is successful in establishing that the Commission decision is null and void, the question of compensation arises. The European Court has jurisdiction over non-contractual claims against the Community by virtue of Article 178 of the EC Treaty. The Court has been instructed by Article 215 of the EC Treaty to develop the law of non-contractual liability of the Community from 'the general principles common to the laws of the Member States' in order to 'make good any damage caused by its institutions or by its servants in the performance of their duties'. A number of principles have been fashioned by the European Court into a rudimentary framework to regulate this matter. In *Sociedade Agro-Pecuaria Vincente* v *EC Council* (1990), the European Court observed that:

'[T]he Court has held in previous decisions that by virtue of Article 215(2) of the [EC] Treaty, the liability of the Community presupposes the existence of a set of circumstances comprising the unlawfulness of the conduct alleged against the institutions, actual damage and the existence of a causal link between the conduct and the alleged damage.'

Article 215 makes no reference to the element of fault in the commission of the act or omission, merely requiring that the Community shall 'make good any damages caused by its institutions or by its servants'. However, the Court has often referred to the requirement of fault in determining the non-contractual liability of the Community: *Toepfer* v *EC Commission* (1965). At the same time, the Court has not invariably required proof of fault and the jurisprudence of the Court has become a little incoherent: *Adams* v *EC Commission* (1985). The necessity of demonstrating fault appears to vary according to the nature of the act upon which liability is alleged.

Where the liability of the Community is being established on the basis of a measure adopted by a Community institution, no liability will fall on the Community unless adoption of the measure constitutes a flagrant violation of a fundamental rule for the protection of the individual. The Court has stressed that, where a legislative measure is concerned, the unlawfulness of the conduct must constitute a 'sufficiently serious breach of a superior rule for the protection of the individual': *Zuckerfabrik Bedburg & Ors* v *EC Council and EC Commission* (1987).

Even although the British customs authorities refused to grant Wooltex application for a licence, the Community will still remain liable even although national authorities were directly responsible for the commission of the tortious act. In *Krohn Import-Export Co* v *European Commission* (1986), the Court established the principle that, where a national authority or body is bound to comply with the instructions of the Commission, a claim for compensation should be addressed to the Commission and not the national authority.

The second requirement for a claim for non-contractual compensation is the existence of injury sustained by the applicant. The degree of injury is also relevant to the calculation of damages. However, the Court has avoided identifying heads of damages and has been content to assess both injury and damages on an ad hoc basis. Where injuries sustained cannot be attributed to the act of a Community institution, no damages may be awarded: *Comptoir National Technique Agricole SA* v *EC Commission* (1975). The Court has also developed a number of rules to govern the issue of the remoteness of damages.

QUESTION FOUR

Recent research by British scientists has revealed that certain types of cling-film may constitute a health hazard when used in a particular fashion. Concerned by this revelation, the British Government decide to prevent imports of cling-film from Germany and Sweden. German and Swedish firms affected by this decision want to seek a remedy. Advise these firms as to their rights and remedies.

Question prepared by the Author

General Comment

A question dealing with a particularly contentious area of Community law.

Skeleton Solution

• Nature of the alleged violation.
• Inability of individuals to sue Member States in the ECJ.
• Complaints to the European Commission.
• Remedy before national courts and tribunals.

Suggested Solution

The EC Treaty requires, in addition to the abolition of customs duties, the removal of all quantitative restrictions and measures having an equivalent effect on imports and exports within the Community: Article 30 EC Treaty. In *Procureur du Roi* v *Dassonville* (1974), the European Court pointed out that 'all trading rules enacted by Member States which are capable of hindering, directly or indirectly, actually or potentially intra-Community trade are to be considered as measures having equivalent effect to quantitative restrictions'. Measures introduced to protect public health are permitted under Article 36, but Member States introducing such measures must show that the purpose of the legislation is in the general interest and is such as to take precedence over the requirement of the free movement of goods which constitutes one of the fundamental rules of the Community: *Cassis de Dijon Case* (1979).

However, individuals and legal persons cannot bring a direct action in the European Court of Justice for judicial review of the actions of a Member State. While individuals and legal persons can raise a direct action against a Community institution under Article 173 of the EC Treaty, a similar right is not created in respect of actions against Member States. The German and Swedish companies could opt for two alternate courses of action. First, they could complain to the European Commission about the measures adopted by the United Kingdom. Second, they could sue the governmental department responsible for the measure on the ground that the department has been responsible for a violation of Community law.

The European Commission may start an investigation into a violation of a Community obligation by a Member State after a complaint has been received from a private individual or a legal person. A complaint from an aggrieved individual to the Commission has a number of advantages over litigation against the government of a Member State in the courts of that Member State. First, the complainer incurs nominal legal costs since the Commission assumes the responsibility for the prosecution of the case. Second, the weight of the Commission behind a complaint is more likely to expedite an out-of-court settlement of the dispute. In addition, the complainer may remain anonymous in the event of the Commission proceeding with the complaint.

At the same time, if the Commission initiates an action on the basis of a complaint from an individual, the success of the Commission in the subsequent litigation will not give the complainer an automatic right to seek damages or compensation for injuries sustained. Further, the Commission retains absolute discretion to decide whether litigation is the appropriate course of action. A private party alleging injury as a consequence of a violation of Community law by a Member State cannot compel the Commission to institute proceedings against that state: *Star Fruit Co SA v EC Commission* (1990).

In the event that the Commission refuses to prosecute the case against the United Kingdom after a complaint by the German and Swedish producers of cling-film, these companies would be obliged to raise an action in the British courts against the responsible governmental department. In such a case, a plaintiff would have to establish that either a remedy for such a breach existed in English law and could be enforced in the English courts or that Community law established such a remedy which the English courts would have to recognise: *Rewe v Landwirtschaftskammer Saarland* (1977).

While the Swedish firm would not be able to rely on Community rights against the UK government, the position is different for the German firm. In the recent decision in *Francovich v Italian Republic* (1993), the European Court held that Member States can be liable to private individuals for failing to comply with Community law if the failure causes injury or damage to those individuals.

The facts of this case may be briefly stated as follows. The plaintiff raised an action in an Italian court claiming damages for loss of salary caused by the failure of the Italian government to establish a fund to pay redundancy payments in the event that an employee is made redundant through the insolvency of his or her employer. The duty to establish such a fund was imposed by a Community directive which Italy had failed to implement.

The Italian court referred the question to the European Court for a preliminary ruling. The European Court replied that, under Community law, states are liable to private individuals for failing to comply with Community law if three conditions are satisfied:

a) the purpose of the Community measure which was not respected by the Member State was to create private rights for individuals;

b) the nature and content of these rights must be identifiable from the terms of the measure; and

c) there must exist a causal link between the failure by the Member State to comply with Community law and the injury sustained by the individual.

In the event that these conditions are fulfilled, the Member State is liable to remedy the consequence of any damage or injury suffered as a result of the denial of Community rights.

Since the principle of Member State responsibility for violations of Community law can be asserted in national courts, which have powers to enforce their decisions, this is likely to be a more effective remedy for the German firm rather than pursuing the complaint to the Commission.

There are two reasons why litigation in the UK courts is the preferred course of action. First, UK courts may issue injunctions to restrain further infringements of the rights of individuals under Community law: see *Kirklees Metropolitan Borough Council v Wickes Building Supplies Ltd* (1992).

Second, the UK courts are empowered to award damages for compensation for any injury suffered as a result of injury directly attributed to the illegal act committed by the Member State.

Of course, in the particular circumstances of this case it would be necessary to establish that the UK's action in establishing the embargo was contrary to provisions of Community law, most likely Article 30.

4 THE PRELIMINARY RULING JURISDICTION OF THE EUROPEAN COURT OF JUSTICE

4.1 Introduction

To ensure the uniform, consistent and harmonious application of Community law throughout the national legal systems of the Member States, the Community Treaties establish a procedure to allow national courts to refer questions of Community law to the European Court for consideration. These references from national courts fall within the preliminary ruling jurisdiction of the Court. Article 177 of the EC Treaty establishes the essential principles and procedures which govern this aspect of the jurisdiction of the European Court.

4.2 Key points

a) *Scope of the preliminary ruling jurisdiction*

Article 177 of the EC Treaty confers jurisdiction on the European Court to render preliminary ruling decisions which relate to:

i)   The interpretation of the Community Treaties.

ii) The validity and interpretation of acts of the Community institutions.

iii) The interpretation of statutes of bodies established by the Council of Ministers where the relevant statutes so provide.

In addition, a number of Conventions among the Member States of the Community provide for preliminary references from national courts to the European Court for the interpretation of intra-Community agreements.

b) *The obligation to request a preliminary ruling – lower courts*

All national courts and tribunals, other than those against which there is no appeal, have discretion whether or not to refer a case involving a question of Community law to the European Court. If the issue arises before a court against whose decision there is no judicial remedy under national law, technically that court is obliged to refer the matter to the European Court: Article 177(3) EC Treaty.

Courts and tribunals which exercise a discretion to refer a question should be satisfied that two preconditions exist before making a reference, namely:

i)   the court or tribunal must believe that the case involves an issue of Community law; and

ii) the court or tribunal must be satisfied that a decision on the question is necessary to decide the merits of the case.

A prima facie question of Community law will arise where a party relies on a provision of a Community Treaty, or a measure of Community law such as a regulation, a directive or a decision, or a precedent of the European Court (and now also the Court of First Instance).

c)   *The obligation to request a preliminary ruling – courts of final instance*

National courts and tribunals of final instance (or last resort) are subject to a different set of obligations as regards seeking preliminary references from the European Court. Article 177(3) of the EC Treaty declares that these courts are bound to refer a question of Community law to the European Court for a preliminary reference.

This absolute duty has been qualified by the European Court itself, particularly in *CILFIT* v *Ministry of Health* [1982] ECR 3415. Where a question of Community law arises before a national court of final appeal, such a court need not refer the matter for a preliminary ruling if the question has already been settled by the European Court. This discretion applies only 'where previous decisions of the [European] Court have already dealt with the point of law in question, irrespective of the nature of the proceedings which led to those decisions, even although the questions at issue are not strictly identical': *CILFIT*, above.

The European Court has also established a number of guidelines to ensure that this privilege is not abused. A court of final instance which decides not to refer a question to the European Court because of an earlier precedent must give special consideration to the 'characteristic features of Community law and the particular difficulties to which its interpretation gives rise'. Special consideration must be given to the following matters:

i)   Community legislation is drafted in several different languages all of which are equally authentic and proper interpretation often involves comparisons with different language versions.

ii) Community law has acquired its own terminology and legal concepts do not necessarily have the same meaning in Community law as in national law.

iii) Every provision of Community law has to be placed in its proper context and interpreted in light of the system established by the Community Treaties, having regard both to its objectives and to the state of the law at that particular point. See *Litster* v *Forth Dry Dock and Engineering Co* [1989] 1 All ER 1134.

In many respects the decision of the European Court in the *CILFIT* case reduces the discretion of courts of last instance to decide questions of Community law themselves because it establishes rigorous criteria for deciding whether or not to refer a question to the European Court.

d) *The nature of the question submitted for a preliminary ruling*

There are no formal requirements regulating the content of a question submitted for a preliminary reference, although obviously the greater the degree of precision, the more accurate the response of the European Court.

The European Court decides whether the requirements of the preliminary reference itself satisfy the terms of Article 177 of the EC Treaty. In the past, the Court has had to decide:

i) whether a body in national law is a court or tribunal for the purposes of Article 177: see *Pretore Di Salo* v *Persons Unknown* [1989] 1 CMLR 71;

ii) whether a reference is premature or may have the effect of precluding a later reference from the same court in the same case;

iii) if the question asked of the Court is too vague, or general, or involves questions of national law; and

iv) if a preliminary ruling is competent in the event that a higher court had already ruled on the matter: see *Society for the Protection of Unborn Children* v *Grogan* [1991] 3 CMLR 849.

The Court will not answer questions considered to be contrived or hypothetical. For example, in *Foglia* v *Novello (No 1)* [1980] ECR 745, the Court declined to answer a reference which it considered contrived on the grounds that there was no real dispute between the parties.

Similarly, in *Meilicke* v *ADV/OGA FA Meyer AG* (1992) The Times 20 October the Court rejected a reference from a German court concerning a dispute that had not yet arisen between the parties but had been made to resolve a hypothetical and abstract point of law.

In fact, as a general principle, the Court has recently become more and more reluctant to accept loose references made by national courts if either the facts stated are too vague or the legal principles sought to be clarified inadequately specified: see *Pretore Di Genoa* v *Banchero*, judgment of 20 May 1993, not yet reported. This represents a reversal of its earlier policy of flexibility in these circumstances.

e) *The authority of a preliminary reference*

The term 'preliminary reference' is somewhat misleading. A preliminary ruling is not an advisory opinion but rather a decision which the referring national court is obliged to apply to the facts of the case: see *Brown* v *Secretary of State for Scotland* 1989 SLT 402. A preliminary reference is binding upon the court which referred the question for consideration in the sense that it represents an authoritative determination of Community law.

Not only are decisions rendered through the preliminary reference procedure binding on the court which referred the question, but they may also be cited as precedents in those Member States which adhere to the principle of stare decisis. Decisions of the European Court are therefore binding as precedents on British courts when they relate to identical points of Community law: *WH Smith Do-It-All & Payless DIY Ltd* v *Peterborough City Council* [1990] 2 CMLR 577.

f) *The functions and responsibilities of the European Court*

The primary responsibility of the European Court in a preliminary reference is to decide the legal merits of the case in terms of Community law. Therefore, the European Court cannot expressly declare that provisions of national law are inconsistent with Community law; this is a matter for the national court. As the Court has expressly observed:

'[T]he Court is not empowered under Article 177 of the [EC] Treaty to rule on the compatibility with the Treaty of provisions of national law. However, it has jurisdiction to provide the national court with all such matters relating to the interpretation of Community law as may enable it to decide the issue of compatibility in the case before it': *Schumacher* v *Hauptzollamt Frankfurt Am Main* [1990] 2 CMLR 465.

The European Court also cannot take notice of the facts of a particular case. Ascertaining the relevant facts is the concern of the referring court: *Simmenthal SpA* v *Amministrazione delle Finanze dello Stato* [1978] ECR 1453.

Equally, the Court refrains from criticising the reasons behind a particular reference although on occasion the Court has rejected references which have been contrived between the litigating parties for the purpose of obtaining a particular ruling. Thus, in *Foglia* v *Novello* [1980] ECR 745, the Court held that it had no jurisprudence to pronounce on the merits of a case where the parties to the principal action had initiated the proceedings for the sole purpose of obtaining a ruling that a particular law of another Member State was inconsistent with Community law.

g) *The relevance of precedents in the jurisprudence of the European Court*

The European Court, in common with other systems of law based on the civilian model of law, does not adhere to the doctrine of precedent. The Court has, however, adopted a policy of referring to earlier decisions in the course of judgments and repeating, occasionally with slight modifications, parts of decisions from earlier relevant cases. This technique ensures consistency throughout the jurisprudence of the Court.

The Court has even recently declined to issue a fresh judgment in a particular case where the facts stated or questions raised are similar to earlier decisions. For example, in *Rochdale Borough Council* v *Anders* [1993] 1 All ER 520, the Court declined to issue a fresh judgement and cited its earlier judgment as authority for its refusal to issue a complete report.

But, in legal theory at least, the previous decisions of the Court do not constitute binding precedents and on occasion the Court has radically departed from its previous course of decisions. Compare *European Parliament* v *EC Council (Re Comitology)* [1988] ECR 5615 with *European Parliament* v *EC Council (Re Tchernobyl)* [1992] 1 CMLR 91.

4.3 Relevant cases

CILFIT v *Ministry of Health* [1982] ECR 3415: Elaboration of the criteria required in order to allow a court of final instance to refuse a preliminary reference to the ECJ.

SA Magnavision NV v *General Optical Council (No 2)* [1987] 2 CMLR 262: Decision relating to the proper timing of an application for a preliminary ruling in the English courts.

WH Smith Do-It-All & Payless DIY Ltd v *Peterborough City Council* [1990] 2 CMLR 577: Description of the function of decisions of the European Court as precedents before English courts and tribunals.

4.4 Relevant materials

H G Schermers & CWA Timmermans (eds), *Article 177 EC: Experiences and Problems* (1987).

A Arnull, 'The Use and Abuse of Article 177 EC' (1989) 52 MLR 622.

H Rasmussen, 'The European Court's Acte Clair Strategy in CILFIT' (1984) 9 EL Review 242.

L N Brown, *The Court of Justice of the European Communities* (third edition, 1989) 169–202.

A Arnull, 'References to the European Court' (1990) 15 EL Rev 375.

4.5 Analysis of questions

Many of the questions relating to the subject of preliminary ruling jurisprudence focus on the nature of the relationship between the national courts and the European Court. Thus, issues such as discretion to refer, the form of the question and the role of the Court in this process are particularly popular.

4.6 Questions

QUESTION ONE

Should the European Court ever refuse a national court's request for a preliminary ruling?

University of London LLB Examination
(for External Students) European Community Law 1990 Q3

General Comment

A difficult essay-type question which, although requiring a narrative answer, refers to a particular topic on which there is little legal authority.

Skeleton Solution

• The provisions of the EC Treaty.
• The policy of the European Court.
• Case law.
• Conclusions.

Suggested Solution

Initially, the European Court adopted an extremely liberal policy regarding the admission of references from national courts and tribunals. No formal examination was undertaken into the admissibility of such cases; see for example, *Simmenthal SpA v Ministry of Finance* (1976). This was due not only to the relatively light case load of the Court during the early years of the Community but also to a desire, on the part of the Court, to influence the evolution of the Community by forging fundamental principles of Community law.

In recent times there have been signs that this policy is about to change due for the most part to the substantial increase in the workload of the Court. Thus, for example, in *Pretore Di Genoa v Banchero* (1993), the Court rejected a preliminary reference from an Italian court on the basis that the facts on which the reference was requested were inadequately stated. Similarly, in *Rochdale Borough Council v Anders* (1993), the Court declined to issue a fresh judgment in this reference because the questions referred had already been addressed in an earlier reference. Nevertheless, in cases raising novel or controversial questions of law, the Court has been keen to address these issues to advance the frontiers of Community law.

In the pursuit of this policy, the European Court has been anxious to admit references in order to have an opportunity to fashion principles of Community law through interpretation. Equally, encouraging national courts to refer cases to the Court served the dual purpose of both ensuring uniform interpretation of Community law and acquainting the national courts with the existence of Community law.

The success or otherwise of this process has depended on the cooperation of the national courts. In order to assist national courts to accept the principle of the supremacy of Community law over national law, the European Court has emphasised the importance of cooperation rather than insisting on the development of a hierarchical structure which placed the European Court above national courts and tribunals. Instead the Court has evolved a careful delimitation of responsibilities between the Community system and the legal systems of the Member States, with the European Court interpreting Community law and the national courts applying this interpretation to the facts of the case before them.

A careful balance has been struck by the European Court between furthering the aims of the Community by ensuring the successful development of the Community legal order and consideration for the sentiments within the national legal systems of the Member States.

The practical utility of this policy, together with a growing awareness within the national courts about the existence of Community law, has meant that the European Court has become a victim of its own success. The sheer volume of references from the national courts has meant that a reference can take up to two years before a decision is rendered. Such a heavy workload also implies that the quality of individual judgments may decrease. Further, the quantity of judgments risks diluting their importance.

Yet in the leading case where the Court declined jurisdiction – *Foglia v Novello (No 1)* (1980) – the European Court did not specifically address this issue. The case itself turned on its particular facts.

In *Foglia* v *Novello*, a reference was made by an Italian court in an action between two Italians who had entered into a sales contract requiring delivery of the goods in France. The contract provided that the buyer would not be responsible for the payment of any taxes imposed in contravention of Community law. The goods were duly delivered. The seller was required to pay a consumption tax in France and claimed reimbursement from the buyer who refused to pay on the ground that the tax was contrary to Community law. Thus, the Italian courts were required to decide whether the French tax was in accordance with Community law.

The Italian court referred the question to the European Court. The Court took exception to this question because it involved a challenge to the sovereign rights of one Member State in a legal forum where the state was not in a position to defend itself.

More importantly, there were a number of grounds for believing that the whole transaction had been contrived in order to present a test case to the European Court. For these reasons, the European Court refused to accept the reference on the basis that there was no genuine dispute between the parties. The Italian court declined to accept this decision and made a second reference to the Court: *Foglia* v *Novello (No 2)* (1981). However the European Court again rejected the reference on the same grounds.

This ruling was subject to a considerable amount of criticism, not least because it interfered with the delicate relationship between the national courts and the European Court. By substituting the criteria of 'a real dispute between the parties' for 'a question on matters of Community law' (as specified by the EC Treaty), the European Court created a ground for reviewing decisions of national courts to refer a case for a preliminary reference. The Court could therefore investigate the reasons for the reference and the relevance of the question referred.

This development broke down the cooperative framework which the European Court had patiently developed throughout the course of its jurisprudence and substituted a more hierarchical structure. In addition, the Court conferred upon itself power to investigate the facts of a case in order to ascertain the intention of the parties. This power trespassed on the role of the national court as the finder of facts.

Logic would suggest, however, that there are circumstances in which the Court should, and indeed has, declined a reference. The first ground relates to instances in which the Court determines that the matter at issue has no connection with Community law. The second ground is where the requirements of Article 177 of the EC Treaty are not satisfied – the reference was not made by a court or tribunal or, alternatively, the question referred does not concern the interpretation of Community law or the validity of a Community measure. The third possibility is when the reference is an abuse of the procedure – an amorphous heading. In *Matthews* (1978), the Court declined jurisdiction when it decided that the questions referred were purely hypothetical and that the parties had attempted to compel the national court to make a reference, thus depriving it of its discretion under Article 177(2). In *Foglia* v *Novello*, it could be argued that jurisdiction had been declined because the Article 177 procedure was being abused because it was being employed to indirectly challenged a French tax when proceedings under Article 169 of the EC Treaty would have been more appropriate.

It could also be argued that fictitious litigation is an abuse of procedure, since mere academic consultation on a hypothetical issue is not the purpose of Article 177 of the EC Treaty. It is, however, difficult to develop reliable criteria for determining the existence of fictitious litigation.

In between the two rulings in the *Foglia* affair, two other references were made to the European Court by courts in Italy: *Chemical Farmaceuticic* v *DAF* (1981); and *Vinal* v *Orbat* (1981). Both cases involved facts similar to those in *Foglia* except that the disputed tax was Italian and not French and the disputes were considered 'not to be manifestly bogus'. In both cases, the European Court accepted the reference. It seems likely that the European Court's real reason for its decision in the *Foglia* cases was comity – a desire not to offend France.

The hostile reception received by the decision of the Court in *Foglia* and the potentially devastating consequences of the ruling on the intra-judicial relationship previously built up by the Court may mean that the European Court will adopt a policy of only reluctantly interfering in matters which fall within the competence of national courts. The Court has, however, attempted to alleviate the workload before it by following another tactic – the development of the acte clair doctrine after the *CILFIT case* (1982). By establishing criteria which allow national courts of final instance to decide cases without reference to the European Court, the Court itself has developed a doctrine which builds on European-national judicial cooperation rather than encroaches on the role of national courts and tribunals in the preliminary reference procedure.

QUESTION TWO

Discuss the purposes of Article 177 EC and evaluate the extent to which these purposes have been achieved. To what extent is Article 5 EC a necessary complement to Article 177 EC?

University of London LLB Examination
(for External Students) European Community Law 1992 Q5

General Comment

A question requiring detailed knowledge of the purpose and function of the Article 177 procedure as well as an insight into the relevance of Article 5 of the EC Treaty in the structure of the Community.

Skeleton Solution

• Purposes of Article 177; assistance in interpretation and uniform application of Community law.
• The pursuit of these objectives through Article 177.
• Relevance of article 5 EC Treaty.
• Limitations: direct actions; *Francovich* decision.

Suggested Solution

Article 177 of the EC Treaty allows national courts to refer questions of Community law to the European Court for interpretation and for pronouncements on the validity and interpretation of acts of the Community organs. Several conventions negotiated among the Community's Member States, such as the Convention on the Jurisdiction and Enforcement of Judgments 1968, also provide that national courts can refer questions of interpretation to the Court for a ruling.

As the European Court itself pointed out in *CILFIT* v *Ministry of Health* (1982), the procedure under Article 177 is designed to encourage 'the proper application and uniform interpretation of Community law in all the Member States'. The mechanism establishes a procedure whereby national courts and the European Court can cooperate to ensure that there is little possibility of decisions of national courts on questions of Community law differing from the judgments of the European Court on the same issues.

Thus, the preliminary ruling procedure allows the Court to maintain an element of consistency on both a geographical level and at a jurisprudential level.

However, it should be noted that Article 177 does not establish a hierarchy between the European Court and national courts. The preliminary ruling procedure does not mean that the ECJ is a court of final appeal on matters of Community law. Rather, Article 177 creates a system whereby national courts and tribunals can seek guidance from the European Court rather than having a decision imposed on them.

An example of this relationship working in practice is the policy of the European Court to only answer questions of Community law. It will not respond to questions of fact or matters requiring an interpretation of national law. In the event that a national court refers a question dealing with points of national law, the European Court merely extracts the relevant points of Community law from the reference before conveying its responses to the national court.

As observed above, the purpose of Article 177 is two-fold. First, to ensure the proper application and effectiveness of Community law and, second, to guarantee the uniform interpretation of Community law throughout the Community.

For present purposes, proper application is synonymous with effective enforcement. Article 177 itself assists to ensure this objective by requiring all national courts of final instance seized of a question of Community law to refer the issue to the European Court for interpretation. While not all lower courts are required to make such a reference, this avenue is, of course, open to them should they wish to do so.

The important point is that Article 177 envisaged all questions of Community law, at least potentially, being interpreted by the European Court. This scheme would ensure proper and effective enforcement by creating an all-embracing scheme to coordinate the implementation of Community law through the European Court.

However, in certain respects, the European Court has contributed itself to the demise of this system. In *CILFIT* v *Ministry of Health*, the Court, under considerable pressure from national courts, developed the doctrine of acte clair. Courts of final instance would no longer be required to make a mandatory reference if previous decisions of the European Court dealt adequately with the point at issue. In other words, if there was an earlier judgment of the court dealing with similar facts, national courts were released from the obligation to refer.

While it is true that the European Court set down rules for the application of the doctrine of acte clair, at the same time it is clear that it has undermined the effective application of Community law. National courts do not feel themselves under so much pressure to refer questions to the European Court. While this development was largely predictable once Community law had grown into a sizeable corpus of law with the assistance of the Court, nevertheless there are undoubtedly side-effects as regards effective enforcement of Community obligations.

On the other hand, the uniform interpretation of Community law has been achieved by the Court actively encouraging national courts to make preliminary references. For example, the Court will accept virtually all cases referred to it by national courts, no matter how trivial, if there is a genuine dispute.

However, this policy of the Court has also had unfortunate and unseen consequences. The present volume of cases was never anticipated and now the average period of delay between the initial reference and a decision on the matter stands at two years. This delay is unacceptable once it is acknowledged that the matter may have been before a national court for some time prior to the reference.

The relationship of Article 5 of the EC Treaty to Article 177 is largely a separate issue. Article 177 is a procedure designed to ensure the effective enforcement and uniform application of Community law in national courts. Article 5 is intended to be a substantive obligation imposed on all governmental organs and agencies of Member States to ensure respect for Community law. Thus, while Article 177 promotes compliance with Community law by national courts and tribunals, Article 5 is a broader obligation imposed on all government organs.

Article 5 has been used extensively by the European Court to keep Member States in line with their Community obligations. For example, this provision forms the basis for the principle of the direct effect of unimplemented directives since the decision of the European Court in *Marleasing SA* v *La Commercial Internacional De Alimentacion SA* (1992). In that case, the European Court held that Article 5 requires all Member States to take all appropriate measures to ensure the fulfilment of their Community obligations and it follows from this that their national laws must be interpreted to achieve this aim.

The same Article also forms the basis for most of the actions brought by the European Commission against Member States for non-implementation of Community regulations and directives: see for example, *EC Commission* v *Belgium (Re the Privileges and Immunities of European Community Officials)* (1989). Equally, actions brought by the Commission for failure by a Member State to abide by the terms of an adverse ruling in the European Court are brought under this provision and not the article providing grounds for the first offence.

The scope of Article 5 is considerable. It applies not only to acts attributable to Member States, but also to their omissions. Thus, in the recent *Francovich* case (1993), the Court held that private individuals have a right to sue their own Member States for damages if the Member State acts in a manner contrary to Community law, if the consequences of such actions cause injury to the individual.

While Articles 177 and 5 can be seen in the broadest context as complementing each other, their relationship is not an essential one. Both serve to ensure compliance with Community law, one from a procedural perspective, the other from a substantive perspective. They are not, however, interdependent on each other.

QUESTION THREE

'If in a case before a national court a point of EC law is sufficiently clear and even if the judge is very knowledgeable about Community law, a ruling by the European Court of Justice could still be sought.' Discuss.

University of Glasgow LLB Examination
1987 Q5

General Comment

A complex question involving an opinion-answer on the part of the student.

Skeleton Solution

• Obligation of national courts to refer to the ECJ.

• Doctrine of acte clair: *CILFIT*.

• Relevant factors in determining whether a reference should be made by a court.

Suggested Solution

Not all national courts are required to submit questions of Community law to the European Court under the preliminary reference procedure established under Article 177 of the EC Treaty. If all courts and tribunals confronted with issues of Community law made such references, the European Court would be unable to function as its case-load would far exceed its capacity. To ensure this does not happen, Article 177 is selective in specifying which courts are obliged to make such a reference and which are not.

Article 177 makes a clear distinction between the obligations of lower courts and the obligations of courts of final instance. Where a question of Community law is raised before a lower court or tribunal, it may, if it considers that a decision on the question is necessary to enable the court to give judgment, request the European Court to render a preliminary judgment on the question. In contrast, where a question of Community law is raised before a court against whose decision there is no judicial remedy under national law, that court is obliged to bring the matter to the attention of the European Court by way of a preliminary reference.

Where a court has discretion whether or not to make a reference, two factors are relevant. First, the court should be satisfied that the case before it involves a question of Community law. Second, the court must believe that a decision from the ECJ is necessary in order to decide the merits of the case.

A number of decisions of the English courts have attempted to modify these two requirements. Thus, in *Bulmer* v *Bollinger SA* (1974), Lord Denning MR claimed that the discretion of lower courts to refer decisions to the ECJ could be subject to practical considerations. A number of 'guidelines' were developed in this case. First, the point must be conclusive of the case. Second, the point must not have been decided by the European Court in a previous decision. Third, if the point of law is reasonably clear and free from doubt, the court need not exercise its discretion to refer the case. Finally, the national court should ascertain the facts of the case before it prior to making a reference to the European Court. These criteria have been applied by the English courts in a number of cases: see Bingham J in *Customs and Excise Commissioners* v *ApS Samex* (1983).

The European Court has, however, held that the discretion of inferior courts to refer a question of Community law to the European Court cannot be fettered by the decisions of superior courts: *Rheinmuhlen* (1974). This principle is applicable regardless of whether inferior courts or tribunals adhere to the doctrine of precedent. Consequently, in light of the criticism drawn by the guidelines laid down by Lord Denning, it is doubtful whether inferior English courts are required to apply the criteria specified in *Bulmer* v *Bollinger* before deciding to refer a case for a preliminary reference.

Whether or not a question should be referred to the European Court by a national court which has discretion in the matter must be decided by the court itself. Doubtless, in practice, a number of factors are taken into consideration. Perhaps the paramount consideration is the expertise of the European Court and the inexperience of the national court. At least one judge has been prepared to concede that 'sitting as a judge in a national court, asked to decide questions of Community law, I am very conscious of the advantages enjoyed by the Court of Justice. It has a panoramic view of the Community and its institutions, a detailed knowledge of the treaties and of much subordinate legislation made under them, and an intimate familiarity with the functioning of the Community which no national judge denied the collective experience of the Court of Justice could hope to achieve': *Customs and Excise Commissioners* v *ApS Samex*, above.

Even if a national judge is sufficiently knowledgeable regarding the applicable Community law, and even if the relevant principles of Community law are apparent, a cogent argument may still be sustained in favour of a preliminary reference. Few British judges possess sufficient knowledge of Community law in order to decide a case concerning the application of Community law, and even fewer would be able to keep abreast of contemporary developments within Community law. Both of these are reasons for remitting a case for a preliminary ruling.

Courts of final instance are subject to a different series of obligations. While Article 177 expressly requires that courts of last resort submit questions of Community law for a preliminary ruling, even these courts exercise a degree of discretion in deciding whether or not to make such a reference. This discretion arises from the decision of the European Court in *CILFIT* v *Ministry of Health* (1982) which established the Community doctrine of acte clair. Courts of final instance are not obliged to submit questions to the ECJ for a preliminary reference if previous decisions of the European Court have dealt with the point in contention. However, even if the national court could exercise an option not to refer under the doctrine of acte clair, naturally it could, of course, continue to make such references if it wished.

Even a court of final instance exercises a degree of discretion whether or not to refer a question to the European Court when the criteria established in the *CILFIT* case are applicable. In such circumstances, even these courts would be wise to take into consideration the factors which lower courts have taken into consideration prior to exercising their discretion to refer.

QUESTION FOUR

'The European Court has on several occasions stated that Article 177 presupposes distinct and separate functions for the national and European courts'; R Plender, *Cases and Materials on the Law of the European Communities* (1989), 178.

Discuss.

Question prepared by the Author

General Comment

A question discussing the relationship between national courts and the European Court vis-à-vis preliminary references.

Skeleton Solution

- Functions and responsibilities of the national courts.
- Functions and responsibilities of the ECJ.
- Relationship between these organs.
- Conclusions.

Suggested Solution

In essence, the national courts and tribunals of the Member States are required to perform three principal functions in references for preliminary rulings from the European Court: to determine issues of fact; to ascertain whether a reference should be made; and to apply the decision of the European Court to the facts of the case. In contrast, the European Court is required to decide the question of European law submitted for reference by the national court.

Only national courts and tribunals exercising a judicial function are entitled to refer a question of Community law to the European Court through the preliminary reference procedure. The European Court decides whether or not a particular body constitutes a court or tribunal for the purposes of Article 177 and the status of the body in national law is irrelevant in this determination. A number of factors are taken into consideration by the Court in this determination, including appointment procedure, rules of procedure, the authority upon which the body has been established, compulsory jurisdiction and whether or not the body applies legal principles. Courts of law clearly qualify under these criteria, as do many administrative tribunals such as the Employment tribunal and the VAT tribunal.

Disciplinary bodies for professional groups may or may not constitute tribunals depending on their authority to render binding decisions of a judicial character and whether the body has been created on the basis of statutory authority: contrast *Borker* (1981) with *Broekmeulen v Huisarts Registratie Commissie* (1981).

The majority of national courts retain discretion whether or not to refer a question of Community law to the European Court. Where an appeal may be lodged against the decision of the court or tribunal, a discretion to refer may be exercised. In contrast, tribunals and courts against which no appeal may be lodged are obliged to refer the matter to the attention of the European Court by way of preliminary references, although this absolute duty has been modified by the jurisprudence of the European Court itself: Article 177(3) EC Treaty.

Courts and tribunals which exercise a discretion to refer a question for a preliminary reference should be satisfied that two preconditions exist: Article 177(2) EC Treaty. First, the court must believe that the case involves an issue of Community law. A prima facie question of Community law will arise where a party relies on a provision of a Community treaty, a measure of Community law such as a regulation, a directive, or a decision, or a precedent of the European Court (and now also the Court of First Instance). Second, the court must be satisfied that a decision on the question is necessary to decide the merits of the case. The decision of an inferior court or tribunal to refer, or not to refer, a case to the European Court may itself be the subject of an appeal.

Courts of final resort are, however, subject to a different series of obligations. The EC Treaty declares that such courts are bound to refer a question of Community law to the European Court for a preliminary reference. However, the absolute duty has been qualified for cases involving questions of European law already settled by the European Court. In such circumstances, it would be an unnecessary repetition to submit a case to the Court for an identical decision. In *CILFIT* v *Ministry of Health* (1982), the Italian Supreme Court asked the European Court to specify the conditions which must prevail before a court of final instance could avoid referring a question of Community law to the European Court. In other words, the Italian court wanted to know whether a preliminary reference had to be made by a court of final instance when the applicable Community law was unambiguous and not subject to a reasonable interpretive doubt.

The European Court held that where a question of Community law had already been settled, national courts of last resort were not obliged to refer the question to the Court. The Court acknowledged that the correct application of Community law may often be so obvious as to leave no scope for any reasonable doubt as to the manner in which the question raised is to be resolved. Where this was the case, the national court was free to decide the point without seeking guidance from the European Court.

The stage of the proceedings at which an application for a preliminary ruling should be made is another issue for the national court to decide. In making a preliminary reference, particular regard should be made to the national system of pleading. The necessity of referring a question under the preliminary ruling procedure would not normally arise until the pleadings have been adjusted and the real questions focused in the pleadings.

Also, the facts should be clear and the arguments on the merits of the case fully developed. A reference to the European Court would be inappropriate in the event that preliminary issues of title, competency and relevancy remain unresolved. Similar comments have been made by way of obiter, to the effect that a reference to the European Court is desirable only after the pursuers have established a prima facie case.

No formal requirements regulate the contents of the questions submitted for a preliminary reference, although obviously the greater the degree of precision, the more accurate the response of the European Court. The main problem in framing a preliminary reference is that the national court might refer a question, the response to which exceeds the jurisprudence of the European Court under Article 177. The European Court has no authority to decide matters of national law, which are issues to be decided solely by the national courts.

Where national courts have inadvertently included questions of national law in a reference, the European Court has generally extracted the pertinent issues of Community law from the reference, bearing in mind the subject-matter of the case. The Court will then apply the relevant principles of Community law and return the case to the national courts to apply the preliminary judgment to the facts of the case.

A preliminary reference is binding upon the court which referred the question for consideration in the sense that it is an authoritative determination of Community law. A preliminary ruling is not merely an advisory opinion and the English courts are obliged to apply the relevant Community law to the facts of the case. Further, decisions of the European Court are binding as precedents on the English courts where they relate to identical points of Community law: *WH Smith Do-It-All & Payless DIY Ltd* v *Peterborough City Council* (1990).

The primary responsibility of the European Court in a preliminary reference is to decide the legal merits of the case in terms of Community law. The Court has express jurisdiction in preliminary references to interpret the Community Treaties, to rule on the validity and interpretation of acts of Community institutions, and to interpret the statutes of bodies established by an act of the Community.

As the Court has expressly observed, 'the Court is not empowered under Article 177 of the [EC] Treaty to rule on the compatibility with the Treaty of provisions of national law. However, it has jurisdiction to provide the national court with all such matters relating to the interpretation of Community law as may enable it to decide the issue of compatibility in the case before it': *Schumacher* v *Hauptzollamt Frankfurt Am Main* (1990).

In the event of a conflict, the Court may only conclude that the provision of national law is 'incompatible' with the relevant Community law. The national court has responsibility to apply the relevant law and to determine whether a plaintiff should prevail or a prosecution should be continued.

Nor does the European Court have jurisdiction to take cognisance of the facts of the case. Ascertaining the relevant facts is the concern of the referring court: *Simmenthal SpA* v *Amministrazione delle Finanze dello Stato* (1978). Equally, the Court is unable to criticise the reasons behind a reference although the Court has adopted a policy of rejecting references which have been contrived for the purposes of obtaining a ruling. Thus, in *Foglia* v *Novello* (1980), the Court held that it had no jurisdiction to pronounce on the merits of a case where the parties to the main action had initiated proceedings for the sole purpose of obtaining a ruling that a particular national law of a Member State was inconsistent with Community law: see also *Foglia* v *Novello (No 2)* (1981). The Court expressed its concern at the use of the preliminary ruling procedure in cases where there was no genuine dispute and where the applicants sought to obtain a judgment on the compatibility of the laws of one Member State in the courts of another Member.

While the European Court and national courts have different competences and responsibilities under the preliminary reference procedure, these frequently overlap.

In such circumstances, a clear cut distinction in functions is impossible to identify. Moreover, the European Court has demonstrated a tangible propensity to extend its competence further into the affairs of national courts. The fact that the responsibilities of each set of courts is not explicitly defined in Article 177 made this eventually inevitable. Whether this is a development which will serve the long-term strategic interests of the European Court is entirely another matter.

5 EUROPEAN COMMUNITY LEGISLATION

5.1 Introduction

A critical distinction is made between primary and secondary sources of Community law. Primary sources consist of the international agreements entered into by the Member States for the purpose of establishing the constitution of the Community. Secondary sources are measures enacted by Community institutions exercising the authority vested in them by the Community treaties. Naturally, primary sources of Community law prevail over secondary sources in the event of a conflict.

5.2 Key points

a) *Primary sources of Community law*

The three Community Treaties, together with a number of international agreements formally amending these Treaties, form the constitution of the Community and are the ultimate source of legal authority within the Community system. These Treaties function as primary sources of law in two ways:

   i) The Community Treaties prescribe the powers of Community institutions to promulgate secondary legislation. Failure on the part of an institution to respect the limits of authority prescribed in the Treaties will render a putative measure null and void: *EC Commission* v *EC Council (Re Generalised Tariff Preferences)* [1987] ECR 1493.

   ii) The Community Treaties, in certain circumstances, establish fundamental principles of Community law which have direct effect and may be relied upon by individuals before national courts and tribunals.

b) *Community agreements with third states*

Each of the three Community Treaties confers authority on the Community to enter into international agreements with third states dealing with matters which fall within the competence of the Community. These agreements are also capable of providing a source of directly applicable principles of Community law: see *Demirel* v *Stadt Schwabisch Gmund* [1989] 1 CMLR 412. The Court has also held that such agreements prevail over inconsistent provisions of national law: *Hauptzollamt Mainz* v *Kupferberg & Cie KG* [1982] ECR 3641.

In certain circumstances, the decisions of bodies established to administer such treaties may also be given such an effect. For example, in *SZ Sevince* v *Staatssecretaris Van Justitie* [1992] 2 CMLR 57 the Court held that a decision made by a body established by virtue of a Community agreement may be directly applicable when, regard being had to its wording and the purpose and nature of the agreement itself, the provision contains a clear and precise obligation.

No decision has yet been rendered on the issue of whether the terms of such agreements would prevail over inconsistent secondary legislation. However, under no circumstances would the European Court support the principle that the terms of such agreements are capable of prevailing over conflicting provisions of the Community Treaties.

c) *Intra-Community agreements*

Article 200 of the EC Treaty requires Member States to negotiate intra-Community agreements to regulate particular subjects including the protection of persons and the protection of individual rights against discrimination, the abolition of double taxation within the Community, mutual recognition of corporations having their seat of incorporation in another Member State, and a system for the reciprocal recognition and enforcement of judgments among Member States.

Four Conventions have been negotiated among the Member States to achieve certain of these objectives:

i) The Convention on Jurisdiction and Enforcement of Judgments in Civil and Commercial Matters 1968.

ii) The Convention on the Law Applicable to Contractual Obligations 1980.

iii) The Convention on the Mutual Recognition of Companies and Bodies Corporate 1968.

iv) The Convention for a European Patent for the Common Market 1975.

In addition, the Lugano Convention on Jurisdiction and the Enforcement of Judgments in Civil and Commercial Matters 1988 extends the terms of the 1968 Jurisdiction and Judgments Convention to the European Free Trade Association (EFTA) countries on the basis of reciprocity with Community Member States. As of October 1993, only the first two of these agreements have entered into force.

In the past, these Conventions have been given effect through the traditional national procedures for the incorporation of international agreements. Within the United Kingdom, this procedure involves the enactment of enabling legalisation. For example, the 1968 Jurisdiction and Judgments Convention has force of law within the United Kingdom by virtue of the Civil Jurisdiction and Judgments Act 1982.

d) *Secondary sources of Community law*

Both the Council of Ministers and the European Commission have authority to enact secondary legislation although in order to do so they must have authority over the particular subject-matter by virtue of the terms of the Community Treaties. Article 189 of the EC Treaty specifies three separate forms of Community secondary legislation:

i) Regulations

A regulation is a general legislative instrument which is binding in its entirety throughout the Community and which is directly applicable within the legal orders of the Member States without the need of intervention on the part of national legislative bodies.

ii) Directives

A directive also has binding effect, but only against the Member State to whom it is addressed and only in relation to the result to be achieved. Directives are not automatically applicable within Member States since Member States exercise a discretion to select the appropriate form of domestic law to incorporate the obligations arising from the directive into national law.

iii) Decisions

A decision is binding in its entirety, but only upon those to whom it is addressed. Decisions may be addressed to both Member States and individuals.

Authority is also conferred upon the Council of Ministers and the Commission to make recommendations and to deliver opinions. Neither of these acts involves the creation of measures which have legal effect.

e) *The distinction between the direct applicability and the direct effect of Community law*

The concept of direct applicability only applies to Community regulations and is derived from Article 189 of the EC Treaty which provides that regulations shall be 'directly applicable in all Member States'. The quality of direct applicability means that regulations are automatically incorporated into the domestic laws of the Member States immediately upon enactment by the appropriate Community institution. Individual and legal persons may therefore rely on rights and duties created by Community regulations before national courts and tribunals.

The quality of direct applicability was only expressly conferred upon Community regulations. Neither individual Treaty provisions nor Community directives were intended to be directly applicable. In fact the EC Treaty expressly provides that the national authorities of the Member States retain discretion in selecting the appropriate instrument of national law to implement Community directives. However, the European Court has significantly modified this provision by establishing the principle of direct effect which applies to Treaty provisions and also directives which have not been implemented by Member States within the prescribed period.

While the principles of direct applicability and direct effect perform the same function – to create enforceable rights on behalf of individuals – each principle applies to different forms of Community legislation.

f) *The direct applicability of Community regulations*

The essence of the principle of direct applicability is that a Community regulation which has entered force may be enforced by or against the subjects of the regulation and that the application of such a measure is independent of any measure of national law: *Bussone* v *Ministry of Agriculture and Forestry* [1978] ECR 2429.

Not all regulations create individual enforceable rights. Frequently regulations are not addressed to individuals but to Member States. In such cases, obligations created under regulations are imposed on Member States and function in the field of public – as opposed to private – law: *Gibson* v *Lord Advocate* 1975 SLT 133. Whether or not a particular regulation creates directly enforceable rights for individuals depends on two factors – the subject-matter of the regulation and the nature of the group to whom it is addressed: *Becker* v *Finanzant Munster-Innenstadt* [1982] ECR 53.

g) *Direct effect and Community Treaty provisions*

No provision of any Community Treaty expressly authorises the use of individual Treaty provisions as a reservoir of legal principles, but from the very formation of the Community the European Court has sought to achieve this object. In *Costa* v *ENEL* [1964] ECR 585, the European Court held that where a Treaty article imposes a clear and unconditional obligation upon a Member State, unqualified by any reservation reserving the right of legislative intervention, such a provision could be capable of direct effect and individual rights could be created which were enforceable in municipal courts.

Three specific conditions are therefore required for a provision of a Community treaty to have direct effect:

i)   The provision being relied upon must be clear and precise: see *Gimenez Zaera* v *Instituto Nacional de la Seguridad Social* [1987] ECR 3697.

ii) The term must be unqualified and not subject to a right of legislative intervention: *Diamantarbeiders* v *Brachfeld & Chougol Diamond Co* [1969] ECR 211.

iii) The obligation must not confer a discretion on either Member States or Community institutions to act: *Salgoil* v *Italian Ministry for Foreign Trade* [1968] ECR 453.

The principle of direct effect has been expressly acknowledged in a number of cases involving the courts of the United Kingdom. See *R* v *Goldstein* [1983] 1 All ER 434; *Garden Cottage Foods Ltd* v *Milk Marketing Board* [1984] AC 130; and *Argyll Group plc* v *Distillers Co plc* [1986] 1 CMLR 764.

The Court will not necessarily give general retroactive validity to Treaty provisions which have direct effect. Thus, in *Defrenne* v *Sabena* [1976] ECR 455, the Court held that the direct effect of Article 119 applied only from the date on which the judgment was rendered, except as regards those litigants who had already instituted legal proceedings: see also *Barber* v *Guardian Royal Exchange Assurance Group* [1990] 2 CMLR 513.

In *Blaizot* v *University of Liège* [1989] 1 CMLR 57, the European Court outlined its policy towards the non-retroactive application of Treaty articles given direct effect. It expressly observed:

' ... in determining whether or not to limit the temporal effects of a judgment it is necessary to bear in mind that although the practical consequences of any judicial decision must be weighed carefully, the Court cannot go so far as to diminish the objectivity of the law and compromise its future application on the grounds of the possible repercussions which might result, as regards the past, from a judicial decision.'

h) *Direct effect and Community directives*

Since Community directives are given legal force through national measures, rights and duties are conferred on individuals only after incorporation into national law. Individuals and legal persons may, of course, rely on rights established by directives after the enabling legislation has been enacted. Further, frequently time limits are placed on implementation in order to ensure that Member States do not postpone incorporation indefinitely.

Where a Member State has failed to adopt a directive within the prescribed time period the European Court has, on certain occasions, been prepared to give direct effect to the contents of unimplemented directives notwithstanding the fact that the Member State has not incorporated the measure into internal law. The rationale for the development of this principle has been expressed by the Court in the following terms:

'It would be incompatible with the binding effect given by Article 189 [of the EC Treaty] to Directives to refuse in principle to allow persons concerned to invoke the obligation imposed by the Directive ... Especially in cases where the Community authorities, by means of a directive, oblige Member States to take a specific course of action, the practical effectiveness of such a measure is weakened if individuals cannot take account of it as part of Community law': *Grad* v *Finanzamt Traunstein* [1970] ECR 825.

Strictly speaking, the provision of an unimplemented directive is not actually given direct effect in the same sense as the application of this concept to Community Treaty provisions. Rather, a Member State is prevented from invoking its own omission or deficiency as a defence to an otherwise competent action.

A number of conditions must be satisfied before direct effect can be given to a term of a Community directive:

i) The term must be sufficiently precise;

ii) The provision in question must specify an obligation which is not subject to any qualification, exception or condition;

iii) The provision must not require intervention on the part of a Community institution or a Member State: see *Van Duyn* v *Home Office* [1974] ECR 1337.

The difference between this test and the analogous test for the direct effect of Treaty provision is that the condition requiring the non-discretionary implementation of the provision is easier to satisfy in the case of directives than for Treaty provisions: see Advocate-General Warner in *R* v *Secretary of State for Home Affairs, ex parte Santillo* [1980] ECR 1585.

Two important limitations are placed on the application of this principle:

i) The principle only applies to directives which are unimplemented after the date set for implementation. The application of directives which have been adopted, but which have not yet entered into force, cannot be anticipated or pre-empted.

ii) The Court has only been prepared to apply this doctrine to the relationship between individuals and the state as opposed to the relationships among individuals themselves. The former is known as 'vertical direct effect' while the latter is known as 'horizontal direct effect'.

In the case, *Marshall* v *Southampton and South West Hampshire Area Health Authority* [1986] ECR 723, the Court confirmed that while a directive might be upheld against defaulting Member States, it cannot be involved directly against other individuals. The rationale for this principle stems from the fact that the concept of the direct effect of directives originates from the doctrine of personal bar.

While the Court of Justice has refused to recognise the concept of the 'horizontal direct effect' of directives, it has sought to achieve the same effect through the process of interpretation. For example, where the Court is interpreting the terms of an unimplemented directive as it applies between private individuals, the Court observed:

'In applying national law, whether the provisions in question were adopted before or after the directive, a national court called upon to interpret it is required to do so, as far as possible, in light of the wording and purpose of the directive in order to achieve the result pursued by the latter...': *Marleasing SA* v *La Commercial Internacional De Alimentacion SA* [1992] 1 CMLR 305.

However, it is not clear what limitations are imposed on this means of indirectly applying unimplemented directives to the relationships between private individuals by way of interpretation. Certainly the UK courts have been reluctant to follow the European Court's lead on this point.

5.3 Relevant cases

Hauptzollamt Mainz v *Kupferberg* [1982] ECR 3641: The terms of Community agreements with third states may be given direct effect if the condition being relied upon is unconditional and precise, and also capable of conferring individual rights.

EC Commission v *United Kingdom (Re Tachographs)* [1979] ECR 419: If a Community Regulation is re-enacted into national legislation in order to provide a greater degree of specification, the legislation must satisfy all the obligations incumbent on the Member State.

SZ Sevince v *Staatssecretaris Van Justitie* [1992] 2 CMLR 57: Direct effect of decisions of bodies set up under the authority of Community treaties with third states.

Marshall v *Southampton and South West Hampshire Area Health Authority* [1986] ECR 723: While vertical direct effect may be given to unimplemented directives, the European Court was unwilling to accept a similar application of the concept of horizontal direct effect.

Von Colson v *Land Nordrhein-Westfahlen* [1984] ECR 1891: Original application of unimplemented directives between private individuals through interpretative means.

Marleasing SA v *La Commercial Internacional De Alimentacion SA* [1992] 1 CMLR 305: Most recent case on implementation of directives through interpretation.

5.4 Relevant materials

L Collins, *European Community Law in the United Kingdom* (fourth edition, 1990) 46–112.

J Steiner, 'Coming to terms with EC Directives' (1990) 106 LQR 144.

PE Morris 'The Direct Effect of Directives: Recent Developments' (1989) Jour Bus Law, 223–45 and 309–20.

D Curtin, 'The Province of Government: Delimiting the Direct Effect of Directives' (1990) 15 EL Rev 195–223.

5.5 Analysis of questions

Within this topic, the direct effect of treaty provisions and unimplemented Community directives is the issue which most frequently arises in examinations. In part this is due to the controversial nature of this doctrine. However, frequently issues which form part of this topic also arise as subsidiary points in questions concerning other matters of Community law. Due to the important nature of this particular part of the syllabus, a student would be well advised to acquire an extensive familiarity with both the fundamental principles of this subject as well as the recent jurisprudence of the European Court.

5.6 Questions

QUESTION ONE

To what extent does Article 189 EC provide an accurate description of the acts which may be taken by the European Community institutions? What suggestions would you make regarding the possible redrafting of Article 189 EC?

University of London LLB Examination
(for External Students) European Community Law 1992 Q2

General Comment

This question concerns the changes brought about through the intervention of the European Court to the various measures that can be enacted by Community institutions.

Skeleton Solution

- The terms of Article 189: regulations, directives, decisions and recommendations.
- Regulations: direct effect/binding in their entirety.
- Directives: no express direct effect but note the rulings of the ECJ.
- Blurring of the distinction between regulations and directives.
- Redrafting proposals: define the various types of measures in light of the jurisprudence of the ECJ.

Suggested Solution

Article 189 of the EC Treaty identifies five different types of measures that may be adopted by the Council of Ministers and the European Commission in the performance of their functions and legal duties. Both organs are permitted to make regulations, issue directives, take decisions, make recommendations and to deliver opinions. Of these, only regulations, directives and decisions have legal effects. Neither recommendations nor opinions have binding legal force.

In practice, regulations and directives are the most important types of acts or measures that can be enacted at the Community level. Decisions, while common in some fields such as competition law, are not a major form of Community measure. Decisions are binding in their entirety, but only upon the entity to whom they are addressed. Decisions may be addressed to Member States but most frequently they are applied to individuals and legal persons.

The description of regulations and directives in Article 189, however, no longer adequately describes the two principal measures used by the Community institutions. It is in this respect that it is open to speculation whether or not Article 189 continues to accurately define the measures that may be taken by Community institutions.

A Community regulation is a general legislative instrument which is binding in its entirety throughout the Community, unless otherwise stated, and which is directly applicable within the legal systems of the individual Member States without the need of intervention on the part of national legislative bodies. Individuals may therefore rely on the terms of a regulation in a national court even though there is no national law giving it effect. The English courts have acknowledged this quality and have been prepared to recognise the force of Community law in this form and to protect individual rights vested in this manner: *R* v *Secretary of State, ex parte Factortame (No 3)* (1989).

Regulations are therefore clearly designed as measures permitting the Community institutions to legislate directly throughout the whole of the Community. This purpose is recognised in s2(1) of the European Communities Act 1972 which requires that all rights and obligations created in accordance with the Community Treaties are 'without further enactment to be given legal effect' within the United Kingdom.

True, occasionally Community regulations are re-enacted by measures of national law to provide greater clarity or to create penalties for failure to comply with the terms of a regulation. However, in such cases, the force of law continues to reside in the regulation and is not superseded by the national measure. Further, if a regulation is so re-enacted, the legislation must satisfy all the obligations incumbent on the Member State. Partial implementation is insufficient.

Thus, in *EC Commission* v *United Kingdom (Re Tachographs)* (1979), the United Kingdom was held in violation of a Community regulation requiring the fitting of tachographs to certain types of vehicle. The regulation required the creation of criminal sanctions for failure to do so but the implementing legislation enacted in the United Kingdom made no such provision. The European Court held the United Kingdom liable for breach of the EC Treaty and declared that it was inconceivable that a Member State could implement a regulation 'in an incomplete or selective manner ... so as to render abortive certain aspects of Community legislation which it opposed or which it considered contrary to its national interests'.

Regulations are therefore the most effective and comprehensive measures that may be adopted by Community institutions. Directives, on the other hand, are expressly declared in Article 189 to have binding effect, but only as against the Member States to whom they are addressed. More importantly, the text of Article 189 implies that directives are not directly effective because the national authorities of each Member State exercise a discretion in selecting the appropriate measure of national law to give effect to the terms of the directive. Directives are therefore, at the same time, less comprehensive in their coverage than regulations and also lack the automatic effect possessed by regulations.

However, the distinction between these two types of measures is no longer clear cut and arguably Article 189 requires redrafting to reflect this fact. There has developed a blurring in both function and effect of regulations and directives caused, for the most part, by the desire on the part of the European Court to render directives more effective.

The European Court has been prepared to give vertical direct effect to directives that have remained unimplemented by Member States after the period provided for the adoption of the directive. In other words, the Court has been prepared to refuse to allow the failure of a state to adopt a directive as an excuse to an otherwise competent action. As the Court pointed out in *Grad* v *Finanzamt Traunstein* (1970):

'It would be incompatible with the binding effect given by Article 189 [of the EC Treaty] to directives to refuse in principle to allow persons concerned to invoke the obligation imposed by the directive ... Especially in cases where the Community authorities, by means of a directive, oblige Member States to take a specific course of action, the practical effectiveness of such a measure is weakened if individuals cannot take account of it as part of Community law.'

But the right to rely on the terms of an unimplemented directive is not absolute. Three conditions must be satisfied before reliance can be placed in the measure. First, the terms of the directive must be sufficiently precise to create directly enforceable legal obligations. Second, the provision must specify an obligation which is not subject to any qualification, exception or condition. Third, the provision must not require intervention on the part of a Community institution or a Member State. These are the necessary preconditions for a regulation to be considered as having direct effect.

There are, however, two major limitations placed on the application of this principle.

Firstly, the principle applies only to directives which remain unimplemented after the date has passed for adoption. The entry into force of directives which have been adopted, but which have not yet entered into force, cannot be anticipated or pre-empted.

Secondly, and more importantly, the Court has only been prepared to apply this doctrine to the relationships between individuals and the state as opposed to the relationships among individuals themselves. In other words, while an individual can evoke an unimplemented directive against national authorities, either as a ground for action or a defence, the rights conferred by the directive cannot be enforced against other individuals. Thus, in *Marshall* v *Southampton and South West Hampshire Area Health Authority* (1986), the Court refused to allow the principle of direct effect to be used by an employee suing her employer for failure to comply with directives concerning equal pay.

The situation has, however, been made even more complex by recent decisions of the Court which, while continuing the policy of refusing to give horizontal direct effect to directives, have nevertheless opened up the possibility of an alternative remedy in such cases. First in *Von Colson* v *Land Nordrhein-Westfahlen* (1984), and more recently in *Marleasing SA* v *La Commercial Internacional De Alimentacion SA* (1992), the Court has given indirect horizontal effect to directives by means of Article 5 of the EC Treaty. This article requires Member States to take all appropriate measures to ensure the fulfilment of the obligations arising out of the EC Treaty.

In the *Marleasing* case, the plaintiffs alleged that a Spanish company had been wound up for the purpose of defrauding its creditors. The company was formed by a founders contract which is an agreement among the participants in the company to establish a company. This was a legitimate means of establishing a company under Spanish law. The plaintiffs claimed that the founders contract was void for lack of consideration, a concept recognised in Spanish company law, and therefore the directors would be liable for its debts.

The grounds on which a company can be annulled are exhaustively listed in Directive 68/151. Lack of consideration is not a ground listed in this directive but the Spanish government had not implemented its terms at the time the dispute arose. The defendants relied on this directive to support the claim that the company could not be wound up for lack of consideration because this was not a ground for declaring a company void under the directive. The Court was asked whether the directive could be given effect as between these two private parties.

While the Court rejected the notion of horizontal direct effect, it observed that Article 5 places Member States under an obligation to give effect to Community obligations. Spanish law had to be interpreted in light of this obligation and this required that Spanish company law should be interpreted in light of the terms of the directive. Since the directive exhaustively listed all the grounds for annulling a company, the Spanish company could not be annulled for lack of consideration.

The effect of this decision is to give indirect horizontal effect to directives. In other words, the Court is prepared to apply the terms of unimplemented directives to the relationships between individuals where this can be achieved by implication. The elaboration of this principle, in many respects, ends the distinction between regulations and directives, but at the moment the actual effects and impact of the Court's decision is not yet clear and requires further elaboration from the Court itself.

As regards the proposed amendment of Article 189, the following suggestions can be made in the light of this background. First, the text of the article should remain unchanged except for the terms referring to directives. This provision should be altered by the addition of further clauses ensuring that unimplemented directives can be relied upon by private individuals as either grounds for action or as a defence to civil actions or prosecution, but only against the state. The requirements for giving effect to such directives should be clearly stated.

In addition, the organs and public bodies that are considered to be emanations of the state should be defined in order to allow limits to be drawn on the principle. There should also be provision prohibiting Member States from relying on unimplemented directives against individuals: see *Officier van Justitie* v *Kolpinghuis Nijmegen BV* (1989).

QUESTION TWO

'To give what is called "horizontal effect" to directives would totally blur the distinction between regulations and directives which the Treaty establishes in Articles 189 and 191.' Advocate-General Slynn in Case 152/84 *Marshall* v *Southampton and South West Hampshire Area Health Authority.*

Discuss.

University of London LLB Examination
(for External Students) European Community Law 1989 Q3

General Comment

A problem concerning the application of the doctrine of direct effect of unimplemented directives which also requires consideration of the relationship between the various secondary sources of Community law.

Skeleton Solution

• The legal effect of Community regulations.
• The legal effect of Community directives.
• The concept of horizontal effect and its consequences.
• Contrast between the effects of regulations and unimplemented directives.

Suggested Solution

Article 189 of the EC Treaty provides that regulations 'shall be binding in their entirety and directly applicable in all Member States'. The quality of direct applicability means that regulations are immediately and automatically incorporated into the legal systems of the Member States without the need for intervention on the part of a legislative body such as the British Parliament. Individuals and legal persons may therefore vindicate rights and duties created by Community regulations before national courts and tribunals. An institution of the Community would pass a regulation when it was deemed undesirable that the national authorities of a Member State should be allowed to intervene in its promulgation.

Community directives do not possess the same quality. In fact, the EC Treaty expressly provides that the national authorities of the Member States retain discretion in selecting the appropriate instrument of national law to implement Community directives. Directives are employed where an institution of the Community intends to create standards which need not be identical throughout the Community.

The essence of the principle of direct applicability is that a Community regulation which has entered force may be enforced by or against the subjects of the regulation and the application of such measures is independent of any measure of national law: *Bussone* v *Ministry of Agriculture and Forestry* (1978). This latter quality is expressly acknowledged in the European Communities Act 1972 s2(1), which requires that all rights and obligations created in accordance with the Community Treaties are 'without further enactment to be given legal effect' within the United Kingdom.

On occasion, Community regulations are, however, re-enacted into national law to provide a greater degree of specification, for example to provide penalties to enforce the contents of the measure. In such cases, the force of law resides in the regulation itself not the national provision: *Variola* v *Amministrazione Italiana delle Finanze* (1973). Further, if a regulation is re-enacted, the legislation must satisfy all the obligations incumbent upon the Member State, partial implementation being insufficient. In *EC Commission* v *United Kingdom (Re Tachographs)* (1979), the British government was held to have violated Community law by not passing legislation making non-compliance with a Community regulation requiring the fitting of tachographs a criminal offence. The European Court held the United Kingdom liable for breach of the Treaty of Rome and declared inconceivable the implementation of a regulation by a Member State 'in an incomplete or selective manner ... so as to render abortive certain aspects of Community legislation which it opposed or which it considered contrary to its national interests'.

Actual penalties prescribed by national law for the enforcement of regulations may vary from one Member State to another. In one case involving the enforcement of Community regulations relating to road transportation, and in particular maximum permitted daily driving periods and compulsory rest periods, the European Court held that no violations of Community law occurred because some Member States adopted a system of strict criminal liability while others had not: *Anklagemyndigheden* v *Hausen and Son I/S* (1990). This conclusion was reached because the regulation in question left significant discretion to the Member States for the implementation of its rules. Naturally where a regulation specifies criminal penalties, such provisions must be strictly observed.

Directives are given force of law through national measures and rights and duties are conferred on individuals only upon incorporation into national law. Individuals and legal persons may rely on the rights and duties contained in directives but merely by virtue of the terms of the incorporating legislation. Frequently, time limits are placed on implementation in order to ensure that Member States do not postpone incorporation indefinitely.

Where a Member State fails to adopt a directive within the specified time period, the European Court has, on certain occasions, given direct effect to the contents of the unimplemented directive notwithstanding the fact that the Member State has not adopted the measure into internal law. This concept has become known as 'vertical direct effect'. Its purpose is to prevent Member States avoiding their Community obligations: *Grad* v *Finanzamt Traunstein* (1970). The concept of direct effect prevents Member States from invoking their own omissions or deficiencies as a defence to an otherwise competent action.

Substantial limitations are, however, placed on the application of the concept of vertical direct effect by the European Court. In the first place, it only applies to directives which remain unimplemented after the date specified for implementation. The application of directives which have been adopted by the Council but which have not yet passed the expiry date for implementation cannot be anticipated or pre-empted. Second, where a plaintiff is attempting to invoke an unincorporated directive against a defaulting state, the directive in question must create an 'unconditional and sufficiently precise' obligation: *Pubblico Ministero* v *Ratti* (1979). Whether an obligation is sufficiently precise depends on the facts of each case: *Marshall* v *Southampton and South West Hampshire Area Health Authority (Teaching) (No 2)* (1990).

However, the European Court has consistently refused to extend the concept to direct effect of unimplemented directives to the relationships between individuals. 'Vertical direct effect' is the term which describes the application of unimplemented directives by individuals against governmental bodies and agencies: *Browne* v *An Bord Pleanala* (1990). 'Horizontal direct effect' applies to the relationship between individuals within a society and the application of unimplemented directives. Since many directives affect areas such as company law, employment law, or consumer protection law, this is a considerable restriction.

In the case *Marshall* v *Southampton and South West Hampshire Area Health Authority* (1986) the European Court confirmed that while a directive might be upheld against defaulting Member States, it could not be invoked directly against other individuals. The Court reasoned that since Article 189 defined the binding nature of directives as against Member States to whom they are addressed, the possibility of relying on a directive before a national court is limited to these subjects. Consequently '[i]t follows that a directive may not of itself impose obligations on an individual and that a provision of a directive may not be relied upon as against such a person'. Thus, while Advocate-General Slynn believed that granting horizontal direct effect to unimplemented directives would blur the distinction between the legal effects of regulation and directives, in fact the Court refused to extend the concept because of a self-limiting clause within Article 189 itself.

While the Court of Justice has refused to recognise the concept of the 'horizontal direct effect' of directives, it has sought to achieve the same effect through other means. Instead of concentrating on the relationship between individuals and the state, the Court has diverted its attention to the obligations of Member States under Article 5 of the EC Treaty.

In a series of cases, most notably *Von Colson* v *Land Nordrhein-Westfahlen* (1984), and more recently *Marleasing SA* v *La Commercial Internacional De Alimentacion SA* (1992), the Court has relied on the obligation of Member States under Article 5 to interpret national law in a manner consistent with unimplemented directives.

Article 5 requires Member States to take 'all appropriate measures ... to ensure fulfilment of the obligations arising out of [the EC] Treaty'. In *Marleasing* (above), the Court was required to answer the question whether Directive 68/151 on company law harmonisation, which had not been implemented in Spain, could be relied upon to override a provision of Spanish law allowing the nullity of a company on the ground of lack of consideration. The directive exhaustively enumerated the grounds on which the incorporation of a company could be declared void. Spanish law therefore contradicted Community law, but the directive remained unadopted.

The Court held that national law must be interpreted in conformity with the directive and any attempt to dissolve a company on grounds other than those set out in the directive was incompatible with Community law. This decision was reached on the basis of a point of interpretation, namely that Spanish law must be interpreted in a manner consistent with Community law.

The impact of this decision has been to give horizontal direct effect to directives in an indirect manner. While the Court expressly rejected the possibility of directives having horizontal direct effect, its method of interpretation arrived at the same effect.

QUESTION THREE

Okeefenokee plc, a subsidiary of a Dutch food company, distributes mineral water and other non-alcoholic drinks in the United Kingdom. Its current stock of products for sale and delivery includes a new drink called Swamp, which is described on the label as 'mineral water' but which consists in fact of carbonated tap water. When visiting her local hypermarket a local authority officer notices the new product. On reading the label, she forms the view that the product contravenes a prohibition contained in a ministerial order on the stocking for sale and human consumption of products which are 'of defective composition'. This expression is not defined in the order.

The officer considers, however, that in taking legal action against Okeefenokee she can rely on EC Council Directive 80/777. This Directive concerns the approximation of the laws of the Member States regarding the exploitation and marketing of natural mineral waters. It obliges Member States to ensure that only waters which meet certain requirements are marketed as natural mineral waters. Swamp does not satisfy these requirements. The deadline for giving effect to the Directive has not expired, and the United Kingdom has still not introduced implementing legislation. Learning of the possibility of legal action against it, Okeefenokee consults you regarding its position under European Community law.

Advise Okeefenokee.

University of London LLB Examination
(for External Students) European Community Law 1990 Q2

General Comment

A problem question which requires the application of the principles behind the doctrine of direct effect to particular facts.

Skeleton Solution

• Legal force of a ministerial order.
• Legal force of directives which have not entered into force.
• Legal force of unimplemented directives.

Suggested Solution

Okeefenokee's liability for the misleading advertising is confined to two separate grounds: under the Ministerial order; and under Directive 80/777.

The Ministerial order is a measure of national law, analogous to an Order in Council. It therefore has force of law within the United Kingdom legal system. However, its provisions are vague. It merely prohibits the stocking for sale and human consumption of products which are 'of defective composition', a term undefined in the Ministerial order. Further, no mention is made of penalties or fines for infringements of the terms of the order. Clearly, Okeefenokee can claim that the Ministerial order is inapplicable to its ventures since it is not engaged in the stocking for sale of products but merely the distribution of particular products throughout the United Kingdom.

The liability of Okeefenokee is therefore limited to possible action under EC Council Directive 80/777. The substance of this directive relates the harmonisation of national laws throughout the Community regarding the exploitation and marketing of natural mineral waters. Under the directive, Member States must ensure that only waters which meet certain standards may be marketed as natural mineral waters. Swamp fails to satisfy these standards. Is Okeefenokee liable under the directive for misleading product advertising?

Council Directive 80/777 has not been implemented in the United Kingdom. Therefore, the local authority officer would have to rely on the doctrine of the direct effect of unimplemented directives in order to institute the legal proceedings against Okeefenokee.

In the particular circumstances of this case, Council Directive 80/777 could not be given direct effect. First, the doctrine of direct effect only applies to directives which remain unimplemented after the date specified for implementation. The application of directives which have been adopted by the Council of Ministers but which have not yet passed the expiry date for implementation cannot be anticipated or pre-empted. Since the deadline for giving effect to Directive 80/777 has not passed, the United Kingdom is not in breach of its obligations under Community law. It is only once a state has failed to fulfil its obligation to implement a Community directive that the doctrine of direct effect comes into operation.

Even after the deadline for the implementation of the directive, the local authority officer could only rely on the Council directive if the United Kingdom passes enabling legislation to incorporate the obligations contained in Directive 80/777. If the deadline passes for the implementation of the directive, and if the United Kingdom has failed to implement the directive, the local authority officer still could not initiate proceedings since she would be unable to rely on the doctrine of the direct effect of unimplemented directives.

The rationale behind the doctrine of direct effect is a doctrine of personal bar (see *Grad* v *Finanzamt Traunstein* (1970). It would therefore be inequitable to allow the national authorities of a state to rely on their omission in order to initiate proceedings. Consequently, national authorities may not rely, as against individuals or legal persons, upon a provision of a directive which has not yet been implemented in national law even although it should have been: see *Officier van Justitie* v *Kolpinghuis Nijmegen BV* (1989). Therefore, in the absence of legislation enacting the directive into English law, no proceedings can be instituted by the local authority officer.

QUESTION FOUR

Craig, Steven and Andrew are qualified surveyors working part-time for their respective employers. Craig is employed by the Department of Health, Steven is employed by British Rail and Andrew is employed by Smith and Western, a private chartered surveyors firm. All three are dismissed by their employers without notice or compensation. Council Directive 90/888 has been adopted by the Council as part of the Community's European Social Charter, and protects the rights of part-time workers. In particular, the directive provides for periods of notice and effective compensation when part-time employees are dismissed. Although the deadline date for the implementation of this directive has passed, the United Kingdom has not enacted legislation to implement the obligations of the directive.

Advise Craig, Steven and Andrew of their respective rights under Community law.

Question prepared by the Author

General Comment

A simple problem requiring the student to recognise the essential elements of the doctrine of direct effect as it applies to unimplemented directives.

Skeleton Solution

• Failure of the UK to implement the directive.
• Doctrine of the direct effect of unimplemented directives.
• Limitations of its application.
• Rights and duties of the respective employees.

Suggested Solution

The United Kingdom is in breach of its obligation under Directive 90/888 for failure to implement the directive in the specified time period. Although a Member State has discretion as to the form and method of implementation of a directive, by failing to implement the directive the United Kingdom has not achieved the desired object of the directive. Consequently, the United Kingdom is in breach of its obligations as defined by Article 5 of the Treaty of Rome.

The deadline for implementation of the Directive 90/888 has passed and so the directive is directly effective vis-a-vis the United Kingdom authorities (*Pubblico Ministero* v *Ratti* (1979). Craig will be able to rely on the terms of the directive against the Department of Health since it is a governmental organ and therefore estopped from relying on contrary provisions of national law: see *Van Duyn* v *Home Office* (1974).

Equally, Steven will be able to enforce the Directive against British Rail because it is a Crown corporation and therefore an emanation of the state: see *Johnston* v *Chief Constable of the Royal Ulster Constabulary* (1986). All bodies and organisations which are subject to the control of the state or which possess special powers beyond those which result from the normal rules applicable to the relations between individuals are emanations of the state for the purposes of the doctrine of the direct effect of unimplemented directives. Accordingly British Rail would not be justified in dismissing Steven and would also be prevented from relying on contrary national law against him.

However, Andrew would not have a similar recourse against Smith and Western. Obviously, Smith and Western, as a private surveyors firm, cannot be considered an emanation of the state and therefore cannot be caught by the principle of the 'vertical direct effect' of unimplemented directives. Application of the terms of Directive 90/888 to the contractual relationship between Andrew and Smith and Western would require recognition of the 'horizontal direct effect' of directives. In *Marshall* v *Southampton and South West Hampshire Area Health Authority* (1986), the European Court confirmed that while an unimplemented directive could be applied against the authorities of a Member State, it could not be invoked against individuals. Therefore, directives are not horizontally effective and one individual may not rely on a directive as against another individual.

In order for Andrew to obtain enforcement of the directive in the United Kingdom, he may try to obtain an Article 177 preliminary ruling from the ECJ as to the interpretation of the directive. However, the mandate of the European Court is limited to interpretation of the terms of directives. It may not directly declare the United Kingdom in breach of its Community obligations. This is a matter for the national court, but national courts are under a duty under Article 5 to ensure that Community obligations are respected.

In light of *Foglia* v *Novello* (1981), Andrew must also ensure that the litigation from which the question arises is genuine otherwise the ECJ will decline jurisdiction.

Alternatively, Andrew may complain to the European Commission in the hope that it will bring an Article 169 action against the United Kingdom. An enforcement action is brought when the Commission considers that a Member State is in breach of a Community obligation. However, whether or not such an action should be brought is essentially a matter for the Commission's consideration. Andrew cannot compel the Commission to initiate an investigation into his allegations: see *Star Fruit Co SA* v *EC Commission* (1990). Nor can Andrew bring a direct action against the United Kingdom.

Andrew can only challenge the negative ruling of the Commission if it issues a formal decision stating that the Commission sees no reason to bring such an action. In the event of such a decision, Andrew could bring a direct action requesting annulment of the refusal to act under Article 169 of the EC Treaty. Naturally, Andrew would have to establish a direct and individual concern in order to acquire standing to bring an action under Article 169.

QUESTION FIVE

The extension of the doctrine of the direct effect of Treaty provisions to international agreements negotiated by the Community itself represents a dangerous development in the jurisprudence of the Court.

Discuss.

Question prepared by the Author

General Comment

A question requiring the student to analyse the recent jurisprudence of the European Court with a view to criticising the direction of the Court in a particular issue.

Skeleton Solution

• The doctrine of direct effect as it applies to the Community treaties.
• Direct effect and Community agreements.
• The implications of this development.

Suggested Solution

No specific provision of any Community Treaty expressly authorises the use of individual Treaty provisions as a reservoir of Community principles, but from the beginnings of the Community, the European Court has sought to achieve this object by developing the principle of the direct effect of Treaty articles. In an early case heard by the Court, the issue was raised whether customs duties introduced after the entry into force of the EC Treaty could be imposed if contrary to the prohibitions on such duties imposed by Article 12 of that Treaty: *Van Gend en Loos* v *Netherlands* (1963). The critical question was whether the applicant, being an individual, could rely on the treaty provision as a principle of Community law enforceable within a national court. The European Court held that, where a Treaty article imposed a clear and unconditional obligation upon a Member State, unqualified by any reservation requiring legislative intervention, such an article was capable of direct effect and individual rights could be created which were enforceable in municipal courts.

Three specific conditions are required for a provision of a Community Treaty to have direct effect: (a) the provision being relied upon must be both clear and precise (see *Gimenez Zaera* v *Instituto Nacional de la Seguridad Social* (1987)); (b) the term must be unqualified and not subject to the requirement of legislative intervention (*Diamantarbeiders* v *Brachfeld* (1969)); (c) the obligation must not create a substantial discretion on either Member States or the Community institutions to act (*Salgoil* v *Italian Ministry for Foreign Trade* (1968)). The existence of alternative remedies for breach of a Treaty provision which has direct effect does not negate or prevent a right of action under Community law based on another principle capable of direct effect. Eliminating those provisions of the Community Treaties which relate to institutional procedures, transition and accession, and the general provisions, a significant number of treaty provisions are capable of having direct effect.

However, the European Court has extended the application of the principle of direct effect, not only to provisions of the three constitutional Community Treaties, but also to the terms of international agreements negotiated between the Community and third states under the authority vested by the common commercial policy. The case *Hauptzollamt Mainz* v *Kupferberg* (1982), provides an illustration of the application of the principle of direct effect to agreements entered into by the Community. Kupferberg, a German importer, was charged duties on imports of Portuguese port which were later reduced by the German Finance Court applying Article 21 of an Agreement between the European Community and Portugal which prohibited, on a reciprocal basis, discriminatory internal taxation between imported and domestic products. The German tax authorities appealed against the decision of the Finance Court and a preliminary reference was made to the European Court.

The European Court held that, since international responsibility for breach of such agreements rested with the Community, the Court must recognise the need to ensure uniform application of these obligations within the Community. The terms of such agreements could have direct effect if the provision being relied upon is unconditional and precise, and also capable of conferring individual rights which could be enforced in national courts or tribunals: see also *Demirel* v *Stadt Schwabisch Gmund* (1989).

The extension of the doctrine of direct effect to treaty provisions other than those contained in the Community Treaties is a disconcerting development for a number of reasons. First, the Court has not indicated the precise status of the principles of law derived from such treaties in the hierarchy of norms in the Community legal order. It is not clear whether such principles prevail over inconsistent Community secondary legislation, although it is clear that such principles prevail over inconsistent provisions of national law. However, it is unlikely that the Court would hold that principles derived from Community agreements prevail over the constitutional Community Treaties.

Second, the potential scope for the creation of new norms of Community law from this particular source is disturbing. While the European Court has been reluctant to deduce directly enforceable rights from international agreements entered into by the Member States prior to the Treaty of Rome (see *International Fruit Company* v *Produktschap voor Groenten en Fruit* (1972)), the same reluctance has not been manifested towards free trade agreements and association agreements concluded by the Community: see *SZ Sevince* v *Staatssecretaris Van Justitie* (1992). The Community maintains more than 50 economic agreements with third states.

Third, recognition of Community agreements as a source of Community law creates an additional degree of difficulty in the process of identifying applicable principles of Community law.

The rationale asserted by the European Court for the expansion of the doctrine of direct effect to Community treaties with third states was the need to protect the European Community from international responsibility for a failure to observe international obligations, where the fault or omission was caused by a particular Member State. Whether or not this is a sufficient pretext for causing such a radical upheaval within the Community legal system is an unanswered question.

6 FUNDAMENTAL PRINCIPLES OF EUROPEAN COMMUNITY LAW

6.1 Introduction

6.2 Key points

6.3 Relevant cases

6.4 Relevant materials

6.5 Analysis of questions

6.6 Questions

6.1 Introduction

The Community Treaties create a new legal order which interacts with the legal systems of all the Member States. This unique form of law required the development of fundamental principles to provide a basis for its proper functioning. Many of these essential principles were not originally stated in the Community Treaties, but have been developed in the jurisprudence of the European Court. The principle of the supremacy of Community law, the protection of human rights within the Community and the standards developed to interpret Community law are all examples of this phenomenon. In contrast, the principles of non-discrimination on the basis of nationality and non-discrimination on the basis of gender were elaborated in the Community Treaties, but have also been substantially developed by the European Court.

6.2 Key points

a) *The supremacy of European Community law*

Neither the Community Treaties or the European Community Act 1972, which gives force to Community law within the United Kingdom, contain express provisions referring to the question of the supremacy between Community law and national law. Notwithstanding this omission, in *Costa* v *ENEL* [1964] ECR 585, the European Court resolved the issue of supremacy between these legal orders in the following terms:

'[T]he law stemming from the Treaty, an independent source of law, [cannot], because of its special and original nature, be overridden by domestic legal provisions, however framed, without being deprived of its character as Community law and without the legal basis of the Community itself being called into question.'

Community law therefore prevails over inconsistent provisions of national law, whether passed before or after the Community Treaties entered into force. Further, as formulated by the Court, the principle of supremacy must be given effect even within the national legal systems of the Member States.

A number of subsequent decisions of the European Court have elaborated on the implications of this doctrine:

i) The principle applies irrespective of whether the inconsistent provision of national law has a civil or criminal character: *Procureur du Roi* v *Dassonville* [1974] ECR 837.

ii) Community law prevails even over inconsistent provisions of the constitutional law of Member States: *Internationale Handelsgesellschaft* [1970] ECR 1125.

iii) The formal source of national law is irrelevant to a determination of supremacy. Both inconsistent statutes and judicial precedents have been declared inapplicable. Even rules of professional bodies may, in certain circumstances, be held inconsistent and thereby inapplicable: *R* v *Royal Pharmaceutical Society of Great Britain* [1989] 2 CMLR 751.

iv) The European Court has extended the principle of supremacy not only to provisions of Community Treaties, but also to Community regulations and, in certain instances, Community directives.

v) Member States are obliged to repeal national legislation found to be inconsistent with Community law: *EC Commission* v *United Kingdom (Re Origin Marking Requirements)* [1985] 2 CMLR 259.

While the European Court has vigorously asserted the supremacy of Community law over national law within the Community legal system, a number of national courts, including those of the United Kingdom, have expressed reservations in relation to this doctrine.

Principles of Community law will prevail over inconsistent provisions of English law enacted prior to 1972 by virtue of the European Communities Act 1972, as amended. The fundamental question is whether British courts will give effect to inconsistent statutes enacted after the entry into force of the 1972 Act. English courts have been cautious in their approach to this problem. In order to avoid potential conflicts, a number of principles have been developed:

i) Statutes of Parliament are to be interpreted in order not to conflict with Community law: *Garland* v *British Rail Engineering Ltd* [1982] 2 All ER 402.

ii) In the event of an inconsistency, such a defect should be attributed to an oversight on the part of the parliamentary draftsmen: *Shields* v *E Coomes (Holdings) Ltd* [1979] 1 All ER 456.

iii) Pre-1972 statutes which are inconsistent with Community law are inapplicable, but the legal basis of this proposition is the 1972 Act: *WH Smith Do-It-All & Payless DIY Ltd* v *Peterborough City Council* [1990] 2 CMLR 577.

The House of Lords recently had to resolve the conflict between the principle of the supremacy of Community law and that of parliamentary sovereignty. The case itself involved the conflict between the Merchant Fishing Act 1988 and the provisions of the EC Treaty prohibiting discrimination on the grounds of nationality.

The House of Lords requested, inter alia, a ruling from the European Court on the interpretation of the EC Treaty in light of the terms of the 1988 Act. The

European Court found, not surprisingly, that provisions of national law could not be allowed to frustrate the proper functioning of Community law. The decision was passed to the House of Lords for application to the facts before it: *R v Secretary of State, ex parte Factortame (No 4)* [1990] 3 CMLR 375; [1991] 1 All ER 70.

Lord Bridge of Harwich, implementing the terms of the ruling, felt obliged to make the following comment on the modification of the principle of parliamentary sovereignty:

'If the supremacy within the European Community of Community law over the national law of Member States was not always inherent in the EC Treaty it was certainly well established in the jurisprudence of the Court of Justice long before the United Kingdom joined the Community. Thus, whatever limitation of its sovereignty Parliament accepted when it enacted the European Communities Act 1972 was entirely voluntary': *R v Secretary of State for Transport, ex parte Factortame (No 4)*.

b) *The interpretation of Community law*

Since the European Court is engaged in the interpretation of treaty law and legislation enacted thereunder, the Court has consistently prescribed the 'teleological' or 'purposive' method for the interpretation or construction of Community law. This is the method used to ascertain the content of international obligations and contrasts with the 'literal meaning' approach preferred by the English courts.

The teleological approach is intended to allow flexibility in the interpretation process by emphasising the purpose of a measure and not its strict terminology. The first step in this process is to ascertain the purpose of the particular legislative measure. Article 190 of the EC Treaty requires that measures of secondary legislation 'shall state the reasons on which they are based'. The purpose of a Community measure therefore can be determined by reference to the preamble or recital which precedes the actual provisions of any Community measure. Once the purpose of the legislation has been identified, its provisions can be interpreted with this purpose in mind.

Section 3(1) of the European Communities Act 1972 specifically requires that any question relating to the meaning or effect of a provision of Community law before a court or tribunal in the United Kingdom is to be treated as a question of law and interpreted in accordance with the provisions laid down by the relevant decisions of the European Court.

The teleological approach to interpretation also means that measures of Community law incorporated into English law must be construed to give effect to the Community measure: see *Elefanten Schuh GmbH v Jacqmain* [1982] 3 CMLR 1. For example, legislation implementing Community directives must be interpreted in light of the purpose of the original measure: *Litster v Forth Dry Dock and Engineering Co* [1989] 1 All ER 1134.

c) *Non-discrimination on the basis of nationality*

Article 7 of the EC Treaty, which will become Article 6 once the Treaty on

European Union is approved, establishes the fundamental principle that 'any discrimination on the grounds of nationality shall be prohibited'. This obligation extends to all activities within the scope of the Treaty and, in particular, to the exercise of the rights of the free movement of goods, persons, services and capital. The same obligation is repeated in a number of subsequent provisions of the EC Treaty which stress the importance of this principle as a fundamental rule of Community law.

The obligation of non-discrimination on the basis of nationality has a number of important effects:

i) This obligation precludes Member States from levying tariffs or charges having an equivalent effect.

ii) No Member State can impose, either directly or indirectly, any form of internal taxation on the products of other Member States in excess of that imposed on identical or similar domestic products.

iii) Member States cannot discriminate between domestic and Community suppliers of services nor between domestic investors and Community investors.

iv) The European Court has extended the principle of non-discrimination not only to the freedom to supply services, but also the freedom to receive services: *Cowan* v *Tresor Public* [1990] 2 CMLR 613.

v) The obligation of non-discrimination applies to the protection of all economic rights falling within the scope of the EC Treaty and, in particular, intellectual and industrial property rights: *Collins* v *Imtrat Handelsgesellschaft mbH* [1993] 3 CMLR 773.

The principle of non-discrimination also applies to workers but merely as factors of production and not as individuals per se. Thus, nationals of Member States are entitled to the same kind of employment protection as nationals of the host state, the same conditions of employment as well as the same social security and tax advantages. Nationals of Community states are also entitled to the benefit of further education on a non-discriminatory basis. Notwithstanding the scope of these rights, migrant workers are not entitled to the benefits of nationality, such as voting rights in governmental elections or to stand for such elections. The fact that Member States have opened their national territory to the migration of workers within the Community does not exclude the power of the individual Member States to regulate the movement of foreign nationals: *Watson* v *Belmann* [1976] ECR 1185.

d) *Non-discrimination on the basis of gender*

Another fundamental objective of the EC Treaty, stated in Article 119, is recognition of the basic principle that men and women should be entitled to receive equal pay for equal work. The European Court has ruled on a number of occasions that Article 119 is capable of having limited direct effect. In particular, in *Defrenne* v *Sabena* [1976] ECR 455, the Court held that Article 119 prohibited direct and overt discrimination, a concept which was identified by reference to the twin criteria of equal work and equal pay which are specified in the article itself.

Unfortunately, the effect of the Court's decision in this case was limited because, according to the Court, the provision could only support claims relating to pay periods after the date of judgment.

'Equal pay' is defined in Article 119 as 'the ordinary basic or minimum wage or salary and any other consideration, whether in cash or kind, which the worker receives, directly or indirectly, in respect of his [or her] employment from his [or her] employer'.

The European Court has defined 'pay' in broad terms. Thus, special travelling allowances, discriminatory retirement dates, discriminatory pension allowances, and discriminatory redundancy payments, have all constituted pay within the meaning of the article.

A number of Community directives have also been adopted by the Community to add substance to the general obligation of non-discrimination in the workplace: see Council Directive 76/207, Council Directive 79/7 and Council Directive 86/613.

Article 119 applies regardless of whether an employee is employed on a part-time basis or a full-time basis. Further, where discrimination is being perpetrated on the basis of a distinction between full-time workers and part-time workers, and the majority of one or other of these categories is predominantly one gender, discrimination contrary to Article 119 may exist: see *Nimz* v *Frie Und Hansestadt Hamburg* [1992] 3 CMLR 699.

Another illustration of de facto discrimination contrary to Article 119 concerned the dismissal of a female employee on account of her pregnancy. In *Webb* v *EMO Air Cargo (UK) Limited* [1994] 2 CMLR 729, the European Court held that Article 119 of the EC Treaty and Directive 76/207 prohibited the dismissal of a female employee who was unable to fulfil the terms of her employment contract due to her absence for maternity leave. The Court found that the maternity leave for her condition could not be equated to a period of absence attributable to a comparable medical condition in a male employee which would justify dismissal.

e) *The protection of human rights in Community law*

Although each Member of the European Community is also a party to the European Convention on Human Rights 1950, this Convention is not part of Community law. But issues of human rights frequently arise before the European Court of Justice. Indeed, the European Court has acknowledged that 'the fundamental rights generally recognised by the Member States form an integral part of [the] Community system': *Nold* v *EC Commission* [1974] ECR 491. In the past, the European Court has considered issues of human rights relating to the following matters:

i)   the right to privacy: *National Panasonic (UK) Ltd* v *EC Commission* [1980] ECR 2033;

ii) freedom to practise a religion: *Prais* v *EC Council* [1976] ECR 1589;

iii) the right to possess property: *Hauer* v *Land Rheinland-Pfalz* [1979] ECR 3727;

iv) the right of lawyer-client confidentiality: *AM & S Europe* v *EC Commission* [1982] ECR 1575;

v) issues of substantive and procedural due process of law: *Musique Diffusion Française SA* v *EC Commission* [1985] ECR 1825;

vi) the right to refrain from self-incrimination: *Heylens* [1987] ECR 4097.

However, notwithstanding the Court's extensive jurisprudence on human rights issues, no allegation that a Community measure is void on the ground that it infringes fundamental human rights has yet been accepted by the European Court as a sufficient ground for declaring a rule of Community law null and void.

f) *The liability of Member States to private individuals for breach of Community law*

There is no provision in the EC Treaty which expressly permits private individuals to initiate proceedings against Member States for breaches by those states of Community law. The impact of this omission was magnified by the apparent reluctance of national courts to grant relief to private individuals under national law for injury occasioned to them by acts of Member States committed in violation of Community law.

To plug this gap, the European Court has recently developed a principle of Community law which provides that national courts are required to grant relief to private individuals who suffer injury as a result of a breach of Community law by a Member State. This principle is destined to become a fundamental principle in Community jurisprudence.

The case in which this principle was definitively established was *Francovich* v *Italian Republic* [1993] 2 CMLR 66. The Court held that a Member State is liable to private individuals for breaches of Community law if three conditions are satisfied:

• the Community obligation is capable of conferring individual private rights. In other words, the obligation must affect the position of private individuals and the applicant must fall within the category of affected individuals;

• the individual is able to establish injury suffered by him or her as a result of the unlawful act; and

• there is proof of causation between the unlawful act and the injury suffered by the individual.

The principle which has been established in this case is that a Member State, and its agencies and organs, are liable for acts which cause injury to private individuals if their actions are contrary to Community law. However, it must be noted that this right must be vindicated in the national courts and private individuals remain unable to bring direct actions against Member States in the European Court.

6.3 Relevant cases

Costa v *ENEL* [1964] ECR 585: The original decision asserting the supremacy of Community law over inconsistent provisions of national legislation.

R v *Secretary of State for Transport, ex parte Factortame (No 1)* [1990] 3 CMLR 807: Decision of the European Court asserting the supremacy of Community law over an inconsistent Act of Parliament enacted after the 1972 Act.

Barber v *Guardian Royal Exchange Assurance Group* [1990] 2 CMLR 513: Pensions which are administered on a discriminatory basis may be contrary to Community law.

Nimz v *Frie Und Hansestadt Hamburg* [1992] 3 CMLR 699: The application of the terms of Article 119 to part-time workers.

Francovich v *Italian Republic* [1993] 2 CMLR 66: The precedent from the European Court establishing the principle of the liability of Member States for breaches of Community law.

R v *Secretary of State for Transport, ex parte Factortame (No 4)* [1990] 3 CMLR 375; [1991] 1 All ER 70: The decision of the House of Lords modifying the doctrine of parliamentary sovereignty in light of the principle of the supremacy of Community law.

6.4 Relevant materials

S Prechal & N Burrows, *Gender Discrimination Law of the European Community* (1990).

J Steiner, 'From Direct Effects to Francovich: Shifting Means of Enforcement of Community Law' (1993) EL Rev 3.

A Robertson, 'Effective Remedies in EC Law Before the House of Lords' (1993) LQR 27.

6.5 Analysis of questions

Questions dealing with the issue of fundamental principles of Community law take many different shapes and forms. However, most frequently such questions take the form of problem-type questions requiring the application of Community law to factual circumstances. Students should be particularly aware of the recent developments surrounding the principle of the supremacy of Community law and the controversy surrounding discrimination on the basis of gender.

6.6 Questions

QUESTION ONE

'The rules of national law which render the exercise of directly enforceable Community rights excessively difficult must be overridden': per Lord Bridge of Harwich in *R* v *Secretary of State, ex parte Factortame (No 3)* [1989] 3 CMLR 1.

Discuss the principle of the supremacy of Community law in the light of the decision by the House of Lords in the *Factortame* case.

Question prepared by the Author

General Comment

A question dealing with the issue of the supremacy of Community law and requiring a descriptive answer.

Skeleton Solution

- The origins of the principle of supremacy: *Costa* case.
- The scope of the principle of supremacy.
- Pre-*Factortame* decisions of the English courts.
- The decision of the House of Lords.
- The implications of the decision.

Suggested Solution

In order to create a supranational organisation with legislative capacity, the Member States of the Community have been required to delegate certain aspects of sovereignty to the European Community. The Community has power to enact laws on those subjects which expressly fall within its competence under the Community Treaties, while Member States continue to retain authority to legislate on all residual matters. However, inevitably, when separate bodies legislate on behalf of the same population, conflicting principles will emerge even though the competence of each body has been strictly defined. In the event of such a conflict, the question of the supremacy of one legal order over the other becomes critical.

No Community Treaty contains express provisions regulating the issue of supremacy between Community law and national law. The only implied reference to the issue of supremacy in the Community treaties is Article 5 of the EC Treaty which imposes an obligation on all Member States to adopt all appropriate measures to ensure that the obligations of the treaty are observed, together with an additional duty to abstain from all acts which might jeopardise achievement of the objectives of the Treaty. The absence of an express supremacy clause suggests that the draftsmen of the Community Treaties did not intend principles of Community law to prevail over national law.

Despite these omissions, the European Court of Justice has adopted an unequivocal position on the question of supremacy between Community law and national law. In *Costa v ENEL* (1964), the Court was asked to decide whether an Italian statute enacted after the creation of the Community could prevail over provisions of the EC Treaty relating to the regulation of state monopolies. At the outset of the case, the Court reaffirmed its decision in an earlier case that the Community Treaties had created a new legal order in the form of the Community, for the benefit of which the Member States had limited their sovereign rights: *Van Gend en Loos v Netherlands* (1963). The Court then continued to resolve the issue of supremacy in favour of Community law on the ground that the objects and purposes of the Community would be frustrated if national law was allowed to deviate from Community law. Community law therefore prevailed over inconsistent provisions of national law, whether passed before or after the Community Treaties entered into force. The principle of supremacy has subsequently become a fundamental principle of

Community law, and must be given effect even in the courts and tribunals of the Member States.

The principle of the supremacy prevails over inconsistent provisions of national law regardless of form or content. In particular, Community law prevails regardless of whether the inconsistent provision of national law has a civil or criminal character. An illustration of the application of the principle to criminal proceedings was the *Scotch Whisky case: Procureur du Roi v Dassonville* (1974). Criminal charges were instituted against a Belgian importer who had imported Scotch whisky from France without a certificate of origin from the British customs authorities. The Belgian Criminal Code prohibited imports into Belgium in the absence of a certificate of origin. However, the importer had acquired the consignment of whisky from agents in France and not directly from the United Kingdom. Obtaining a certificate of origin in these circumstances was both difficult and expensive.

The importer was prosecuted and a Belgian criminal court asked the European Court for a ruling on whether provisions of the EC Treaty provided a defence to these charges. The Court held that this requirement was unduly onerous and contravened Article 30 of the EC Treaty. Since the provision of the Belgian criminal code conflicted with Community law, no charges could be brought on this ground against the importer without contravening Community law.

A more complex problem arises when provisions of Community law are alleged to be inconsistent with guarantees of human rights enshrined in the constitutions of Member States. In *Internationale Handelsgesellschaft* (1970), the European Court had to decide whether Community law prevailed over provisions of German constitutional law embodying fundamental principles of human rights. The European Court upheld the supremacy of Community law, but qualified this decision by asserting that fundamental principles of human rights were also part of Community law.

The principle of supremacy applies to a number of different forms of Community law. Clearly the most obvious application of the principle is inconsistency between national law and a provision of a Community Treaty. However the Court has also extended the doctrine to conflicts between provisions of national law and Community regulations: *Neumann v Hauptzollamt Hof* (1967). In addition, the Court has even upheld the supremacy of unimplemented directives which are capable of direct effect over inconsistent provisions of national law: *Marshall v Southampton and South-West Hampshire Area Health Authority* (1986).

As a corollary to the principle of supremacy, Member States are obliged to repeal national legislation found to be inconsistent with Community law: *EC Commission v United Kingdom (Re Origin Marking Requirements)* (1985). The European Commission bears primary responsibility for ensuring that Member States are brought before the European Court to resolve allegations of inconsistencies. Member States are obliged under Article 5 of the EC Treaty to adhere to the rulings of the European Court and amend or repeal offending provisions of national law. Where individuals or legal persons wish to challenge the consistency of national law with measures of Community law, the appropriate course is to raise an action in the national court of the offending Member State against the responsible national authority. Although national courts are obliged to ensure that the principle of supremacy of Community law is respected, an application to the European Court for a preliminary reference on the question may be a more appropriate course of action.

According to the decisions of the English courts before the *Factortame (No 4)* case (1990), principles of Community law will prevail over inconsistent provisions of English law enacted prior to 1972 by virtue of the 1972 Act itself: *WH Smith Do-It-All & Payless DIY Ltd* v *Peterborough City Council* (1990). However, the jurisprudence of the English courts became contorted when efforts were made to reconcile the principle of the supremacy of Community law with inconsistent statutes enacted after the 1972 Act. Clearly such statutes should override the 1972 Act by virtue of the constitutional principle that subsequent parliamentary statutes prevail over inconsistent prior statutes.

In order to avoid potential conflicts between Acts of Parliament and Community law, a series of principles of interpretation were derived to assist in the application and construction of inconsistent provisions. Thus, statutes of Parliament are to be interpreted in such a manner as not to conflict with Community law: *Garland* v *British Rail Engineering Ltd* (1982). In the event of an inconsistency, such a defect should be attributed to the oversight of the parliamentary draftsmen. On this basis, even Lord Denning was prepared to embrace the principle of Community supremacy in *Shields* v *E Coomes (Holdings) Ltd* (1979) where, after referring to the *Costa* case and the *Simmenthal* case, he declared that '[i]f ... a tribunal should find any ambiguity in the statutes or any inconsistency with Community law, then it should resolve it by giving primacy to Community law'. However, in a rejoinder to this dictum the qualification was made that this principle only applies in the event of accidental oversight and not when Parliament has expressed a deliberate intention to repudiate Community law. A clear intention on the part of Parliament to violate Community law would be given effect by the courts.

Until recently, the courts had managed to avoid a direct confrontation between Community law and an inconsistent Act of Parliament. However, in *R* v *Secretary of State, ex parte Factortame (No 3)* (1989), the courts were confronted with the question whether the Merchant Shipping Act 1988 conflicted with Community law. The plaintiffs in this case were Spanish nationals who owned a number of fishing vessels registered as British under the previous Merchant Shipping Act. The Merchant Shipping Act 1988 radically altered the conditions under which non-British nationals could register vessels in the United Kingdom. Vessels registered under the previous legislation were required to re-register under the 1988 Act. The vessels owned by the plaintiffs failed to satisfy one or more of the conditions for registration introduced by the 1988 statute, including the requirement that the vessels should be owned, managed or controlled by British nationals.

The plaintiffs brought an action on the basis that the 1988 Act violated Community law by depriving them of enforceable Community rights. The Queen's Bench Division referred the substantive issue to the European Court for a preliminary ruling and ordered that, pending final judgment, the application of the statute should be suspended. The Secretary of State appealed this decision to the Court of Appeal which set aside the order by the earlier court suspending the Act. The plaintiffs appealed to the House of Lords against the decision of the Court of Appeal.

The House of Lords dismissed the appeal on the grounds that no English court had power to make an order declaring an Act of Parliament not to be the law until some uncertain future date. However, the question whether Community law empowered or obliged an English court, irrespective of the position under national law, to provide effective interim protection of putative rights under Community law was referred to the European Court for a preliminary ruling. Further, in deciding that the matter should be considered by the European Court of Justice, Lord Bridge of Harwich, commenting on the nature of Community law, stated that rules of national law which render the exercise of directly enforceable Community rights excessively difficult or virtually impossible must be overridden. The question was thereafter submitted by way of a preliminary reference to the European Court for consideration.

In its decision on the merits of the case, the European Court concluded that Community law precludes the application of a rule of national law which would constitute an obstacle to the adoption of Community law: *R* v *Secretary of State, ex parte Factortame* Case (1990). Community law must be interpreted as meaning that if a national court considers that the sole obstacle precluding it from granting interim relief is a rule of national law, it must set aside the national rule. This was a resounding endorsement of the principle that Community law prevails over English law regardless of the constitutional obstacles to the implementation of this policy. Further, in common with courts throughout the Community, English courts are obliged to give effect to the decisions of the European Court obtained through the preliminary reference procedure.

Once the decision of the European Court was returned to the House of Lords, that court was required to apply the decision of the facts of the case. In doing so, Lord Bridge of Harwich felt compelled to address public criticisms of the House of Lords and its readiness to accept the principle of the supremacy of Community law. In particular, he observed:

'Some public comments on the decisions of the ECJ, affirming the jurisdiction of the courts of the Member States to override national legislation if necessary to enable interim relief to be granted in protection of rights under Community law, have suggested that this was a novel and dangerous invasion by a Community institution of the sovereignty of the UK Parliament.

But such comments are based on a misconception. If the supremacy within the EC of Community law over the national law of member states was not always inherent in the EC Treaty it was certainly well established in the jurisprudence of the ECJ long before the UK joined the Community. Thus, whatever limitation of its sovereignty Parliament accepted when it enacted the European Communities Act 1972 was entirely voluntary': *R* v *Secretary of State, ex parte Factortame (No 4)* (1990).

Hence the House of Lords has accepted that the doctrine of parliamentary sovereignty has been modified by the principle of the supremacy of Community law although it is not entirely clear how wide an inroad has been made as a consequence of the *Factortame* saga.

QUESTION TWO

How and when can conflicts arise between rules of national law and rules of Community law? How should such conflicts be resolved in the view of the European Court of Justice? Discuss with reference to ECJ caselaw.

University of London LLB Examination
(for External Students) European Community Law June 1993 Q3

General Comment

Another straightforward essay-type question requiring a narrative answer. How and when conflicts arise can best be demonstrated through examples showing the circumstances giving rise to such situations. The policy of the European Court towards the issue is clear-cut and presents no obstacle to answering the question. However we are not asked for the views of the national courts which should only be alluded to in passing.

Skeleton Solution

- Outline of the measures of Community law on which the European Court has conferred the quality of supremacy.
- Types of incompatible national provisions: statutes, judicial decisions, administrative practices – civil and criminal proceedings.
- Occasions when conflicts arise: before the ECJ (Article 169 cases and 177 references) and national courts.
- Principle of supremacy as elaborated by the ECJ and adopted by the UK courts in *Factortame*.

Suggested Solution

The European Community legal system does not function independently or separately from the legal systems of the Member States. The provisions of the EC Treaty and Community measures often cover the same subject-matters as national legislation. However, none of the Community Treaties contains provisions expressly regulating the issue of supremacy between Community law and national provisions in the inevitable event of conflict.

This inevitability has required the European Court to develop principles to regulate the relationship between inconsistent provisions of Community law and national law. With varying degree of reluctance, the courts of most of the Member States have gradually accepted these principles and have applied them in cases in which conflict arises.

How conflicts can arise

Conflicts between provisions of Community law and those of national law can arise in a number of circumstances. The most obvious is when a state enacts a statute incompatible with a directly enforceable provision of a Community Treaty. Within the United Kingdom, it has been accepted that a UK statute, enacted prior to or after 1972, if inconsistent with a provision of a Community Treaty, cannot prevail over Community provisions: *R v Secretary of State, ex parte Factortame (No 3)* (1989).

There is no logical reason why a statute inconsistent with a Community regulation, or the terms of an illegitimately unimplemented directive should be treated any differently. Lord Bridge of Harwich recognised as much when, in rendering the judgment in *Factortame*, supra. In fact, decisions have been forthcoming from the European Court holding that effect must be given to unimplemented directives capable of direct effect in preference to provisions of national law; see *Pubblico Ministero v Ratti* (1979).

It is not only statutory law which may be incompatible with provisions of Community law. The formal source of national law is irrelevant in the event of inconsistency. Both inconsistent statutory instruments and judicial decisions have been considered by the European Court. Even rules of professional bodies may, in certain circumstances, be held to conflict with measures of Community law; see *R* v *Royal Pharmaceutical Society of Great Britain* (1989).

The possibility of conflict exists irrespective of whether the national law has a civil or a criminal character. For example, Community law may offer a defence to a prosecution if the accused can establish that the charges conflict with Community law. For example, in *Procureur du Roi* v *Dassonville* (1974), the accused successfully relied on Article 30 of the EC Treaty as a defence to a charge of importing goods without the proper documentation.

Conflicts can even arise between provisions of a country's constitutional law and Community law. Even in these circumstances, the European Court has refused to accept that provisions of national law – even of a constitutional nature – prevail over Community law; see *Internationale Handelsgesellschaft* (1970).

The points in time when conflicts arise

As to the time when conflicts between the two different sets of legal principles occur, generally, this is when either the European Court or a national court is required to rule on the application of Community law to a series of facts before it.

The European Court will consider this matter when either an application is made under Article 169 or when the preliminary ruling procedure of Article 177 of the Treaty is invoked by a national court.

In the event that the issue arises when proceedings are initiated against a Member State under Article 169, the Member States in question are required to repeal national legislation held inconsistent with Community law; see *EC Commission* v *United Kingdom (Re Origin Marking Requirements)* (1985). The European Commission bears primary responsibility for ensuring that Member States are brought before the European Court on this basis when in its view a conflict arises.

Member States are obliged under Article 5 of the EC Treaty to adhere to the rulings of the European Court and to amend or repeal offending provisions of national law.

The alternative means whereby conflicts come before the European Court is when a preliminary reference is made. Interestingly, the European Court has no jurisdiction under Article 177 to interpret a provision of national law and is therefore unable to declare a particular national statute or rule to be incompatible with Community law. Instead, the European Court considers itself able to provide the national court with all matters relating to the interpretation of Community law as may enable it to decide the issue of compatibility in the case before it; see *Schumacher* v *Hauptzollamt Frankfurt Am Main* (1990).

In the event of a conflict, the Court may only conclude that the relevant provisions of national law appear 'incompatible' with Community law. It is the responsibility of the national court to ensure that the relevant Community law is applied and to determine whether a plaintiff, the prosecution or the defence should prevail.

If a national court decides not to make a preliminary reference to the European

Court, then the other situation when a conflict will arise is when the national court or tribunal is required to rule on the point.

Resolution of the conflict in the view of the ECJ

According to the European Court, conflicts between Community law and provisions of national law should always be resolved in favour of the Community rules. In one of its earliest decision, the Court declared:

'[T]he law stemming from the Treaty, an independent source of law, cannot, because of its special and original nature, be overridden by domestic legal provisions, however framed, without being deprived of its character as Community law and without the legal basis of the Community itself being called into question': *Costa* v *ENEL* (1964).

Community law therefore prevails over inconsistent provisions of national law whether enacted before or after the Community Treaties entered into force. Further, as formulated by the Court, the principle of supremacy must also be given effect within the national legal systems of the Member States.

The Court has consistently maintained this principle throughout the course of its jurisprudence. For example, most recently, the European Court was asked by the House of Lords for a ruling on whether that court was required to grant interim relief in a case in which provisions of the Merchant Shipping Act 1988 were challenged as being incompatible with Community law.

In its decision, the European Court held that 'any legislative, administrative or judicial practice' which might impair the effectiveness of Community law is incompatible with Community law and cannot be applied by a national court. Hence, a national court which would normally grant interim relief in such circumstances, if it were not for a rule of national law to the contrary, is required 'to set aside that rule': *R* v *Secretary of State, ex parte Factortame (No 1)* (1990).

In is therefore clear that the European Court will not entertain the prospect of any provision of national law, even of constitutional validity, prevailing over an inconsistent provision of Community law. Hence, this is one of the most vigorously asserted principles formulated by the European Court and there are no circumstances to date in which a conflict between a Community rule and a national rule has been resolved in favour of the national rule.

QUESTION THREE

Explain and assess, using examples drawn from at least two different areas of EC law, the European Court's approach to the interpretation of the EC Treaty.

University of London LLB Examination
(for External Students) European Community Law 1989 Q2

General Comment

A question requiring a student to demonstrate the application of a fundamental principle of Community law by reference to the jurisprudence of the European Court.

Skeleton Solution

• The approach of the ECJ to interpretation.
• Examples from the jurisprudence of the Court.
• Effect of this jurisprudence on the UK courts.

Suggested Solution

Since the European Court is engaged in the interpretation of treaty law and legislation enacted thereunder, the Court has consistently prescribed the 'purposive' or 'teleological' method for the interpretation or construction of Community law. This contrasts with the 'literal meaning' approach adopted by the English courts towards the interpretation of statutes.

The teleological approach is intended to allow flexibility in the interpretation process by referring to the purpose of a measure and not the strict terminology. The first step in this process is to ascertain the context of the legislation by reference to its purpose. Thereafter the meaning ascribed to terms is derived by reference to the objects sought to be achieved by the particular legislation. Article 190 of the EC Treaty requires that measures of secondary legislation 'shall state the reasons on which they are based'. The object of a Community measure may therefore be ascertained by reference to the preamble or recitals which precede the actual terms of any Community measure. The object is borne in mind when considering particular terms of the measure.

The European Court has used this teleological approach of interpreting provisions of law in order to pursue a policy of deliberate judicial activism. Many principles of Community law have been derived in this manner. Equally, the European Court has been frequently criticised for expanding the competence of the Community without specific textual authority: see H Rasmussen *On Law and Policy in the ECJ* (1986).

One clear example of this was the approach of the Court in the ERTA case (*EC Commission* v *EC Council* (1971). In this case, the Court had to decide whether Member States required the participation of the European Community in order to enter into an international agreement with non-Community states regarding transport policy in Europe. In determining the competence of the Community to enter into international agreements, the Court examined Article 210 which confers legal personality on the European Community. This provision could not, according to the Court, be given effect unless the objectives of the Community as a whole were taken into account. The objectives of the Community are defined in Part I of the EC Treaty. Since the Community must have competence to pursue its fundamental objectives, the Court held that, in conducting its external affairs, the Community enjoyed capacity to establish international obligations with third countries over the whole field of objectives defined in Part I of the Treaty.

The immediate consequence of this judgment was a dramatic growth in the external competence of the Community. The Court had ruled that the capacity of the Community extended to those matters contained within its objectives. Member States therefore no longer retained competence to enter into international obligations concerning such issues without the participation or consent of the European Community. Such a radical extension of the powers of the Community was achieved by the European Court adopting a teleological approach to the interpretation of the Community treaties.

A similar approach to interpretation was demonstrated by the European Court in the *Woodpulp Case* (1988). The Community Treaties make no comment on the possible extra-territorial application of Community competition policies to undertakings resident outside the Community. However, a number of firms in Finland, Sweden and Canada entered into a cartel to fix the prices of woodpulp charged to customers inside the Community. The only way of preventing these undertakings from maintaining the cartel was to apply Community law to their activities even though their head offices were outside the Community.

In order to achieve this objective, the European Court examined Article 85 of the EC treaty which deals with unfair competitive practices and declared that in order to prevent circumvention of Article 85, Community law had to be applied extraterritorially. The basis for this decision was pragmatism. If the applicability of the prohibitions laid down under the Community competition law were made to depend on the place an agreement was formed, the result would be to give commercial enterprises an easy means of evading their Community obligations. In other words, if the Court did not accept the principle of the extra-territorial application of competition law, the purpose of Article 85 would be significantly undermined.

The European Communities Act 1972 specifically requires that any question relating to the meaning or effect of a provision of Community law before a court or tribunal in the United Kingdom shall be treated as a question of law and determined in accordance with the provisions laid down by relevant decisions of the European Court. British courts and tribunals are therefore obliged to adopt this style of interpretation when applying Community law, whether in the form of Treaty provisions, directives or regulations.

A teleological approach to interpretation also means that measures of Community law adopted into UK law must be construed to give effect to the Community directives: see *Von Colson* v *Land Nordrhein-Westfahlen* (1984); and *Elefanten Schuh GmbH* v *Jacqmain* (1982). Therefore, legislation incorporating Community directives must be interpreted in the light of the original measure. This principle was clearly endorsed in *Litster* v *Forth Dry Dock and Engineering Co* (1989). The plaintiffs brought an action for compensation based on a claim of unfair dismissal. They had been employed by a ship repairing company which fell into receivership and was subsequently sold. The employees were dismissed by the company in receivership one hour prior to the transfer of ownership in the yard to the purchasers. No compensation for redundancy was paid to the employees on the basis that no money was available to pay wages. One hour after the dismissal notices were served the transfer to the new owners took effect.

According to the terms of the Transfer of Undertakings (Protection of Employment) Regulations 1981, transfers of ownership do not automatically terminate contracts of employment if the employees were employed 'immediately before the transfer' of the business. The statutory instrument containing these regulations implemented a Community directive designed to protect the rights of workers unfairly dismissed. The plaintiffs claimed that, despite being dismissed by the company in receivership, the new owners were obliged to pay compensation for the statutory period of notice since the pursuers were immediately employed before the takeover. The Employment Regulations were silent on this particular matter.

The Industrial Tribunal upheld the claim and ordered the new owners to pay compensation and this decision was upheld on appeal to the Employment Appeal Tribunal. The new owners appealed this decision and the appellant court allowed the appeal on the grounds that the pursuers were not employed immediately before the transfer of business. The case was referred to the House of Lords on an appeal against this decision. The House of Lords applied a purposive construction to the relevant regulation in order to give effect to the terms of the Council directive, the objective of which was to protect the rights of employees in the event of a change of employer. Consequently, the pursuers were entitled to seek compensation from the new owners and the appeal was allowed.

British courts and tribunals are therefore bound to give a teleological construction to provisions of Community law. Further, in construing legislation implementing Community directives, the courts are also required to refer to the terms of the original directive in order to give effect to its objectives, even though the implementing legislation makes no reference to the subject.

QUESTION FOUR

John, a UK national married with two children, and Laura, a UK national married with two children, move from Glasgow to Brussels and enter the service of the Commission of the European Communities. When both receive their salary slips, Laura notices that she has not been given the expatriate allowance which John has received. Upon enquiry, she is told by the Commission Personnel Administration office that such expatriate allowances are given to 'heads of households', that is, to husbands only. Laura would like to seek a remedy. Advise.

University of Glasgow LLB Examination
1987 Q8

General Comment

A problem involving the application of the principle of non-discrimination on the ground of gender.

Skeleton Solution

• Article 119 of the EC Treaty.
• Jurisprudence of the Court: *Defrenne*.
• Definition of pay.

Suggested Solution

Laura will be able to claim equal pay with John on the basis of Article 119 of the Treaty of Rome. This Article prohibits discrimination when men and women receive unequal pay for equal work carried out at the same establishment of service, be it private or public.

In *Defrenne* v *Sabena* (1976), the European Court held Article 119 prohibited direct and overt discrimination, a concept which was identified by reference to the criteria of equal work and equal pay specified in the article. Unfortunately, the effect of this

117

provision was limited because, according to the Court, the provision could only support claims relating to pay periods after the date of judgment.

Article 119 of the EC Treaty is based on the related concepts of equal pay and equal work. Equal pay is defined as 'the ordinary basic or minimum wage or salary and any other consideration, whether in cash or kind, which the worker receives, directly or indirectly, in respect of his [or her] employment from his [or her] employer'. The Court has tended to define pay in broad terms. Thus a special travel allowance, discriminatory retirement dates, discriminatory pension allowances, and discriminatory redundancy payments, have all been held as pay within the meaning of the article. A right to equal pay would be limited in value unless linked to a means of determining a comparable employment position and a Council directive specifies the procedure for making this determination.

The principle of gender non-discrimination applies to both public and private entities. Equally, since the principle of sexual equality at work is an element of Community social policy, it applies regardless of a transborder element. In order to establish discrimination, it is not necessary that two people are performing the same employment functions simultaneously. Where a man began employment with a company and is replaced by a woman in the same position or vice versa, there would be discrimination if the pay of the latter employee was below that of the former. The Court has however been willing to examine factors unconnected with sexual discrimination for an explanation of any discrepancies.

Directives have also been adopted by the Community to add substance to the general obligation of non-discrimination on the basis of gender in the workplace. For example, Council Directive 75/117 related to the approximation of the laws of the Member States relating to the application of the principle of equal pay for men and women.

Presuming that Laura is engaged in equal work with John, the fact that John receives an 'expatriate allowance' appears to be gender discrimination despite the fact that the payment is made to heads of household, since this is merely a synonym for men. As an immediate consequence of this discrepancy, Laura's contract of employment is less favourable than John's. The House of Lords decision in *Hayward* v *Cammel Laird Shipbuilders Ltd* (1988) considered this question in the context of s1(2)(c) of the Equal Pay Act 1970 which was enacted to implement Article 119. The court held that the principle of equal pay entitled women to equality where a woman's contract of employment contained a term that was less favourable than a similar term in a man's contract. This would be the case even if the contract conferred an additional benefit upon her which was not conferred on the man.

Laura should therefore be entitled to a similar allowance. However Laura will only be able to rely directly on Article 119 insofar as the discrimination against her is direct and overt. Where this is not the case, she must have recourse to the national law that implements Directive 75/117. This directive is an expansion of the principle of equal pay for work of equal value. If the national law has failed to correctly implement this directive, she will still not be able to rely on it as against private citizens: see *Foster* v *British Gas* (1987).

Adrian, a UK national, applied for a position as a hovercraft pilot with HoverManche, a French state-owned company which runs the hovercraft cross-Channel link between Calais and Dover.

His application for the position was rejected on the grounds that the French Code du Travail Maritime requires all hovercraft pilots to have French nationality. The justification given for this requirement by the French authorities is that the safety of the vehicles would be compromised unless all crew embers speak French and are able to effectively communicate among each other and with the Hovercraft base control.

Adrian's French lawyers advise him that he will not be able to reverse this decision in the French courts. Do you agree and, in particular:

a) Can Adrian bring proceedings in the French courts to reverse this decision?

b) Can Adrian request the European Commission to intervene on his behalf to challenge the Code du Travail Maritime? and

c) What remedies are available to Adrian at the European Court level in the event that the Commission declines to proceed against France on the basis of the complaint?

Question prepared by the Author

General Comment

This question involves a number of different points of law, most of which are procedural matters. The focus of the question is on the rights and remedies of private individuals against other private individuals and Community institutions at both the national and Community level.

Skeleton Solution

a) • Article 48(1) EC Treaty and Article 4 Regulation 1612/68.
   • Duty of national courts to protect and enforce Community rights for individuals: *Factortame (No 2)*.

b) • Breach of Community law by the French authorities.
   • Rights of private individuals to make complaints to the European Commission.
   • Nature of the complaint.

c) • No right to initiate proceedings under Article 173.
   • Possibilities of raising an action under Article 175(3) EC Treaty for failure to act.
   • Difficulties of private individuals bringing actions under Article 175.

Suggested Solution

a) The first issue to resolve is whether Adrian can challenge the decision of HoverManche SA refusing his application for the position as a hovercraft pilot.

This will depend on whether he has directly enforceable Community rights on which he can depend and whether the French courts are required to enforce these rights.

Article 48 of the EC Treaty provides that Community nationals are entitled to exercise the freedom of movement for the purposes of seeking and accepting employment in other Community states. This article has the quality of direct effect and may be relied on by individuals before national courts to establish rights: see *Van Duyn* v *Home Office* (1974).

In addition, Council Regulation 1612/68 (1968), elaborates on this freedom by providing that any national of a Member State may exercise the right to take up an activity as an employed person and to pursue such activity within the territory of another Member State in accordance with its employment law. The exercise of this right is to be free from discrimination on the grounds of nationality.

This measure is a Community regulation and is automatically applicable in all Member States. Private individuals may rely on its terms to establish Community rights by virtue of Article 189 EC Treaty. Therefore, Adrian has a Community right not to be discriminated against on the grounds of nationality when applying for the position with HoverManche. HoverManche has engaged in unlawful discrimination under Community law for which it will be required to pay the necessary compensation.

The French courts are also under an obligation to protect and enforce Adrian's Community rights in cases brought before them. This is a well-established principle, recently reiterated by the European Court in *R* v *Secretary of State, ex parte Factortame (No 2)* (1991). As the Court in this case observed:

'In accordance with the case law of this Court, it is for the national courts, in application of the principle of co-operation laid down in Article 5 of the EC Treaty, to ensure the legal protection which persons derive from the direct effect of provisions of Community law.'

Under Community law, Adrian will therefore be able to challenge the decision by HoverManche, rejecting his application on the basis of discrimination, in the French courts.

However, while Community law has vested Adrian with the right to be protected from discrimination the exact procedural rules applicable and the remedies available in the French courts are matters for those courts to decide. National courts have the discretion to specify the appropriate procedure and remedy to facilitate the presentation of the claim subject to the overriding need to protect the Community rights of individuals: see *Rewe* v *Hauptzollamt Kiel* (1981).

b) The European Commission has primary responsibility for ensuring that the provisions of the EC Treaty and the measures adopted under its authority are applied at national; Article 155 EC Treaty. Private parties are permitted to make complaints to the Commission if they believe that their Community rights are being infringed. However, there is no express provision of the EC Treaty to regulate such complaints.

Adrian should send a complaint to the Commission in Brussels outlining the facts of his case, the applicable substantive national law and the position under

Community law. The complaint itself should identify the French Republic as the party in breach of Community law and not HoverManche since the source of the mischief is the French Code du Travail Hovermaritime. As a general principle, the Commission cannot bring direct proceedings in the European Court against private parties, the appropriate forum for such proceedings being the national courts.

In fact Adrian has a solid case against the French government. Other than Article 48 itself, Article 3(1) of Council Regulation 1612/68 (1968) provides that national provisions of law, whether the result of legal regulation or administrative action, are inapplicable if they limit the rights of workers to take up and pursue employment. Similarly, Article 4 of the same regulation declares that national provisions which restrict the number or percentage of foreign nationals in employment positions are inapplicable to Community nationals.

France has already been caught engaging in employment policies discriminating against other Community nationals. In *EC Commission* v *France (Re Code du Travail Maritime)* (1974), the European Commission prosecuted France for restricting the proportions of foreign crew members on French vessels to certain limits. The European Court held France in violation of both Article 48 and Article 4 of the Regulation. This is a strong precedent in favour of Adrian's argument.

France justifies the discrimination on the basis that French nationals are required to ensure effective communication. Linguistic requirements are rarely permitted to justify discrimination unless such requirements are part of a policy of promoting a national language and, even in this case, the requirements must be applied in a proportionate and non-discriminatory manner.

In this case, no such justification can be put forward by France. The requirement is an unjustifiable measure quite simply because even if Adrian can speak French he will not be allowed access to the post. The nature of the restriction is based on nationality and not linguistic ability.

Hence, the Commission may bring France before the European Court on the basis of Adrian's complaint. The proceedings would be brought under Article 169 of the EC Treaty for failure to comply with its obligations under Community law. The substantive basis for the proceedings is not only breach of Article 48 of the EC Treaty and Article 4 of the Regulation but also Article 7 (general prohibition on discrimination on the grounds of nationality) and Article 5 (requirement of Member States to ensure fulfilment of Community obligations) of the EC Treaty.

c) In the event that the European Commission refuses to respond to Adrian's complaint, the sole legal basis on which he could proceed would be under Article 175(3) of the EC Treaty. This allows private parties to bring Community institutions before the European Court for failure to act.

The European Commission retains virtually absolute discretion as to the appropriate course of action to follow in the event of a notification by a private person of a violation of a Community obligation. A private party alleging injury as a consequence of such a violation by a Member State cannot compel the Commission to initiate proceedings against that state: *Star Fruit Co SA* v *EC Commission* (1990).

Hence, Adrian must rely on the terms of Article 175 and the argument that, by failing to proceed with the complaint, the Commission has failed to act. This is a notoriously difficult course of action to follow and private parties are rarely successful in this type of action. This is because the conditions which must be satisfied for success are particularly onerous.

Once the Commission has indicated that it intends not to proceed with the complaint, Adrian must bring its attention to the alleged omission, namely the failure to proceed against France on the basis of his complaint. Thereafter the European Commission has two months to define its position. This does not require the adoption of a particular measure. For example, where the Commission has explained its position and justified its non-activity in terms which are consistent with its obligations under the EC Treaty, the Court has held an action for failure to act inadmissible; *Alfons Lutticke GmbH* v *EC Commission* (1966).

Adrian must also demonstrate that the Commission was under a clear legal duty to take specific measures and failed to honour this duty. While the behaviour of France indicates a breach of Community law, it is not clear that the Commission is obliged to proceed if it does not agree with his submissions.

Finally, it is necessary for Adrian to demonstrate that the measure which the Commission is allegedly required to adopt would have been specifically addressed to him. It is not enough that the measure is of direct and individual concern to Adrian. He is trying to convince the Commission to bring France before the European Court for a judgment addressed to France requiring repeal of the Code du Travail Hover Maritime. Hence, it is unlikely that he is in the precise legal position of a potential addressee of a legal measure which the Commission has a duty to adopt with regard to him: see *Lord Bethell* v *EC Commission* (1982).

It is therefore not possible for Adrian to force the Commission to respond to his complaint and it is unlikely that, in the event that the Commission refuses to pursue the matter, Adrian would be successful in an action under Article 175(3) of the EC Treaty for failure to act.

7 THE APPLICATION OF COMMUNITY LAW IN THE UNITED KINGDOM

7.1 Introduction

Community law does not function detached from the legal systems of the Member States, but forms an integral part of each of these individual systems. Principles of Community law may be enforced in the national courts and tribunals of each of the Member States of the Community, including the courts and tribunals of the United Kingdom. Further, within the United Kingdom, even accepted constitutional doctrines and precepts require modification in order to facilitate the reception of Community law. This chapter deals with the attitude of the British government towards its Community obligations and the reaction of British courts and tribunals to Community law.

7.2 Key points

a) *Incorporation of Community law into the United Kingdom*

Community law became part of the law of the United Kingdom by virtue of the European Communities Act 1972 (1972 c68). Section 2(1) of this statute provides:

'All rights, powers, liabilities, obligations and restrictions from time to time created or arising by or under the Treaties, and all such remedies and procedures from time to time provided for by or under the Treaties, as in accordance with the Treaties are without further enactment to be given legal effect or used in the United Kingdom shall be recognised and available in law, and be enforced, allowed and followed accordingly.'

The European Communities Act 1972 was amended by the European Communities (Amendment) Act 1986 (1986 c58) in order to give force to the changes to the Community Treaties made by the Single European Act 1986.

Similarly the 1972 Act was again amended by the European Communities (Amendment) Act 1993 (1993, c32) to give effect to the Treaty on European Union 1992.

b) *The effect of the European Communities Act 1972, as amended*

The European Communities Act makes no distinction between Community law enacted before the entry into force of the statute and Community law established after this date. Consequently, in legal proceedings before national courts and tribunals in the United Kingdom, the jurisprudence of the European Court may be invoked regardless of whether the decision in question was rendered before or after 1972. Similarly, Community legislation has force within the United Kingdom regardless of the date of adoption by the Council or Commission.

Judicial notice of all decisions of the European Court has also been taken and matters concerning the interpretation and application of Community law are to be treated as questions of law and not questions of fact, as would be the case if Community law was to be considered 'foreign law' under English conflict of law principles: s3(2) 1972 Act.

c) *Ministerial powers to implement subordinate legislation*

Section 2(2) of the 1972 Act allows designated Ministers to make subordinate legislation for the purposes of implementing Community obligations. This provision allows Ministers to fulfil the obligations of the United Kingdom as a consequence of Community directives. In addition, Ministers may provide criminal sanctions in order to enact certain Community measures.

This prerogative is restricted by a number of limitations on the prerogatives of Ministers to enact subordinate legislation. Ministers are not allowed to enact measures which:

i) impose or increase taxation;

ii) create new criminal offences punishable by more than two years of imprisonment;

iii) sub-delegate legislative authority to other bodies or persons; or

iv) introduce subordinate legislation having a retroactive effect.

Power to enact subordinate legislation may only be exercised by the Minister responsible for the administration of the particular Community subject-matter.

d) *Parliamentary control over Community secondary legislation*

Primary control over Community legislation is exercised by Parliamentary Committees which examine and comment on draft proposals for Community legislation. Each House of Parliament has established select committees to evaluate the implications and ramifications of Community legislation on the political and legal constitution of the United Kingdom.

i) The House of Commons Select Committee on European Secondary Legislation

The House of Commons Select Committee on European Legislation is better known as the 'Scrutiny Committee'. This committee has been given the following mandate by resolution of the House of Commons:

'To consider draft proposals by the Commission of the European Communities for legislation and other documents published for submission to the Council of Ministers or to the European Council whether or not such documents originate from the Commission.'

The Scrutiny Committee reports on whether or not such proposals raise issues of significant legal or political importance and gives reasons for its opinion.

ii) The House of Lords Select Committee on the European Communities

The House of Lords has established a parallel body known as the Select Committee on the European Communities. The mandate of this body has been given in the following terms:

'To consider Community proposals, whether in draft or otherwise, to obtain all necessary information about them, and to make reports on those which, in the opinion of the committee, raise important questions of policy or principle, and on other questions to which the committee consider that the special attention of the House should be drawn.'

The House of Lords Committee functions through a number of sub-committees which deal with individual subjects of relevance to the Community such as finance, law and external relations. On a number of occasions, the House of Lords Committee has produced reports of exceptional quality and detail concerning the functions of the Community.

iii) Authority of the Select Committees

Neither the House of Commons nor the House of Lords Select Committees has direct influence over the Community decision-making processes. Control over the final content of Community legislation is maintained on the basis of the principle of ministerial responsibility: see the Second Report from the Select Committee on European Secondary Legislation, HC 463–I, xii–xv (1972–73).

The Council of Ministers of the Community is composed of one representative from each Member State. In the case of the United Kingdom representative, he or she will be the Minister of the Crown with responsibility for the particular subject-matter upon which Community legislation is being passed. As a consequence of the Parliamentary convention of ministerial responsibility, the same Ministers participating in the Council are also answerable to the British Parliament. This dual responsibility ensures that the scrutiny of Parliament over Community secondary legislation continues.

e) *The reception of Community law by the British courts*

The courts and tribunals of the United Kingdom have reacted positively towards the reception of Community law as part of the UK legal system. The following are the main instances of this attitude:

i) The courts have been willing to utilise the procedures established for preliminary references to the European Court.

ii) The House of Lords itself has embraced the teleological approach to the interpretation of Community law as opposed to the literal approach used in the interpretation of English law: see *Litster* v *Forth Dry Dock and Engineering Co* [1989] 1 All ER 1134.

iii) UK court will apply Community law without prompting from the European Court: see *Kirklees Metropolitan Borough Council* v *Wickes Building Supplies* [1992] 3 WLR 170.

iv) The House of Lords has accepted the principle of the supremacy of Community law over inconsistent UK statutes, whether enacted before or after the European Community Act 1972: *R* v *Secretary of State for Transport, ex parte Factortame (No 4)* [1990] 3 CMLR 375; [1991] 1 All ER 70.

7.3 Relevant cases

Bulmer v *Bollinger SA* [1974] 2 All ER 1226: Lord Denning's much criticised attempt to formulate rules to regulate the discretion of British courts to refer questions of Community law to the European Court.

Bourgoin SA v *Ministry of Agriculture, Fisheries and Food* [1985] 3 All ER 585: An attempt to obtain damages for a failure on the part of the British government to observe Community law.

Litster v *Forth Dry Dock & Engineering Co* [1989] 1 All ER 1134: Application by the House of Lords of the teleological approach to interpretation adopted by the European Court.

Kirklees Metropolitan Borough Council v *Wickes Building Supplies* [1992] 3 WLR 170.

R v *Secretary of State for Transport, ex parte Factortame (No 4)*, above.

7.4 Relevant materials

L Collins, *European Community Law in the United Kingdom* (fourth edition, 1990).

L Gormley, 'The Application of Community Law in the United Kingdom' (1986) 23 CML Rev, 287.

Lord Fraser, 'Scrutiny of Community Legislation in the United Kingdom Parliament' in J Bates (ed), *In Memoriam JDB Mitchell* (1983) 29.

M Hoskins, 'Garden Cottages Revisited: The Availability of Damages in the National Courts' (1992) 13 ECL Rev 256.

7.5 Analysis of questions

Questions concerning this subject often focus attention on the implication of the reception of Community law within the English legal system and the possibility of enforcing Community rights within English courts and tribunals. Students should therefore be familiar with the relationship between Community law and the British Parliament as well as the jurisprudence of the English courts concerning questions of Community law.

7.6 Questions

QUESTION ONE

'The way Regulations and Directives are implemented in the United Kingdom shows that the United Kingdom Parliament is no longer totally sovereign.' Discuss.

University of Glasgow LLB Examination
1989 Q6

General Comment

A general question requiring an answer which describes the relationship between the British legal system and Community law.

Skeleton Solution

- Enactment of Community Directives and Regulations.
- Force of these instruments in the United Kingdom.
- Parliamentary controls on the content of Community law.
- Impact of the Single European Act.

Suggested Solution

Community law takes two main forms – Regulations and Directives. A Regulation is binding in its entirety and is directly applicable in all Member States without legislative intervention. In other words, it may be enforced before a national court without the necessity for any statutory authority, either in the form of an Act of Parliament or a statutory instrument (such as an Order in Council). A Directive, on the other hand, is also binding, but only upon the Member State to whom it is addressed, and the method of implementation is left to the discretion of the individual Member State. However, this is subject to the doctrine of the direct effect of Community Directives, according to which Directives that have not been implemented by a Member State within the requisite period may be given vertical direct effect: *Marshall* v *Southampton and South West Hampshire Area Health Authority* (1986).

The fact that Community Regulations and, under certain circumstances, Directives may have direct effect within the United Kingdom has given rise to the charge that the British Parliament is no longer sovereign. This allegation is also often supported by reference to the principle that Community law prevails over the national laws of the Member States: *Costa* v *ENEL* (1964). Since the European Community has power to enact measures which are automatically enforceable within the United Kingdom, and since these measures take precedence over national law, this argument has a certain degree of cogency.

However, the assertion that the British Parliament is no longer sovereign because of this competence on the part of the Community ignores a number of critical points concerning the relationship between the European Community and the British legal system.

European Community law has force of law within the United Kingdom legal system merely by virtue of the European Communities Act 1972, as amended. This is an ordinary statute of Parliament with no additional legal significance, although it has considerable political implications. This statute may be repealed or amended by subsequent Acts of Parliament. In fact, the 1972 Act was amended by the European Communities (Amendment) Act 1986, which gave effect to the changes instituted by the Single European Act. A later Act of Parliament which expressly repealed the 1972 Act would be interpreted by the English courts as effective and would be applied by them according to its terms: *Shields* v *E Coomes (Holdings) Ltd* (1979).

The British Parliament therefore retains ultimate authority to repeal the 1972 Act and to reacquire total and absolute sovereignty over national legal affairs.

However, while the 1972 Act remains in force, in practice the British Parliament has deliberately delegated some of its sovereignty to the European Community, notwithstanding the authority of Dicey's principle of absolute parliamentary sovereignty. The concept of sovereignty is relative. Only once a state has divested itself of its organic powers, and placed itself under the authority of another state, can it be said that it has lost its sovereignty.

Even the authority which has been delegated to the Community by virtue of the 1972 Act has not been unconditionally conferred. A number of safeguards remain which allow the British Parliament to control the content of Community legislation.

Most importantly, the principal legislative body of the Community is the Council of Ministers, which is composed of representatives from the Member States. Each British government Minister whose portfolio contains a subject of Community concern represents the interests of the United Kingdom in the Council of Ministers. Since Ministers of the Crown are also responsible to the British Parliament in accordance with the constitutional convention of ministerial responsibility, the British Parliament can influence the behaviour of Ministers voting in the Council.

This influence is exercised through a number of procedural devices. In particular, each House of Parliament has established Committees to supervise the implementation of Community secondary legislation such as Regulations and Directives. The purpose of these bodies is to examine and comment on draft proposals for Community legislation and to evaluate the implications and ramifications of the legislation on the political and legal constitution of the United Kingdom.

Parliamentary influence over the content of Community secondary legislation has actually been consolidated by virtue of the resolution of the House of Commons, made on 30 October 1980. This resolution declares that no Minister of the Crown should consent to any proposal for Community legislation in the Council of Ministers before the House of Commons Select Committee has had an opportunity to examine the proposal.

This general rule is subject to two exceptions. First, where the Committee has indicated that such consent need not be withheld, such as in the case of matters of trivial relevance, the approval of the Committee is not necessary. Second, where the Minister, for special reasons, decides that consent should not be withheld, approval may also be given to a proposed measure. In the latter case, the Minister in question is obliged to explain his or her decision to the House of Commons at the first available opportunity.

This scrutiny procedure does, however, suffer from a number of defects. Theoretically, not all Regulations and Directives require unanimous approval in the Council of Ministers. The adoption of some proposals only requires unanimity. Therefore, measures may be adopted by the Council in the face of opposition from the British representative. But, under the formula adopted by the Luxembourg compromise, where the very important interests of a Member State are at stake, that Member State may require unanimous voting in the Council, notwithstanding the express terms of the Treaty. This requirement is, however, qualified as regards voting requirements concerning the implementation of the internal market programme under the amendments made by the Single European Act since these amendments were adopted without reservation of the right of Member States under the Luxembourg compromise.

Another gap in this system of supervision is the practice of the Council to delegate responsibility for the implication of certain policies to the Commission. Often, this authority includes power to enact subordinate legislation. However, while in theory this represents a limitation on the sovereignty of the United Kingdom, in practice such grants of authority are confined to enacting administrative measures which do not have significant legal or political implications.

The fact that certain measures of Community law have direct applicability within the United Kingdom and prevail over inconsistent measures of national law, does not imply that the British Parliament is no longer sovereign. The enactment of the 1972 Act establishes no more significant fetters on the exercise of the powers of Parliament than a number of the constitutional conventions which already restrict the sovereignty of Parliament. The fact that Parliament can repeal the legislation, and continues to effectively supervise the exercise of the powers conferred on the Community under the 1972 Act, adequately demonstrates that Parliament continues to remain sovereign.

QUESTION TWO

Among all the Member States of the European Community, the United Kingdom has demonstrated the greatest reluctance to observe the obligations imposed by the Community Treaties and the duties created thereunder. Discuss.

Question prepared by the Author

General Comment

A narrative question requiring a descriptive answer.

Skeleton Solution

- The nature of the obligation to respect Community law; Article 5 EC Treaty.
- The record of the United Kingdom.
- Examples of deviance from the principles of Community law.
- The record of the United Kingdom in contrast to other Member States.

Suggested Solution

Violations of Community obligations may arise from both positive acts and omissions on the part of Member States. Article 5 of the EC Treaty requires Member States to take all appropriate measures to ensure respect for Community obligations and to 'abstain from any measure which could jeopardise the attainment of the objectives of this Treaty'. Acts and omissions by Member States may also contravene the express provisions of the Community Treaties or may infringe the contents of measures of secondary legislation lawfully enacted under the Community Treaties.

A common ground of action against a Member State is the existence of national legislation which is incompatible with either the Community Treaties or Community legislation. For example, in 1988, the United Kingdom enacted the Merchant Shipping Act 1988 which requires that a number of conditions must be satisfied before a fishing vessel can be registered as British. A fishing vessel is eligible for registration only if the vessel is British-owned, is managed or operated from the United Kingdom, or is owned by a British company. The European Commission took the view that this legislation constituted discrimination on the basis of nationality, contrary to Articles 7, 52 and 221 of the EC Treaty. After entering into unsuccessful discussions with the United Kingdom, the Commission initiated proceedings against the United Kingdom for enacting legislation which contravenes the terms of the Community Treaties: see *EC Commission* v *United Kingdom* (1990).

Member States may also be held to have infringed Community law as a result of the enactment of secondary legislation. Thus, in *France* v *United Kingdom* (1979), the European Court held that the United Kingdom had violated its Community obligations by enacting an Order in Council which imposed a minimum mesh size for fishing. This requirement was held to contravene Community law on the ground that appropriate consultations had not been held prior to the enactment of the measure.

Administrative practices may also be held to contravene Community law. Customs measures and practices are most susceptible to action by the Commission for failure to observe Community law. For example, in *Conegate* v *HM Customs & Excise* (1986), the United Kingdom customs authorities took the view that inflatable dolls manufactured in Germany could not be imported into the United Kingdom on the ground that they were indecent and therefore contrary to the rules established for the administration of imports. The European Court held that such practices contravened Community law because the United Kingdom did not prohibit the manufacture of such products within the United Kingdom and consequently such practices constituted a measure having an equivalent effect to a quantitative restrict.

Proceedings are also frequently initiated against Member States for failing to implement measures of Community law, and in particular Directives. The United Kingdom has often been taken to the European Court for failing to implement directives, particularly in relation to gender discrimination; for example, *Marshall* v *Southampton and South West Hampshire Area Health Authority* (1986). However, in part this possibility has been mitigated by the doctrine of vertical direct effect adopted by the Court.

Neither the constitutional structure of a Member State nor pre-existing provisions of national law constitute a defence against a Member State for the enforcement of

Community law. This is so even when a constituent part of a Member State – such as a region or a province – exercises exclusive authority over a particular subject-matter, independently of the control of the central government: *EC Commission* v *Belgium* (1989). As the Court itself has pointed out, responsibility for the performance of Community obligations rests with Member States. Consequently, the liability of a Member State arises whatever the agency of the state whose action or inaction is the cause of the failure to fulfil its obligations, even in the case of a constitutionally independent institution.

A Member State may even theoretically be liable for the acts of judicial bodies or tribunals for rendering decisions which are contrary to Community law. Thus a refusal of a national court of final instance to refer a question of Community law under the preliminary reference procedure could constitute a violation of Community law, unless the conduct of the court could be justified under the criteria established in *CILFIT* v *Ministry of Health* (1982). This applies despite the fact that the constitutions of a number of Member States rest on the doctrine of the separation of powers. During the 10 year period between 1980 and 1990, the United Kingdom and Denmark had the least enforcement actions initiated against them. While Denmark had less than 20 actions brought against it in the European Court, the United Kingdom had less than 25. These statistics contrast extremely favourably against those of a number of the original Member States of the Community. Italy was the Member State which was the subject of most actions, with approximately 200 actions initiated against it. France and Belgium maintained equally unimpressive records with around 100 enforcement actions during the same 10 year period. Consequently, it is completely inaccurate to suggest that the United Kingdom is the worst offender in respecting its Community obligations.

Further, the United Kingdom also maintains an impeccable record as regards implementing the adverse decisions of the European Court when cases are decided against its favour. Since the European Community is an organisation based on the rule of law, it is wholly appropriate that disputes between the United Kingdom and the Commission be settled through litigation. It is, however, indefensible that some states refuse to implement the decisions of the Court in full knowledge that they are contravening their Community obligations. The fact that the United Kingdom rarely, if ever, adopts such a policy is a reflection of the true commitment of the United Kingdom to the spirit and idea of the Community.

QUESTION THREE

In *Bulmer* v *Bollinger SA* [1974] 2 All ER 1226, Lord Denning MR elaborated a number of guidelines to assist English courts and tribunals in respect of their obligations under Article 177 of the EC Treaty. Outline the scope and nature of these guidelines and comment on their influence on the evolution of English jurisprudence on this point.

Question prepared by the Author

General Comment

A difficult question requiring a detailed knowledge of the jurisprudence of the courts in respect of Article 177 of the EC Treaty.

Skeleton Solution

• The nature of the guidelines.
• Implications of the guidelines.
• Criticism of the guidelines.

Suggested Solution

Immediately following the accession of the United Kingdom to the European Community, a need was felt among the English judiciary to specify the rules regulating applications for preliminary rulings under Article 177 of the EC Treaty. Article 177 does not elaborate on the occasions and conditions under which English courts and tribunals exercising a discretion to refer a question for a preliminary ruling should make an application to the European Court. In order to fill this gap, Lord Denning elaborated a number of guidelines in *Bulmer* v *Bollinger SA* (1974), in an attempt to establish consistency among the English courts when referring a case for a preliminary reference.

Four primary guidelines were laid down. First, before a reference is made, the point of Community law upon which there is doubt must be conclusive of the case. In other words, the case must turn on the point of Community law invoked. Where Community law is immaterial to a decision, no application should therefore be made. Second, account must be taken of the previous jurisprudence of the European Court on the matter. Thus, if the European Court has decided the point in a previous case, there would be no need to make a reference. Third, the acte clair doctrine applies insofar as it is unnecessary to refer a question of Community law to the European Court if the answer is reasonably clear and free from doubt. Fourth, the facts of the case should be decided before any reference is made.

Lord Denning also indicated that a number of subsidiary factors should be taken into account prior to a court exercising discretion to refer a case. In particular, the time required to obtain a ruling from the Court and the importance of not overburdening the Court should be considered in the context of the case. Also, the difficulty and importance of the point of Community law involved are relevant considerations as is the expense of obtaining a preliminary ruling. Finally, the wishes of the parties are important considerations in deciding whether or not a case should be referred.

These guidelines have been repudiated by academics and criticised by the European Court as wholly inappropriate. They symbolise the resistance of the English judiciary to the reception of Community law. Article 177 does not instruct the courts of the Member States to formulate rules to regulate its application. As the European Court has pointed out 'Article 177 is essential for the preservation of the Community character of the law established by the Treaty and has the object of ensuring that in all circumstances this law is the same in all States of the Community': *Rheinmuhlen* (1974).

By establishing rules to regulate applications under Article 177, Lord Denning deviated from this important principle of Community law. If the English judiciary applied the guidelines established in *Bollinger*, this could create chaos, since the courts of other Member States may decide to apply different criteria. The result could easily be the non-uniform application of Community law throughout the Community.

In the absence of common rules to regulate preliminary references, the Community legal system itself may be liable to fragment and could even be submerged by principles of national law. The function of regulating the discretion of the courts of Member States to refer a question is a matter which is best left to the European Court.

The European Court has already made it clear that a court exercising discretion to refer a case need only consider two factors: that the reference is necessary to decide the case and that a judgment cannot be rendered without deciding the point of Community law. Discretion to decide these two points resides with the court or tribunal itself. Only if the exercise of this discretion was completely wrong, based on these two factors, could a decision based on this discretion be reversed on appeal: *Rheinmuhlen*, above. Further, in a hierarchical legal system based on the doctrine of precedent, no superior court can bind a lower court to follow guidelines which fetter the discretion of the lower court by compelling it to consider factors other than the two stated in Article 177 itself.

Notwithstanding this criticism, the English judiciary have shown no intention of abandoning these guidelines laid down by Lord Denning. For example, in *English-Speaking Union of the Commonwealth* v *Commissioners for Customs and Excise* (1981), the London VAT Tribunal stated that, although it had been inclined to seek a ruling from the European Court, it had declined to do so after having regard to the guidelines expressed in *Bollinger*. In particular, the fact that the sums involved were small had been a decisive factor in persuading the court to decline the reference.

Similarly, in *Customs and Excise Commissioners* v *ApS Samex* (1983), Bingham J expressly applied the guidelines laid down by Lord Denning in deciding that a reference should be made to the European Court to decide whether or not certain practices of the commissioners of customs and excise infringed Community law. However, ironically, Bingham J applied the guidelines in a manner which favoured an application to the European Court as opposed to declining such a reference. Indeed, Bingham expressly referred to the advantages enjoyed by the European Court in interpreting questions of Community law and clearly considered that the guidelines expressed by Lord Denning should be applied with this factor in mind.

The guidelines laid down by Lord Denning are a clear example of how national courts can interfere with the functioning of the Community legal system. By meddling in areas outside their competence, national courts and tribunals can severely affect the uniform interpretation and application of Community law throughout the common market. The responsibility for elaborating rights and duties under Community law resides exclusively with the European Court.

8 THE FREE MOVEMENT OF GOODS

8.1 Introduction

8.2 Key points

8.3 Relevant cases

8.4 Relevant materials

8.5 Analysis of questions

8.6 Questions

8.1 Introduction

The creation of a more efficient market through the reduction of obstacles to transnational commerce has always been a fundamental aim of the European Community. The need to achieve the free movement of goods, persons, services and capital throughout the Community was recognised as an express goal of the EC Treaty and was reaffirmed by the Single European Act. Of these freedoms, the free movement of goods has traditionally been acknowledged as being of paramount significance. The free movement of goods implies that goods can move from one Community country to another without having to pay customs duties or charges having an equivalent effect to customs duty and also that goods will not be subject to quantitative restrictions when moving from one Community country to another.

8.2 Key points

a) *Elimination of customs duties between Member States*

The six original Member States of the Community agreed to a series of progressive reductions in the customs duties which existed between them prior to the EC Treaty, culminating in the elimination of all customs duties on both import and export transactions; Articles 13–16 EC Treaty. Customs duties were officially eliminated between the original six on 1 July 1968.

States acceding to the Community are obliged, as a condition of membership, to eliminate all customs duties between them and the other Member States over negotiated transitional periods. The United Kingdom, Ireland, Denmark, and Greece have all eliminated customs duties for intra-Community trade in goods, while Spain and Portugal removed such restrictions on 1 January 1993. Subject to limited derogations for certain products, particularly agricultural goods, Austria, Sweden and Finland were required to remove all customs duties for trade in goods between the countries of the European Community and themselves by 1 January 1995, as a requirement of the 1994 Treaty of Accession.

Article 12 of the EC Treaty expressly prohibits the re-introduction of any custom duties on imports and export for goods passing between Community states.

b) *Elimination of charges having an equivalent effect to customs duties*

Member States are also obliged to eliminate all 'charges having an equivalent effect to customs duties' on imports and exports and to refrain from re-introducing such charges on intra-Community transactions. No definition of 'charges having an equivalent effect' is elaborated in the EC Treaty and interpretation of this term has been left to the European Court. While the Court has elaborated on the nature of this concept in a number of cases, it has most recently stated that:

'[A]ny pecuniary charge, whatever its designation and mode of application, which is imposed unilaterally on goods by reason of the fact that they cross a frontier, and is not a customs duty in the strict sense, constitutes a charge having equivalent effect to a customs duty': *EC Commission* v *Germany (Re Customs Inspection Fees)* [1990] 1 CMLR 561.

Not all charges imposed on goods crossing a frontier between Member States will be deemed to have an equivalent effect to a customs duty. In particular, an expense will not be prohibited as a charge having an equivalent effect in three separate circumstances:

i)   If the charge relates to a general system of internal dues applied systematically within a Member State without discrimination between domestic and imported products: *Denkavit* v *France* [1979] ECR 1923.

ii) If the charges constitute payment for a service in fact rendered and the charge is proportionate to the costs of receiving that service: *EC Commission* v *Denmark* [1983] ECR 3573.

iii) If the charges are levied in accordance with the terms of a Community measure. In this case, a number of conditions must be satisfied: *Bauhuis* v *Netherlands* [1977] ECR 5.

Charges levied under the authority of Community legislation for services actually rendered (category (iii) above) do not constitute charges of equivalent effect if four conditions are satisfied:

i)   the charges do not exceed the actual costs of the services rendered in connection with the charge;

ii) the inspections are obligatory and uniform for all products throughout the Community;

iii) the charges are prescribed by Community law in the general interest of the Community; and

iv) the service promotes the free movement of goods by neutralising obstacles which arise from unilateral measures of inspection.

c) *Elimination of quantitative restrictions between Members*

A quantitative restriction is a national measure that restrains the volume or amount of imports or exports, not by artificially raising the costs of importing or exporting (as would be the case with a tariff or export tax), but by placing direct or indirect limits on the physical quantity of the imports or exports that may enter or leave the market. The most common example of a quantitative restriction is a quota.

Quantitative restrictions between the original six Member States were gradually phased out and acceding Members must observe a similar obligation: Articles 30–36 EC Treaty. Article 30 of the EC Treaty prohibits the re-introduction of quantitative restrictions on imports while Article 34 imposes the same obligation for exports.

The explicit prohibition on the introduction of quotas is periodically violated. For example, in 1978, the United Kingdom restricted imports of Dutch potatoes while France imposed an embargo on sheepmeat from the United Kingdom. Similarly, in 1982, the United Kingdom limited imports of French UHT milk by establishing a quota. Each of these actions resulted in litigation before the European Court: *EC Commission* v *United Kingdom (Re Imports of Dutch Potatoes)* [1979] ECR 1447; *EC Commission* v *France (Re Sheepmeat from the UK)* [1979] ECR 2729; and *EC Commission* v *United Kingdom (Re Imports of UHT Milk)* [1983] ECR 230.

d) *Measures having an equivalent effect to quantitative restrictions*

Article 30 of the EC Treaty also prohibits all measures having an equivalent effect to quantitative restrictions. The concept of 'measures having an equivalent effect to quantitative restrictions' should be distinguished from that of 'charges having an equivalent effect to customs duties'. Charges having an equivalent effect to customs duties impose direct costs on imported products while measures having an equivalent effect to quantitative restrictions are national measures – either legislative or administrative – which affect the amount (quantity or volume) of products imported.

Again the EC Treaty contains no definition of the concept of measures having an equivalent effect. In order to fill this vacuum, the European Court has adopted the following definition:

'All trading rules enacted by Member States which are capable of hindering directly or indirectly, actually or potentially, intra-Community trade are to be considered as measures having an effect equivalent to quantitative restrictions': *Procureur du Roi* v *Dassonville* [1974] ECR 837; reaffirmed in *Dansk Denkavit* v *Ministry of Agriculture* [1990] 1 CMLR 203.

The term 'measures having an equivalent effect' includes all laws and practices attributable to public authorities as well as government funding of activities which have the effect of restricting imports. For example, in 1982, the Irish government was held responsible for infringement of Article 30 because it financed a 'Buy Irish' campaign which encouraged consumers to purchase goods produced in Ireland in preference over competitive goods from Community countries: *EC Commission* v *Ireland (Re Discriminatory Promotional Policies)* [1982] ECR 4005.

Article 30 and the relevant legislative measures also apply to the activities of local and regional government agencies which are required to respect the terms of such measures. The European Court will not permit any distinction to be drawn between measures enacted at local, regional or national level as long as the enacting authority exercises the necessary legislative competence. A Member

State cannot therefore argue that it bears no liability for infringements of Article 30 caused by the actions of such agencies: *Aragonesa De Publicidad Exterior SA and Ors* v *Departmento De Sanidad Y Seguridad Social De La Generalitat De Cataluna* [1994] 1 CMLR 887.

The first Community Directive enacted to reduce measures having an equivalent effect was clearly intended to eliminate measures discriminating between domestic and imported products: Commission Directive 70/50, OJ Sp Ed 17 (1970). This Directive addressed measures, other than those equally applicable to domestic and imported products, which hinder imports that would otherwise have taken place, including measures which make importation either more difficult or most costly than the disposal of domestic production. Practices deemed unlawful under this Directive included:

i)   measures designed to specify less favourable prices for imports than for domestic prices;

ii) practices which establish minimum or maximum prices below or above which imports are prohibited or reduced;

iii) standards which subject imports to conditions relating to shape, size, weight or composition and which cause imported products to suffer in competition with domestic products; and

iv) laws which restrict the marketing of imported products in the absence of an agent or representative in the territory of the importing Member State.

e) *Exceptions to restrictions on quantitative restrictions and measures having an equivalent effect*

Specific exceptions to Article 30 of the EC Treaty are made by Article 36. Quantitative restrictions and measures having equivalent effect on either imports or exports may be permitted in four circumstances:

i)   The protection of public morality, public policy and public security

Restrictions justified on the basis of public morality have frequently been upheld by the European Court. In fact, the Court allows a considerable degree of discretion (or 'margin of discretion') on the part of Member States to make such determinations: see *R* v *Henn and Darby* [1979] ECR 3795.

The concept of public policy is capable of a greater application than public morality, although surprisingly few measures have been justified on this ground. The leading case is *R* v *Thompson* [1978] ECR 2247, where the European Court upheld convictions for fraudulently importing gold coins into the United Kingdom on the basis that such practices circumvented the right of a state to mint coinage for circulation, a prerogative traditionally recognised as involving the fundamental interests of the state.

ii) The protection of the health and life of humans, animals or plants

Restrictions for the protection of the life and health of humans, animals and plants are permitted if two conditions are satisfied:

• the restriction must be necessary for the protection of public health and

137

not a disguised form of discrimination: *EC Commission v Germany* [1979] ECR 2555; and

- the degree of regulation imposed by the measure must be proportionate to the need to maintain the effective protection of the health and lives of human beings: *Centrafarm* [1976] ECR 613.

The principle of proportionality requires that the power of a Member State to prohibit or restrict imports should be restricted to measures necessary to attain the legitimate aim of protecting health: *Officier van Justitie v Sandoz BV* [1983] ECR 2445.

iii) The protection of national heritage

Member States can maintain restrictions necessary to protect national treasures which have artistic, historic, or archaeological value. This exception, however, only applies to treasures which remain in the public domain. As a general rule, only works of art which have not been placed on the market may benefit from this exception. Thus, in *EC Commission v Italy (Re Protection of National Treasures)* [1968] ECR 423, the European Court held that an export tax introduced by the Italian government could not be justified as a measure intended to protect national heritage because the items in question had entered the commercial market and had become sources of revenue for the national authorities.

iv) Protection of industrial and commercial property

National legislation may be maintained to protect the intellectual property rights of patent holders, licensees and copyright holders. The European Court has held that measures to protect patent holders may only be maintained if the products have been manufactured without the permission of the holder of the intellectual property right: *Centrafarm*, above. Such protection cannot be afforded where the imported product has been lawfully placed in circulation by the property right holder, or with his consent, in the Member State from which it has been imported.

f) *Mandatory requirements as additional exceptions to the prohibition on measures having equivalent effect*

In addition to the express exceptions enumerated in Article 36, the European Court has acknowledged that, in the marketing of products, Member States may regulate marketing activities as long as the objectives of the regulatory measures are legitimate. Most notably, in the *Cassis de Dijon Case* [1979] ECR 649, the Court expressly observed that national laws imposing 'mandatory requirements' are permissible in certain circumstances.

Five types of mandatory requirements may be imposed by Member States on the free movement of goods:

i) Fiscal supervision requirements: These are rules to ensure that the currency of a state is not undermined.

ii) Measures protecting public health: It is unclear how this requirement relates to the express exemption under Article 36 which provides for the protection of public health.

iii) Measures to ensure the fairness of commercial transactions: This includes laws to protect consumers from fraudulent or negligent misrepresentations and deceptive practices: see *GB-INNO-BM* v *Confederation du Commerce Luxembourgeois* [1991] 2 CMLR 801.

iv) Consumer protection: This was the type of measure with which the *Cassis de Dijon Case* itself was concerned. The Court has developed a number of precedents in this area and one example is provisions intended to protect the environment: see *EC Commission* v *Denmark (Re Returnable Containers)* [1989] 1 CMLR 619.

v) Protection of national or regional socio-cultural characteristics: This was the justification given by the European Court in permitting Member States to decide the rules to regulate the opening of shops and stores on Sundays: see *Stoke-on-Trent City Council* v *B & Q plc* [1993] 1 All ER 481.

The rights of Member States to introduce such mandatory requirements are not unfettered. In particular, such measures must not constitute an unjustified or arbitrary means of discrimination: *EC Commission* v *Germany (Re German Sausages)* [1989] 2 CMLR 733.

Also, the restrictions will not be allowed if they are more restrictive than necessary to attain the objective of the measure. For example, in *Italy* v *Nepoli* [1992] 2 CMLR 1, the European Court held that national rules limiting the minimum fat content of cheese could not be justified as a mandatory requirement based on consumer protection because consumers could be adequately protected by appropriate labelling of the product.

Finally, the burden of justifying such restrictions rests with the national authorities.

g) *Discriminatory domestic taxation*

Article 95 of the EC Treaty expressly prohibits Member States from imposing – directly or indirectly – internal taxes of any kind on Community products if such taxes exceed those imposed on identical or similar domestic products. This provision only applies to the levying of internal taxes where imported goods compete with domestic products. If there are no similar products, or no products capable of being protected, the prohibition in Article 95 is inapplicable. The products must therefore be in actual or potential competition.

The degree of competition required was illustrated in *EC Commission* v *United Kingdom (Re Wine and Beer Tax)* [1983] ECR 2265, which concerned British internal taxation policy on wines and beer. The United Kingdom imposed greater taxes on wine products, which were almost exclusively imported, than on beer products, which were mainly domestically produced. The Commission argued that, since wine and beer were conceivably interchangeable products, this tax differential created an artificial separation of the market which had the effect of de facto discrimination. The European Court agreed with this submission and held that beer and wine were competing products and therefore the United Kingdom was guilty of discrimination by levying different levels of tax.

h) *Harmonisation of barriers to trade*

Measures having an equivalent effect to quantitative restrictions form the greatest obstacles to the free movement of goods within the Community. These measures fall into three categories:

i)   physical barriers to trade – for example, the systematic stopping and checking of goods and people at national frontiers;

ii) technical barriers to trade – for example, national legislation regulating product standards, conditions of marketing, or the protection of public health or safety;

iii) fiscal barriers to trade – for example, the divergence in types and rates or indirect taxes levied on goods within the Community.

The EC Treaty specifically identifies the harmonisation (or approximation) of the laws of the Member States in order to remove these obstacles as an objective of the Community: Article 3(h) EC Treaty. Articles 100, 100A and 235 of the EC Treaty confer authority on the Community to enact legislation to harmonise such measures and standards throughout the Community. A number of Community measures have been adopted to eliminate such barriers through harmonisation. Products which satisfy such standards are entitled to unimpeded entry into the markets of all Member States.

Where Community legislation has been enacted to harmonise the legislation of the Member States, as regards a particular restriction based on Article 36, any additional requirements imposed under national law which extend or exceed those contained in the Community measure are not permitted: see *Dansk Denkavit* v *Ministry of Agriculture* [1990] 1 CMLR 202.

However, it is only when Community legislation provides for complete harmonisation that recourse to Article 36 itself is no longer justified: *Oberkriesdirecktor Des Kreises* v *Handelsonderneming Moorman* [1990] 1 CMLR 656.

i) *The single internal market programme*

The Single European Act also introduced the single market programme, also known as the 1992 programme. The internal market is defined as:

'an area without internal frontiers in which the free movement of goods, persons, services and capital is ensured in accordance with the provisions of the [EC Treaty]': Article 8A EC Treaty.

The programme itself was a package of measures designed to eradicate barriers to trade and measures having an equivalent effect to quantitative restrictions. The deadline for the achievement of this goal was set for 31 December 1992. A total of 282 measures were introduced to tackle barriers to trade in the areas of customs, tax, public procurement, capital movements, company law, employment, transport and safety standards.

As noted above, the target set for the enactment of all proposals was 31 December 1992. While the Council was unable to adopt all the measures proposed by the Commission under the programme, around 95 per cent of this total was in fact enacted.

As part of its post-1992 agenda, the Commission has reaffirmed its commitment to having all the proposals adopted by the end of 1993. In addition, the Commission established a committee to consider its post-1992 strategy which recently rendered its report. This group made a number of recommendations:

i) where a satisfactory degree of harmonisation has been achieved through directives, these should be converted into regulations which have direct effect;

ii) a legislation co-ordination unit should be established within the Commission to ensure the consistency of implementing legislation;

iii) the manner in which private individuals obtain redress for breaches of Community law by Member States should be reviewed; and

iv) a co-operative approach to the enforcement of internal market legislation should be adopted throughout the Community to reinforce the mutual confidence between the Member States and the Commission.

These four guidelines will provide the principles for the future evolution of the internal market programme.

j) *Trade in goods from non-Community states*

Goods entering the Community from non-Community countries are subject to the Common Customs Tariff (CCT) which is a comprehensive Community-wide regime for assessing customs duties on non-EC goods. The CCT supersedes the individual tariff schedules and customs laws of the Member States, although the Community relies on national customs officials to enforce its provisions. The present CCT is based on Council Regulation 2658/87 OJ L256/1 (1987).

Article 10(1) of the EC Treaty provides that products from third countries shall be considered to be in 'free circulation' within the Community if:

i) the relevant import formalities have been completed;

ii) any customs duties or charges having an equivalent effect have been levied; and

iii) the goods have not benefited from a total or partial drawback of such duties or charges.

According to Article 9(2) of the EC Treaty, once foreign goods are in free circulation, they may not be subject to customs duties, quantitative restrictions or measures having an equivalent effect during intra-Community trade; see *Grandes Distilleries Paureux* v *Directeur des Services Fiscaux* [1979] ECR 975.

8.3 Relevant cases

EC Commission v *Germany (Re Customs Inspection Fees)* [1990] 1 CMLR 561: Definition of the concept of 'charges having an equivalent effect to customs duties'.

Dansk Denkavit v *Ministry of Agriculture* [1990] 1 CMLR 203: Definition of the concept of 'measures having an equivalent effect to quantitative restrictions'.

R v *Henn and Darby* [1979] ECR 3795: Exception to the restrictions on quantitative measures for reasons of public morality.

Oberkreisdirecktor Des Kreises Borken v *Handelsonderneming Moormann BV* [1990] 1 CMLR 656: Where Community Directives provide for the harmonisation of measures to ensure public health, the exceptions contained in Article 36 cannot be relied upon and checks must be carried out within the framework of the Directives.

GB-INNO-BM v *Confederation du Commerce Luxembourgeois* [1991] 2 CMLR 801: A case assessing the legitimacy of national measures regulating advertising with Community law.

EC Commission v *Denmark (Re Returnable Containers)* [1989] 1 CMLR 619: Any mandatory requirements based on legitimate rationales must nevertheless remain proportionate to the objectives sought to be achieved.

Stoke-on-Trent City Council v *B & Q plc* [1993] 1 All ER 481: An assessment of the rights of Member States to regulate Sunday trading.

Italy v *Nepoli* [1992] 2 CMLR 1: Appropriate labelling of a product can be a sufficient means of protecting consumers without the need to prohibit the sale of goods.

8.4 Relevant materials

L W Gormley, *Prohibiting Restrictions on Trade Within the EEC* (1985).

P Oliver, *Free Movement of Goods in the EEC* (1988).

R Barents, 'Internal Market Unlimited: Some Observations on the Legal Basis of Community Legislation' (1993) CML Rev 85.

D Chalmers, 'Free Movement of Goods Within the Community: An Unhealthy Addiction to Scotch Whisky (1993) ICLQ 269.

E L M Voelkers, *Barriers to External and Internal Community Trade* (1993).

N Green, *The Legal Foundations of the Single European Market* (1992).

8.5 Analysis of questions

Students should be familiar with the basic principles behind the concept of the free movement of goods, including the prohibitions on customs duties, charges having an equivalent effect to customs duties, as well as the elimination of quantitative restrictions and the abolition of measures having an equivalent effect to quantitative restrictions. In addition, an understanding of the relationship between these principles and the objectives of the internal market programme initiated by the Single European Act is desirable.

8.6 Questions

QUESTION ONE

Martin NV exports TV aerials from the Netherlands to the United Kingdom. It enters into a contract with Nairn Ltd to supply 1,000 aerials a month. The first shipment from Martin to Nairn is stopped by United Kingdom customs authorities. The authorities state that:

a) United Kingdom law requires that such products be inspected at the port, the inspection has been carried out and a fee is now due;

b) the aerials are made partly of an aluminium alloy which United Kingdom legislation prohibits from being used in the United Kingdom for reasons of consumer protection;

c) the strength of the aerials is below that required by standards adopted by the United Kingdom pursuant to the procedure permitted by Article 100A(4).

Advise Martin NV as to any rights and remedies which it may have under European Community law.

University of London LLB Examination
(for External Students) European Community Law 1992 Q6

General Comment

A problem-type question requiring the student to analyse the facts presented in light of Articles 30 and 36 of the EC Treaty. There appear to be no real difficulties presented by the facts of the question and so a familiarity with the basic elements of this part of the syllabus should secure a reasonable score.

Skeleton Solution

- General principles relating to the free movement of goods.
- Restrictions on customs duties and charges having similar effect: Article 12.
- Restrictions on the use of quantitative restrictions and measures having equivalent effect: Articles 30 and 36.
- Exemptions for Member States from the rigours of harmonising legislation under Article 100A.

Suggested Solution

There are three separate measures preventing Martin NV from importing the aerials from the Netherlands into the United Kingdom: inspection charges; consumer protection legislation; and product technical standards. While each of these measures constitutes a barrier to trade in terms of the free movement of goods, each is subject to different Community rules. It is therefore necessary to consider each measure separately.

Article 12 of the EC Treaty expressly prohibits the introduction of any customs duties, or charges having an equivalent effect to customs duties, on imports and exports from different Member States of the Community. This provision has been given direct effect by the European Court and may therefore be founded upon by private individuals in national courts without reference to the European Court.

Charges having equivalent effect to customs duties have been defined by the European Court as 'any pecuniary charge, whatever its designation and mode of application, which is imposed unilaterally on goods by reason of the fact that they cross a frontier, and is not a customs duty in the strict sense': *EC Commission* v *Germany (Re Customs Inspection Fees)* (1990). A charge imposed on importation which has the effect of discriminating between domestic goods and similar goods of Community origin, and which cannot be justified by provisions in the EC Treaty or Community legislation, will therefore amount to a charge having equivalent effect.

Charges having an equivalent effect can only be justified in three circumstances: (a) if the charges relate to a general system of internal levies applied systematically within a Member State and without discrimination; (b) if the charges constitute payment for a service in fact rendered and are in proportion to the costs of receiving that service; and (c) if the charges are levied under the authority of a Community measure harmonising customs procedures.

According to the facts of this case as presented in the question, UK law requires inspection of these products at the port of entry and a charge is due for such an inspection. It is unlikely that such inspections are made of domestically-produced aerials and there is therefore a presumption that such charges are unlawful under Community law. Further, although the charge imposed was for a service rendered, in the event that this charge is disproportionate to the costs of rendering the service, again the charge may be illegitimate.

Further, no direct benefit accrued to either Martin NV or Nairn Ltd by virtue of the inspection. Community law requires that the importer receives some benefit from the service which has not happened in this case. Obviously a direct benefit will not accrue to an importer if the charges are made in the interests of the inspecting state: *EC Commission* v *Italy (Re Customs Administrative Charges)* (1989).

In these circumstances, it is unlikely that Martin or Nairn will be liable for the charges and the appropriate action can be raised on these grounds to reject such a claim.

The second barrier to import is the fact that the aerials are made of an aluminium alloy prohibited under United Kingdom consumer protection legislation.

Article 30 of the EC Treaty prohibits quantitative restrictions on imports along with all measures having an equivalent effect to quantitative restrictions. Measures having an equivalent effect to quantitative restrictions have been defined as 'all trading rules enacted by Member States which are capable of hindering directly or indirectly, actually or potentially, intra-Community trade': *Procureur du Roi* v *Dassonville* (1974). All rules enacted by a Member State to regulate trade, and which have the effect of hindering commerce, may contravene Article 30 unless they can benefit from an exception to this rule.

In the *Cassis de Dijon* case (1979), the European Court considered the question of national restrictions affecting the free movement of goods. It concluded that, in the absence of Community-wide measures of harmonisation, Member States retain authority to enact laws and regulations in relation to products but only so far as such provisions are necessary to satisfy 'mandatory requirements' and the defence of the consumer. However, such measures cannot be discretionary, disproportionate to the objectives which they seek to achieve, or in conflict with Community law.

At the same time, there is a presumption that if goods satisfy the safety standards established in one Member State, they will satisfy the counterpart standards in other Member States.

The first question is whether the measure constitutes a disguised form of discrimination. This is unlikely because the alloy is prohibited from being used in the manufacture of similar products within the United Kingdom.

Whether the measure is disproportionately excessive in relation to the object which it seeks to achieve depends largely on the quality of the material. If it is inherently dangerous or toxic an absolute ban on its use is not disproportionate. If, however, scientific evidence does not support the theory that the material is dangerous, it is far less likely that such an absolute ban could be justified.

There is no suggestion that the material is the subject of regulation at the Community level and we must therefore presume that the prohibition on use is not contrary to Community law.

In the event that the prohibition does not satisfy these conditions, the British authorities may rely on Article 36 of the EC Treaty which allows measures designed to ensure the protection of the health and lives of humans. Naturally, however, in order to rely on this provision, the United Kingdom would have to establish that the material presents a genuine threat to the health of the general population.

The final measure preventing importation is the technical standards relating to the strength of the aerials.

From the facts presented, it appears that Community-wide measures have been adopted to harmonise these standards otherwise the United Kingdom could not have made use of the Article 100A exception.

Article 100A provides that a Member State may derogate from the application of a harmonisation measure enacted to secure the internal market so long as the justification for the derogation can be based on either the terms of Article 36 or on the ground that it relates to the protection of the environment or working conditions. If the United Kingdom has secured such a derogation, the exception will be legitimately based on one of these grounds.

However, derogations must be notified to the Commission and if this has not been properly done the exception cannot be relied upon by the British government. It must therefore be verified that the appropriate procedures have been complied with by the United Kingdom.

The second ground which may be founded upon by Martin stems from the fact that often such derogations are of a temporary nature. In other words, Member States are allowed to rely on the derogation only for a particular period. If the period of authorisation has expired, the derogation will no longer be valid and the measures cannot be justified.

QUESTION TWO

Hillfarm plc, a British company which exports lamb, wishes to enter the French market. Its principal product is lamb chops, packed in cube-shaped packages designed for supermarkets. It is convinced that it can compete with French producers with regard to the quality and price of the product. It hesitates to invest, however, because it has been advised that French law requires that all lamb sold in France, regardless of its place of production, must satisfy three requirements:

a) it must undergo a health inspection for which a small charge is made;

b) it must be packed in triangular-shaped packages, because tests conducted at major universities have shown that this form of packaging tends to prolong the shelf-life of meat and to be associated generally by consumers with meat of the highest quality; and

c) it must be sold only in supermarkets offering equal space to French lamb, because
    in the view of the French government, such a policy is necessary to encourage
    local production and to protect the rural environment in the mountainous regions
    of the country.

Advise Hillfarm plc as to its position under EC law, assuming that there is no relevant
legislation under the Common Agricultural Policy.

University of London LLB Examination
(for External Students) European Community Law 1989 Q6

General Comment

Another problem-type question requiring the application of legal principles to a
factual situation.

Skeleton Solution

• The concept of charges having an equivalent effect to customs duties.
• Measures having an equivalent effect to quantitative restrictions.
• Compatibility of these actions with EC law.

Suggested Solution

Three particular practices impede Hillfarm from penetrating the French market:
health inspection charges; packaging requirements; and preferential purchasing
requirements.

Article 12 of the EC Treaty expressly prohibits the re-introduction of any customs
duties, or any charges having equivalent effect to customs duties, on imports and
exports. This provision has been given direct effect and may be founded upon by
individuals before national courts: *Van Gend en Loos* v *Netherlands* (1963). Charges
having an equivalent effect to customs duties have been defined by the European Court
as 'any pecuniary charge, whatever its designation and mode of application, which is
imposed unilaterally on goods by reason of the fact that they cross a frontier, and is
not a customs duty in the strict sense, constitutes a charge having an equivalent effect
to a customs duty': *EC Commission* v *Germany (Re Customs Inspection Fees)* (1990). A
charge imposed on goods in transit across a frontier which discriminates between
domestic and foreign goods, and which is not justified by provisions in the EC Treaty
or Community legislation will therefore amount to a charge having an equivalent effect.

Charges having an equivalent effect may only be justified in three circumstances: (a)
if the charges relate to a general system of internal dues applied systematically within
a Member State, without discrimination between domestic and imported products; (b)
if the charges constitute payment for a service in fact rendered and are in proportion
to the costs of receiving that service; or (c) if the charges are levied in order to fulfil
obligations imposed by Community law.

In this particular case, the health charges levied by the French government may be
lawful under Community law since the charge is made for a service actually incurred,
and the service is rendered on both domestic and imported lamb products. However,
Hillfarm must receive a specific benefit from the charge. A direct benefit will not

accrue to an importer if the charges are made in the interests of the state *(EC Commission* v *Italy (Re Customs Administrative Charges)* (1989)), or if the charge has been levied to ensure the health of animals in transit for public policy reasons: *EC Commission* v *Belgium (Re Health Inspection Charges)* (1984).

Package requirements are prima facie measures which have an equivalent effect to quantitative restrictions. Such measures may only be lawful if they satisfy two conditions: (a) the purpose of the measure is in the general interest of the public; and (b) the interest of the public takes precedence over the requirement of the free movement of goods, which constitutes one of the fundamental rules of the Community: *Cassis de Dijon Case* (1979). Commission Directive 70/50 expressly identifies measures which subject imported products to conditions regarding shape as a measure of equivalent effect to a quantitative restriction. However, the fact that the particular measure under examination is applied without discrimination between foreign and French lamb products may mitigate the application of this provision: *Oosthoek Case* (1982). Nevertheless it may be possible to have the measure declared incompatible with Community law on the basis that the measure constitutes an obstacle to Community trade because it exceeds what is necessary to ensure the attainment of the objective which is sought by the measure: *Torfaen Borough Council* v *B & Q* (1990).

Preferential purchasing policies are also prima facie measures which have an equivalent effect to quantitative restrictions: *EC Commission* v *Ireland* (1982). The French government are pursuing a policy of promoting French goods over imported goods by requiring that lamb sold in supermarkets must be 50 per cent French lamb. Such policies, even though they may be in the general public interest, do not prevail over the principle of the free movement of goods since they result in discrimination between imported and domestic goods. Commission Directive 70/50 clearly prohibits measures which 'hinder the purchase by individuals of imported products, or encourage, require or give preference to the purchase of domestic products'. Clearly the French policy of imposing a mandatory requirement of 50 per cent French meat contravenes this rule.

QUESTION THREE

Pietrasanta SpA is a leading Italian producer of modernistic etchings on a stone background. It contracts with the Rock & Hard Place Cafe in London to supply 10 etchings per month for a trial period of a year for sale in the cafe to customers and passers-by. The first shipment arrives at Southampton in May 1991 but is refused entry by the customs authorities on the grounds that: (a) the customs authorities consider some of the etchings to be pornographic and not entitled under United Kingdom legislation to be sold in the country; (b) the etchings are produced using a chemical which is not permitted for use in any products marketed in Britain; and (c) the products are produced with a dye which according to United Kingdom legislation cannot be used on products sold in the country because it is deemed to cause serious harm to the environment.

Advise Pietrasanta of any rights which it may have under European Community Law.

University of London LLB Examination
(for External Students) European Community Law 1991 Q5

General Comment

A problem type question requiring the student to analyse the facts presented in the light of Articles 30 and 36 of the EC Treaty. There appear to be no hidden traps in the question. A familiarity with the basic elements of this part of the syllabus should ensure that a good mark is scored in this question.

Skeleton Solution

- Article 36 exceptions to Article 30.
- *R* v *Henn and Darby*; *Conegate* v *HM Customs*.
- Community measures of harmonisation.
- *German Beer Purity Case*.
- Title VII of the EC Treaty and Articles 130s and 130t.
- Principle of proportionality.

Suggested Solution

Member States are prohibited under Article 30 of the EC Treaty from introducing or maintaining quantitative restrictions or measures having an equivalent effect, subject to the exceptions established in Article 36. These exceptions relate to matters such as the protection of intellectual property rights, national heritage and treasures, public health, and also public morality, public policy and public security.

From the facts presented, the first objection of the UK customs authorities is that the etchings in question constitute pornographic material that cannot be sold in the United Kingdom. Article 36 of the Treaty certainly appears to support the right of Member States to reject goods of a pornographic nature and the European Court has allowed a considerable degree of discretion (or the 'margin of discretion') on the part of the Member States to make such judgments.

For example, in *R* v *Henn and Darby* (1979), a prohibition on the importation of pornographic materials from other Community countries into the United Kingdom was upheld by the Court despite the fact that such material was freely available in other Member States. The Court is not therefore willing to accept an argument that Community wide standards of morality exist, instead leaving Member States to decide this matter themselves.

There is, however, one exception to this policy on the part of the Court. If a Member State allows the sale of such material within its territory when manufactured by domestic producers, import prohibitions are not justified. This is because permitting import restrictions would allow discrimination in favour of nationals.

Thus, where the importation of erotic inflatable dolls manufactured in the Community was prevented by the British customs authorities, the Court held that the absence of legislation within the United Kingdom prohibiting the manufacturing of such goods created unjustifiable discrimination: *Conegate Ltd* v *HM Customs and Excise* (1986). Consequently, a Member State may not rely on the public morality exception to prohibit importation when its own legislation contains no similar prohibition on the manufacturing or marketing of the same goods within its territory.

In the present case, it is likely that the fact that UK law prohibits the sale of these goods would be sufficient to justify the import restriction, although Pietrasanta SpA would be free to argue that the goods in question are not pornographic under the definition provided in the legislation, and on this basis, argue that the import restriction was discriminatory.

The second ground for rejecting the goods is the public health exception also contained in Article 36. Two main principles have been developed by the Court to ascertain whether or not measures to protect the health and safety of the public are justified.

First, the restriction must be necessary for the protection of public health and not a disguised form of discrimination. In the *German Beer Purity Case* (1988), the Court held that a German measure prohibiting the import of beers containing additives or preservatives was contrary to Community law because the restriction was excessive and constituted a measure of arbitrary discrimination. In particular, the Court pointed out that, if a product satisfies the health and safety requirements of one Member State, there is a presumption that it will satisfy the standards of other Member States.

Second, the effect of the restrictions imposed must be proportionate to the aim sought to be achieved. The principle of proportionality therefore requires that the power of a Member State to limit imports should be restricted to what is necessary to attain the protection of public health: *Officier van Justitie* v *Sandoz BV* (1983).

If the etchings are produced by using a chemical that is banned in the United Kingdom, it is necessary to consider whether the use of the chemical is permitted in other Member States and whether the present state of scientific research into the chemical can justify such a prohibition. Insofar as there are uncertainties at the present stage of scientific research, it is for the Member States to decide what degree of protection is required, having regard to the principle of the free movement of goods.

Thus, if the scientific advisory bodies of the Community have certified that the chemical is safe for this use, it will be difficult for the United Kingdom to justify the ban. Similarly, if there is a Community measure of harmonisation, such as a regulation or directive, authorising the use of the chemical, national measures under Article 36 cannot be justified: *Oberkreisdirecktor Des Kreises Borken* v *Handelsonderneming Moorman BV* (1990).

If the etchings are produced in a manner that complies with Community standards, there is an irrefutable presumption that that the goods conform to an adequate standard of quality and safety. In such cases, national measures restricting imports on the grounds of the protection of public health are not justified.

The final ground upon which the rejection of the etchings is based is because the dyes in the product are deemed to cause serious damage to the environment.

National measures to protect the environment are probably justified under Article 36 as necessary to protect public health and, at least until 1986, Member States retained exclusive competence to enact legislation in this field. The Single European Act altered the EC Treaty by adding Title VII on environmental protection. Article 130s empowers the Council to take action to protect the environment, but Article 130t does not exclude the possibility of more stringent action on the part of Member States.

However, measures adopted by Member States to protect the environment must still comply with the principle of proportionality. Thus, in *EC Commission* v *Denmark* (1989), the Court held that a Danish system of requiring manufacturers to package their products in returnable containers was found to be disproportionate to the objective pursued and the restriction of 3,000 hl per producer per annum for the production of beer and soft drinks in non-approved containers was contrary to Article 30.

The United Kingdom authorities may therefore justifiably impose such restrictions for the purposes of protecting the environment, but an absolute ban on the use of the dye would have to be justified by a threat of a particularly serious nature.

QUESTION FOUR

Discuss the legal principles which form the basis of the European internal market envisaged by Article 8A EC and evaluate the legislative mechanisms available for the implementation of these principles. In your answer you should also consider what other legal means, if any, might be necessary to achieve European economic integration.

University of London LLB Examination
(for External Students) European Community Law 1992 Q8

General Comment

An essay-type question requiring a narrative answer on the subject of the internal market programme. The question has three distinct parts and the answer must address each of these aspects of the question individually.

Skeleton Solution

• Legal basis for the internal market programme: Article 8A.
• Fundamental principles of the programme.
• Legislative procedures for the enactment of appropriate legislation.
• Suggested improvements to the existing process.

Suggested Solution

The Single European Act 1986 introduced a number of new policy objectives for the European Community by amending the EC Treaty. Of these, one of the most significant and successful was the initiation of a programme designed to create a single internal market. Article 8A of the EC Treaty, as amended, defines the internal market as 'an area without internal frontiers in which the free movement of goods, persons, services and capital is ensured in accordance with the provisions of the [EC Treaty]'. The deadline for the achievement of this goal was set as 31 December 1992.

The internal market programme is designed to eliminate or reduce all major physical, technical and fiscal barriers to trade thereby attaining free movement of goods, persons, services and capital. The programme entails an extensive legislative agenda harmonising national legal provisions relating to customs procedures, taxation, public procurement, capital movements, company law, intellectual property, employment and investment. These measures are required because the existing disparities between each of the Member States in these areas impede the creation of a harmonious and consistent environment for the production and sale of goods and the conduct of commerce.

Within the Community, physical barriers to the free flow of goods presently exist for many reasons such as to enforce national quotas for certain products, to collect VAT and excise duties, to carry out health inspections and checks, to operate the Community system of compensation under the Common Agricultural Policy, to ensure compliance with transportation regulations and to collect statistical information.

To reduce the effect of these barriers and to facilitate the free movement of goods, simplified customs procedures have been adopted. The adoption of the Single Administrative Document (SAD) is intended to reduce delays caused by the multiple processing of customs forms. The introduction of common border posts (banalisation) where all formalities are confined to a single stopping point between each Member State has been introduced to pave the way for the eventual removal of all systematic controls at frontiers.

It is the existence of technical barriers to the construction of the internal market that causes the greatest problems. These barriers result in standards and conditions which retard the practical exercise of the four freedoms. Technical barriers to trade in goods include the diversity of national regulations and standards for testing products or for the protection and safety of the consumer, the duplication of product testing and certification requirements (such as exist in the pharmaceutical industry) and the reluctance of public authorities to open their procurement contracts to the nationals of other Member States.

There are two fundamental legal principles behind the elimination of the technical barrier to the proper functioning of the free movement of goods. These are the principle of equivalence and the principle of harmonisation.

The principle of equivalence or mutual recognition requires that, once a product has been manufactured in one Member State, it is capable of being sold without restrictions throughout the Community. In other words, if a product meets the technical or safety standards of one Member State, there is a presumption that it will meet the counterpart requirements in other Members. The use of this principle was sanctioned in the *Cassis de Dijon* case (1979) and was also reiterated in the *German Beer Purity* case (1988).

The second principle is that of harmonisation. This requires that measures standardising technical and safety requirements within the Community are adopted at the Community level. Generally, this requires the passing of Community legislation. The SEA ensures that legislation for this purpose will receive expedited passage by lowering the voting requirements in the Council of Ministers to enacting such measures to majority voting.

Where harmonising legislation is not absolutely required, the Commission has expressed its intention to rely on the principle of equivalence as applied by the European Court to attack remaining barriers. A substantial amount of Community

151

legislation pertaining to the harmonisation of technical standards, mostly in the form of directives, has been passed to approximate technical standards on products.

Failure to achieve the four freedoms before the Single European Act was widely attributed to the legislative process which existed within the Community prior to 1986. In order to realise the achievement of these four goals, it was necessary to liberate the legislative process from the stranglehold of the requirement for unanimity among all Member States. Article 100A of the EC Treaty, as amended, introduced qualified majority voting for all proposed legislation enacted to secure the internal market. Measures enacted under Article 100A are designed to approximate or harmonise national measures relating to technical barriers to trade.

Measures designed to tackle the problem of fiscal barriers and proposals relating to the free movement of persons or the rights and interests of employed persons are specifically excluded from the scope of Article 100A. Adoption of measures relating to these subjects will continue to require unanimity under Article 100 of the EC Treaty. Further, Article 100A(4) of the Treaty allows a Member State to derogate from measures enacted on a majority vote if the measure is alleged to adversely affect the security or welfare of that Member State.

At the same time, measures enacted under Article 100A are subject to the cooperation procedure which requires that the Commission fully consult the European Parliament as regards proposed legislation. The cooperation procedure adds a second reading stage for certain types of proposed legislation. Under the cooperation procedure, responsibility for the initiation of proposals continues to reside in the European Commission which formulates proposals taking into account the views of the European Parliament, before submitting the proposals to the Council of Ministers for approval.

The Council of Ministers is then required to reach a 'common position' on the measure acting by majority voting. The common position is referred to the European Parliament which can approve the Council position, reject the position, or amend the Council's position. If the position is amended, the Commission has one month to consider the amendments proposed by Parliament with a view to taking these into account when amending its proposal.

There is little doubt that the amended legislation procedure has contributed significantly to the passage of legislation to create a single internal market. Member States can no longer veto such measures because the requirement of unanimity has been removed. Similarly, the European Parliament has made a significant contribution to the content of proposed legislation.

Yet, at the same time, the creation of the Article 100A process has opened the door to potential abuse of the legislative process. Thus, frequently Member States and the Commission clash on the legitimate basis for a particular measure. Naturally, if a measure is based on a provision of the Treaty that requires unanimity, it is easy for the Commission to assert that the proper legal basis for the measures is Article 100A and thereby substitute majority voting for unanimity.

For example, the European Commission suggested that the controversial Fifth Company Directive on the Statute for European Companies could be enacted by means of Article 100A and not Article 100 as originally proposed. The difference was that unanimity was required under Article 100 but qualified voting applied to measures processed through Article 100A. The United Kingdom government threatened to take this matter to the European Court if the European Commission tried to follow this route. Eventually, the European Commission withdrew its proposals on this matter.

Legislation is a potent means of achieving European economic integration. Community regulations and directives can effectively harmonise whole areas of national laws. However, their are limits to the effectiveness of legislation. For example, Community legislation must rest on some form of political consensus within the Community that the measure is necessary and appropriate. Often there is a feeling that the European Commission is too far ahead of this political consensus in its proposals. The result is conflict among the Member States and the Community institutions.

At the same time, the creation of a single market will not, by itself, significantly advance the cause of European economic integration. This is clear because the concept of the internal market is considerably more refined than that of a common market which in turn is significantly looser than a European union of states. The internal market programme concentrates on achieving the basic goals of the free movement of goods, labour, services and capital. This reflects a desire on the part of the Member States to achieve at least a bare minimum level of economic integration to sustain the momentum towards true economic, political and monetary union among the Member States.

Action is required in other fields such as social policy, cultural relations, and social interaction. This implies that a number of important political decisions must be made. Political and monetary union can only occur when there is a sufficient degree of economic and social integration among the peoples of Europe.

QUESTION FIVE

Consider the following from the point of view of Community law:

a) legislation by a Member State imposing a financial levy on all books published in a foreign language published within or imported into the country.

b) legislation by a Member State requiring all novels sold in the country to state on the title page the nationality of the author;

AND

c) legislation by a Member State banning the sale of all alcoholic drinks but permitting freely their manufacture in private households.

University of London LLB Examination
(for External Students) European Community Law June 1993 Q6

General Comment

This is a three-part question concerning the application of Articles 30 and 36 of the EC Treaty with the exception of part (a) which requires consideration of the concept of charges having an equivalent effect to customs duties. The issues raised are relatively novel and require a moment of reflection prior to answering the question properly.

Skeleton Solution

a) • The terms of Article 30, de facto discrimination and the exceptions contained in Article 36.

   • Article 12 and the principle of charges having an equivalent effect.

b) • The *Cassis de Dijon Case* and the principle of mandatory requirements.

   • The requirements of non-discrimination and proportionality.

c) • The principles behind the ECJ decision in *Stoke-on-Trent* v *B & Q plc*.

   • Concept of socio-economic function and the requirements on non-discrimination and proportionality.

Suggested Solution

a) A distinction must be drawn between the financial levy imposed on the books published within a Member State and the levy or charge imposed on the importation of foreign language books into the Member State.

Article 30 of the EC Treaty prohibits quantitative restrictions and measures having equivalent effects to quantitative restrictions. Measures having an equivalent effect have been defined by the European Court as 'all trading rules enacted by Member States which are capable of hindering, directly or indirectly, actually or potentially, intra-Community trade': *Procureur du Roi* v *Dassonville* (1974).

Quite clearly the legislation imposing a financial levy on books published within the Member State would fall into this category if it in some way limited the sale of foreign language books within the country. While prima facie the financial levy applies to both national and foreign publishers of foreign-language books, in practice this measure amounts to discrimination because its impact will be felt disproportionately by foreign producers. Few publishers within the Member State will be engaged in the publication of foreign language books in comparison to producers in other Member States who will mainly produce publications in their own langauge.

Hence, although the measure is not discriminatory on the face of it, in effect it will cause discrimination by burdening foreign producers with higher costs than those incurred by national producers publishing in their own language. This is an example of de facto discrimination as opposed to de jure discrimination.

By causing discrimination between national and non-national producers, the legislation constitutes a measure which hinders trade between Member States and which therefore constitutes a measure having an effect equivalent to a quantitative restriction contrary to Article 30.

The Member State cannot rely on the terms of Article 36, which contain the exceptions to the general principle prohibiting measures having an equivalent effect to quantitative restrictions. The law cannot be justified on the basis of an attempt to protect public morality, public policy, the protection of national heritage or to protect industrial or commercial property.

In particular, the exception relating to the protection of national heritage does not extend to linguistic protection and in any event it is unlikely that this objective would be secured by the imposition of a financial levy.

In addition to violating Article 30, it is also likely that the financial levy imposed on the importation of foreign language books infringes Article 12 of the EC Treaty. This provision prohibits all charges having an equivalent effect to customs duties. These are defined as 'any pecuniary charge, whatever its designation and mode of application, which is imposed unilaterally on goods by reason of the fact that they cross a frontier': *EC Commission* v *Germany* (*Re Customs Inspection Fees*) (1990).

If the legislation imposes a charge on the importation of the foreign language books when they cross the frontiers into the Member State, this will involve a violation of Article 12 unless the charge relates to a general system of internal dues applied systematically within a Member State without discrimination between domestic and imported products: *Denkavit* v *France* (1979).

Clearly in this case the pecuniary charge is not non-discriminatory even although it applies to both national publishers and foreign publishers quite simply because it causes de facto discrimination.

b) The legislation of the Member State requiring all novels sold in the country to state on the title page the nationality of the author also requires scrutiny under Article 30 to verify whether or not it amounts to a measure having an equivalent effect to a quantitative restriction.

This requirement will violate Article 30 if it amounts to a rule capable of hindering intra-Community trade. In essence, the measure amounts to a marketing requirement and it is well settled in the jurisprudence of the European Court that obstacles to movement of goods within the Community resulting from national laws relating to the marketing of products are acceptable if they are required to satisfy 'mandatory requirements' relating in particular to the protection of public health, the fairness of commercial transactions and the defence of the consumer; see *Cassis de Dijon Case* (1979).

In other words, the Member State would have to demonstrate that the requirement was necessary to ensure the fairness of commercial transactions or to protect consumers from unfair trade practices. It is unlikely that the Member State would be successful in establishing that either of these conditions was applicable. The requirement does not serve a purpose which could be said to be in the general interests of the public and the objective of the measure is not of sufficient magnitude to take precedence over the obligation of Member States to ensure the free movement of goods.

Any such mandatory requirement must remain proportionate to the objective sought to be achieved and cannot cause discrimination between foreign and domestic goods. It is unlikely that either of these conditions is satisfied by the legislation requiring novels to state the nationality of the author. If anything, the requirement is an attempt to indulge in de facto discrimination by encouraging consumers to purchase books written by authors from Member States. There can be few other reasons for the introduction of such a measure.

c) This legislation must also be assessed against the obligations contained in Article 30. It the *Cassis de Dijon Case*, supra, the European Court first hinted that Article 30 could apply to measures within a Member State regulating the production and marketing of a product without any overt manifestation of discrimination between domestic and imported goods.

The Court held that, in the absence of Community rules relating to the production and marketing of alcohol products, it was for the Member States themselves to regulate all matters relating to the production and marketing of alcohol and alcoholic beverages within their territories. Further, it was a legitimate purpose of such regulations to protect the health of the consumer.

Only if the mandatory requirements imposed on the production and marketing of the products were disproportionate to the object sought to be achieved, or amounted to discrimination, is there a violation of the terms of Article 30.

The legislation presumably is based on the need to protect the public from the dangers of alcohol abuse and therefore has a legitimate aim. Allowing individuals to manufacture alcohol in their own private households is consistent with this objective since the overall impact of the measure would be to dramatically reduce alcohol consumption throughout the population.

The measure also affects the sale of both domestic and imported products equally and does not create any overt form of discrimination in favour of national products. The marketing of the alcoholic drinks is not made more difficult than the marketing of national products.

In addition, there is a solid argument that the measure is not disproportionate to the objective sought to be achieved, namely a reduction in the amount of alcohol consumed by the population. The protection of the public from alcohol abuse may justifiably warrant such measures. In assessing the proportionality requirement it is also necessary to weigh the national interest in attaining that aim against the Community interest in ensuring the free movement of goods.

National rules restricting the sale of alcohol therefore pursue an aim which is justified under Community law. These rules reflect choices relating to particular national socio-cultural characteristics. It is therefore for the Member States to select the proper means of regulating alcohol consumption in compliance with the requirements of Community law and in particular the principle of proportionality; see *Stoke-on-Trent City Council* v *B & Q plc* (1993).

9 THE FREE MOVEMENT OF PERSONS

9.1 Introduction

9.2 Key points

9.3 Relevant cases

9.4 Relevant materials

9.5 Analysis of questions

9.6 Questions

9.1 Introduction

The free movement of labour is recognised by the EC Treaty as essential to achieve the goal of a common market. The essence of this freedom is the abolition of discrimination between nationals and workers from other Community Member States as regards employment, remuneration and other conditions of work. In the realisation of this object, a distinction is made between 'workers' and 'self-employed persons'. 'Workers' enjoy the freedom of movement, while 'self-employed persons' enjoy the freedom of establishment. Both freedoms serve the same purpose – the liberalisation of the supply of labour.

9.2 Key points

a) *The freedom of movement of workers*

Article 48 of the EC Treaty regulates the free movement of workers. It creates four rights which are inherent in the exercise of this freedom:

i) the right to accept offers of employment actually made;

ii) the right to move freely within the territory of Member States for this purpose;

iii) the right to reside in a Member State for the purpose of employment in accordance with the provisions governing the employment of nationals of that State as laid down by law, regulations or administrative action;

iv) the right to remain in the territory of a Member State after having been employed in that State, subject to conditions laid down by the European Commission.

Article 49 authorises the Council of Ministers to issue regulations and directives to implement Article 48. However, this has not prevented the European Court from declaring that Article 48 has direct effect; see *EC Commission* v *France* [1974] ECR 359 and *Van Duyn* v *Home Office* [1974] ECR 1337.

Acting in pursuance of the authority vested by Article 49, the Council introduced the concept of the free movement of workers in three stages:

i) Council Regulation 15/61 (1961): This established the principle that every national of the Community was free to take employment in another Member State provided that no suitable employee was available among the work force of that State.

ii) Council Regulation 38/64 (1964): This reduced the level of preference enjoyed by workers with the national labour force.

iii) Council Regulation 1612/68 (1968): This legislation, which continues to remain in force in an amended form, eliminated preferences and established the full freedom of movement for workers.

b) *Definition of 'worker' under Community law*

The right to the freedom of movement is expressly restricted to 'workers' under Article 48. Whether a person qualifies as a worker depends on whether or not he or she satisfies the relevant criteria laid down in Community law. See *Lawrie-Blum* v *Land Baden-Wurttemberg* [1986] ECR 2121.

In order to qualify as a worker under Article 48, a person must be employed. The essential feature of an employment relationship is that, for a certain period of time, a person performs services for and under the direction of another person in return for which he or she receives remuneration. The term 'worker' therefore includes all persons engaged in a contract of employment, including executives, salaried employees and manual workers.

The definition of 'worker' is not restricted to full-time employees. A person who is employed on a part-time basis may acquire the right of freedom of movement provided that he or she pursues an activity as an employed person which is 'effective and genuine': *Levin* v *Staatssecretaris van Justitie* [1982] ECR 1035. Even a worker who is engaged in part-time employment, and who receives public assistance to supplement his or her income, may exercise this right: *Kempf* v *Staatssecretaris van Justitie* [1986] ECR 1741.

Although not strictly workers in the true sense of that term, students enjoy special rights due to the vocational nature of their studies. A special regime has been introduced to regulate their right to exercise this freedom. In particular, Council Directive 93/96/EEC (1993) confers on students the right of residence when pursuing their studies in Member States other than their own.

c) *Prohibitions on discrimination*

Council Regulation 1612/68 (1968) is intended to harmonise national legislation regulating employment by removing any measures discriminating between national and Community workers. This objective is achieved by creating the following rights and duties:

i) Any national of a Member State may, irrespective of his place of residence, exercise the right to take up an activity as an employed person, and to pursue such activity within the territory of another Member State in accordance with the employment law of that State.

ii) A worker has the right to take up available employment in a Member State with the same priority as a national of that State.

iii) National employment legislation will be inapplicable if it limits applications for employment or offers of employment in a discriminatory manner, or is designed to exclude Community nationals from employment positions.

iv) A worker who seeks employment in a foreign Member State shall receive the same assistance there as afforded to nationals by the employment offices of that State.

v) A worker who is a national of a Member State may not be treated differently from national workers by reason of his nationality in respect of conditions of employment, including remuneration and tenure.

vi) Spouses and dependants are entitled to accompany the worker to the place where he or she intends to exercise the right of free movement.

However, although Community countries have created the principle of the free movement of persons, Community law has not excluded the power of Member States to adopt measures enabling the national authorities to have an exact knowledge of population movements affecting their territory: *Watson* v *Belmann* [1976] ECR 1185.

d) *Rights of workers exercising the freedom of movement*

Council Directive 68/360 (1968) abolishes restrictions on the movement and residence of workers within the Community. Under this Directive, workers may exercise the freedom of movement on production of a valid identity card or passport.

Also, workers taking up employment in another Member State are entitled to a residence permit as proof of the right of residence: Article 4(2). This permit must be renewed unless justified reasons may be given for not doing so: Article 10.

A valid residence permit may not be withdrawn from a worker solely on the ground that he is no longer in employment due to illness or involuntary unemployment.

When a worker travels from one Community country to another for the purpose of obtaining employment, the whole gambit of Community rights under the principle of the free movement of workers is activated. This includes the right of the spouse of a Community worker to return with his or her spouse to their original Member State.

Once inside the home country, the individual and his or her spouse are entitled to exercise the right of free movement and cannot be prevented from doing so on the grounds of nationality: *R* v *Immigration Appeal Tribunal and Singh, ex parte Secretary of State for the Home Department* [1992] 3 CMLR 358.

The right to remain after ceasing employment applies to employees and self-employed persons who have decided to retire. Council Directive 90/365/EEC requires Member States to grant the right of residence to nationals of other Member States who have been employed or self-employed and are recipients of an invalidity or early retirement pension, an old age pension or a pension in respect of industrial accident or disease. Entitlement to this right requires the individual to prove to the national authorities that he or she receives sufficient income from these sources as not to be a burden on the social security system of the host state.

e) *Employment in the public service*

Article 48(4) exempts employment in the public sector from the scope of the free movement of workers. The Member States of the Community all vary from each other in their characterisation of public service. For the purposes of the application of this exemption, whether or not a position constitutes employment in the public service depends on whether or not:

'the posts in question are typical of the specific activities of the public service in so far as the exercise of powers conferred by public law and responsibilities for safeguarding the general interests of the State are vested in it': *EC Commission v Belgium (Re Public Service Employment)* [1980] ECR 3881.

Therefore, in order for this exemption to apply, it must be shown that the persons employed are charged with the exercise of powers conferred by public law or, alternatively, have been given responsibility for protecting the special interests of the state. See also *EC Commission v Italy (Re Public Service Employment)* [1987] ECR 2625.

f) *Derogations*

Article 48(3) limits the exercise of the free movement of workers on the grounds of public policy, public security and public health. Council Directive 64/221 (1964) creates rules to regulate the exercise of discretion conferred on Member States.

i) Public policy

Restrictions on the right of a Community worker to enter the territory of another Member State, to reside there, or to move around that state, cannot be imposed unless his or her presence or conduct constitutes a genuine and serious threat to public policy: *Rutili v Minister of the Interior* [1975] ECR 1219. If the conduct of a worker poses a threat to public policy, the reasons for this conclusion must be given to the worker in order to allow him or her decide whether or not such a judgment may be challenged.

This restriction applies not only to workers crossing frontiers, but may also allow a Member State to restrict the movements of a national within its own territory. In *R v Saunders* [1979] ECR 1129, the European Court held that the United Kingdom could lawfully require a British national to reside outside England and Wales for three years as a condition of a suspended sentence for theft.

Measures taken on the ground of public policy (as well as public security) shall be based exclusively on the conduct of the individual concerned and no other grounds. Further, previous criminal convictions are not in themselves sufficient grounds for the adoption of such measures: Article 3(2) Council Directive 64/221 (1964).

ii) Public security

The exception on the ground of public security implies that restrictions may be imposed on the free movement of persons for the purpose of securing the safety of the state and society in the face of violence, disturbances and threats to the peace, whether they emanate from within or outside the Member State.

iii) Public health

Restrictions on the movement of persons based on the ground of public health have been codified in Directive 64/221. This lists the only diseases and disabilities which justify refusing entry into a territory or a refusal to issue a residence permit. Diseases or disabilities occurring after a residence permit has been issued do not justify a refusal to renew the permit.

Diseases which are considered to constitute a danger to the pubic health include tuberculosis of the respiratory system, syphilis, and other infectious diseases or contagious parasitic diseases. Disabilities which constitute a threat to public health include drug addiction and profound mental disturbance.

g) *Rights of the family of a Community worker*

Under Article 10 of Council Regulation 1612/68 (1968), a worker is entitled to take his or her spouse, together with their dependants, to the country where the right of free movement is being exercised. In addition, the right to take up employment is extended to the family of the worker.

A number of other rights are granted to the family of a worker exercising the right of free movement:

i) The worker and his family are entitled to all the benefits and rights accorded to national workers in relation to housing matters.

ii) The children of the worker are entitled to education and vocational training as nationals of the Member State concerned.

iii) The children of Community workers are entitled to access to further education on the same basis as nationals. This right extends to grants for tertiary education: see *Brown* v *Secretary of State for Scotland* [1988] ECR 3205.

iv) Council Directive 77/486 (1977) provides for special free tuition to facilitate the initial reception of children into the new Member State, including training in the official languages of the state.

Council Directive 68/360 (1968) supplements these rights by requiring the abolition of restrictions on the movements and residence of workers and their families.

h) *Social security*

Article 51 of the EC Treaty instructs the Council of Ministers to draw up legislation in the field of social security in order to facilitate the free movement of workers. In the pursuit of this objective, Community legislation should ensure two primary objectives:

i) aggregation of all periods of employment in which contributions had been made to social security funds; and

ii) payment of benefits to persons resident in the territories of Member States.

A substantial number of Community measures have been introduced in order to regulate the social security of migrant workers. Council Regulation 1408/71 (1971) applies to sickness benefit, maternity benefit, invalidity benefit, old age and survivor's benefits, workmen's compensation, occupational illness benefit, death grants, unemployment benefit and family benefit. However, the Regulation applies only to social security schemes and not public assistance benefits. This Regulation has been extended by Council Regulation 1390/81 (1981) to self-employed persons and their families.

i) *Freedom of establishment – EC Treaty provisions*

Article 52 of the EC Treaty provides that 'restrictions on the freedom of establishment of nationals of a Member State in the territory of another Member State shall be abolished by progressive stages'. The freedom of establishment is the right to take up and pursue activities as a self-employed person. The right of establishment also includes the right of Community nationals to participate in existing firms and businesses as the nationals of the host state.

Article 52 has been given direct effect insofar as it prohibits discrimination on the basis of nationality: *Reyners* v *Belgian State* [1974] ECR 631. Thus Article 52 is intended to ensure that self-employed persons are treated in another Member State in the same way as nationals of that Member State. The rules regarding the freedom of establishment not only extend to the self-employed person, but also to his or her family.

Article 53 prohibits Member States from introducing new restrictions on the right of establishment, unless such restrictions are justified by other provisions of the Treaty. Article 54 provides the authority for the Council of Ministers to enact Community legislation to abolish the existing restrictions on the freedom of establishment within the Community.

The Treaty provisions concerning the right of establishment do not apply to activities conducted wholly within a single member State by its own nationals. It is necessary to establish a nexus between the facts and a Community measure, such as a directive harmonising standards in order to achieve such an effect: *Ministerio Fiscal* v *Lopez Brea* [1992] 2 CMLR 397.

j) *The freedom of establishment – secondary legislation*

The general programme for the implementation of the right of establishment programme requires considerable Community legislation to harmonise qualifications throughout the Community. Since the practice of most professions requires the possession of relevant qualifications, a failure to recognise equivalent qualifications obtained in one Member State can amount to an effective obstacle to the exercise of the freedom of establishment in another Member State.

Community legislation equating professional qualifications has been introduced on a profession-by-profession basis.

i) Lawyers

Council Directive 89/48 (1989) establishes a general system for the mutual recognition of qualifications, including those of lawyers.

ii) Architects

Professional qualifications regarding architecture have been harmonised by Council Directive 85/384 (1985).

iii) Doctors

A number of measures have been passed by the Council to implement the freedom of establishment of doctors, including Council Directives 75/362, 75/363 and 86/457.

iv) Veterinary surgeons

Veterinary surgeons have a right to establishment by virtue of Council Directives 78/1026 and 78/1027.

All these Directives deal with the mutual recognition of formal qualifications to facilitate the effective exercise of the right of establishment. A number of other Directives have been adopted in relation to other professions under the single internal market programme.

Where a profession has been the subject of harmonising legislation, Member States are prohibited from implementing these measures in a manner likely to prevent their proper functioning: see *EC Commission* v *Germany (Re Restrictions on the Legal Profession)* [1989] 2 CMLR 677. Even where a profession has been subject to harmonising measures to equate different professional qualifications from institutions and professional bodies in Member States, a state is still required to ensure that the right of individuals under Article 52 are not infringed: see *Haim* v *Kassenzahnarttliche Vereinigung Nordrhein* [1994] 2 CMLR 169.

The position as regards professional qualifications that have not been the subject of harmonising legislation is that Member States are entitled to specify the conditions required for appointment to such positions to ensure that appointees possess sufficient knowledge and qualifications subject to the proviso that there can be no discrimination on the grounds of nationality: see *UNECTEF* v *George Heylens* [1989] 1 CMLR 901.

The European Court has in fact held, on a number of occasions, that Member States will violate their Community obligations if they indulge in discrimination in favour of their own nationals when regulating professional activities within their territories: see, for example, *EC Commission* v *Luxembourg (Re Access to the Medical Profession)* [1992] 3 CMLR 124.

9.3 Relevant cases

Kempf v *Staatssecretaris van Justitie* [1986] ECR 1741: A person who pursues part-time employment, and who receives supplementary benefits to his income, is still a worker for the purposes of the freedom of movement of workers.

Rutili v *Minister of the Interior* [1975] ECR 1219: Definition of the concept of 'public policy' as contained in the exception to Article 48.

R v *Immigration Appeal Tribunal and Singh, ex parte Secretary of State for the Home Department* [1992] 3 CMLR 358: Once a worker has activated his or her right of free movement, his or her spouse is also automatically entitled to exercise the gambit of Community rights provided under this freedom.

EC Commission v *Germany (Re Restrictions on the Legal Profession)* [1989] 2 CMLR 677: A Member State is not entitled to place greater restrictions than necessary on Community measures liberalising professional services.

EC Commission v *Luxembourg (Re Access to the Medical Profession)* [1992] 3 CMLR 124: Consideration of the legality of requiring a presence for the exercise of the right of establishment.

9.4 Relevant materials

D Edwards, 'Establishment and Services: An Analysis of the Insurance Cases' (1987) 12 EL Rev 231.

D Pickup, 'Reverse Discrimination and the Free Movement of Workers' (1986) 23 CMLR 135.

J Hardoll, 'Article 48 of the EC Treaty and Non-National Access to Public Employment' (1988) 13 EL Rev 223.

9.5 Analysis of questions

The free movement of workers is a common subject for examination. Issues which frequently arise within this topic include the scope of the right itself, exceptions to the general rules, and the right of establishment. Although this topic is not particularly complex, students should be aware that questions from this area of the syllabus generally take the form of problem-type questions.

9.6 Questions

QUESTION ONE

Kirsten, a Danish national with a degree in civil engineering, seeks employment in Italy. She is offered a part-time job with Verona City Council. Kirsten is informed by her lawyer that she is not eligible for that job because under the current Italian law the City Council may employ only Italian nationals, since the job is considered to be in the public service. She is also told that her rate of pay would be lower than that paid to full time city engineers and that she would have to retire at the age of 55 while the male civil engineers retire at the age of 60.

Advise Kirsten on the relevant points of Community law.

University of London LLB Examination
(for External Students) European Community Law June 1993 Q7

General Comment

Two separate issues are raised in this question. The first is the right of a Community national to seek employment in another Member States which involves the application of Article 48 and the related secondary legislation. The second is the issue of equal pay for part-time workers which is an Article 119 issue. In this connection, there is also recent caselaw from the ECJ with which the student must be familiar in order to respond properly.

Skeleton Solution

• Free movement of persons: Article 48 and Regulation 1612/68.
• Eligibility and equality in employment.
• Article 48(4) exception: employment in the public sector.
• Equal pay: Article 119 and the ECJ in the *Nimz* case.

Suggested Solution

Article 48 of the EC Treaty establishes the right of Community workers to travel from their own country to another Member State for the purposes of seeking and accepting offers of employment. Community workers are also entitled, by virtue of the same provision, to reside in that Member State to exercise the right to work and to remain in the territory of the Member State after having been employed there. These basic rights have been supplemented by a considerable volume of supporting secondary legislation.

The rights bestowed by Community law under the freedom of movement of workers are conferred only on those individuals who qualify as 'workers' in terms of Article 48. A worker is a person engaged in a contract of employment which will be the case should Kirsten accept the terms of the contract presently being offered to her by Verona City Council. It is irrelevant for the purposes of Community law that the contract is part-time. As the Court has pointed out a person who is employed on a part-time basis may acquire the right of freedom of movement provided that he or she pursues an activity as an employed person which is 'effective and genuine'; see *Levin v Staatssecretaris van Justitie* (1982).

One of the fundamental rights conferred by the principle of the free movement of workers is that all discrimination based on nationality as regards the conditions of employment, remuneration and other conditions, is to be abolished by virtue of Article 48(2) of the EC Treaty. This obligation has been given effect in secondary legislation by Council Regulation 1612/68 (1968).

According to Article 1 of this Regulation, workers are entitled to take up employment in the territory of a Member State with the same priority as nationals of that state. Employment contracts must be issued in accordance with the provisions of the law in force and, in particular, without any discrimination. National provisions are expressly declared inapplicable when they limit the rights of workers to take up and pursue employment.

These rights are, however, subject to the overriding exception stated in Article 48(4) which expressly declares that the obligation of non-discrimination on the grounds of nationality does not apply to employment in the public service. However, this exception is not as general as might first be believed.

First, the proviso does not apply to all types of employment in the public sector. In *EC Commission* v *Belgium* (1980), the European Court found that the Article applied only to those posts which required direct or indirect involvement in exercising powers 'conferred by public law and duties designed to safeguard the general interests of the state and other public authorities.' These posts normally involve some form of allegiance to the state.

Hence, the Court cited a range of positions which fell outside this exception including train drivers, plumbers and nurses. On the other hand, works supervisors and office supervisors were considered as falling within the exception since they involved safeguarding the interests of the state.

The job that has been offered to Kirsten is that of a civil engineer with Verona City Council. The factors which operate against any assumption that this is a post which falls within Article 48(4) are that there is no particular element of allegiance to the state required of a civil engineer and that her position is a minor one with no supervisory functions or responsibilities. It is therefore more than likely that the position does not fall within Article 48(4) and that the exception contained therein is inapplicable.

It should also be noted that once Kirsten has been accepted for the position, no discrimination on the grounds of nationality may be perpetrated in terms of the conditions of employment applicable once appointed; see *Sotgiu v Deutsche Bundespost* (1974). Kirsten would therefore be well-advised to accept the terms of her offer, ignore her lawyer's advice, and rely on her Community rights under the freedom of movement of persons once appointed.

Kirsten may rely on a different set of Community rights in order to challenge the gender discrimination encountered in her conditions of employment. Article 119 of the EC Treaty sets out these rights and basically provides that both genders must receive 'equal pay for equal work'. This provision has been given direct effect in a whole host of cases; see for example *Defrenne v Sabena* (1976). This basic provision has also been supplemented by considerable secondary legislation, mainly in the form of directives.

In order to be successful, Kirsten will have to establish that two conditions exist. First, that she is not receiving equal pay, as defined in Community law, for equal work. Second, that the discrimination is based on a distinction between genders.

'Equal pay' is defined in Article 119 as 'the ordinary basic or minimum wage or salary and any other consideration, whether in cash or kind, which the worker received, directly or indirectly, in respect of his [or her] employment from his [or her] employer'. The European Court has defined 'pay' in very broad terms indeed. Thus, special allowances, discriminatory retirement periods, pension allowances and redundancy payments, all constitute pay within the meaning of the Article.

Quite clearly, the fact that she is to be paid at a lesser rate than full time male colleagues doing essentially the same job amounts to discrimination unless there are objective criteria on which such discrimination may legitimately be based. Similarly, the fact that female employees are required to retire prior to the dates set for their male counterparts has, for some considerable period, been considered contrary to the equal pay for equal work principle; see for example, *Marshall v Southampton and South West Hampshire Area Health Authority* (1986); *Barber v Guardian Royal Exchange Assurance Group* (1990).

One defence which might be offered by Verona City Council is that, because Kirsten will be employed on a part-time basis, and her male counterparts work on a full-time basis, then Kirsten is not doing equal work to that of her male colleagues. The European Court has recently considered this issue in *Nimz* v *Freie Und Hansestadt Hamburg* (1992). In this case, the plaintiff was a part-time worker paid at a lesser rate than her full-time male colleagues. The question asked of the European Court on a preliminary reference was whether both sets of employees were engaged in equal work in terms of Article 119.

The Court held that whether part-time and full-time work in the same general role amounted to equal work under Article 119 was to be determined on the basis of objective criteria which are unrelated to any discrimination on the ground of gender. In this context, the amount of experience acquired by a full-time employee in relation to that acquired by a part-time employee was significant insofar as the full-time employee can more quickly gain experience. Whether or not this is the case depends on the relationship between the nature of the work performed and the experience gained from the performance of that work on completion of a certain amount of working hours.

In practical terms, the Court's decision is in essence a statement that the more complex, the more skilled and the less repetitive or mundane the work involved in the position, the more likely that a distinction between part-time workers and full-time workers will be justified on the basis that the two positions do not involve similar work. Other factors which will support the argument that, despite the part-time/full-time distinction, both are engaged in equal work, include the same hourly rates of pay, the same degree of job responsibility and the same job description.

Kirsten must also establish that the discrimination is based on gender. As regards her pay her case will be assisted if she can demonstrate that an overwhelming proportion of full-time employees are male while the majority of part-time employees are female. Her case would also be reinforced if she could demonstrate that part-time male colleagues were being paid at the same rate as their full-time counterparts. On the other hand, if the majority of part-time workers are male, and if they are paid at the same rate as Kirsten, the onus would be on Kirsten to demonstrate that there is still discrimination.

The requirement that female employees must retire at 55 while their male colleagues are permitted to work until the age of 60 is a clear-cut violation of Article 119. The retirement requirement applies regardless of the nexus between the gender of the employee and the particular position which is involved. There is an across-the-board policy that male employees retire at 60 and female employees at 55 regardless of job responsibilities and positions. Policies such as these have, for some considerable period, been considered to violate Article 119; see *Defrenne*, supra.

QUESTION TWO

In 1987, Sabena, a German national, accepted a position as a translator in a British bank in London. Over the course of the next three years, Sabena developed an addiction for cocaine. After a raid on her flat in London, the police recovered a small amount of cocaine and she was subsequently convicted for the unlawful possession of drugs. The Home Office has refused to renew Sabena's residence permit and have threatened her with deportation in the event that she does not leave the United Kingdom of her own free will.

Advise Sabena of her rights under Community law.

Question prepared by the Author

General Comment

A variation on the general theme of the free movement of workers.

Skeleton Solution

• Right of free movement of workers.
• Exceptions on the grounds of public policy.
• Relevance of convictions.
• Right to challenge the decision to refuse renewal.

Suggested Solution

Based on the presumption that Sabena is a 'worker' for Community purposes, she would normally be entitled to exercise the right of freedom to work in any Member State by virtue of her German nationality. This applies even if she works part-time so long as her work is not simply 'marginal': *Kempf* v *Staatssecretaris van Justitie* (1987). Even although her residence permit has expired, it should be automatically renewable under Article 6(1) of Council Directive 68/360. However, Council Directive 64/221 does allow a Member State to refuse to issue or renew a residence permit in certain circumstances, or to expel the holder of a residence permit on the grounds of public policy, public security or public health. This right is subject to the condition that such grounds are not invoked to serve economic ends: Article 2(2).

Article 3 of Directive 64/221 states that measures taken on grounds of public policy shall be based exclusively on the personal conduct of the individual involved. In this case, we shall assume that the refusal by the Home Office to renew the residence permit is based on criteria of public policy.

However, this article continues to the effect that previous criminal convictions do not, ipso facto, justify the taking of such measures. Thus, in *Bonsignore* v *Oberstadt-Direcktor for the City of Cologne* (1975), the European Court considered the case of an Italian worker in Germany who had been convicted and fined for the unlawful possession of a pistol. The plaintiff had accidentally shot another person and, upon conviction, was ordered to be deported by the German authorities. The Court held that exceptions to the principle of the free movement of workers had to be construed strictly. Deportation (which obviously prevents such freedom of movement for the person concerned), should be consequent on the behaviour of the individual, not for the purpose of deterring others from unlawful behaviour.

Although previous convictions alone will not automatically justify the deportation of a worker, such convictions may indicate a propensity to behave in a manner contrary to public policy or security. Thus, in *R* v *Bouchereau* (1977), a French worker who had been convicted of possessing dangerous drugs for the second time, was lawfully expelled from the United Kingdom. However, the European Court did point out that to justify expulsion, the threat to public safety must be genuine and serious: see also *ex parte Santillo* (1980).

It is even possible that a worker can be refused admittance to a Member State, and therefore presumably expelled from such a state, even although he or she has not committed any offence, if the work in which they are engaged in the host state, although not unlawful, is regarded by the host state as being socially harmful and thus contrary to public policy: *Van Duyn* v *Home Office* (1975).

In the present case, Sabena can certainly argue that her conviction for the unlawful possession of cocaine is not sufficient to justify her expulsion from the United Kingdom. For example, she could claim that her drug problem was under control and she was undertaking drug rehabilitation. It could then be argued that her past drug problems do not indicate any harmful future propensity.

It should also be noted that even if Sabena has become a drug addict, this disability would not, by itself, justify her exclusion. The Annex to Directive 64/221 does indeed set out a list of diseases and disabilities including drug addiction, from which a Member State is entitled to protect its citizens by prohibiting entry to a worker from another Member State who is suffering from such a disease or disability. However, Article 4(2) of this Directive states that, where such diseases or disabilities occur in respect of a worker from another Member State after a residence permit has been obtained, such an eventuality will not justify a refusal to renew the permit or the expulsion of the worker affected by the disease or disability.

Clearly, therefore, Sabena will have grounds for challenging the Home Office's decision in the English courts. Also, in accordance with Article 9 of Regulation 64/221, except in the case of urgency, if there is no substantive right of appeal to a court, or where the appeal cannot have suspensory effect, the administrative authorities of the host state cannot expel a national of another Member State, or refuse to renew a residence permit, until those administrative authorities have sought an opinion from the 'competent authorities' of the host state, this body being independent of the administrative authorities and before which the person concerned must have an opportunity to argue their case as are allowed by the domestic law of the host state.

QUESTION THREE

Grunhild, who recently graduated from university in Germany with a degree in biochemistry, seeks employment in England. She receives an offer of employment with a public-sector company in Manchester, which is willing to employ her part-time on a monthly salary and also to offer her regular freelance work as a technical consultant. While she is considering this offer, she is informed by the British immigration authorities that she is not eligible for either the salaried employment or the freelance work, because:

a) United Kingdom legislation provides that the company in question may employ only British nationals;

b) the part-time salaried position is considered to be employment in the public service, as it involves frequent meetings with government officials in London;

c) according to the company's rules, the rate of pay for freelance consultants varies according to the gender of the consultant, with the daily rate for women being approximately 80 per cent of that for men, and the United Kingdom government does not wish to put pressure on the company to change its rules as a change in its salary structure might increase its operating costs.

Advise Grunhild as to her position under EC law.

University of London LLB Examination
(for External Students) European Community Law 1989 Q7

General Comment

Another problem-type question requiring the student to demonstrate knowledge of the principles behind the free movement of workers.

Skeleton Solution

- Rights of part-time workers under Community law.
- Prohibitions on discrimination.
- Public service exception.
- Gender discrimination issue.

Suggested Solution

For the purposes of the question, it is assumed that Grunhild is a citizen of Germany, and therefore a national of a Community country. Article 48 of the EC Treaty establishes the right of free movement throughout the Community for the purpose of obtaining employment. In particular, Community workers are entitled to accept offers of employment actually made and to reside within a Member State for the purpose of exercising this right.

Whether or not Grunhild is a worker entitled to the right of free movement is a question of Community law. Grunhild has received an offer of part-time employment together with a supplementary offer of freelance work. A person employed part-time may qualify as a worker under Community law so long as he or she pursues an activity as an employed person and so long as that employment is both genuine and effective. In *Levin* v *Staatssecretaris van Justitie* (1982), the European Court held that the concept of worker must be interpreted in order to allow activities on a part-time basis to be included within its scope.

Further, even if Grunhild is paid less than at subsistence level, she would still qualify as a worker for the purposes of the right to free movement. The European Court has held that a person in genuine and effective part-time employment cannot be excluded from the sphere of application of Article 48 merely because the remuneration derived is below the minimum level of subsistence: see *Kempf* v *Staatssecretaris van Justitie* (1986).

As a worker under Community law, Grunhild is entitled to the rights conferred by Article 48, as supplemented by Community legislation. As Article 1 of Council Regulation 1612/68 (1968) states, any national of a Member State may, irrespective of his or her place of residence, exercise the right to take up an activity as an employed person, and to pursue such activity in accordance with the provisions of the national law of that Member State.

However, the immigration authorities have suggested that national legislation provides that the company may only employ British nationals. Such a measure infringes two Community provisions. First, Article 48(2) of the EC Treaty requires the abolition of any discrimination based on nationality between the workers of the Member States as regards remuneration and other conditions of employment. Further, this provision has been given direct effect by the European Court: *EC Commission v France* (1974). The absolute nature of this prohibition has the effect of rendering inapplicable legislation which impedes equal access to employment to the nationals of all Member States.

Second, Article 3 of Council Regulation 1612/68 declares that any national law which excludes Community nationals from applying for positions within the Member State is inapplicable if it discriminates between nationals and foreign Community workers. This prohibition applies particularly to laws which restrict the number or percentage of foreign nationals in any company or firm.

However, the company offering the position to Grunhild functions in the public sector. Article 48(1) expressly excluded employment in the public service from the scope of the freedom of movement of workers. The question which arises is whether employment within this company constitutes employment in the public sector.

Although there is no definition of 'public service' either in the EC Treaty or in secondary legislation, the European Court has held that whether or not a position is within the public sector depends on whether the post in question is typical of the specific activities of the public service and involves either the exercise of the powers conferred by public law or responsibility for safeguarding the general interests of the state: *EC Commission v Belgium* (1980).

The immigration officials have asserted that the position falls within the public sector because it involves frequent meetings with government officials. However, this does not imply that the position which was offered to Grunhild involved the exercise of powers conferred by public law. This is extremely unlikely considering that Grunhild is a biochemist. Equally, it seems unlikely that the post entails a responsibility for safeguarding the interests of the state. Such an allegation could only be sustained if the research in which Grunhild was about to engage was of a secret nature.

In these circumstances, it is extremely unlikely that the British authorities could successfully claim that the position offered to Grunhild was exempt from the scope of Article 48 by virtue of the fact that it constituted employment in the public service.

Nor could the fact that the company indulges in discrimination justify the refusal of the British authorities to grant Grunhild a residence permit. In fact such practices constitute a violation of Article 119 of the EC Treaty which states the principle that men and women should receive equal pay for equal work. Grunhild would therefore be able to claim that she was a victim of gender discrimination on the basis that Article 119 of the EC Treaty has direct effect and Community secondary legislation has created additional rights.

The United Kingdom could also be guilty of failing to observe its obligations under Article 5 of the EC Treaty by allowing a public sector company to indulge in discrimination. The European Court has consistently upheld the direct effect of Article 119 and the failure on the part of the British government to implement Community legislation preventing such discrimination may render the United Kingdom liable. In this situation, the appropriate course of action is for the European Commission to bring proceedings against the United Kingdom before the European Court for failing to observe its Community obligations.

Grunhild is also entitled to exercise the right of establishment. The right of establishment is a separate right from the right to free movement. It applies to self-employed persons establishing businesses in another Member State. The offer of freelance work could allow Grunhild to claim that she is a self-employed person and entitled to the right of establishment.

If such a claim was successful, Grunhild could rely on Article 52(2) of the EEC Treaty to establish her right to take up and pursue activities as a self-employed person. The same provision requires Member States to extend the same treatment to foreign community nationals as is given to their own nationals as regards conditions of employment. Not only are Member States obliged to abolish existing discriminatory provisions, but under Article 53, Member States may no longer introduce new restrictions on the exercise of the right of establishment by foreign Community nationals. The British legislation clearly prevents Grunhild from exercising her right of establishment, and is therefore also challengeable on that basis. Consequently, it appears that Grunhild would be successful in challenging these restrictions on the employment of Community nationals, either on the basis of the right of free movement or because they infringe the right of establishment.

QUESTION FOUR

To what extent is it true to say that if a person is admitted to the practice of law in one Member State, he or she is entitled to practise in all the other Member States?

University of London LLB Examination
(for External Students) European Community Law 1992 Q7

General Comment

A popular question requiring consideration of the implications of the right of establishment for the legal profession.

Skeleton Solution

- The complexities of the present legal position.
- The primary legislation.
- Case law.
- Proposed amendments.

Suggested Solution

It is not yet possible to make a categorical statement that once a person is qualified to practise law in one Community Member State, he or she may practise law in another Member State. This lack of clarity is partially due to the uncertain scope of

Article 52 of the EC Treaty which establishes the right of establishment and Article 59 which regulates the right to provide services, which implies a more temporary arrangement. The European Court has, however, stressed the parallels between Articles 48 (free movement of workers), 52 and 59 and that the three Articles comprise an integrated whole: *Procureur de Roi* v *Royer* (1976).

Council Directive 77/249 has helped to clarify the matter. It is concerned with the recognition of the lawyer coming from another Member State as a lawyer, and to offer him the opportunity of acting as a lawyer in the host state. It is thus only concerned with the freedom to provide services (although it has been introduced as a result of Articles 57 and 66 of the EC Treaty) and has no effect on the right of establishment in a host state, with all the consequent benefits for the immigrant's family. This would require mutual recognition of qualifications which has not yet been achieved (in contrast see Directives 75/362 and 75/363 on the mutual recognition of medical qualifications).

A lawyer is permitted to practise in another Member State under the Directive but this freedom is subject to various conditions. First, under Article 4(1), activities of representing a client in legal proceedings or before public authorities in a Member State must be carried out under the conditions laid down for lawyers established in that state, but there are exceptions against requirements for a residence qualification and the necessity for registration with any organisational body. Article 5 of the Directive also permits supplementary conditions to be imposed on the foreign lawyer with respect to procedural details consequent to legal representation. Actual appearance before a foreign court is, however, likely to be hampered by linguistic difficulties. Second, when giving legal advice, certain basic rules of the host state are imposed on foreign lawyers in addition to the professional rules of the Member State of origin: Article 4(4). Third, the foreign lawyer can be excluded from making wills in the host country and can be refused the right to represent an employer if he is a salaried lawyer-employee: Article 6.

The effects of this Directive have been largely superseded by the development of a considerable body of jurisprudence by the Court which is intended to offer greater freedom to the foreign lawyer. In *Reyners* v *Belgian State* (1974), the leading case in this area, the plaintiff was a Dutch national resident in Belgium. He had been born in Belgium, educated there, and taken his Docteur en Droit Belge, only to be finally refused admission to the Belgian bar on the grounds of his Dutch nationality. The European Court held that the prohibition of discrimination contained in Article 52 of the EC Treaty, concerned the right to establishment, was directly applicable as of the end of the transitional period, despite the opening words of the text of the Article. The Court expressed the view that the aim of Article 52 was intended to be facilitated by the Council of Ministers through the introduction of a legislative programme, but the direct effect of the provision was not made dependent on the initiation of such a programme.

The European Court went one stage further in *Thieffery* v *Paris Bar Council* (1977). That case showed that even in the absence of Directives under Article 57, recognition of foreign legal qualifications may be required under Article 52 which prohibits discrimination on the grounds of nationality. Thieffery, a Belgian national, held a Belgian law degree recognised by the University of Paris as equivalent to a French law degree. He also acquired the qualifying certificate for the profession of advocate, but the Paris Bar Council refused to allow him to undergo practical training on the ground that he did not possess a French law degree. The European Court held that such a refusal could amount to discrimination under Article 52 of the EC Treaty.

The next case, *Ordre des Advocats* v *Klop* (1985) appears to put foreign lawyers in a better position than national lawyers. Article 52 of the EC Treaty et seq were held by the European Court to preclude the denial to a national of another Member State the right to enter and to exercise the profession of advocate solely on the ground that he maintains chambers in another Member State (a national lawyer can only maintain one set of chambers within the national territory). The host state's rules of conduct, however, apply to the foreign lawyer providing they do not discriminate between the national and the foreign lawyer: *Gulleng* v *Ordre des Advocats* (1988).

Directly applicable rights derived from Article 52 secure the foreign lawyer a greater degree of freedom to practise, while dodging the pitfalls arising from rights derived from the Directive. Naturally, the derogations to Article 52 also apply to the freedom of establishment of lawyers. The 'official authority' exception in Article 55 was raised in the *Reyners* case, above. The European Court, while tacitly acknowledging that the occasional exercise of judicial power by an advocate would amount to the exercise of an official authority, declared that this would not be the case with respect to the advocate's other responsibilities and so the part of the EC Treaty relating to establishment was applicable. Certain functions of notaries public might fall within the ambit of Article 55.

Council Directive 89/48, which establishes a general system for the mutual recognition of higher education diplomas, was adopted by the Council of Ministers on 21 December 1988. As from 1 January 1991, lawyers qualified in the United Kingdom and in the rest of the Community will, in principle, be able to practise anywhere in the Community, provided that they have obtained a diploma following a minimum of at least three years university training, the completion of the relevant professional training and some relevant professional experience in the country of origin or host country.

Member States are not, however, permitted to use these requirements to impose more onerous professional requirements on non-national lawyers than are imposed on national lawyers. Thus, in *EC Commission* v *Germany (Re Restrictions on the Legal Profession)* (1989), the European Court held that Germany was not entitled to require foreign lawyers practising in Germany to be supervised at all times by a German lawyer to ensure that the foreign lawyer received the necessary experience. Such a requirement was disproportionate to the object sought to be achieved which was the protection of the public from inadequately qualified legal advisers.

The Directive permits derogations to this basic principle if there are major differences in the education and training of the migrant and the training received by people qualified in the intended host state. The legal profession is specifically identified as falling into this category so that the 'compensatory mechanism' provisions apply. In the case of lawyers, the Member State can choose whether the migrant lawyer should satisfy an adaptation period, extending to a maximum of three years duration, or should pass an aptitude test.

10 FREEDOM TO PROVIDE SERVICES

10.1 Introduction

10.2 Key points

10.3 Relevant cases

10.4 Relevant materials

10.5 Analysis of questions

10.6 Questions

10.1 Introduction

The freedom to provide services allows individuals and companies to move throughout the Community and, at least in theory, to supply their services without being prevented from doing so by national legislation or administrative practices. This requires the abolition of the numerous technical barriers to foreign suppliers of services. In particular, the removal of regulatory mechanisms which require suppliers of services to maintain a presence in a Member State is necessary, along with the harmonisation of company law throughout the Community and the creation of rules to regulate public procurement.

10.2 Key points

a) *The scope of the freedom to supply services*

Article 59 of the EC Treaty requires Member States to progressively abolish restrictions on the freedom to provide services in respect of suppliers who are established in a state of the Community other than that of the person for whom the services are intended.

Services are deemed to include activities of an industrial character, activities of a commercial character, the services of craftsmen, and the supply of professional services.

Article 63 of the EC Treaty confers upon the Council of Ministers, acting on the proposals of the Commission, authority to enact Community legislation to achieve the abolition of existing restrictions on the freedom to provide services within the Community. Substantial Community legislation has been passed to achieve the harmonisation of the national rules governing the supply of services. This legislation has been supplemented by a number of important decisions of the European Court.

The scope of the term 'services' is broad and in *Society for the Protection of Unborn Children Ireland Ltd* v *Grogan* [1991] 3 CMLR 849, the European Court held that medical services, including abortion clinics, were services within the meaning of Article 59.

b) *The right to receive services*

Although the EC Treaty contains no express right, the European Court has held that Article 59 also entails the right to receive services. Thus, the freedom to provide services includes the freedom of a recipient of services to go to another Member State in order to receive a service: *Luisi and Carbone v Ministero del Tesoro* [1984] ECR 377. This right may be exercised without obstruction from restrictions based on discrimination between domestic and foreign recipients.

The right to receive services has important ramifications, particularly as regards the rights of tourists. If Community law guarantees a person the freedom to enter another Member State for the purposes of receiving services, this right must be exercised in accordance with Article 7 of the EC Treaty which prohibits discrimination on the basis of nationality. Recipients of services are therefore entitled to the full protection of the law of the Member States, including the right to compensation in the event of a criminal assault: *Cowan v Tresor Public* [1990] 2 CMLR 613.

Procedural safeguards for non-residents are, however, permitted for the administration of justice in certain circumstances. Thus a rule requiring a non-resident plaintiff to lodge security for costs as a condition for continuing an action was held to be justifiable discrimination by the European Court on the ground that the rule was designed to allow the enforcement of judicial orders: *Berkeley Administration Inc v Arden McClelland* [1990] 2 CMLR 116.

c) *Community legislation implementing free movement of services*

The Community has adopted the instrument of Community Directives for achieving the establishment of the free movement of services. Since the purpose of these directives is to harmonise national legislation, these measures have been passed on an activity-by-activity basis. The aim is to eliminate all national measures causing discrimination between national suppliers of services and foreign Community suppliers.

The most common national restriction on the free movement of services is the requirement that the supplier must be resident within the Member State in order to lawfully provide a service. Generally, this requirement is justified on the basis of the need to regulate certain services, such as banking, insurance, investment and telecommunications.

The European Court has taken the view that Article 59 has direct effect and abolishes all discrimination against a person providing a service by reason of his or her nationality or the fact that he or she is resident in another Member State, although exceptions to this rule do exist: *Maria van Binsbergen v Bedrijfsvereniging voor de Metaalnijverheid* [1974] ECR 1299. A requirement of residence is not, however, incompatible with the EC Treaty where it has as its purpose 'the application of professional rules justified by the general good'.

Rules relating to the organisation, qualifications, professional ethics, supervision or liability of suppliers of services may therefore be justified where the person who is supplying the services would escape from the ambit of these rules by being established in another Member State. But, the requirement of residence in the territory of the Member State where the service is provided can only be allowed as an exception where the Member State is unable to apply other, less restrictive, measures to ensure respect for these rules: *Gerardus Coenen* v *Sociaal Economische Raad* [1975] ECR 1547.

d) *Community regulation of the supervisory powers of Member States*

While the European Court has recognised the abilities of Member States to supervise certain commercial activities for the public interest, such supervision must be administered in a non-discriminatory manner. Article 59 has been held to abolish all discrimination against the person providing the service by reason of his or her nationality or place of residence. Therefore, a Member State may not impose more onerous obligations on foreign suppliers of services than on national suppliers. Thus, the issue of a licence or supervision by competent authorities must be made available to both foreign and domestic suppliers of services on an equal basis: *Ministere Public* v *Waesmael* [1979] ECR 35; *Alfred John Webb* [1981] ECR 3305.

Restrictions based, directly or indirectly, on discrimination between foreign and domestic suppliers of services will rarely be upheld by the European Court. Further, restrictions of an administrative nature cannot justify any derogation from the principle of the free movement of services, since such restrictions prevent the exercise of one of the fundamental freedoms of the EC Treaty: *EC Commission* v *Germany (Re Regulation of the Insurance Sector)* [1987] 2 CMLR 69.

e) *Non-discriminatory access to public procurement*

Public procurement is the process through which national governmental agencies such as the central government, or local authorities, place contracts for the supply of goods or services. The Department of Trade and Industry estimates that over 15 per cent of the gross domestic product of each Member State of the Community consists of purchases of goods and services by governments and associated bodies and agencies. If these contracts were excluded from the scope of the right to supply services throughout the Community, a serious limitation would be placed on the exercise of this right.

The Community has adopted a number of Directives to provide access to public procurement contracts by Community suppliers of services not resident in the Member State where the services are to be performed. These rules vary according to whether the contract relates to public supply contracts or public work contracts:

i) Public supply contracts: These relate to the provision of goods for the use of governmental organs and are regulated by Council Directive 77/62 (1977), as amended by Council Directive 80/767 (1980) and Council Directive 88/295 (1988).

ii) Public works contracts: These are contracts relating to the construction of buildings and premise and are regulated by Council Directive 71/305 (1971), as amended by Council Directive 89/440 (1989).

iii) Public service contracts: These are contracts for the supply of services and are regulated by Council Directive 92/50 (1992).

A number of additional directives have been enacted by the Council of Ministers in order to achieve the objective of the internal market programme. This Community legislation aims to liberalise public procurement to the same extent as the supply of goods.

f) *Harmonisation of company law*

One of the principal restrictions on the freedom to provide services is the requirement that a supplier must establish a legal presence, generally in the form of an incorporated body, prior to engaging in the supply of services. The harmonisation of company law has therefore been assumed as a primary goal for the achievement of the free movement of services as well as the freedom of establishment.

According to Article 66 of the EC Treaty, companies formed in accordance with the law of a Member State and having their registered office, central administration or principal place of business within the Community shall be treated in the same way as natural persons who are nationals of Member States. While in theory this principle seems simple enough, in practice companies are creatures of the legislation of Member States and are subject to different rights and duties in different states of incorporation. It is difficult to see how a company formed under British law could move its operations to France and still be able to exercise its legal rights and duties under UK law. Rights and duties of companies are, on the whole, non-transferable and companies shifting operations would generally be required to reform under the law of the state to which they are relocating.

In order to approximate the company laws of the Member States for the purpose of harmonising the rights and obligations of companies throughout the Community, a convention, together with a number of regulations and directives, has been adopted.

The Convention on the Mutual Recognition of Companies and Bodies Corporate 1968 was negotiated to give effect to the mutual recognition of companies but, as yet, it has not entered force. In essence it provides that companies formed under the law of one contracting party shall be recognised in another as having the capacity accorded to them by the law under which they were formed, subject to certain derogations.

In addition, a considerable number of directives have been adopted to harmonise company law throughout the Community:

i) Council Directive 68/151 (1968): Requires companies operating in the Community to disclose certain information in the annual accounts.

ii) Council Directive 77/91 (1977): Concerns the formation and maintenance of capital.

iii) Council Directive 78/855 (1978): Relates to mergers between companies incorporated in the same Member State.

iv) Council Directive 78/660 (1978): Regulates the contents of the annual accounts of public and private companies.

v) Council Directive 83/349 (1983): The presentation of consolidated accounts.

vi) Council Directive 84/253 (1984): Deals with the professional qualifications of statutory auditors.

vii) Council Directive 88/627 (1988): Specifies the information which must be published when a major holding in a listed company is acquired.

Each of these directives requires national legislation to incorporate them into the domestic laws of the individual Member States.

g) *Free movement of capital*

Article 67 of the EC Treaty instructs the Member States to progressively abolish all restrictions on the movement of capital between Member States, but only to the extent necessary to ensure the proper functioning of the common market. This provision is designed to remove any discriminatory barriers to the movement of capital which might inhibit freedom to invest capital, particularly for the purpose of providing services.

The free movement of capital is less developed than the other freedoms (free movement of goods, free movement of workers, freedom of establishment and freedom to provide services). Article 67 does not have direct effect and therefore cannot be relied upon by individuals to establish directly enforceable rights: *Casati* [1981] ECR 2595. The European Court has observed that, although Article 67 is considered one of the four fundamental freedoms, its function is closely linked with the economic and monetary policies of the Member States. Since Community cooperation in these fields, particularly monetary union, has been until recently less spectacular than in other areas, the provision cannot, at the moment, be given direct effect.

In fulfilment of the internal market programme, a Council Directive on Capital Movements was adopted in June 1988 and applies to most Member States from 1 July 1990. Spain, Ireland, Greece and Portugal were given extensions until 31 December 1992, to complete the transition.

The objective of the directive is the liberalisation of capital movements by eliminating exchange controls. No limits can be placed on the amount of capital transferred between Member States after the transition period. All restrictions on the actual transfer of capital are abolished, as are all measures which limit the carrying out of underlying transactions (such as trade in goods or the payment of services).

Member States faced with economic problems may be allowed to re-impose restrictions on the movement of capital in exceptional circumstances such as the short-term movement of capital on an exceptional scale, causing disruption of monetary and exchange rate policies.

Member States are also urged to endeavour to attain the same degree of liberalisation in their transactions with third countries as in their transactions with other Member States.

10.3 Relevant cases

Binsbergen v *Bedrijfsvereniging voor de Metaalnijverheid* [1974] ECR 1299: Scope of the right of Member States to restrict the supply of services to those resident within the territory of the Member State.

EC Commission v *Germany (Re Regulation of the Insurance Sector)* [1987] 2 CMLR 69: Considerations of an administrative nature cannot justify derogations from the application of Article 59.

The Queen v *HM Treasury and Commissions of Inland Revenue, ex parte Daily Mail and General Trust plc* [1988] 3 CMLR 713: Neither Article 52 nor 58 of the EC Treaty confer rights on a company incorporated in one Member State to transfer its central management and control to another Member State without re-incorporating.

Casati [1981] ECR 2595: Article 67 of the EC Treaty relating to the free movement of capital does not have direct effect.

10.4 Relevant materials

D Edward, 'Establishment and Services: An Analysis of the Insurance Cases' (1987) 12 EL Rev 231.

L Gormley, 'Public Works Contracts and Freedom to Supply Services' (1983) 133 NLJ 533.

R Hodgin, 'Case Law of the Court of Justice' (1987) 24 CML Rev 273.

10.5 Analysis of questions

The free movement of services is an area of the syllabus which incorporates an extensive number of seemingly divergent subjects. Students must acquaint themselves thoroughly with all aspects of this topic before attempting a question relating to the free movement of services. Among the more popular areas with examiners are the harmonisation of company law, the legal effect of Article 59 and the problem of discrimination between domestic and Community suppliers of services.

10.6 Questions

QUESTION ONE

Michelle is a British national. She travels to France as a tourist and is mugged by a gang of French youths. Her passport and money are stolen and her holiday is ruined. She discovers that in France there exists a criminal injuries compensation scheme, but is shocked to discover that, as a non-French national, she is not entitled to recover any financial damages from the scheme. Advise Michelle.

University of Glasgow LLB Examination
1989 Q9

General Comment

A problem-type question requiring the application of Community law to a set of hypothetical facts.

Skeleton Solution

• Limitations on the rights of individuals under the free movement of workers principle.

• The right to supply services and the right to receive services.

• Decision of the Court of Justice in *Cowan*.

• Limitations of this decision.

Suggested Solution

Article 7 of the EC Treaty establishes the general principle that any discrimination on the grounds of nationality shall be prohibited, but this prohibition is expressly restricted to those subjects which fall within the scope of the Treaty itself. In other words, the prohibition on discrimination does not apply by virtue of the fact that a person is a Community national, but only if the discrimination is perpetrated against an individual exercising his or her rights under Community law.

The principle of non-discrimination is also expressly reformulated in the Treaty provisions regulating the free movement of workers where a positive obligation is placed on Member States to eradicate this form of discrimination. But, the right to non-discriminatory treatment essentially applies to persons as factors of production and not individuals per se. Thus, nationals of Member States are entitled to the same degree of employment protection as nationals, the same conditions of employment as well as the same social and tax advantages: *Wurttembergische Milchverwertung-Sudmilch AG v Salvatore Ugliola* (1969). Further, this principle has been extended to the provision of further education on a non-discriminatory basis: *Blaizot v University of Liège* (1989).

Notwithstanding the scope of these rights, migrant workers are not, however, entitled to the benefits which nationality confers, such as voting rights in governmental elections or to stand for election. The fact that Member States have opened their national territory to the migration of workers within the Community does not mean that they are obliged to extend the benefits of citizenship to migrant workers. In fact, the European Court has expressly held that Member States continue to exercise their powers to regulate the movement of foreign nationals: *Watson v Belmann* (1976).

Since the principle of the free movement of workers would not confer any rights on Michelle in her circumstances, the alternative is to seek redress through the application of Article 59 which establishes the right to provide services. The European Court has, in the past, held that the right to provide services also implies the right to receive services: *Luisi and Carbone v Ministero del Tesoro* (1984). Thus, consumers are entitled to receive services from suppliers of services and, in the exercise of this right, the principle of non-discrimination on the basis of nationality prohibits discrimination between foreign and domestic consumers.

Since tourists are recipients of services, Michelle can claim that, in exercising her right to receive services in France, she is entitled to protection from the French legal system on a non-discriminatory basis. The freedom to travel to receive services therefore implies that the tourist is entitled to the same protection of the law as nationals of that Member State.

The European Court elaborated on the doctrine of non-discrimination as it applies to recipients of services in *Cowan* v *Tresor Public* (1990). This case involved a British national who, while visiting his son in Paris, was assaulted and robbed outside a Metro station by a number of assailants, thereby sustaining severe injuries. The assailants were never apprehended and as a result a claim was initiated for compensation under the appropriate provision of the French Penal Code. This provision, however, specified that victims of violent attacks must either be French nationals or holders of a French identity card in order to claim compensation. The claimant was therefore disqualified from making a claim.

An action was brought in the French Commission D'Indemnisation Des Victims D'Infractions (the equivalent of the Compensation Board for Victims of Crime) in order to review this decision. The Commission referred the matter to the European Court for a preliminary ruling on the question of whether foreign nationals of Member States are entitled to claim compensation for criminal injuries.

The European Court held that the non-discrimination provisions of the Treaty of Rome extend to the free movement of services and in particular the freedom to receive services. Since the victim was a tourist, and thereby a recipient of services in France, the Court held that that he was entitled to protection from harm, and compensation in the event of an infraction, on the same basis as nationals.

Since it is virtually impossible for a foreign national to enter another country without taking advantage of local services, this decision extends the protection of the law of each Member State to nationals of other states. Procedural safeguards for non-residents are, however, permitted in certain circumstances.

Michelle would therefore be entitled to make a claim for compensation before the appropriate French compensation board, and would be entitled to any remedy available to a French national. Whether or not such compensation extends to financial damage and not merely physical injury depends on the terms of the French Penal Code itself.

QUESTION TWO

Wren Construction plc has recently become aware of the existence of an advertisement soliciting tenders for the construction of a local town hall outside Paris. In addition, the advertisement also tenders a contract for the supply of office furniture after the completion of the construction project. Snug Bug, a British subsidiary of Wren Construction, manufactures office equipment. The director of Wren Construction seeks your advice on the following points:

a) What rights does Community law confer on Wren Construction and Snug Bug if they decide to tender for these contracts?

b) Can the French local authority responsible for the construction of the building discriminate in favour of French contractors? and

c) What remedies are available to Wren Construction and Snug Bug in the event that the contracts are awarded contrary to Community law.

Advise Wren Construction and Snug Bug on their rights under Community law.

Question prepared by the Author

General Comment

Another problem-type question, this time dealing with the complexities of public procurement.

Skeleton Solution

- The Community Directives on public works contracts.
- The Community Directives on public supply contracts.
- Principles behind these instruments of Community law.

Suggested Solution

The rules relating to public procurement vary according to whether the contract relates to public supply contracts or public works contracts.

Public supply contracts relate to the provision of goods for the use of governmental organs and are regulated by the Directive of 1977 on Public Procurement (77/62), as amended by Directive 80/767 (1980) and Directive 88/295 (1988). Public works contracts are regulated by Council Directive 71/305 (1971), as amended by Council Directive 89/440 (1989). These are contracts relating to offers for construction of buildings and premises.

The Directives for the public procurement of goods and services all have the same objective: the gradual elimination of discrimination among suppliers for governmental agencies. Three common themes run throughout this legislation: transparency, increasing the scope of applications and compliance.

Supply contracts for governmental bodies must be published in the appropriate section of the Official Journal. Such contracts must refer to European standards which avoids the possibility of introducing discriminating national standards.

Sectors which were formerly excluded from the ambit of earlier Community procurement requirements are opened up to foreign tendering, including water, energy, transport, and for supplies, telecommunications. Proposals before the European Parliament would further reduce excluded sectors.

In addition, a complaints procedures have been established in order to provide remedies against public bodies discriminating in favour of local suppliers. An Enforcement Directive (Council Directive 89/665 (1989)) has been adopted to ensure the proper compliance of these requirements. This permits unsuccessful applicants to petition the Commission to investigate a matter and also provides for the review procedure in local courts ultimately culminating in compensation for parties which have been unlawfully discriminated against.

The contract which Wren Construction seeks to tender for is a public works contract. Council Directive 71/305, as amended, requires governmental agencies to tender such contracts to Community suppliers of services when two conditions are satisfied: the government agency falls within the scope of the Directive; and the contract is valued over the minimum required.

The Directive applies to all State, regional and local, authorities governed by public law. A body established by public body means any body established for the specific purpose of meeting the needs of the general public and not having an industrial or commercial character. A list of bodies to which the Directive applies forms Annex I to the Directive. For present purposes, it can be assumed that the construction of the local town hall is a function of either the local or regional government, both of which fall within the scope of the Directive.

The second condition relates to the value of the contract. As amended, the threshold for the public tendering of works contracts has been raised to five million ECU. Such contracts have to be advertised in the Official Journal for tender by any supplier from any Member State. All the legislation required to implement this scheme has been passed.

If these two conditions are satisfied, the substantive provisions of Directive 89/440 are applicable to the contract. A specific procedure must be followed for the tendering of the contract. First, the contract must be advertised in the Official Journal of the Community. Second, any supplier who submits an offer which is rejected must be informed of the reasons why the offer was rejected. Third, a number of criteria are established for the award of the contract. An acceptance by the government agency must be on the basis of the lowest price or, the most economically advantageous tender. In determining the most economically advantageous tender, the government agency is required to consider a number of criteria including price, period of completion, running costs, profitability and technical merit.

Aggregation rules are also specified which prevent governmental agencies from breaking down contracts into lesser amounts in order to fall below the thresholds. In particular, these rules concentrate on renewal contracts and sub-divided contracts. By dividing public works contracts, the governmental authorities may be able to create a number of individual contracts which fall below the five million ECU threshold for tendering public supply contracts.

The contract for the supply of office furniture which is sought by Snug Bug is also subject to Community legislation, and in particular Council Directive 77/62. Again this Directive is applicable only to certain governmental agencies and according to minimum price thresholds. Again the Directive is applicable to government agencies regulated by Annex I to the Directive, which would again include the local or regional authorities in this case.

However, in this case, a threshold is applicable. A minimum threshold of 200,000 ECU is specified for supply contracts subject to the Community rules.

Again, if a public supply contract fulfils these criteria, a number of obligations must be satisfied by the tendering authority. First, the contract must be published. Second, specifications must be given in European standards where possible. Third, the same criteria for awarding contracts must be observed as was the case in public works contracts.

The aim of these Directives is to eliminate discrimination between domestic and other Community suppliers of services. Therefore, if the contracts fall within the scope of these Directives, the governmental authorities or agencies cannot indulge in discrimination against Wren Construction or Snug Bug.

These Directives also establish complaints procedures which unsuccessful tenderers can utilise in order to obtain redress in the event that discrimination has been perpetrated. However, in general, remedies will be sought through national courts, according to national standards and procedures, and this gives rise to the problem that complete harmonisation in this field has not be achieved.

QUESTION THREE

The Commission has embarked on an extensive programme of harmonisation of company law and many Directives it has proposed have been adopted. However, proposals for granting employees certain rights to participate in the corporate decision-making process is proving to be one of the stumbling blocks on the way to complete harmonisation. Discuss.

University of Glasgow LLB Examination
1989 Q4

General Comment

A narrative question requiring an answer outlining the main features of the Community company law harmonisation programme.

Skeleton Solution

• The harmonisation programme.
• Directives on company law.
• The proposed Fifth Directive.
• British objections to the Fifth Directive.

Suggested Solution

The field of company law is no stranger to Community law. However, since in the past Community law relating to companies has taken the form of Directives which have been incorporated into the United Kingdom by domestic legislation, this has not been a completely visible phenomenon. The First EC Directive of 1968 (68/151) required that companies operating within the Community were obliged to disclose certain information in the annual accounts and was implemented in the Companies Act 1980 and the Companies Act 1985.

The Second Directive of 1976 (77/91) was also implemented by this legislation and in fact to date a total of nine directives have been adopted [Third Directive of 1978 (78/855); Fourth Directive of 1978 (78/660); Sixth Directive of 1982 (82/891); Seventh Directive of 1983 (83/349); Eighth Directive of 1984 (84/253); Eleventh Directive of 1989 (89/528); and Twelfth Directive of 1989 (89/101)].

In addition two directives have been adopted in relation to the banking industry (Bank Branches Directive of 1989 (89/117); Bank Accounts Directive of 1986 (86/635)).

While these directives have been mainly confined to information and data in the accounts of public bodies, the remaining directives which have been proposed are not so restrictive and in fact, if adopted, would signal a radical transformation in existing UK company law.

The Fifth Directive of 1983 (83/185) forms the core of the proposed harmonisation of European company law and, at this moment, the proposals are under discussion at the Second Reading Stage of the Council Working Group. As it stands at present, this tentative directive proposes to introduce a two-tier management structure for companies, a scheme which is already familiar to most continental Member States. Instead of a company being under the direction of one managing body – the Board of Directors – there would be two different bodies: the Management Organ (or Executive Organ) which would make the management decisions of the corporation; and the Supervisory Organ, which would supervise the actions of the Management Organ.

The Supervisory Organ would have the power to authorise certain actions by the Management Organ including transfers of business, mergers, closures and structural changes and it would be entitled to receive a written report of the company's affairs every three months. It would have exclusive power to appoint and dismiss members of the Management Organ.

In relation to the appointment and dismissal of members of the Supervisory Organ, a number of alternative procedures would be possible where the company has more than 1,000 employees: appointment and dismissal could be carried out by the shareholders and employees, by the shareholders acting alone, or by co-option (which, in some cases, would be subject to veto by employees).

In the face of British opposition to this proposal, a short-term concession has been made. Where this two-tier structure would be impractical to enforce then, as a short term measure, a single-tier structure based on the Management Organ could be adopted provided that different members undertake distinct management and supervisory roles.

The British government also opposes this harmonised company structure on a number of other grounds. First, the participation of workers in the management of companies, while common in continental companies, is alien to the British conception of management within limited liability companies.

Second, the directive requires detailed disclosure of information in the minutes of meetings held at the management level.

Third, in order to secure the independence of auditors, company accounts can only be audited by the same accounting firm after a certain period of time has elapsed. Auditors cannot be retained for periods longer than one year unless the required period has elapsed since the company inspected the accounts.

11 EUROPEAN COMPETITION LAW – ARTICLE 85 EC TREATY

11.1 Introduction

11.2 Key points

11.3 Relevant cases

11.4 Relevant materials

11.5 Analysis of questions

11.6 Questions

11.1 Introduction

Articles 85 and 86 of the EC Treaty are the pillars of the Community competition policy. Each of these articles addresses different forms of anti-competitive behaviour. Article 85 (the subject of this chapter) prohibits agreements and concerted practices among private commercial bodies if they affect trade between Member States and distort, prevent or restrict competition. Article 86 (the subject of the next chapter) prohibits commercial practices by one or more enterprises where such practices amount to an abuse of a dominant position with the Community. These two provisions therefore seek to achieve separate objectives. Article 85 attempts to eradicate unfair commercial practices which result from collaboration between enterprises while Article 86 strikes at companies taking advantage of dominant or monopoly positions in the market-place.

11.2 Key points

a) *The subjects of European Community law*

Both Articles 85 and 86 apply to 'undertakings' although this term is not expressly defined. The European Court has, however, defined an undertaking as:

'a single organisation of personal, tangible and intangible elements, attached to an autonomous legal entity and pursuing a long-term economic aim': *Mannesmann* v *High Authority* [1962] ECR 357.

This definition embraces all natural and legal persons engaged in commercial activities, whether profit-making or otherwise. The fact that an entity is a non profit-making organisation is irrelevant for the purpose of identifying an undertaking: *Heintz van Landewyck Sarl* v *EC Commission* [1980] ECR 3125. The critical characteristic is whether or not the entity is engaged in economic or commercial activities.

The application of European competition law is not restricted to undertakings located within the Community, but extends to undertakings whose registered offices are situated outside the Community: *Beguelin* v *GL Imports Export* [1971]

ECR 949. This is because European competition law is not concerned with the behaviour of entities but rather the effects of such behaviour on the competitive environment within the Community. See the *Woodpulp Cartel Case* [1988] 4 CMLR 901.

b) *Commercial practices prohibited by Article 85 EC Treaty*

Article 85(1) of the EC Treaty addresses different forms of concerted behaviour between two or more undertakings and specifically provides:

'The following shall be prohibited as incompatible with the common market: all agreements between undertakings, decisions by associations of undertakings, and concerted practices which may affect trade between Member States and which have as their object or effect the prevention, restriction or distortion of competition within the Common Market, and in particular those which:

a) directly or indirectly fix purchase or selling prices or any other trading conditions;

b) limit or control production, markets, technical development, or investment;

c) share markets or sources of supply;

d) apply dissimilar conditions to equivalent transactions with other trading parties, thereby placing them at a competitive disadvantage;

e) make the conclusion of contracts subject to acceptance by the other parties of supplementary obligations which, by their nature or according to commercial usage, have no connection with the subject of such contracts.'

All agreements, decisions and practices prohibited under Article 85(1) are automatically void unless exempt from the scope of this subsection by virtue of Article 85(3).

The Article itself specifically enumerates a number of examples of anti-competitive behaviour in order to illustrate the types of conduct which the provision is intended to limit.

i) Price fixing

Practices which have the effect of directly or indirectly fixing buying or selling prices for products are incompatible with competition policy. This includes arrangements whereby undertakings agree on the particular trading conditions which are applicable to their business dealings, such as discounts or credit terms. Another example of prohibited practices is agreements to fix prices and to apportion markets: *Re Italian Flat Glass Suppliers* [1992] 5 CMLR 502.

ii) Limitation or control of production

Quotas on production and supply cartels are contrary to competition policy, as are arrangements to control marketing, technical development or investment. An illustration of this type of practice is the setting of volume targets for production: *PVC Cartel Case* [1992] 4 CMLR 357.

iii) Allocation of markets

Practices which allow potential competitors to apportion a market in a particular product amongst each other on a mutually exclusive basis are prohibited. This practice is condemned when the apportionment is made on the basis of either geography or product ranges: see *Siemens-Fanne* [1988] 4 CMLR 945; and *ACF Chemiefarma NV* v *EC Commission* [1970] ECR 661.

iv) Application of dissimilar conditions

By applying dissimilar sales conditions to identical transactions one undertaking may place another at a competitive disadvantage. For example, an agreement to provide one purchaser with more advantageous purchasing conditions than another purchaser would result in unfair discrimination.

v) Imposition of supplementary obligations

Agreements requiring the fulfilment of supplementary obligations which, by their nature or commercial usage, have no connection with the original subject matter of a contract, are prohibited. For example, agreements which require a buyer of one product or service to purchase another product or service unconnected with the first transaction would amount to the imposition of a supplementary obligation.

This list of anti-competitive behaviour is intended to illustrate the most common forms of conduct which will infringe Article 85(1) and is not intended to be exhaustive.

c) *Agreements, decisions by associations of undertakings and concerted practices*

Article 85 identifies three separate arrangements which may contravene competition law: agreements, decisions, and concerted practices. Each of these concepts refers to a different form of commercial practice among undertakings.

i) Agreements

The term 'agreements' includes all contracts in the sense of binding contractual obligations, whether written, verbal, or partly written and partly verbal. Further, an arrangement between two or more parties may constitute an agreement for the purposes of Article 85(1) even although the arrangement in question has no binding legal effect: see *Atka A/S* v *BP Kemi A/S* [1979] CMLR 684.

Unrecorded understandings, the mutual adoption of common rules, and so-called 'gentlemen's agreements' are also agreements for the purposes of competition law: *Boehringer* v *EC Commission* [1970] ECR 769.

Agreements which prevent, distort or restrict competition are classified either as horizontal agreements or vertical agreements. Horizontal agreements are arrangements made between competitors or potential competitors while vertical agreements are arrangements between undertakings at the differing stages of process through which a product or service passes from the manufacturer to the final consumer.

Illustrations of horizontal agreements include agreements dividing markets among competitors, price fixing, export and import bans, cartels, and boycotts.

Examples of vertical agreements include exclusive distribution agreements, exclusive patent licensing agreements, exclusive purchasing agreements, and tying.

ii) Decisions of associations of undertakings

The concept of decisions of associations of undertakings refers to the creation of rules establishing trade associations, as well as any other formal or informal decisions or recommendations made under such rules.

Prohibited decisions of trade associations would include recommending prices, fixing discounts, collective boycotts and the negotiation of restrictive contract clauses. A recommendation by a trade association may constitute a decision, even although such acts are not binding under the constitution of the association in question: see *Vereeniging van Cementhandelaren* v *EC Commission* [1972] ECR 977.

iii) Concerted practices

The term 'concerted practice' refers to commercial cooperation in the absence of a formal agreement. The European Court has defined a concerted practice as:

'a form of coordination between enterprises that has not yet reached the point where it is a contract in the true sense of the word but which, in practice, consciously substitutes practical cooperation for the risks of competition': *Imperial Chemical Industries* v *EC Commission* [1972] ECR 619.

Manufacturers and producers are, of course, entitled to take into consideration prices set for similar goods by competitors. It is only when potential competitors deliberately and intentionally agree to coordinate pricing policy that a concerted practice arises.

Commercial cooperation will likely amount to a concerted practice if it enables the entities under investigation to consolidate their market positions to the detriment of the principle of free movement of goods within the Community and the freedom of consumers to select products: *Cooperatieve Vereeniging 'Suiker Unie' UA* v *EC Commission* [1975] ECR 1663.

It is contrary to the rules on competition contained in Article 85 for a producer to cooperate with its competitors in order to determine a coordinated course of action relating to pricing policy, particularly if this cooperation ensures the elimination of all uncertainty among competitors as regards matters such as price increases, the subject matter of increases, and the date and place of increases.

d) *Effect on trade between Member States*

No agreement, decision or concerted practice may be held contrary to Community competition law unless it affects patterns of trade between Member States. As the European Court has observed:

'It is only to the extent to which agreements may affect trade between Member States that the deterioration in competition falls under the prohibition of Community law contained in Article 85; otherwise it escapes the prohibition': *Consten and Grundig* v *EC Commission* [1966] ECR 299.

This requirement is intended to enable a distinction to be drawn between unfair commercial practices which have only national ramifications and those practices which have Community implications.

The effect of an agreement on trade between Member States is ascertained by reference to the principle of free movement of goods and, in particular, the realisation of the objective of creating a single market among all the Member States of the Community. An agreement, decision or practice will affect trade between Member States if it is capable of constituting a threat, either direct or indirect, actual or potential, to the freedom of trade between Member States in a manner which might harm the attainment of the objective of a single market between states: *Remia BV* v *EC Commission* [1985] ECR 2545.

Actual harm need not be established. It is sufficient that the agreement is likely to prevent, restrict or distort competition to a sufficient degree: *Société Technique Minière* v *Maschinenbau Ulm GmbH* [1966] ECR 235.

It should also be noted that there is no need for there to be any overt cross-border element in the transaction for an arrangement to affect trade between Member States. Thus, arrangements between producers to set target prices for the sale of products, even although they applied in only one Member State, have been considered by the Commission to infringe Article 85(1): *Cementhandelaren* v *EC Commission* [1972] ECR 977.

There is no violation of Article 85 if an agreement or practice has only a negligible effect on trade between Member States. Early in the jurisprudence of competition law, the European Court held that:

'[A]n agreement falls outside the prohibition in Article 85 when it has only an insignificant effect on the markets, taking into account the weak position which the persons concerned have on the market of the product in question': *Frans Volk* v *Vervaercke* [1969] ECR 295.

Insignificant agreements escape the prohibition of Article 85 because their relative effect on trade between Member States is negligible.

e)   *The object or effect of preventing, restricting or distorting competition within the Community*

Agreements, decisions and practice are only prohibited under Article 85 if, in addition to satisfying all other relevant criteria, they have as their object or effect the prevention, restriction or distortion of competition within the Community. Such arrangements may have either the object or the effect of distorting competition. These options are clearly intended to be alternative, not cumulative, tests.

An agreement will have the object of distorting competition if, prior to its implementation, it can be determined that the agreement would prevent or restrict competition which might take place between the parties to the agreement: *Consten and Grundig* v *EC Commission* [1966] ECR 299. If an agreement does not have the object of restricting competition, whether or not an agreement has the effect of distorting competition may be determined by market analysis.

f) *Activities outside the scope of Article 85(1)*

An agreement, decision or practice may be excluded from the scope of Article 85(1) on four principal grounds: (i) where an agreement has been given negative clearance by the Commission; (ii) where an agreement is of minor importance; (iii) where an agreement regulates relations between undertakings to which the competition rules are inapplicable; and (iv) where agreements and practices benefit from the exemptions under Article 85(3).

i) Negative clearance

An undertaking proposing to enter into an agreement or engage in a practice which might be considered to restrict, prevent or distort competition may apply to the Commission for negative clearance in respect of the arrangement. Negative clearance is a determination made by the Commission that, on the basis of the facts in its possession, it believes that there are no grounds under Article 85(1) for action to be taken against the submitted agreement, decision or practice.

In order to obtain negative clearance, the undertakings submitting the application must prove that the agreement, decision or practice is excluded from the scope of the applicable competition provision. Negative clearance is therefore not strictly a separate ground for exclusion from the competition provisions of the EC Treaty, but rather certification that an agreement or practice, in the opinion of the Commission, falls outside Community competition law.

Frequently, instead of making a formal decision on a matter, the Commission may notify the undertaking by correspondence that no action is required to conform to the terms of Article 85(1). Such correspondence is known as a 'comfort letter'. It offers no absolute protection from investigation by the Commission, particularly where the facts submitted by the undertaking vary from the true facts of the case. But, if an investigation is subsequently initiated, the statement may be pleaded in mitigation should an infringement be established.

ii) Agreements of minor importance

Agreements which would otherwise be caught by Article 85(1) may nevertheless be exempt from its scope if they are incapable of affecting trade between Member States or restricting competition to any appreciable extent. This principle is known as the de minimus rule and was originally conceived by the European Court in the *Volk Case* above. Agreements fall outside the prohibition of Article 85(1) if they have an 'insignificant effect' on the market in such products.

The Commission has published a notice intended to establish guidelines for the application of the de minimus rule, the basis of which is the jurisprudence of the European Court in this subject. The Commission has indicated that, in normal circumstances, agreements would fall outside Article 85(1) by virtue of the de minimus rule, if two conditions can be established:

• market share: the goods or services which are the subject of the agreement and its immediate substitutes do not constitute more than 5 per cent of the total market for such goods or services in the area of the common market affected by the agreement; and

- turnover: the aggregate annual turnover of the undertakings participating in the arrangement does not exceed 200 million ECU (approximately £135 million): Commission Notice Concerning Agreements, Decisions and Concerted Practices of Minor Importance (1986).

The intention of the notice is to allow small and medium sized undertakings to benefit from the rule exempting minor agreements from the rigours of Article 85(1).

iii) Commercial relations to which competition rules do not apply

The competition rules established under Article 85 do not apply to two particular commercial relationships: between principals and agents; and between parents and subsidiaries.

From the beginning of Community competition policy administration contracts entered into between principals and commercial agents have been traditionally excluded from the scope of Article 85(1) so long as the agent is concerned with the simple negotiation of transactions on behalf of the principal: Commission Notice Relating to Exclusive Dealing Contracts with Commercial Agents (1962). While the non-application of Article 85(1) to such relationships legally has the form of a group negative clearance, the application of competition rules to such relations is clearly contrary to the policy of promoting competition throughout the Community.

A subsidiary which is under the control of a parent company is not considered to be capable of anti-competitive behaviour in relation to its parent since it has no autonomous decision-making capacity. Restrictive agreements and anti-competitive concerned practices between parents and non-autonomous subsidiaries are therefore not subject to the rules of Community competition law. As the European Court has explicitly ruled:

'Article 85 is not concerned with agreements or concerted practices between undertakings belonging to the same concern and having the status of parent company and subsidiary, if the undertakings form an economic unit within which the subsidiary has no real freedom to determine its course of action on the market, and if the agreements or practices are concerned merely with the internal allocation of tasks as between the undertakings': *Hydrotherm Geratebau* v *Andreoli* [1984] ECR 2999.

Two conditions are therefore required in order to avoid the application of Article 85(1) on this basis:

- The subsidiary cannot have any real freedom to dictate its own course of action in the market place. Control over the conduct of a subsidiary is determined by reference to the size of the shareholding held by the parent.
- The restrictive agreement itself must relate only to the allocation of responsibilities and tasks between the parent and the subsidiary.

iv) Exempt agreements and practices

Article 85(3) specifically creates criteria for exempting agreements, decisions and concerted practices from the effects of Article 83(1). Agreements and practices which satisfy the exemption criteria established by Article 85(3) are not void under Article 85(2) nor subject to the imposition of fines. Two positive and two negative tests must be satisfied for an agreement to be exempt and the onus is on the applicant to establish these conditions are present:

- the agreement, decision or practice must contribute to improving the production or distribution of goods or promoting technical or economic progress;
- a fair share of the resulting benefit must accrue to the consumer;
- the agreement or practice must not impose any restrictions which go beyond the positive aims of the agreement or practice; and
- these restrictions must not create a possibility of eliminating competition in respect of a substantial part of the products in question.

Two types of exemption are granted on the basis of the authority of this provision: (1) individual exemptions which are issued on the basis of an individual application; and (2) block exemptions which are applicable to categories of agreements. Subject to review by the Court of First Instance and thereafter the European Court itself, the European Commission has exclusive authority to create exemptions on the basis of Article 85(3).

The procedure for obtaining an individual exemption is specified in Council Regulation 17/62. Individual exemptions are granted in the form of Commission decisions. These decisions are issued for a limited period and may be conditional on the fulfilment of certain obligations. A decision may be renewed if the relevant conditions continue to be satisfied. The Commission may revoke or amend a decision granting an individual exemption in the event of a change of circumstances. Naturally an individual exemption will only be granted if the four conditions on Article 85(3) are satisfied.

To reduce the bureaucratic burdens imposed by applications for individual exemption, the Commission is empowered to establish group exemption categories: Council Regulation 19/65 and Council Regulation 2821/71. The Commission has enacted a number of Regulations in order to grant group exemption to a number of types of agreements including exclusive distribution agreements, exclusive purchasing agreements, patent licensing agreements, motor vehicle distribution and servicing agreements, specialisation agreements, research and development agreements, franchising agreements, and know-how agreements.

If an agreement falls within the scope of a group exemption under a Commission regulation, the parties to the agreement are not required to notify the Commission of the agreement and the parties cannot be fined by the Commission for violating competition law on that basis.

g) *Remedies through the national courts*

Articles 85 and 86 of the EC Treaty have direct effect and may be relied on by private individuals against other private parties in the national courts. Three remedies in particular should be noted:

i) These provisions may form the basis for an action of damages against the party indulging in anti-competitive practices for injury caused to the business activities of the plaintiff: *Garden Cottage Foods Ltd* v *Milk Marketing Board* [1984] AC 130.

ii) Article 85(2) declares that any agreement contrary to Article 85(1) is void. The European Court has however applied the doctrine of severability to this provision and only those terms of an agreement which are contrary to the article are void and the rest remain in force: *Delimitis* v *Henninger Bräu AG* [1992] 5 CMLR 210.

iii) An infringement of Article 85(1) may also form the basis of an action of injunction to prevent the party allegedly infringing competition law from continuing to do so.

In order to develop co-ordination between the Commission and the national courts in this area, the Commission has recently published a Notice to National Courts on the Application of Articles 85 and 86 (1993). This Notice sets out in detail the procedure which national courts should follow if an allegation of an infringement of Community competition law arises before them.

In fact, the Commission has adopted a deliberate policy of encouraging private parties to use domestic court procedures rather than complaining direct to the Commission by declining to investigate complaints unless there are important 'Community considerations' to be taken into account. This policy has been supported by the European Court: see *Automec* v *EC Commission* [1992] 5 CMLR 431.

11.3 Relevant cases

ICI v *EC Commission* [1972] ECR 619: Definition of the concept of concerted practice, together with the identification of the requisite criteria.

Remia BV v *EC Commission* [1985] ECR 2445: Decision of the European Court applying the test necessary to identify whether or not an agreement has an effect on trade between Member States.

Metro v *SB-Grossmarkte GmbH* v *EC Commission (No 2)* [1986] ECR 3021: Identification of the scope of the requirement that an agreement must have the effect of distorting competition before contravening Community competition law.

Woodpulp Cartel Case [1988] 4 CMLR 901: An example of the application of the principle of extraterritoriality to Community competition law by the European Court.

Re Italian Flat Glass Suppliers [1992] 5 CMLR 502: the Commission is permitted to apply Articles 85(1) and 86 to the same parties and the application of these articles is not mutually exclusive.

Delimitis v *Henninger Bräu AG* [1992] 5 CMLR 210: a classic case for the identification of the relevant market in investigations conducted under Article 85.

11.4 Relevant materials

D G Goyder, *EC Competition Law* (1993).

I Van Bael & J-F Bellis, *European Competition Law* (1990).

V Korah, *EC Competition Law and Practice* (1991).

C W Bellamy et al, *Common Market Law and Competition* (1993).

R Goebel, 'Metro II's Confirmation of the Selective Distribution Rules' (1993) 24 CMLR 605.

J Shaw, 'Group Exemptions and Exclusive Distribution and Purchasing Agreements' (1985) 34 ICLQ 190.

L Brittan, 'The Future of EC Competition Policy' (1993) EBL Rev 27.

11.5 Analysis of questions

European competition law is perhaps the most complex element of the Community law syllabus, not only due to the nature of the subject-matter, but also because the principles of competition law have been mainly developed by the European Commission and the ECJ. However, it is an extremely popular area for examiners. Students should therefore be familiar with the terms of Article 85(1), the types of agreement prohibited by Article 85, and the exceptions to Article 85.

11.6 Questions

QUESTION ONE

What is meant by the expression 'concerted practice', and what role does this concept play in EC competition law?

University of London LLB Examination
(for External Students) European Community Law 1991 Q4

General Comment

A straightforward question requiring elaboration of one of the basic concepts of Community competition law.

Skeleton Solution

- Co-ordination of commercial behaviour.
- Degree of co-operation required to establish a concerted practice.
- The secretive nature of concerted practices and the problem of evidence.
- The policy of the Commission and the existence of a presumption given certain circumstances.

Suggested Solution

Article 85(1) identifies three separate practices which may contravene Community competition law: agreements, decisions and concerted practices. Each of these concepts refers to a different form of commercial practice or arrangement among parties.

The term 'concerted practice' refers to forms of commercial co-operation that exist in the absence of a formal agreement. More precisely, a concerted practice, according to the European Court, is:

'... a form of co-ordination between enterprises that has not yet reached the point where it is a contract in the true sense of the word but which, in practice, consciously substitutes practical co-operation for the risks of competition': *ICI v EC Commission* (1972).

The essence of a concerted practice is co-operation. Naturally, manufacturers, producers, distributors and suppliers take into account the pricing policies and marketing strategies of competitors when calculating the price of goods and this is an acceptable practice. It is only when a conscious decision is taken to co-ordinate marketing policy that an arrangement becomes a concerted practice.

But, a concerted practice need not involve a detailed and concise plan or strategy. Lesser degrees of co-operation are sufficient. However, some form of direct or indirect contact with the object of influencing actual or potential competition is necessary to establish a concerted practice. Such contacts frequently take the form of negotiations, conferences, discussions, exchanges of views, the swapping of policy documents and communication of market sensitive information.

Concerted practices are only prohibited under Community competition law if they affect trade between Member States and prevent, restrict or distort the conditions of competition within the Community. Only if a concerted practice produces anti-competitive effects can it be challenged under Community law.

A concerted practice will probably be contrary to Community law if it enables the parties involved to secure their positions in a market, or allows them to increase their respective shares of a market. Equally, a concerted practice is prohibited if it interferes with the free movement of goods or diminishes the freedom of the consumer to select between products: see *Sugar Cartel Cases* (1975) and (1976). Also, if parties co-operate to ensure the elimination of all uncertainty in relation to matters such as price increases, supply, and the date and place of changes in marketing strategies, it is likely that the parties will be engaging in unlawful conduct.

The nature of a concerted practice is essentially secretive, and the Commission has largely been engaged in identifying practices, not by way of notification, but after investigations into certain economic sectors. This involves comparisons of actual market conditions with the normal conditions prevailing in particular sectors.

For example, in the *Dyestuffs Case* (1972), the European Court held that the Commission had been correct in inferring the existence of a concerted practice from the coincidence of price increases. The timing of such rises could not logically be explained by reference to the normal market conditions of the sector since such conditions rarely, if ever, produced parallel, yet independent, price rises.

Evidence of a concerted practice is usually circumstantial, there generally being no documents to prove the intended course of action. This has led the Commission to assume a policy of requiring undertakings to explain their conduct in suspicious circumstances.

By way of illustration, in the *Woodpulp Cartel Case* (1988), the Commission demonstrated the existence of a concerted practice by showing that the price of certain products bore no relationship to either supply or demand. This scenario could not be adequately explained by the parties under investigation. Since commodity prices in general fluctuate wildly in relation to changes in supply and demand, there was a prima facie case of a concerted practice.

QUESTION TWO

British Breweries plc is an important producer of beer in the United Kingdom. Statistics show that British Breweries account for some 12 per cent of all beer sold in the United Kingdom but that its British Brewlite is especially successful and accounts for 40 per cent of all non-alcoholic beer consumed in the UK.

British Breweries want to establish a German subsidiary but have been advised that most retailers in Germany have agreed to purchase non-alcoholic beer only from the German Brewers' Association. The Association checks the quality of its members' products. However, there is a two-year trading requirement in Germany before a new brewery can be admitted to the Association.

Advise British Breweries as to the significance, if any, of EC law for each of the above aspects of its business.

adapted from University of London LLB Examination
(for External Students) European Community Law 1990 Q7

General Comment

A problem-type question involving the application of Article 85 to hypothetical circumstances.

Skeleton Solution

- Is there a prohibited practice?
- Does this practice affect trade between Member States and distort competition?
- Application of individual or group exemption.
- Alternative methods of challenge.

Suggested Solution

In order to ascertain whether or not a practice infringes Community competition policy, three separate determinations must be made: (1) the activity in question must constitute an agreement, decision or concerted practice as prescribed by Article 85(1); (2) the practice must affect trade between Member States; and (3) the practice must prevent, restrict or distort competition.

Both the German beer retailers and the German Brewers Association (GBA) are undertakings for the purpose of Article 85(1). All natural and legal persons engaged in economic activities constitute undertakings, regardless of whether or not they are profit-making or otherwise. The fact that the GBA is a non-profit making organisation would be irrelevant for the purpose of identifying it as an undertaking.

Article 85(1) addresses decisions of associations of undertakings, whether formal or informal. Therefore any decision made by the GBA – as an association of undertakings – is subject to review under Community competition law. Further, its decisions need not be legally binding. In the case, *Re Fire Insurance* Case 45/85, the Commission applied Article 85 to a 'recommendation', described as 'non-binding' by an association of insurers in Germany, that premiums for various classes of policy be raised by a stipulated percentage. The conclusive factor is the ability of the association, in fact if not in law, to determine the conduct and behaviour of its members.

It is also immaterial whether the GBA is publicly or privately established. Competition law makes no distinction between public and private commercial bodies for the purpose of identifying undertakings. The term applies to all state bodies engaged in commercial activities: *IAZ* v *EC Commission* (1983). Furthermore, GBA's rules themselves are a product of an agreement and thus potentially contravene Article 85.

Naturally, the decisions of the GBA affect trade between Member States. A decision will affect trade between Member States if it is capable of constituting a threat, either direct or indirect, actual or potential, to the freedom to trade between Member States in a manner which might harm the attainment of the objectives of a single market: *Remia BV* v *EC Commission* (1985). The fact that the GBA effectively prevents foreign sellers from entering the German non-alcoholic beer market is more than sufficient to establish that its decisions affect trade between Member States.

Article 85(1) refers to decisions which 'have as their object or effect the prevention, restriction or distortion of competition' within the common market, to an appreciable degree. It is sufficient that a decision of an association of undertakings has as its object the restriction of competition without this necessarily representing the common intention of the parties: see *Consten and Grundig* v *EC Commission* (1966).

Competition is clearly severely restricted if not prevented by the two year trading requirement imposed in Germany by the GBA. Since most retailers purchase non-alcoholic beer only from members of the GBA, any brewery attempting to enter the market would have to trade for two years, selling to a very limited number of retailers – a venture which would not be commercially viable. The two year trading requirement acts as a disincentive to new competitors entering the market and effectively closes the market to new entrants to the market. It is immaterial that the arrangement is a vertical agreement between undertakings operating at different levels.

Since the two year trading requirement does not appear to be covered by any of the block exemptions, and presumably has not been granted an individual exemption, only the de minimus rule would apply. However, the sheer magnitude of the domination of the market suggests that the de minimus defence would be inapplicable.

British Breweries should therefore be advised to make a complaint to the Commission under Regulation 17/62, Articles 3(1) and 3(2). British Breweries is a party with a sufficient legitimate interest. If the Commission decides not to initiate proceedings and notifies British Breweries accordingly, British Breweries will have sufficient locus standi to bring an action for annulment under Article 173. Further, if the Commission takes no action British Breweries can bring Article 175 proceedings.

GBA could seek an exemption under Article 85(3) for the decision, primarily on the ground that the two year trading requirement ensures that any new brewer is a reliable, quality producer of non-alcoholic beers. This supervision process, it could be argued, contributes to improved production which inevitably benefits the consumers and retailers.

However, these arguments are likely to fail for three reasons. First, the benefit of the two year trading requirement is not strictly economic. Second, a two year requirement goes substantially beyond what is absolutely necessary to achieve the objectives regarded as beneficial. Third, the measure has resulted in the elimination of a substantial degree of competition.

British Breweries could also challenge the decision of the GBA on the ground that it breaches the right of an undertaking to establish itself anywhere in the Community under Article 52 of the EC Treaty.

QUESTION THREE

Outline the origins and evolution of the de minimus rule which exempts small businesses from the application of Article 85 of the EC Treaty.

Question prepared by the Author

General Comment

A narrative question requiring a descriptive answer.

Skeleton Solution

• Origins of the de minimus rule – effect on trade between Member States.
• Jurisprudence of the Court.
• Commission regulations.

Suggested Solution

No agreement, decision or concerted practice may be held contrary to Community competition law unless it affects patterns of trade between Member States. Commercial practices are capable of infringing Article 85 only to the extent to which they affect trade between Member States. This requirement is intended to enable a distinction to be drawn between unfair commercial practices which have only national ramifications and those practices which have Community implications.

Consequently, there is no violation of Article 85 if an agreement or practice has only a negligible effect on trade between Member States. Early in the jurisprudence of competition law, the European Court held that an agreement falls outside the prohibition in Article 85 when it has only an insignificant effect on the markets, taking into account the weak position which the persons concerned have in the market for the product in question: *Frans Volk* v *Veraercke* (1969). Insignificant agreements therefore escape the prohibition of Article 85 because their relative effect on trade between Member States is negligible.

In order to benefit from this de minimus ruling two conditions have to be satisfied by an agreement, decision or practice. First, the products covered by the agreement must constitute an insignificant part of the market for identical and similar products. Second, the turnover of the undertakings involved must not exceed limits which would allow them to exercise a strong influence over the market in the product: *Distillers Co* v *EC Commission* (1980).

'Insignificant effect' has not been defined by the Court, but in *Miller* v *EC Commission* (1978), an agreement extending to approximately 5 per cent of the total market in sound recordings in Germany was held to be sufficient to be caught by Article 85(1). See also *AEG* v *EC Commission* (1983).

In addition, undertakings entering into agreements which concern volumes of sales which might qualify under the de minimus rule will not escape the prohibition if one or more of the undertakings involved are of sufficient importance for their behaviour to be considered capable of influencing patterns of trade. The Court has tended to refuse to apply the de minimus rule, even though the market share of the products involved in the agreement is relatively small, if large undertakings are concerned. In *Musique Diffusion Française* v *EC Commission* (1983), the Court held that, although the two undertakings involved maintained market shares of less than 4 per cent in the relevant markets, the agreement was not excluded from Article 85(1) under the de minimus rule because the relevant market in the products was fragmented and the market shares of the applicants of London LLVby brand were greater than their competitors.

Similarly, in *Distillers Co* v *EC Commission* above, the Court refused to apply the de minimus rule to a product which constituted a mere fraction of the market in spirits in the UK but which was manufactured by a large undertaking involved in the marketing of a variety of other spirits.

The European Commission has in fact codified the jurisprudence of the European Court by publishing guidelines which establish specific thresholds for the application of Article 85. The Commission has published a notice intended to establish guidelines for the application of the de minimus rule, the basis of which is the jurisprudence of the European Court in this subject: Commission Notice Concerning Agreements, Decisions and Concerted Practices of Minor Importance (1986).

The Commission has indicated that, in normal circumstances, agreements would fall outside Article 85(1) by virtue of the de minimus rule, if two conditions can be established:

a)   market share: the goods or services which are the subject of the agreement and its immediate substitutes do not constitute more than 5 per cent of the total market for such goods or services in the area of the common market affected by the agreement; and

b)   turnover: the aggregate annual turnover of the undertakings participating in the arrangement does not exceed 200 million ECU (approximately £140 million).

The intention of the notice is to allow small and medium sized undertakings to benefit from the rule exempting minor agreements from the rigours of Article 85(1).

In order to calculate the market share of a product, it is necessary to determine the relevant market. This implies the identification of both a relevant product market and a relevant geographical market. The relevant product market consists of the market for the particular product together with the market for products which are identical or substantially equivalent to the particular product. Identical and substantially equivalent products must be interchangeable with the original product. Whether or not this requirement is satisfied must be judged from the perspective of the consumer, normally taking into account the characteristics, price and intended use of the products. However, in certain cases it is perfectly possible that a particular product can constitute a separate market by itself: *United Brands* v *EC Commission* (1978).

The relevant geographical market is the area within the Community in which the agreement produces its effects. There is a presumption that this area is the whole territory of the Community if the products which are the subject of the agreement are regularly bought and sold in all Member States. Where the products cannot be bought or sold in a particular part of the Community, or are bought and sold only in limited quantities or at irregular intervals in a part of the Community, that part is disregarded for the purposes of ascertaining the geographical market.

The relevant geographical market will be narrower than the whole Community if: (a) the nature and characteristics of the product (such as prohibitive transport costs) restrict its mobility; or (b) the free movement of the product within the Community is hindered by barriers to entry into national markets resulting from state intervention and non-tariff barriers. In such cases the relevant geographical territory is the national territory of origin.

QUESTION FOUR

It has been suggested that Article 85 EC is intended only to support the rules for the movement of goods. Comment on this suggestion in the light of the case law of the European Court of Justice, particularly the judgment in *Consten and Grundig* v *Commission*.

University of London LLB Examination
(for External Students) European Community Law 1992 Q3

General Comment

A question dealing with two separate areas of Community law but both concerning trade in goods. To answer the question, it is necessary to compare and contrast the policy reasons behind Community competition law with the principle of the free movement of goods.

Skeleton Solution

- Purposes of European competition law and policy.
- Relationship between Article 85 and the provisions relating to the free movement of goods.

- Decision of the ECJ in *Consten and Grundig*.
- Limitations applying to the relationship.

Suggested Solution

Article 85 of the EC Treaty prohibits all agreements, decisions and concerted practices between commercial enterprises if they affect trade between Member States and have, as their object or effect, the prevention, restriction or distortion of competition within the Community. Together with Article 86, this provision forms the basis of the competition policy of the Community.

The purpose of Article 85 is relatively straightforward; it is intended to prevent commercial parties erecting barriers to trade between Member States by means of private agreements or contracts. For example, if a British company and a German company are both engaged in the production or supply of the same goods and agree not to sell their products in the national market of the other party, goods would not flow from Germany to the United Kingdom and vice versa. In the absence of competition both companies could set their prices in their respective markets without reference to the prices charged by the other. This would undoubtedly have the effect of depriving consumers of lower prices which generally result from competition between producers and supplies.

Agreements fixing prices, controlling or limiting production, or permitting price discrimination are potentially anti-competitive because they prevent or restrict distortion. Each of these arrangements impedes the normal free flow of goods by erecting artificial barriers to trade.

There is little doubt that, at least theoretically, competition policy and the principle of the free movement of goods are related because both seek to reduce barriers to trade within the Community.

It will be recalled that Article 8A of the EC Treaty introduced the concept of an internal market, defined as an area 'without internal frontiers in which the free movement of goods ... is ensured'. Article 12 prohibits customs duties and any charges having equivalent effect on the flow of goods between Member States while Articles 30 and 34 prevent the imposition of quantitative restrictions and measures having an equivalent effect on imports between Member States.

These are measures taken by the relevant national authorities of each Member State for particular purposes. These rules, and the objective which they seek to achieve, namely the free movement of goods, would be circumvented if private parties were allowed to substitute private barriers to prevent effective competition and the free movement of goods. The decision of the European Court in *Consten and Grundig* v *EC Commission* (1966) supports this view.

In this case, Grundig, a German manufacturer of electrical equipment, entered into a distribution agreement with Consten, a French distributor. This agreement appointed Consten as Grundig's exclusive agent in certain regions of France. However, a French competitor imported Grundig's products, in free circulation in Germany, into France where they were sold at prices beneath those being offered by Consten.

Consten brought an action in the French courts to prevent its rival from importing in this manner, but the European Commission objected to this procedure and commenced an investigation into the commercial activities of Consten. The Commission found that the distribution agreement was contrary to Article 85(1) because the agreement had the effect of distorting competition in the Community because it restricted trade. Both parties brought an action against the Commission in the European Court to have this decision annulled.

The Court held that an agreement could only be contrary to Article 85(1) if it affected trade between Member States. It is only to the extent that an agreement affects trade between Member States that the deterioration in competition caused by the agreement falls within Article 85; otherwise it would escape the prohibitions contained in Article 85(1).

To assess whether an agreement affects trade between Member States, it is necessary to assess whether an agreement is capable of constituting a threat, either direct or indirect, actual or potential, to the free movement of goods between Member States in a manner which might harm the attainment of the objectives of a single market among the Member States. In other words, the degree to which an agreement affects trade between Member States is determined by reference to the amount of distortion it causes to the achievement of the free movement of goods.

If commercial agreements do not impede the free flow of goods from Member States, they do not fall within the scope of Article 85(1). But, for this condition to be satisfied, it is not necessary that there is actual trade between parties situated in different countries. In the past, the Commission and the Court have held that agreements between two or more parties in the same Member State may be anti-competitive even though there is no element of transnational trade. For example, in *Cementhandeleren* v *EC Commission* (1972), the Court held that a price fixing cartel between cement manufacturers in the Netherlands was contrary to Article 85 even though no participant was from outside the Netherlands, simply because the effect of the cartel inside the Netherlands prevented or impeded imports from other Member States.

Similarly, in *Delimitis* v *Henninger Bräu* (1992), the Court held that an exclusive supply agreement between a bar owner and a brewery was contrary to Article 85(1) even though both parties conducted business in Germany because of the cumulative effect of similar agreements between the brewery and various third parties.

The degree to which competition law and the principle of the free movement of goods complement each other is also evidenced by the fact that the operation of both is primarily in the interest of the consumer. Naturally, it is in the interests of the consumer that no customs duties, quantitative restrictions or measures having an equivalent effect are imposed on goods since these would merely increase the final price or limit the choice of goods available to consumers. Competition between producers and suppliers also has the overall effect of lowering average prices.

However, while the relationship between Article 85 and the principle of the free movement of goods is certainly tangible, it may be going too far to suggest that Article 85 is intended only to support the rules for the free movement of goods. The purpose of Article 85 is wider than mere support for the principle of the free movement of goods. It provides a comprehensive framework for the operation of an effective Community policy on competition.

The purpose of competition policy in a market economy is more than merely protecting consumer interests. It is intended to promote efficiency by allowing businesses to compete with each other, generally on fair terms and without one or the other having an unfair competitive advantage. It would be grossly unfair, for example, for a number of businesses to group together and pool their resources merely for the purposes of eliminating a competitor from the market.

The EC Commission itself has observed that Articles 85 and 86 are intended to provide a commercial environment where competition is not distorted: *EC Competition Policy in the Single Market* (2nd ed, 1989). In other words, competition policy provides a level playing field throughout the Community where companies can compete in the knowledge that their competitors are subject to similar commercial and trading conditions.

Further, Article 85 applies not only to goods, but also to the supply of services. It is therefore equally applicable to the freedom to provide services as it is to the free movement of goods. In the past, for example, banking services have been the subject of investigation by the Commission: see *Zuchner v Bayerische Vereinsbank* (1981). Similarly, in *Ahmed Saeed Flugreisen v Zentrale zur Bekämpfung Unlauteren Wettbewerbs* (1990), the economic activity under review was the supply of airline services. So, there is no logical restriction of Article 85 to its relationship with the principle of the free movement of goods.

QUESTION FIVE

Examine any one of the block exemptions adopted by the Commission and, in particular comment on the problems which it is designed to solve, the benefits which the exemption brings and any difficulties created by this procedure.

Question prepared by the Author

General Comment

A difficult question requiring the student to demonstrate detailed knowledge of the application of competition law.

Skeleton Solution

• Authority for the creation of block exemptions.
• Description of a block exemption – one vertical, one horizontal.
• Functions of block exemptions.

Suggested Solution

Article 85(3) specifically creates criteria for exempting agreements, decisions and concerted practices from the effects of Article 85(1). Agreements and practices which satisfy the exemption criteria established by Article 85(3) are not void under Article 85(2) nor subject to the imposition of fines.

Two types of exemption are granted on the basis of the authority of this provisions: (1) individual exemptions which are issued on the basis of an individual application; and (2) block exemptions which are applicable to categories of agreements. Subject to review by the Court of First Instance and thereafter the European Court itself, the European Commission has exclusive authority to create exemptions on the basis of Article 85(3).

To reduce the bureaucratic burdens imposed by applications for individual exemption, the Commission is empowered to establish group exemption categories: Council Regulation 19/65 (1965). The Commission has enacted a number of Regulations in order to grant group exemption to a number of agreements including exclusive distribution agreements (Commission Regulation 1983/83 (1983)), exclusive purchasing agreements (Commission Regulation 1984/83 (1983)), patent licensing agreements (Commission Regulation 2349/84 (1984)), motor vehicle distribution and servicing agreements (Commission Regulation 123/85 (1985)), specialisation agreements (Commission Regulation 417/85 (1985)), research and development agreements (Commission Regulation 518/85 (1985)), franchising agreements (Commission Regulation 4087/88 (1988)), and know-how agreements (Commission Regulation 556/89 (1989)). If an agreement falls within the scope of a group exemption under a Commission regulation, the parties to the agreement are not required to notify the Commission of the agreement and the parties cannot be fined by the Commission for violating competition law on that basis.

Each block exemption contains specific and particular criteria which must be satisfied in order for an agreement to take advantage of the exemption. Many of the exemptions are mutually exclusive and occasionally an agreement will fail to qualify as an exempt agreement because it falls within two mutually exclusive categories. At the same time a number of exemptions overlap and reliance may be placed on one or other option to obtain exemption for an agreement.

Group exemptions have been created for both horizontal and vertical agreements. An example of group exemption applicable to a horizontal agreement is the specialisation agreement block exemption. Specialisation agreements are agreements whereby the parties agree among themselves who should manufacture certain products. By relinquishing production of certain goods, the participating undertakings can concentrate on manufacturing those products which remain on their respective production lines. Competition is restricted because the parties refrain from independently manufacturing certain items.

In order to qualify for exemption under this provision, an agreement must satisfy all the following conditions: (a) the agreement must be between small and medium sized undertakings, measured on the basis of market share and turnover; (b) the commitment to specialise must be reciprocal which means that an obligation on only one of the parties to refrain from production of a certain item would not qualify for group exemption; (c) the commitment must refer only to the nature of the products, so any quantitative limitation of production does not fall within the group exemption; (d) certain additional clauses must be agreed which are essential to implement the commitment to specialise, including a non-competition clause and exclusive purchasing and distribution commitments; and (e) commitments with regard to prices are not allowed in the context of the group exemption.

The purpose of this group exemption is to allow small and medium-sized firms to improve their production processes and thereby strengthen their competitive positions in relation to larger firms.

Vertical agreements may also be the subject of group exemptions. A typical example of such a group exemption is the exclusive distribution agreements block exemption. This group exemption applies to three situations: (i) where the supplier and the distributor agree that the distributor should supply a certain area; (ii) where the distributor agrees to purchase goods exclusively from the supplier; and (iii) where the supplier agrees to supply the distributor exclusively, and the distributor agrees to purchase exclusively from the supplier.

In order to be exempt, such agreements must fulfil the following principal conditions: (a) the agreement can involve only two parties; (b) the products must be supplied for resale; (c) the sales area must be either a defined part of the Common Market or the entire Common Market; (d) the only permitted restriction on the supplier is the obligation not to sell to other resellers in the sales area allocated to the exclusive distributor; (e) the distributor must agree to purchase all his requirements from the supplier; (f) the agreement must not involve competing manufacturers, since this might lead to market sharing; and (g) there must be no effort by the parties to create absolute territorial protection for the distributor. In other words, parallel imports of the goods must remain possible.

Although agreements which satisfy these conditions are automatically exempt, the Commission retains the right to withdraw the benefit of the group exemption in particular cases such as, for example, a distributor abusing an exemption by charging unreasonable prices.

12 EUROPEAN COMPETITION LAW AND MERGER CONTROL – ARTICLE 86 EC TREATY

12.1 Introduction

This chapter will deal mainly with the restraints imposed on commercial practices by Article 86 of the EC Treaty and also the regulation of mergers within the Community by competition law. In addition, a number of other matters of general competition law will be considered in order to provide a comprehensive description of the Community competition policy scheme. This includes the proper procedure for the initiation of a complaint, the determination of infringements, the powers of the Commission to investigate complaints, and the imposition of fines. These matters are equally relevant to the application of Article 85 as well as Article 86, but are included in this chapter to avoid duplication and repetition.

12.2 Key points

a) *Commercial practices prohibited by Article 86 EC Treaty*

Article 86 of the EC Treaty prohibits practices which constitute an abuse of a dominant position within the Community market. Article 86 expressly provides:

'Any abuse by one or more undertakings of a dominant position within the common market or in a substantial part of it shall be prohibited as incompatible with the common market in so far as it may affect trade between Member States. Such abuse may, in particular, consist in:

a) directly or indirectly imposing unfair purchase or selling prices or other unfair trading conditions;

b) limiting production, markets or technical developments to the prejudice of consumers;

c) applying dissimilar conditions to equivalent transactions with other parties, thereby placing them at a competitive disadvantage;

d) making the conclusion of contracts subject to acceptance by the other parties of supplementary obligations which, by their nature and according to commercial usage, have no connection with the subject of such contracts.'

Article 85(1) and 86 are not mutually exclusive. The Commission has discretion in selecting the appropriate instrument to enforce competition policy. Consequently, the possibility that both Articles 85 and 86 may be applicable to a particular case cannot be ruled out: *Ahmed Saeed* v *Zentrale zur Bekämpfung* [1990] 4 CMLR 102.

The existence of a dominant position per se is not prohibited under Article 86, only any abuse of the market power which usually accompanies such a position. Article 86 is not intended to penalise or punish efficient forms of economic behaviour. On the contrary, Article 86 seeks to discourage the acquisition or maintenance of a dominant position through anti-competitive practices which create artificial competitive conditions.

b) *The existence of a dominant position*

The concept of dominant position is not defined in the EC Treaty but, in effect, is analogous to the existence of a monopoly in a particular sector of the economy. The European Court has defined dominant position in the following terms:

'Undertakings are in a dominant position when they have the power to behave independently, which puts them in a position to act without taking into account their competitors, purchasers or suppliers. That is a position when, because of their share of the market, or of their share of the market combined with the availability of technical knowledge, raw materials or capital, they have power to determine prices or to control production or distribution for a significant part of the products in question': *Continental Can Co* v *EC Commission* [1973] ECR 215.

Article 86 does not, however, only apply to the activities of single companies. For example, in *Re Italian Flat Glass Suppliers* [1992] 5 CMLR 502, the European Court held that the provision could be applied to three Italian glass producers. The number of parties is not the critical factor although in investigations under Article 86 this number does tend to be small. The important element is the position of the parties in the relevant market and their behaviour.

The two key relevant concepts in establishing the existence of a dominant position are: (i) the definition of the market; and (ii) the calculation of market share.

i) Definition of the relevant market

The relevant market is defined in terms of both the relevant product market and the relevant geographical market.

To identify a product market it is necessary to isolate the product under investigation from similar products in the market. For this purpose, the Commission identifies the relevant product together with all other products which may be perfectly substituted for the product under investigation. Jointly these products constitute the relevant product market: see, for example, *AZKO Chemie BV* v *EC Commission* [1993] 5 CMLR 197. The test for ascertaining substitutable products depends on whether or not:

'there is a sufficient degree of interchangeability between all the products forming part of the same market in so far as a specific use of such products is concerned': *Hoffmann La Roche & Co AG* v *EC Commission* [1979] ECR 461.

The relevant geographical market has been defined by the European Court as the area:

'where the conditions are sufficiently homogeneous for the effect of the economic power of the undertaking concerned to be evaluated': *United Brands* v *EC Commission* [1978] ECR 207.

In general, the relevant geographical market will be assumed to be the whole of the Community. Only if the existence of impediments to cross-border trade, such as physical, technological, legal or cultural non-tariff barriers, can be established will the relevant geographical market be reduced. Further, as the single internal market programme proceeds, it is less likely that such artificial barriers will be permitted to reduce the geographical market from the whole territory of the Community.

ii) Calculation of market share

No particular share of a market is required to prove the existence of a dominant position. In the *United Brands Case* above, the European Court stated that the fact that an undertaking possessed around 40 per cent of the relevant market was not itself sufficient to establish market dominance. Other factors contributed to the determination that United Brands maintained a dominant position, including the facts that the company controlled its own shipping fleet, could regulate the volume of the product entering the Community regardless of weather conditions and subjected distributors to rigorous restrictive covenants.

On the other hand, in the *Continental Can Case*, the Commission decided that a company with a share of approximately 50 per cent of the relevant market occupied a dominant position.

iii) Investigation period for determination of market share

The period selected for the calculation of market share and the determination of a dominant position must be sufficient to facilitate the proper appraisal of market conditions, dominant position and the alleged abusive practice. Failure to properly assess these conditions may lead to the partial or complete annulment of any Commission measures designed to penalise findings of abuse: see *BPB Industries & British Gypsum* v *EC Commission* [1993] 5 CMLR 32.

c) *Abuse of a dominant position*

Abuse is an objective concept which relates to the behaviour of the undertaking alleged to be in a dominant position. It is behaviour which modifies the structure of a market in such a way as to reduce the levels of competition or retard the growth of competition in a particular economic area.

Article 86 lists a number of practices which are specifically identified as perpetrating such abuse, including:

i) Directly or indirectly imposing unfair purchase or selling prices or other unfair trading conditions: see for example, *Bodson* v *Pompes Funebres* [1988] ECR 2479.

ii) Limiting production, markets or technical development to the prejudice of consumers.

iii) Applying dissimilar conditions to equivalent transactions with other trading parties, thereby placing them at a competitive disadvantage: see *San Pellegrino SpA* v *Coca-Cola Export Corp* [1989] 4 CMLR 137.

iv) Making the negotiation of contracts subject to acceptance by the other parties of supplementary obligations which, by their nature or according to commercial usage, have no connection with the subject of such contracts.

This catalogue is intended to be illustrative and, in common with the list elaborated in relation to Article 85(1), is not exhaustive.

It should also be noted that refusals to act can be just as anti-competitive and are equally as liable to be found in violation of Article 86: See *Independent Television Publications Ltd* v *EC Commission* [1991] 4 CMLR 745.

d) *Merger control in the European Community – the original provisions*

The Community competition provisions make no express reference to the control of mergers among undertakings in the Community. Notwithstanding this omission, the Commission has been prepared to apply both Articles 85(1) and 86 to mergers and takeovers. For example:

i) A dominant position in the manufacturing or distribution of a product or service may also lead to abuse where one producer or supplier is able to absorb competitors by way of an acquisition or merger: *Tetra Pak Rausing SA* v *EC Commission (No 1)* [1991] 4 CMLR 334.

ii) Article 85(1) may be applied to acquisitions of shareholdings where a company acquires a minority stake in a competitor as leverage for the coordination of marketing strategy between the two undertakings: *British American Tobacco & RJ Reynolds Industries Inc* v *EC Commission* [1986] ECR 1899.

iii) Article 85(1) may also be infringed if a company enters into a joint venture or acquires an interest in a third company where the other principal shareholder is in a related field of business.

iv) Consortium bids may also violate Article 85 if the consortium involves competitors seeking to acquire a competitor or attempting to influence its behaviour.

Notwithstanding the application of these provisions to individual cases, until 1990, the European Commission had no specific mandate to investigate mergers or acquisitions within the Community.

e) *Merger control in the European Community – the Merger Control Regulation 1990*

After a series of controversial takeovers in the early 1980s, the Council of Ministers agreed to adopt Community legislation conferring authority on the Commission to investigate takeovers and mergers above a certain threshold. Council Regulation 4064/89 (1989) was enacted for this purpose and came into force in September 1990.

The Regulation uses the term 'concentration' to refer to mergers and takeovers. A concentration arises where either: (a) two or more previously independent undertakings merge into one; or (b) one or more persons already controlling at least one undertaking acquire, whether by purchase of securities or assets, direct or indirect control of the whole or part of one or more other undertakings.

Article 1 of the Regulation confers regulatory jurisdiction upon the Commission over all mergers involving a 'Community dimension'. A concentration has a 'Community dimension' where:

i) the aggregate worldwide turnover of all the undertakings concerned is more than ECU 5,000 million; and

ii) the aggregate Community-wide turnover of each of the undertakings concerned is more than ECU 250 million.

Aggregate turnover is calculated on the basis of amounts derived by the undertakings concerned in the preceding financial year from the sale of goods or the supply of services during the course of ordinary trading activities. Deductions are permitted for sales rebates, value added tax and other taxes directly related to turnover.

Certain types of mergers are expressly excluded from the jurisdiction of the Commission by virtue of the regulation itself. A concentration has no Community dimension where, despite satisfying both the necessary criteria, all of the undertakings involved make more than two-thirds of its aggregate Community-wide turnover within one and the same Member State. In such cases, the concentration has no Community dimension.

Even if a merger is approved by the Commission, Member States retain a veto over mergers in particularly sensitive sectors of their national economies. Member States may take appropriate measures to protect legitimate national interests such as public security, the plurality of the media and the maintenance of prudent rules for the conduct of commerce. However, such measures are subject to the requirement that they must be compatible with the general principles and other provisions of Community law.

Concentrations with a Community dimension must be notified to the Commission not more than one week after the conclusion of the agreement, or the announcement of a public bid, or the acquisition of the necessary controlling interest. If a merger is by consent, the notification must be made jointly by all the parties involved. In all other cases, including contested acquisitions, the notification to the Commission must be made by the acquiring undertaking.

The Commission is empowered to impose fines on persons, undertaking or associations of undertakings if they intentionally or negligently fail to notify the Commission of a concentration with a Community dimension. These fines can range from ECU 1,000 to ECU 50,000.

Once a concentration with a Community dimension is notified, two options are available to the Commission:

i) The Commission can conclude that the concentration does not fall within the scope of the Regulation and must record such a finding by means of a decision.

ii) It can find that the concentration falls within the scope of the Regulation. In such a case, it may adopt one of two alternative courses of action:

- declare that the concentration, while within the scope of the Regulation, is not incompatible with the common market and will not therefore be opposed; or
- find that the concentration falls within the Regulation and is incompatible with the common market in which case it is obliged to initiate proceedings.

In each of these cases, the Commission must make its decision within one month of the notification.

To appraise the compatibility of a concentration with the common market, the Commission must evaluate the implications of the concentration in the light of the need to preserve and develop effective competition within the common market, taking into account, inter alia, the structure of all the relevant markets concerned and the actual or potential competition from other undertakings both within and outside the Community. In making this assessment, the Commission must consider the market position of the undertakings concerned, their economic and financial power, the opportunities available to both suppliers and consumers, access to supplies and markets, the existence of legal or other barriers to the entry of the product into particular markets, the interests of intermediate and ultimate consumers, as well as technical and economic development and progress.

f) *Determination of infringements of European Competition law*

The Commission may investigate alleged anti-competitive behaviour either on an ex proprio motu basis, or at the instance of interested parties. Interested parties permitted to notify the Commission of anti-competitive behaviour include Member States, undertakings and individuals who are affected by the alleged infringement of the competition rules: see *BMW Belgium SA* v *EC Commission* [1979] ECR 2435.

Although the Commission has discretion whether or not to pursue an investigation after allegations have been made by interested parties, it is obliged to notify a petitioner if no action is to be taken. If the Commission reaches the conclusion that no action is warranted, it must at least have conducted a proper preliminary investigation and cannot dismiss a complaint without exhausting the proper standard of appraisal in such an investigation: see *SA Asia Motors France* v *EC Commission* [1994] 4 CMLR 30.

In conducting its investigations, the Commission has a right to obtain all necessary information from the competent authorities of Member States as well as from undertakings and associations subject to investigation. The owners of undertakings or, in the case of companies, the persons authorised by the articles of association to represent incorporated bodies, are obliged to supply such information.

g) *Commission's powers to conduct investigations*

The Commission's powers to investigate are contained in Council Regulation 17/62 and can be broadly classified as follows:

i) Power to obtain information from the parties involved in the investigation;

ii) Power to conduct inspections;

iii) Power to convene hearings; and

iv) Power to grant interim relief.

i) Power to obtain information

Under Article 11(1) of the Regulation, in carrying out its duties, the Commission may obtain 'all information necessary' for the purposes of the investigation from interested private parties and the governments and competent authorities of the Member States.

The scope of information 'necessary' for the purposes of conducting the investigation falls broadly within the discretion of the Commission to decide: *Samenwerkende Elektriciteits Produktiebedrijven NV (SEP)* v *EC Commission* [1992] 5 CMLR 33.

ii) Conduct of inspections

Again the Commission's powers to conduct on-the-spot investigations are extensive. Article 14(1) of the Regulation allows Commission officials to:

• Examine the books and business records of the company;

• To take copies of books and business records;

• To ask for oral explanations on the spot; and

• To enter any premises, land or means of transport of parties under investigation.

The Commission exercises these powers in two stages. First, Commission officials visit premises with a simple mandate from the Commission authorising inspection. If these officials are refused access to premises or records, the Commission may adopt a decision under Article 14(3) requiring companies to submit to investigations authorised by the decision.

The Commission may proceed with a search after obtaining the necessary permission from the national authorities and can impose fines on companies for failing to comply with the Commission's requests. The European Court has held that such searches must be subject to procedural safeguards. In particular:

'if the Commission intends, with the assistance of the national authorities, to carry out an investigation other than with the cooperation of the undertakings concerned, it is required to respect the relevant procedural guarantees laid down by national law': *Hoechst AG* v *EC Commission* [1988] 4 CMLR 430.

iii) Power to convene hearings

The Commission is required to allow interested parties an opportunity to present their arguments and views directly to its officials. The procedures for the convening of hearings to discharge this obligation are regulated by Commission Regulation 99/63 (1963).

The main purpose of holding such meetings is to allow parties to make representations in their favour at various stages in the proceedings.

iv) Power to grant interim relief

No such power is expressly conferred in Regulation 17/62, but the Commission has been deemed to possess an inherent power to issue decisions providing interim relief to complaining parties to prevent injury caused by the anti-competitive practices of business competitors: *Camera Care* v *EC Commission* [1980] ECR 119.

The Court of First Instance has recently confirmed that the Commission can adopt interim measures of protection if the following three conditions were satisfied:

- The practices against which a complaint was lodged were prima facie likely to infringe Community law;
- Proven urgency existed; and
- There is a need to avoid serious and irreparable damage to the party seeking relief: *La Cinq* v *EC Commission* [1992] 4 CMLR 449.

h) *Power to fine*

According to Article 15 of Council Regulation 17/62, as amended, the Commission may impose fines ranging from ECU 1,000 to ECU 1,000,000 or a sum in excess of this limit but not exceeding 10 per cent of the turnover, against any undertakings found in violation of Articles 85(1) and 86. In addition, fines can be imposed for the supply of false or misleading information, for the submission of incomplete books or other documents or for refusal to submit to an investigation.

The policy of the Commission towards fining is a matter which is influenced by many factors. However, the following factors are considered most relevant to such a determination:

i)   The size of the companies engaged in the anti-competitive behaviour: see *Belasco* v *EC Commission* [1991] 4 CMLR 96.

ii) The steps taken by the party to mitigate the infringement prior to the decision imposing fines has been rendered: see *National Panasonic* v *EC Commission* [1980] ECR 2033.

iii) The nature of the infringement. For example, the Commission considers certain practices, such as predatory pricing, to be particularly repugnant to Community competition policy: see *Tetra Pak Rausing SA* v *EC Commission (No 1)* [1991] 4 CMLR 334.

The Commission also has authority to require undertakings to adopt particular courses of action including:

i)   discontinuing infringements of Articles 85(1) and 86;

ii) discontinuing action prohibited under Article 8(3) of Regulation 17/62;

iii) supplying completely and truthfully any information requested under Article 11(5); and

iv) submitting to any investigation ordered under the investigative powers of the Commission.

While the Commission has authority to fix the amount of the fine, the national authorities concerned enforce the decision by virtue of Article 192 EC Treaty in accordance with their rules of civil procedure.

12.3 Relevant cases

United Brands v *EC Commission* [1978] ECR 207: Identification of the criteria applied in order to determine the relevant product market.

Cooperatieve Vereniging 'Suiker Unie' v *EC Commission* [1975] ECR 1663: The relevant geographic market is the whole of the Community unless the pattern and volume of production allow for a determination otherwise.

Hoffman La Roche & Co AG v *EC Commission* [1979] ECR 451: Illustration of the practices deemed to be dominant.

Continental Can v *EC Commission* [1973] ECR 215: Description of the concept of abuse.

PVC Cartel Case [1992] 4 CMLR 357: The European Commission must abide by the terms of its own rules of procedure and failure to do so will result in any decision being declared null.

Tetra Pak Rausing SA v *EC Commission (No 1)* [1991] 4 CMLR 334: The record fine for anti-competitive practices under European Community competition law.

La Cinq v *EC Commission* [1992] 4 CMLR 449: Principles behind the grant of interim measures of relief by the Commission.

Hilti v *EC Commission* [1992] 4 CMLR 16: Identification of the relevant product markets for the purposes of ascertaining the dominant position of an undertaking.

12.4 Relevant materials

D R Price, 'Abuse of a Dominant Position' (1990) 3 ECLR 80.

L Gyselden et al, 'Article 86 EC: The Monopoly Power Measurement Issue Revisited' (1986) 11 EL Rev 134.

P J P Verloop, Merger Control in the European Community (1993).

M Reynolds, 'EC Commission's Policy on Fines' (1992) EBL Rev 262

V Korah & P Lasok, 'Philip Morris and Its Aftermath: Merger Control?' (1988) 25 CMLR 333.

J S Venit, 'The "Merger" Control Regulation: Europe Comes of Age ... or Caliban's Dinner' (1990) 27 CMLR 7.

W Elland, 'The Mergers Control Regulation (EC) No 4064/89' (1990) 3 ECLR 111.

12.5 Analysis of questions

In common with the regulation of commercial practices under Article 85, the application of the concept of abuse of a dominant position is particularly complex. The following examples consider some of the more complex issues, but, at a minimum, students should understand basic concepts such as 'abuse' and the 'relevant market'. Familiarity with the investigation procedure is also extremely important.

12.6 Questions

QUESTION ONE

British Breweries plc is an important producer of beer in the United Kingdom. Statistics shown that British Breweries account for some 12 per cent of all beer sold in the United Kingdom but that its British Brewlite is especially successful and accounts for 40 per cent of all non-alcoholic beer consumed in the UK.

a) British Breweries has been negotiating with County Beers Ltd with a view to merger. County Beers is the principal other producer of non-alcoholic beers and after merger the new company, British County Breweries, will control 65 per cent of the market in non-alcoholic beer.

b) British Breweries includes in its standard supply contract a requirement that pubs and other purchasers must display prominently its non-alcoholic beer and advertising materials. The advertising materials offer consumers 'healthy drinking discounts' whereby the more non-alcoholic beer they buy, the lower the price they have to pay. Since the healthy drinking discounts were introduced two years ago, British Breweries' sales have doubled and several small-scale producers of non-alcoholic beers have gone out of business.

Advise British Breweries as to the significance, if any, of EC law for each of the above aspects of its business.

adapted from University of London LLB Examination
(for External Students) European Community Law 1990 Q7

General Comment

A problem question requiring the application of Article 86 to hypothetical facts.

Skeleton Solution

• British Breweries as an undertaking.
• Do the practices affect trade between Member States?
• Application of Article 86 – dominant position and abuse.

Suggested Solution

a) British Breweries is clearly an undertaking for the purposes of Article 86, as is County Beers Ltd. Further, Article 86 covers all sectors of the economy and the sale of drink is not covered by any derogation to the Treaty. Therefore, whether the proposed merger amount would to an abuse of a dominant position depends on whether the criteria established under Article 86 are satisfied.

The acquisition of a competitor by a company which maintains a dominant position in the market may infringe Article 85 if the merger results in an abuse of a dominant position, and this abuse affects trade between Member States.

British Breweries could feasibly argue that, since its activities only take place in the United Kingdom, trade between Member States is not affected. In this case, British law would apply and not Community competition law. However, in *Hugin v EC Commission* (1979), the European Court stated that the test for effect on trade is whether the practice constitutes a threat to the freedom of trade between Member States in a way that might harm the attainment of a single market. In other words, it is only necessary that it is possible to foresee with a sufficient degree of probability that the practice in question would influence, directly or indirectly, actually or potentially, the pattern of trade between Member States.

The broad wording of this test means that it is not difficult for the Commission to establish that an effect on trade exists. Activities by an undertaking which create artificial divisions of the national market have been found to have an indirect effect on trade, for example, by making it harder for imports to penetrate the market; see *Cementhandelaren* v *EC Commission* (1972). Specifically, under Article 86, the European Court has held that where a dominant company refused to sell chemicals to the smaller company which sold almost all of its production outside the common market, that the requirement of an effect on trade was satisfied by the impairment of the competitive structure in the Community. A similar test was applied in the *Woodpulp Case*. Thus, it would seem likely that Community law would apply to the activities of British Breweries, unless it could prove that its activities fell within the de minimus standard. In view of the market share held by British Breweries, this argument is likely to fail.

Next, it is necessary to ascertain whether British Breweries holds a dominant position, a term not defined in the EC Treaty, but which has been interpreted to mean an overall independence of behaviour on the market 'which puts [undertakings] in a position to act without taking into account their competitors, purchasers or suppliers': *Continental Can* v *EC Commission* (1973). Absolute domination is not necessary.

There are two tests to establish a dominant position: (a) the identification of the relevant market; and (b) the assessment of the strength of the undertaking in question on the market.

It would be in British Breweries' interest to define the relevant market as broadly as possible, such as the market for all drinks, alcoholic and non-alcoholic, or at least the market for non-alcoholic drinks. In *United Brands* v *EC Commission* (1978), the Court had to decide whether bananas should be regarded as an independent market in themselves or, alternatively, part of the general market for fresh fruit. In this case, the Court adopted the test of limited interchangeability and decided that the banana could be 'singled out by such special features distinguishing it from other fruits that it is only to a limited extent interchangeable with them and it is only exposed to their competition in a way that is hardly perceptible'.

The same argument may be used to distinguish alcoholic beer from non-alcoholic beer, the latter being developed expressly for its non-alcoholic content. Following the Court's reasoning in *Michelin* v *EC Commission* (1983) which distinguished the market in retreaded tyres from the market in replacement tyres, it could be argued that although other soft drinks are to some extent interchangeable with non-alcoholic beer, and hence in competition with such beer, sales of soft drinks do not sufficiently undermine the sales of non-alcoholic beer, which has been specifically developed for its similarity to beer and not just as another soft drink.

In assessing the strength of an undertaking in a market, the most important factor is the size of the undertaking's share of the relevant market. Market shares have normally been relatively high. In the *Continental Can Case*, above, the undertaking accounted for 50–60 per cent of the market in Germany for meat tins, 80–90 per cent of fish tins and 50–55 per cent for metal closures for glass jars. In *Hoffman La Roche* v *EC Commission* (1979), the undertaking held an 80 per cent share of the vitamin market. However, in *United Brands*, above, the Court was content to hold a figure of 40–45 per cent of the relevant market as constituting a dominant position. The Commission has said that a dominant position will usually be found once a market share of the order of 40–45 per cent is reached, but cannot be ruled out even as regards shares of between 20 and 40 per cent.

Furthermore, the rest of the market is likely to be fragmented – County Beers holds a 25 per cent share and the remaining 35 per cent is likely to belong to smaller producers. This factor underlines British Breweries' dominance.

Although nothing is known about British Breweries' financial resources or its performance, these factors suggest that the Commission would have a strong case for establishing the existence of a dominant position after merger.

However, to violate Article 86, British Breweries must be abusing their dominant position. One possible abuse is the takeover of competitors. The EC Treaty does not contain any explicit merger control provision equivalent to Article 66 of the ECSC Treaty. However, in the *Continental Can Case*, above, the European Court established the principle that a merger which causes the strengthening of a dominant position may amount to abuse. In that case the undertakings under investigation had acquired control of two other companies. The Commission decided that the merger with one amounted to an abuse of a dominant position because it was a potential competitor and the effect of the acquisition was to practically wipe out competition. Although the decision of the Commission was subsequently annulled on the ground that the facts had not been adequately analysed, the Court confirmed that Article 86 would be applicable in such circumstances.

For a merger to fall within the prohibition of Article 86, two conditions must be satisfied. First there must be a pre-existing dominant position to be abused – this has already been shown to be probable in British Breweries' case. It is possible that Article 86 also includes the case where a single merger operation between two leading firms results in the creation of a dominant position of such magnitude as to substantially fetter competition. If British Breweries are not deemed to hold a dominant position, its merger with County Beers would mean that the combined forces of the two undertakings would constitute a dominant position, although whether a 65 per cent share of the market is of sufficient magnitude is debatable. Article 86 cannot apply to mergers falling short of dominance even if these seriously affect competition.

Also, in the *Continental Can Case*, the Court spoke of strengthening an undertaking's position to a point where all the remaining operators in the market are dependent upon it. In the light of developments in cases such as *Michelin* and *Hoffman La Roche*, it is unlikely that the Court would insist that a merger would have such a drastic effect before it would qualify as abuse.

Given this reasoning, it seems likely that the proposed merger would attract the prohibition in Article 86. British Breweries would therefore be well advised to notify the Commission of the proposed merger under Regulation 17 and seek a negative clearance under Article 2 to be assured that there are no grounds for intervention.

Two further matters should also be noted. First, since *BAT and Reynolds* v *EC Commission* (1986), transfers of ownership and in particular minority acquisitions which result in the coordination of the behaviour of independent companies constitute a breach of Article 85. This reasoning could be applied to the British Breweries and County Beers merger. Second, Regulation 4064/89 has come into force and requires prior notice to the Commission of mergers and acquisitions. The language of this regulation reflects the existing law and the pre-existing law will continue to be used extensively.

b) Tying arrangements may also constitute an abuse of a dominant position. As illustrated by Article 86(d), where a person is required to accept, as a condition of entering into a contract, 'supplementary obligations which, by their nature or according to commercial usage, have no connection with the subject of such contracts', a prima facie infringement of competition law arises. The requirement that public houses and other purchasers must display British Breweries products and also advertisements in a prominent position appears to fall inside Article 86(d).

Such conditions may, however, be sanctioned by commercial usage. For example, the inclusion of a meal in the price of an airline ticket is an accepted use of tying. The onus would therefore be on British Breweries to establish that such conditions are an accepted commercial practice.

But, in this particular case the advertising goes beyond describing the attributes of the non-alcoholic beer by offering financial incentives towards its purchase, thus locking the consumer into the purchase of a single brand name, to the exclusion of other products. The main objection to tying is that it enables an undertaking with a dominant position in the market to gain a competitive advantage. Therefore, it is likely that the practices of British Breweries as regards the ancillary conditions for purchasers would fall foul of Article 86.

Even if British Breweries are not deemed to be abusing a dominant position, these contract terms may fall foul of Article 85(1)(e) (see *Delimitis* v *Henninger Bräu AG* (1992)). The Brewers could, however, try to bring themselves within one of the existing exceptions to Article 85(1). By arguing that these contractual terms were necessary to establish non-alcoholic beer on the market, using the analogies drawn from two cases – *Société Technique Minière* v *Maschinenbau Ulm GmbH* (1966) and *Pronuptia* (1986) – such contractual terms might escape possible contravention of the competition provisions.

Alternatively, British Breweries could seek an exemption from liability under Article 85(3) by arguing that the contractual terms contribute to improving the production or distribution of goods. British Breweries is likely to be on weaker ground here since the Commission insists that the gain to welfare must exceed what could have been achieved without the restriction on competition: see *Re Ford Werke* (1984). In British Breweries' case, competition has clearly been restricted since several small-scale producers have gone out of business.

QUESTION TWO

Fruit Ltd, an English company, has developed a fruit called Peach Delight, which is a cross between a peach and an apricot. It has become extremely popular in shops and supermarkets. Foreign rivals have also developed the Peach Delight, but Fruit Ltd still retains a 48 per cent share of the total Peach Delight market in the European Community, although this only constitutes a five per cent share of the total market for fresh fruit.

Fruit Ltd only supplies its Peach Delight to shops which agree to sell only Peach Delight and no other soft fruit. It also insists on charging retailers 75p per Peach Delight. (Production and cultivation costs amount to only 5p per fruit).

a) The European Commission have started an investigation into Fruit Ltd's activities. Advise Fruit Ltd as to how Community law might affect its conditions of sale.

b) Pete Robinson, a small Surbiton grocer, wishes to stock Peach Delight. However, Fruit Ltd has refused to supply him with the fruit because he refuses to comply with Fruit Ltd's conditions. Mr Robinson asks for your advice on the relevant position in European Community law.

University of London LLB Examination
(for External Students) European Community Law June 1993 Q5

General Comment

This is a problem-type question requiring the application of the relevant law to the hypothetical facts presented. The necessary figures are provided to establish the position of the hypothetical company on the market and the facts stated evidence abuse. However, exactly what the examiner requires by way of an answer is not well stated.

Skeleton Solution

• Outline of the requirements for establishing an infringement of Article 86: dominant position, abuse, effect on trade between Member States
• Establishing a dominant position: relevant product market, relevant geographical market, market share
• Abusive behaviour: conditions and requirements
• Penalties, sanctions, etc imposed by the Commission

Suggested Solution

a) Fruit Ltd should be advised that, should its activities amount to a dominant position within the Community for the production and sale of Peach Delight, then the two practices which it is presently engaged in – namely refusal to supply and excessive pricing – are likely to amount to an abuse of that position under Article 86 of the Treaty.

To assess whether the European Commission will find an abuse of a dominant position, it is necessary to calculate whether or not Fruit Ltd has a dominant position within the relevant market for its product and to apply the criteria used by the Commission and the Court to decide whether these two practices amount to an abuse.

Existence of a dominant position

The first step towards determining the existence of an abuse of a dominant position is to ascertain whether or not Fruit Ltd possesses a dominant position in terms of Article 86. This requires examination of two factors: (i) identification of the relevant market; (ii) calculation of Fruit Ltd's market share.

i) Relevant market

The relevant market is defined in terms of both the product market and the geographical market.

To identify the relevant product market it is necessary to isolate the product under investigation from similar products in the market-place. For this purpose, the relevant product includes the actual product under consideration together with all other products which may be substituted, in terms of production and use, for the actual product. In this particular case, the relevant product is therefore Peach Delight and all other fruits which can be considered substitutes.

The test for identifying substitutable products depends on whether or not there is'a sufficient degree of interchangeability' between all the products forming part of the same market; *Hoffmann La Roche & Co AG v EC Commission* (1979). Where a product is interchangeable with the product under investigation, then that product too forms part of the relevant product market.

Whether another product is sufficiently interchangeable with the product under investigation, and hence part of the relevant product market, is measured by two factors. First, the objective physical characteristics of the product must be similar to the product under consideration, in this case Peach Delight. Second, the competitive conditions and the structure of the supply and demand for the product on the market must also be similar to those for Peach Delight.

For fresh fruit, the Court has already ruled that the important physical qualities which require consideration are the characteristics of the product gauged in terms of appearance, taste, softness and ease of handling: *United Brands* v *EC Commission* (1978). So, it is possible that, on the basis of this test, both peaches and apricots will be included within the scope of the relevant market since the Peach Delight is a hybrid of both of these. However, much will depend on the factual physical features of the Peach Delight.

As regards competitive conditions, the Court, in the *United Brands* case, supra, considered four factors to be germane in identifying interchangeable products in terms of this condition, namely;

– the degree to which the principal product is affected by falling or increasing prices of other fruits;

– the purchasing habits of consumers relative to expenditure on the principal product compared to other types of fresh fruit;

– the existence of special purchasing groups such as sectors of the community
which consider the principal product to be a necessary dietary requirement;
and

– growing season for the particular product relative to other fruits.

So, if other fruits share similar pricing patterns, purchasing habits of
consumers, and the growing seasons of the Peach Delight, they will be
considered relevant products in the event that their physical characteristics are
also sufficiently similar.

In these circumstances, it is likely that peaches and apricots will also be
included in the relevant product market along with Peach Delight since
products which are produced by means of cross-fertilisation generally share
some features in common with the products from which they have been
produced.

The relevant geographical market is considerably more easy to ascertain. The
relevant geographical market is defined as the area within the Community
'where the conditions are sufficiently homogeneous for the effect of economic
power of the undertaking concerned to be evaluated'; *United Brands*, supra.
The geographical market will be the whole Community unless there are factual
reasons for limiting the area to a lesser size while still satisfying the criterion
of being 'a substantial part' of the Community.

Factors generally relied on to limit the geographical scope of the relevant
geographical market include impediments to cross-border trade such as
physical, technological, legal or cultural barriers to trade, the lack of adequate
transportation facilities, or the inability to extend distribution or supply
networks into certain regions.

The facts presented in the question state that Fruit Ltd has a 48 per cent
share of the total Peach Delight market in the Community and is the sole
Community supplier. Hence, there is no reason for believing that factors
limiting the scope of the geographical market exist and the geographical
market is therefore the whole of the Community.

Applying both the tests for the relevant product market and the relevant
geographical market to the facts stated in the question, the relevant market is
therefore probably the market throughout the Community for Peach Delight,
apricots and peaches.

ii) Market share

We are informed that Fruit Ltd has a market share of 48 per cent in the total
Peach Delight market in the Community and a 5 per cent share of the market
for fresh fruit. Since it is the sole Community producer for Peach Delight, the
remaining market share in that product must be imported from non-
Community producers.

Since the relevant product market will most likely include peaches and
apricots, the market share held by Fruit Ltd in the relevant product market will
be less than 48 per cent and higher than 5 per cent. The exact share will have
to be calculated in light of the statistics for the markets in apricots and peaches.

Naturally the market share held by Fruit Ltd is the critical factor in establishing whether or not it possesses a dominant position. But no absolute percentage share of the relevant market has ever been considered by the Court or the Commission to definitively establish the existence of a dominant position. Thus, in the *United Brands* case, above, a market share of 40 per cent was considered sufficient to establish dominance. However, the Commission has in the past taken the view that a market share of 20–40 per cent of the relevant market may constitute dominance if certain circumstances are shown to exist.

Hence, it is more likely than not that Peach Delight will be considered to have a dominant position in the market.

Existence of an abuse of position

Abuse of a position is an objective concept which relates to the behaviour of the company under investigation. Article 86 itself identifies some of the practices which may be considered abuse. These include directly or indirectly imposing unfair purchase or selling prices or other unfair trading conditions.

Fruit Ltd is possibly guilty of two forms of abusive practices: refusing to supply purchasers with Peach Delight unless they agree to sell no other soft fruits; and charging excessive prices relative to production costs.

Fruit Ltd's refusal to supply is a flagrant abuse of its dominant position. Companies and producers cannot use their positions within particular markets to impose their unreasonable terms and conditions of sale on customers. Dominant companies may only refuse to supply customers where there is an objectively justifiable reason for such a refusal. Where an order is made in the ordinary course of trade and can be easily satisfied, a dominant company cannot flex its economic muscle to impose unfair terms on customers; see *Hilti* v *EC Commission* (1992).

Fruit Ltd is also guilty of abusing its dominant position by charging excessive prices. Prices are excessive if they bear no 'reasonable relation to the economic value of the product supplied': *General Motors* v *EC Commission* (1975). The test of excess pricing involves a comparison between the selling price of the product and the costs of production, thereby disclosing the margin of profit.

Fruit Ltd makes each Peach Delight at a cost of 5p, including both cultivation and production costs. Even once distribution costs, marketing expenditure, commissions, etc, are deducted Fruit Ltd cannot justify the profit margin which results after charging 75p for each fruit. Therefore, it is likely that they have also abused their dominant position by engaging in excessive pricing.

Consequences of a determination of abuse of position

It is extremely likely that the Commission will find Fruit Ltd guilty of an abuse of a dominant position. This will result in two immediate consequences. First, the Commission is empowered to impose fines and second, the Commission can issue a cease and desist order to compel Fruit Ltd to discontinue its present conditions of sale policy.

The Commission is authorised to impose fines up to ECU 1,000,000 or, alternatively, a sum in excess of these limits but not exceeding 10 percent of the annual turnover of a company found to have violated Article 86. The Commission assesses the quantum of fine according to the nature of the anti-competitive practices found to exist, the duration of the practices and the market position of the company infringing the Article.

In this particular case, Fruit Ltd must be advised that a heavy fine can be expected, specifically because of the nature of its anti-competitive practices. It should therefore immediately engage in a damage limitation exercise by introducing a competition compliance programme, revise its terms and conditions of sale to remove both abusive practices and assist the Commission to the greatest extent possible throughout the course of its investigation.

b) In theory at least, Mr Robinson can rely on the terms of both Articles 85 and 86 of the EC Treaty. Article 85 prohibits anti-competitive agreements contravening its terms while Article 86 prohibits companies and undertakings abusing their dominant positions. These articles are not mutually exclusive and it is perfectly possible that a particular practice may infringe both provisions; see *Re Italian Flat Glass Suppliers* (1992).

If Mr Robinson wishes to rely on Article 85(1) he must establish that there exists an agreement between himself and Fruit Ltd. Thus, for example, if an agreement previously existed according to which Mr Robinson agreed to Fruit Ltd's conditions of sale, and this was terminated because Mr Robinson refused to comply with these terms, Article 85(1) would probably apply.

However, he would be on more solid ground under Article 86 of the EC Treaty. As noted above, Fruit Ltd are in flagrant violation of the obligation contained in that provision not to engage in an abuse of its dominant position. The abuse in question has had a direct effect on the trading activities of Mr Robinson and it is likely that he would be able to establish injury, in particular by the refusal to sell unless the unfair trading conditions are accepted.

Mr Robinson has two separate remedies available. First, he can complain to the European Commission that Fruit Ltd is abusing its dominant position. Such a complaint has a number of advantages. The Commission would assume responsibility for pursuing the matter should it decide that the complaint is valid. Hence, Mr Robinson would incur nominal expenses by proceeding in this manner.

On the other hand, he cannot compel the Commission to pursue the complaint and, even if the Commission brought the matter to a successful conclusion, he would not be automatically entitled to compensation for injury suffered as a result of the anti-competitive practice.

The alternative course of action is to raise proceedings in the English courts directly against Fruit Ltd. First, an application for an interlocutory injunction to restrain the refusal to supply can be made by a plaintiff; see *Garden Cottage Foods v Milk Marketing Board* (1984).

Second, an action for damages for injury caused can be commenced on the ground of breach of statutory duty against Fruit Ltd on the basis of injury suffered to Mr Robinson's business by the refusal to supply; see *Commission Notice on Co-operation with National Courts in the Enforcement of Community Competition Law*

1993. This would probably provide the best relief to Mr Robinson against the abuses being perpetrated by Fruit Ltd.

QUESTION THREE

Two American airline corporations, together with two other airline companies – one Canadian and one Swiss – have negotiated an agreement to fix the price of airline tickets for transatlantic flights from London. The purpose of this agreement is to put a British airline company, which offers transatlantic flights at a substantially discounted rate, out of business.

This agreement was submitted to the European Commission who, after an investigation, issued a comfort letter. This assurance was subsequently withdrawn after the Commission had realised the full implications of the agreement. No hearing was held by the Commission prior to the withdrawal of the comfort letter.

What are the legal implications of this situation under Community competition law?

Question prepared by the Author

General Comment

A question requiring a description of the rights and duties of undertakings as regards competition law.

Skeleton Solution

- Effect of a comfort letter.
- Right to challenge the decision of the Commission.
- Extra-territorial application of Community law.
- Breach of an essential procedural requirement.

Suggested Solution

Article 15(5) of Regulation 17/62 provides that fines for infringement of Community competition policy shall not be imposed in respect of acts taking place after notification to the Commission following an application for exemption and before the decision of the Commission has been reached regarding the application. However, Article 15(6) of Regulation 17/62 then specifies that the above provision shall not have effect where the Commission has informed the undertakings concerned that after a preliminary examination it has formed the view that the practices infringe Community competition policy.

It is now clear that notification by the Commission, as above, since it defines the legal position of the parties involved, will be regarded by the European Court as a decision: *Cimenteries* v *EC Commission* (1967). Because a notification by the Commission of its conclusion is tantamount to a decision by the Commission, the parties affected by it can apply to the Court under Article 173, within the prescribed period, to have it quashed. Since decisions, inter alia, must specify the reasons on which they are based, such reasons must, consequently, be set out in any decisions made under Article 15(6) of Regulation 17/62. Otherwise this will be a ground for annulment of the decision by the Court.

All four parties to the agreement under consideration in this question will have standing to seek a review of the decision contained in the letter. Article 173(2) of the EC Treaty provides that any legal or natural person may institute proceedings in the Court against a decision addressed to that person. Clearly then, the actual addressee of the decision has standing to challenge it before the Court.

Further, Article 173(2) provides that a natural or legal person shall have standing to challenge a decision, inter alia, addressed to another person where that decision is of direct and individual concern to the first person. There can be no doubt that the airline companies, though not addressees of the letter-decision, would also, by passing the test laid down by the Court in *Plaumann v EC Commission* (1963), have standing to initiate proceedings before the Court to annul the Commission's decision. The Plaumann test, in regard to the problem under consideration, is whether the decision affects the applicant 'by reason of circumstances in which they are differentiated from all others so that they are individually distinguished'. Clearly, the decision does affect them.

The four non-Community organisations must be advised that the Commission does not hesitate to apply Community competition law to undertakings situated outside the territory of the Community if the operations of such undertakings have an unlawful effect within that territory: see the *Woodpulp Cartel Case* (1988). The European Court has resolutely supported the Commission in its attempts to acquire the extra-territorial application of competition law. Clearly therefore any argument raised before the Court questioning the competence of the Commission in this regard will be dismissed.

However, the four companies will be on much firmer ground in claiming that the Commission has sought no comments or advice from them. Article 19 of Regulation 17/62 provides that before taking certain decisions, including a decision under Article 3, which requires undertakings to terminate infringements of competition law, the Commission shall give the undertakings involved an opportunity to be heard on the matters under consideration. If the non-Community undertakings can convince the Court that the letter-decision of the Commission amounts to a decision of the type covered by Article 19, and that they were denied an opportunity to be heard, this would be a ground for the Court to quash the decision.

Where the European Court has reviewed the legality of an act under Article 173 of the EC Treaty, such actions may be held void if the action is well founded. Accordingly, if the act concerned in this problem – the Commission's decision that the notified agreement does not qualify for exemption – is annulled by the Court, then presumably the application for exemption will be reinstated and given continued immunity from fines unless and until the Commission adopts a valid final decision to reject the application.

QUESTION FOUR

Describe the powers of the European Commission to conduct investigations into alleged violations of Community competition policy.

Question prepared by the Author

General Comment

A general essay type question on the powers of the Commission to conduct investigations.

Skeleton Solution

- Authority of the Commission's powers – Regulation 17/62.
- Power to compel evidence.
- Sanctions for refusal to cooperate.
- Fines and penalties.

Suggested Solution

The basic provision that governs investigations against undertakings for breaches of Articles 85 and 86 is Council Regulation 17/62 (1962). The Commission may initiate proceedings on its own initiative or in respect to a complaint by a 'natural or legal person claiming a legitimate interest' or in response to a notification by the undertaking in question.

During investigation proceedings, the Commission has certain fact finding powers to determine whether or not the undertaking is in breach of Community competition law. These are of a two-fold nature, as provided for in Articles 11 and 14 of Regulation 17/62.

Under Article 11, the Commission may obtain all necessary information from the governments and competent authorities of the Member States and from undertakings and associations of undertakings. This is effected by means of an informal request being made with a specified date for reply. Despite the non-compelling nature of this request, an undertaking may still be fined should it be subsequently discovered that the undertaking gave an incorrect response to a question posed by the Commission.

If an undertaking refuses to reply, the Commission may adopt a decision ordering the supply of information under Article 11(5) of Regulation 17. If the undertaking continues to refuse to comply, it may again be fined under Article 15(1)(b), or it will be made the subject of a periodic payment under Article 16(1)(c).

By virtue of Article 14, the Commission may enter the premises of an undertaking, examine and take copies of, or extracts from, books and business records and ask for oral explanations on the spot.

Once the Commission has acquired authority to conduct an investigation, an undertaking is subject to an obligation to cooperate fully with the Commission. If an undertaking fails to cooperate, the Commission can adopt a decision under Article 14(3) requiring an undertaking to cooperate. Refusal risks a fine or a periodic payment.

The Commission has an option whether to proceed on the basis of Article 14(2) or 14(3). It is not a two stage procedure as is the case under Article 11. Such investigatory action may also be taken against subsidiaries of undertakings if they are deemed to be a single economic unit.

Undertakings are entitled to claim legal professional privilege with regard to certain documents. This right was recognised by the European Court in *AM & S v EC Commission* (1982). It relates to communications made for the purposes and in the interests of the client's right of defence and extends to earlier written communications which have a relationship to the subject-matter of the procedure. However, this privilege may only be claimed for communications emanating from independent lawyers established in the Community. This excludes in-house lawyers and lawyers from non-EC countries.

If the status of a document is disputed, the Commission may adopt a decision ordering disclosure. This decision may, of course, be challenged under Article 173 of the EC Treaty.

Once the Commission considers that it has collected sufficient material to initiate proceedings, it will do so by sending the undertaking a statement of objections. It will inform the undertaking of the basis and the facts which the Commission consider violate Articles 85 or 86. After the statement of objections has been issued, the undertaking may examine the Commission files relating to the case, except for business secrets and internal documents.

The undertaking will be invited to reply to the statement within a specified period, normally about three months. It may request an oral hearing, which is governed by Commission Regulation 99/63 (1963). This would enable it to further develop its written submissions.

Where the Commission has decided that an undertaking has indeed infringed Articles 85 or 86, under Article 3(1) of Regulation 17/62, it may order this state of affairs to be terminated and specify the steps to be taken, which may even include an order to supply.

If the Commission believes that the infringement of the competition rules was negligent or intentional, it may fine an undertaking between 1,000 and 1,000,000 ECU or up to 10 per cent of the previous year's turnover. The quantum of the fine will depend on such factors as the duration and gravity of the infringements and the degree of cooperation by the undertaking throughout the course of the investigation: see *Chemiefarma* v *EC Commission* (1970).

Proceedings may also be terminated by means of a comfort letter. This will state that the file on an investigation is closed pending a change of legal or factual circumstances (such as the existence of fresh evidence). Such a letter is of no legal import and it is questionable whether the Commission is bound by such a letter even in the absence of a change of circumstances: see *Frubo* v *EC Commission* (1975).

If an undertaking wishes to appeal the decision of the Commission, recourse lies to the Court of First Instance, which exercises jurisdiction in this particular field.

13 EUROPEAN COMMUNITY POLICIES

13.1 Introduction

To ensure that the objectives of the European Community are achieved, the EC Treaty authorises the creation of a number of Community policies. These policies facilitate economic integration among the Member States and ensure that the purposes of the common market are not undermined or eroded by the existence of inconsistent national policies. Although some of the Community policies were originally specified in the Community Treaties, a number of other policies, including environmental protection policy and monetary policy, have evolved as a consequence of the functions of the Community. This chapter will deal with the principal Community policies other than competition policy which forms an independent chapter of the WorkBook, and the common commercial policy, which forms a substantial portion of the chapter dealing with the external relations of the Community.

13.2 Key points

a) *The Community transport policy*

The adoption of a common policy in the sphere of transportation is sanctioned by Article 3 of the EC Treaty and Articles 74 to 84 provide the guidelines for the implementation of this policy. The common transport policy extends to carriage of goods and persons by road, rail and inland waterways.

Article 75 allows the Council, acting on a proposal from the Commission, to establish:

i) common rules applicable to international transport to or from the territory of Member States or passing across the territory of one or more Member States;

ii) conditions under which non-resident carriers may operate transport services within a Member State; and

iii) any other appropriate provisions.

The implementation of a common transport policy is, of course, an essential element in achieving the goal of the free movement of goods.

i) Carriage of goods by road

Council Regulation 1018/68 (1968) allocated quotas of Community-wide permits among Member States. These permits enable the holders to convey goods by road between Member States. This system has been revised with substantial increases in the levels of quotas. At present, Council Regulation 3621/84 (1984) contains the relevant allocations.

The Council has also adopted common rules for certain types of vehicles which are exempt from requiring a permit.

ii) Road passenger transport

The basic measure regulating the carriage of passengers is Council Regulation 117/66 (1966). This establishes common definitions for international services and a system largely free from bureaucracy.

Both the carriage of goods and passengers are subject to rules relating to the maximum permitted number of hours for drivers. Council Regulation 3820/85 (1985) now governs the maximum number of permitted hours, although the actual figures have been altered from time to time. Criminal penalties may be imposed under the authority of Community Regulations in the event that drivers exceed maximum permitted daily driving periods or are not allowed compulsory rest periods: see *Anklagemyndigheden* v *Hausen and Son I/S* [1990] ECR 2911. Other Regulations concern matters such as drivers' qualifications and minimum levels of training.

iii) Railway transportation

Although in theory the Community transport policy extends to railway transportation, in practice, national railway systems do not often extend beyond the boundaries of Member States. Nevertheless, a number of Regulations have been passed to deal with issues such as competition between railways and other forms of transportation, the fixing of rates for the international carriage of goods by rail, and investment in railway network systems.

iv) Inland waterways

A number of important rivers, including the Rhine and the Danube, flow through Europe and pass through a number of Member States. Council Directive 76/135 (1976) provides for the mutual recognition of navigation licences issued for vessels using inland waterways. This regulation requires that a certain minimum amount of information is set out in the licence.

v) Air transportation

A number of cases before the European Court have confirmed that air transport falls within the scope of the common transport policy: *EC Commission* v *France (Re Air Transport)* [1974] ECR 35; and *Ministère Public* v *Asjes* [1986] ECR 1425. Matters such as competition, tariffs, noise emission and airline schedules are subject to the Community transport policy.

The Community has also introduced a number of measures designed to create a common air transportation policy. Three Council measures form the core of this policy:

- Council Regulation 3975/87 (1987) which specifies the implementation of Community competition policy in this economic sector: see *Ahmed Saeed Flugreisen* v *Zentrale zur Bekämpfung Unlauteren Wettbewerbs* [1990] 4 CMLR 102;
- Council Regulation 3976/87 (1987) which exempts certain agreements under Article 85(3) of the EC Treaty; and
- Council Decision 87/602 (1987) which deals with the sharing of passenger capacity and access of carriers to scheduled air routes within the Community.

Other recent Council measures deal with the sharing of revenues, computer reservation systems and ground handling services.

b) *The Community social policy*

Title III of Part Three of the EC Treaty (Articles 117 to 127) deals with the social policy of the Community, together with the related matter of the European Social Fund. In general, the Community social policy is mainly confined to matters relating to the treatment of Community workers, including the elimination of gender discrimination and equal pay. Article 118 obliges the Commission to promote closer cooperation between Member States as regards employment, labour law, working conditions, vocational training, social security, the prevention of occupational accidents, and the related rights of association and collective bargaining.

The Single European Act augmented this provision with Article 118A which requires the Council to enact Directives harmonising national measures concerning improvements in conditions relating to the health and safety of workers.

The Treaty on European Union contains a separate Agreement on Social Policy. Social policy objectives were included as an appendix rather than in the main provisions of the Treaty because of the inability of the United Kingdom and the other 11 Member States to reach a consensus of the principles applicable to Community social policy.

In fact the actual terms of the Agreement are vague. But the emphasis of its terms is on working conditions, training, education, equality between genders and social security. The Agreement specifies that the Commission may make proposals to the Council in these areas for measures to give effect to the objectives contained in the Agreement. Nonetheless, the Agreement itself contains few provisions which can be seen as having direct effect.

Once the Treaty on European Union has been finalised, including the supplementary protocol, the European Commission will most likely embark on a programme of regulations and directives intended to give effect to the stated policy objectives. It will be this package which will give actual legal substance to the social provisions of the Treaty on European Union.

c) *The Community fisheries policy*

The EC Treaty does not expressly sanction the creation of a common fisheries policy (CFP). However, since Article 38 of the Treaty defines agricultural products to include the products of fisheries, the common fisheries policy was developed as a subsection of the common agricultural policy. However, in practice it is organised on an independent basis: see *France* v *United Kingdom (Re Fishing Mesh)* [1979] ECR 2923.

The territorial scope of the common fisheries policy extends to the fishing zones of all the Member States. A Council Resolution of 1976 urged Member States to adopt a 200 mile fishing limit along the Atlantic and North Sea coasts and Council Regulation 507/81 (1981) provides the legal authority to extend exclusive fishing zones.

The essence of the common fisheries policy is the principle of non-discrimination on the ground of nationality. Council Regulation 101/76 (1976) extended the principle of non-discrimination to access to the fishing grounds of Member States by vessels registered in other Member States. This general principle is subject to four exceptions:

i)   Member States are entitled to maintain an exclusive fishing zone for their own nationals up to a maximum of 12 nautical miles;

ii) Previously existing arrangements made between Member States prior to the CFP in reserved waters can be continued;

iii) Special restrictions are imposed on large fishing vessels in the 'Orkney/Shetlands box'; and

iv) Unlimited access to Portuguese and Spanish waters will not be established until 2002.

The Community regulates fishing activities within Community waters by limiting fish catches, introducing measures of price support and quality control, establishing measures for conservation, and negotiating access agreements with third countries. These matters now fall within the exclusive competence of the Community: *EC Commission* v *United Kingdom* [1981] ECR 1045.

i)   Total allowable catches

     Council Regulation 170/83 (1983) grants authority to the Council to set total allowable catches on an annual basis. The total allowable catch is calculated on the basis of scientific research into the volume and quantity of fishing stocks. Mathematically, the allowable catch is determined on a global basis, then by reference to species of fish and area, and then this allowance is allocated among the Member States.

ii) Price support and quality control

     The Council sets guide prices annually according to the species of fish, taking into account market conditions, as well as the supply and demand for the product. An intervention price is also established, but in the context of the CFP this is known as the 'withdrawal price'. The withdrawal price is the price at which the Community will purchase fish products by way of intervention buying.

     Quality control is maintained by a Community scheme to facilitate the mutual recognition of producer organisations within Member States: Council

Regulation 105/76 (1976). Producer organisations generally purchase the products from fishermen and adopt measures designed to improve product quality.

iii) Conservation

Conservation of fishing resources is achieved through three Council Regulations: 3440/84 (1984), 1866/86 (1986) and 3094/86 (1986). These regulations specify technical measures designed to conserve fishing stocks. Conservation measures include minimum mesh sizes, restrictions on types of fishing gear, restrictions on the size of vessels, minimum fish sizes, and the designation of closed areas and closed seasons.

iv) Access agreements

Access agreements allowing non-Community vessels to fish in Community waters fall within the scope of the common commercial policy. The Community has exclusive authority to enter into agreements with third states to regulate access by foreign fishermen: *Kramer* [1976] ECR 1279.

In the pursuit of this policy, the Community has entered a number of international agreements to regulate access, including the Northwest Atlantic Fisheries Convention 1978 and the Northeast Atlantic Fisheries Convention 1981.

d) *The Community environmental policy*

A Community policy for the protection of the environment was not originally included in the EC Treaty. However, the Single European Act amended the Treaty by adding Title VII to Part Three (Articles 130r to 130t) which regulates environmental policy.

According to Article 130r, Community action relating to the environment should have three main objectives:

i)   to preserve, protect and improve the quality of the environment;

ii) to contribute towards protecting human health; and

iii) to ensure a prudent and rational utilisation of natural resources.

Community measures relating to the environment are to be based on a number of principles, including the principle that preventative action should be taken, that environmental damage should be rectified at source, and that the polluter should pay for damage to the environment.

The Council of Ministers has authority, acting on the proposals of the European Commission, to adopt measures on behalf of the Community to tackle issues of environmental protection.

To date, Community measures relating to the environment have been confined to three main areas: public health, atmospheric pollution, and the disposal of waste. Regulations in the field of public health deal, for example, with the quality of drinking water and the cleanliness of beaches. A number of Directives also deal with allowable levels of emissions from industrial plants. Finally, Community legislation has been introduced to regulate the acceptable levels of by-products from waste disposal processes.

Again, the Treaty on European Union will revamp the Community's environmental protection policy. This policy will, in the future, be based on four principles:

i) the preservation, protection and improvement of the quality of the environment;

ii) the protection of human health;

iii) the prudent and rational utilisation of natural resources;

iv) the promotion of measures at the international level to deal with regional or worldwide environmental problems: Article 130r EC Treaty, as amended.

The Community's policy in this area is to be dictated by a number of legal concepts, including the 'polluter pays' principle and that of preventative action. In addition, environmental damage should, where possible, be rectified at its source.

13.3 Relevant cases

EC Commission v *France (Re Air Transport)* [1974] ECR 35: Member States no longer possess capacity to enact measures which regulate subjects which fall within the competence of the Community.

R v *Kirk* [1984] ECR 2689: The European Court quashed the conviction of a Danish fisherman on the ground that unilateral quotas could not be introduced by a Member State even when the Council had failed to agree on revised terms for a common fisheries policy.

Pesca Valentia v *Ministry of Fisheries and Forests* [1988] 1 CMLR 888: Member States are entitled to require that a specified minimum proportion of the crews of ships registered in the Member State are nationals of that state.

EC Commission v *Denmark (Re Returnable Containers)* [1989] 1 CMLR 619: Environmental considerations may justify limitations on the free movement of goods so long as the objectives to be achieved are not disproportionate to the restrictions imposed.

Knichem Base and Others v *Commune di Cinisello Balsamo* [1991] 1 CMLR 313: Directives enacted to implement the policy of environmental protection may be given direct effect.

13.4 Relevant materials

D Lasok, *The Law of the Economy of the European Communities* (1981) 335–392.

13.5 Analysis of questions

Questions relating to the common policies of the Community rarely refer to particular decisions of the European Court. Instead, knowledge of general concepts and principles is usually required. Students should therefore be familiar with the general scope and framework of the various Community policies. In particular, an understanding of any recent events or changes within the structure or content of each particular policy is desirable.

13.6   Questions

QUESTION ONE

What contribution can the European Community make to the development of Community wide measures to protect the environment?

University of Glasgow LLB Examination
1989 Q8

General Comment

A narrative question requiring an answer describing the present state of the Community environmental policy.

Skeleton Solution

• The provisions of the EC Treaty relating to the protection of the environment.
• The subjects regulated by Community measures.
• Future content of the policy.
• Impact of the policy on the protection of the environment.

Suggested Solution

Protection of the environment is an apt illustration of the growing competence of the Community in areas which were, for some considerable time, presumed to be outside the scope of the economic nature of the EC Treaty. Prima facie, the protection of the environment is an issue which is only remotely related to the regulation of economic activities. However, the Community has vigorously assumed the duty of protecting the environment, on the ground that such activities will improve the quality of life within the Community.

Prior to the Single European Act of 1986, the Community had been involved in regulating certain aspects of environmental protection under the guise of consumer protection. However, the Single European Act conferred unambiguous authority on the Community to regulate issues of environmental concern by amending the EC Treaty to contain a whole section dealing with the environment. This section consists of three articles (Articles 130r to 130t).

Article 130s authorises the Council of Ministers to pass legislation, acting on a proposal from the Commission, to protect the environment. Further, Article 130t provides that the adoption of such measures shall not preclude Member States from introducing more stringent protective measures so long as these are compatible with the EC Treaty. In other words, measures enacted in pursuit of a common environmental policy are intended to be minimum standards and do not remove the power to legislate on such matters from the individual Member States. In fact the Community has been given a wide mandate to harmonise laws throughout the Community to protect the environment, and the potential for protecting the environment is significant.

The wide scope of the competence of the Community in this field is clear from Article 130r. The Council is authorised to enact legislation to achieve three separate goals. First, a policy of preserving, protecting and improving the quality of the environment is to be vigorously pursued. Second, measures to protect human health are to be introduced. Third, the prudent and rational utilisation of natural resources is to be encouraged.

Further, in enacting such provisions, a number of principles are to be borne in mind, including the principle that prevention is better than cure, that environmental damages should be rectified at source, and that polluters should be held financially responsible for their unlawful acts. The discretion of the Council to enact measures in this field is therefore substantially unfettered.

The Community has already made a substantial contribution to the protection of the environment by targeting three areas of concern: public health, atmospheric pollution, and the disposal of waste.

Measures designed to protect the health of consumers from dangers stemming from pollution in drinking water were enacted as early as 1975. Council Directive 75/440 (1975) regulated the standards for drinking water and, in particular, the maximum permissible levels of harmful substances. This Directive was subsequently replaced by Council Directive 80/778 (1980) which expanded on these minimum requirements. Annex I to the Directive lists the substances which are considered harmful along with maximum admissible concentrations in drinking water. Deviation from these standards must be justified by an emergency and can only be sustained for the minimum amount of time necessary to restore the quality of water: see *Criminal Proceedings Against Persons Unknown* Case (1989).

A number of other Directives have been passed in connection with the pollution of water. Thus, Directive 76/160 (1976) concerns the quality of bathing waters and the standard of beaches, the latter being a subject on which the United Kingdom has frequently been threatened with prosecution in the European Court. Other Directives deal with the maximum permissible amounts of pollutants which can be discharged into the environment.

The regulation of air pollutants is a matter which has been controlled by more recent measures. Council Directive 88/609 (1988) identified the most toxic substances and limits the emission of these substances from combustion plants. Other Directives tackle the problems of emissions from incinerating plants and the quality of air. The problem of exhaust emissions from vehicles has not escaped the rigours of regulation. Member States are required to ensure that unleaded petrol is freely available throughout their respective territories and limits on emissions from new cars have been set. A comprehensive measure has been recently adopted to limit the volume of emissions from new cars with less than 1.4 litre cylinder capacity: see Council Directive 89/458 (1989).

Also, the disposal of waste and unwanted bi-products is considered by the Community to fall within the scope of its mandate to protect the environment. Council Directive 75/442 (1975) established standards of the protection of public health during waste disposal processes and has been given direct effect by the European Court: see *Knichem Base* v *Commune di Cinisello Balsamo* (1991). Community legislation regulates the amount of noxious substances that can be released into the atmosphere during this process, in terms of both volume and chemical composition. The transportation of dangerous chemicals, spillage from which would endanger the environment, has also been controlled. However, as yet a comprehensive Community regime for the reduction of noxious emissions has not been adopted.

Strictly speaking, the subject of noise pollution does not fall within the scope of the Community policy of environmental protection. However, the Community has been relatively successful in introducing standards to regulate the sound emissions from certain products including the exhausts of motor vehicles and motorcycles, the noise of garden tools and agricultural machinery, industrial machinery, and even the noise levels emitted from subsonic aircraft.

While the Community has authority to embark on a comprehensive programme of environmental protection, it has preferred to tackle the issue on an industry-by-industry, or subject-by-subject basis, the result being a somewhat piecemeal approach to the issue. A number of critical issues continue to remain unregulated at the Community level, including the levels of permissible radiation from nuclear power stations and the maximum levels of pollutants which can be discharged into the seas and oceans surrounding the Community. While the Community was widely expected to make a substantial contribution to the protection of the environment, progress has not been dramatic. The length of time taken to introduce measures has also been the subject of criticism.

The contribution made by the Community to the protection of the environment will ultimately depend on the willingness of the Member States to impose restrictions on their industries. Inevitably, such requirements will affect the profitability of industries. To date, Member States have appeared unwilling to burden their domestic industries with these extra costs and the immediate consequence has been an environmental protection programme of limited impact.

QUESTION TWO

The masters of two German fishing vessels were prosecuted for offences committed under the West Coast Herring (Prohibition of Fishing) Order 1981, a statutory instrument enacted under the authority of a British statute. Both masters were convicted for violating prohibitions on fishing in designated waters off the British coast and their catches confiscated. In addition, a fine of £30,000 was imposed on both masters.

Advise the fishermen of their rights under Community law with a view to appealing both the fines and the confiscation of their catches.

Question prepared by the Author

General Comment

A rare problem-type question requiring the student to understand the fundamental nature of one particular Community policy.

Skeleton Solution

• Authority of the Prohibition Order – Community or national law?
• Competence of the Community in this field.
• Compatibility of the convictions with Community law.
• Possible appeal to the ECJ under Article 177.

Suggested Solution

Since the creation of the common fisheries policy, competence to regulate fishing in the exclusive economic zones of the Member States has been exercised at the Community level. In other words, the Council of Ministers, acting on proposals from the European Commission, enacts Community measures to regulate such matters as total allowable catches, quotas, access by foreign fishermen, conservation and structural policy.

Member States no longer maintain capacity to enact measures of domestic law which affect matters which fall within the competence of the common fisheries policy unless such measures have been promulgated with the consent of the Community: *Gewiese & Mehlich* v *MacKenzie* (1984). Therefore, if the Order in Council has been passed under the authority of a British statute, the Order may be challenged on the ground that it infringes a principle of Community law.

The basis of the Community common fisheries policy is the principle of non-discrimination between nationals of Member States in Community fishing waters. Community legislation has also been passed to implement this obligation: Council Regulation 101/76 (1976). However, at the same time the Community has responsibility for regulating fishing within Community waters and may therefore pass legislation to conserve fishing stocks, which could involve a ban on fishing in certain areas: see *EC Commission* v *United Kingdom* (1981). In particular, the Community is empowered to establish total allowable catches which establish limits on the quantity of fish which may be caught in certain areas.

While the Community is responsible for setting quotas, enforcement of these measures usually falls within the competence of the individual Member States. Thus, even though the German fishermen have been prosecuted under British law, it is possible that this national legislation has been promulgated to incorporate a measure of Community law, such as Regulations and Directives, into British law. In these circumstances, the authorities of the United Kingdom are allowed to conduct prosecutions to uphold the Community rule of law.

If the Order in Council was enacted as enabling legislation for a Community measure, it must satisfy a number of criteria. First, the legislation must satisfy all the obligations incumbent upon the Member States and partial implementation is insufficient. For example, in *EC Commission* v *United Kingdom (Re Tachographs)* (1979) the British government was held to have violated Community law by not passing legislation making non-compliance with a Community regulation a criminal offence. The European Court held the United Kingdom liable for a breach of Community law and declared inconceivable the implementation of a regulation by a Member State 'in an incomplete and selective manner so as to render abortive certain aspects of Community legislation which it opposed or which it considered contrary to its national interests'.

Therefore, the German captains may challenge the convictions on the basis that the Order in Council is a measure of national law which contravenes Community law, but if the Order has been introduced with the consent of the Community, or if it implements a Community measure, the convictions may not be overturned on the basis of a European defence.

Further, where a Community measure specifies that Member States have discretion as to the type of criminal penalty which may be imposed upon those found to have violated the measure in question, it is not possible to challenge the implementing legislation on the ground that different Member States have applied different criminal sanctions. Thus, in *Anklagemyndigheden* v *Hausen and Son I/S* (1990), the European Court held that the fact that some Member States imposed strict criminal liability to enforce a Regulation while others did not constitutes a ground to challenge the implementing instrument of national legislation. This conclusion was reached because the regulation in question left considerable discretion to Member States for its implementation. Naturally, where a regulation specifies particular criminal penalties, such provisions must be strictly observed. However, it is rare for Community legislation to require particular criminal sanctions.

The two German captains should therefore be advised to appeal their convictions to the superior criminal courts if it can be established that the Order in Council infringes Community measures implementing the common fisheries policy. In particular, a reference from the European Court under Article 177 of the EC Treaty would be most appropriate in these circumstances. In this respect it should be remembered that preliminary references may be made from both criminal and civil courts to the European Court.

14 THE EXTERNAL RELATIONS OF THE EUROPEAN COMMUNITY

14.1 Introduction

14.2 Key points

14.3 Relevant cases

14.4 Relevant materials

14.5 Analysis of questions

14.6 Questions

14.1 Introduction

The Member States of the European Community have transferred considerable external sovereignty to the Community for the purpose of conducting economic and commercial relationships with non-Community states. The European Community, on behalf of the individual Member States, negotiates trade and economic agreements with third countries and administers the various trade protection mechanisms to protect industry within the Community from unfair foreign competition. The European Commission and the Council of Ministers are the bodies responsible for the conduct of the Community's external affairs. Authority to exercise powers to regulate external affairs is vested in the Community by virtue of Common Commercial Policy (CCP) provisions of the EC Treaty.

14.2 Key points

a) *The international legal personality of the European Community*

The European Community has limited international personality and has entered a substantial number of bilateral and multilateral agreements with third states. In addition, the Community participates in a number of international organisations, including the General Agreement on Tariffs and Trade (GATT) (now the World Trade Organisation).

Article 210 of the EC Treaty expressly declares that '[t]he Community shall have legal personality'; see also Article 75 ECSC Treaty and Article 101 Euratom.

b) *Types of international agreements entered into by the Community*

Express capacity to enter international agreements is granted under Articles 113 and 238 of the EC Treaty. In addition, Article 228 specifies the procedure for the negotiation of such agreements. Agreements between the Community and third states may be classified according to form and content into four groups:

i) multilateral trade agreements, primarily negotiated within the context of the General Agreement on Tariffs and Trade;

ii) bilateral free trade agreements;

iii) association agreements, which are usually concluded with states about to become members of the Community; and

iv) development and assistance agreements with developing states.

These agreements vary, in both content and legal structure, according to the relationship which is to be regulated by a particular agreement.

c) *Capacity of the European Community to enter into international obligations*

The Community does not exercise unlimited capacity to enter into international agreements on behalf of its Member States. Where the subject matter of an agreement is unrelated to the objectives and purpose of the Community, the Community has no competence to act. Unfortunately, the distinction between those subjects which concern the Community under the terms of the three Community Treaties and other issues of international concern is not clear cut. Often an international agreement will regulate issues of Community concern as well as unrelated issues: for example the United Nations Convention on the Law of the Sea 1982.

If the subject matter of an international agreement falls completely within the competence of the Community, the Community has exclusive capacity to negotiate the agreement and the individual Member States have no authority to negotiate. Such agreements are known as 'Community Agreements'.

Where an international agreement contains provisions relating to matters within the competence of the Community, and also issues which fall outside the scope of the Community Treaties, both the Member States and the Community participate in the negotiating process and ratify the final agreement. Such agreements are known as 'mixed agreements'. For example in *Re Uruguay Round Final Act* [1995] 1 CMLR 205, the European Court confirmed that the Community had exclusive competence to conclude the WTO agreements concerning trade in goods but shared competence with Member States in two other sectors. Since the Community did not have exclusive competence over all the matters contained in the agreement, a mixed agreement was required and the Member States also ratified the terms of the agreement.

The Member States of the Community may be parties to international treaties, in their own right, concerning matters not related to the Community. Even though all the Member States participate in such agreements, if the subject matter bears no relation to issues of Community concern, the obligations are assumed by the Member States alone. These agreements are known as 'International Agreements Assumed by the Member States'. An example of such an agreement is the European Convention on Human Rights 1950 which, despite participation by all Community Member States, is not an agreement of Community concern.

i) Community agreements

The Community has express capacity to enter into two forms of international agreements without the participation of the Member States in the negotiating process:

- Article 113 of the EC Treaty authorises the Community to enter commercial agreements relating to tariff and trade matters for the purpose of achieving the objectives of the Common Commercial Policy. This authority expressly extends to export aids, credit and finance, and matters relating to multilateral commodity agreements.
- Article 238 authorises the Community to negotiate with third states, unions of states or international organisations, association agreements creating reciprocal rights and obligations, and facilitating common action through special procedures.

While the capacity to enter association agreements under Article 238 is relatively defined, the exercise of power under Article 113 has a potentially greater application since no explicit parameters have been set in relation to its application.

In order to define the scope of the Community's power under Article 113, the European Commission has sought a number of opinions from the European Court. In *EC Commission* v *EC Council (Re ERTA)* [1971] ECR 263, the Court held that authority to enter international agreements not only arose from the express provisions, but also provisions of the EC Treaty which require the negotiation of international agreements for their achievement. As a result, the Court decided that:

'the Community enjoys the capacity to establish contractual links with third countries over the whole field of objectives defined in Part One (Articles 1 to 8) of the [EC] Treaty.'

The rationale for extending the competence of the Community was the need for the Community to assume and carry out contractual obligations towards third states affecting the whole sphere of the application of the Community legal system.

This decision, along with a number of subsequent judgments of the Court, established the doctrine of implied powers. These implied powers supplement the express powers of the Community to enter into international agreements. Whether an agreement with a third state in negotiated by the Community on the basis of an express power or an implied power makes no difference to its status as a 'Community Agreement'.

ii) Mixed agreements

Since Member States have not conferred upon the Community their absolute sovereignty to negotiate treaties and in fact continue to exercise those powers not transferred to the Community, a conflict may arise where an international agreement contains provisions which fall within the competence of both the Community and the individual Member States. Implementation of such agreements requires joint action and such agreements are concluded simultaneously by the Community and the Member States.

In these mixed agreements, each party acts in its own name, undertaking to perform the obligations which fall within its competence. Mixed agreements may be concluded by the Community, acting with the participation of the Member States, under either Article 113 or Article 238.

Mixed agreements have been used extensively to implement the numerous treaties between the Community and developing countries, namely Yaounde I (1964), Yaounde II (1969), Lome I (1975), Lome II (1979), Lome III (1984) and Lome IV (1989).

iii) International obligations assumed by the Member States

The Member States of the Community were parties to a number of international agreements prior to the conclusion of the treaties forming the Community, including the European Convention on Human Rights 1950 and the General Agreement on Trade and Tariffs.

The Community is deemed to succeed to treaties concluded before the Community Treaties only if they contain matters within the competence of the Community. In one case relating to the status of the GATT in Community law, the Court declared that:

'in so far as under the EC Treaty the Community has assumed the powers previously exercised by the Member States in the area governed by the GATT, the provisions of that agreement have the effect of binding the Community': *International Fruit Company* v *Produktschap voor Groenten en Fruit* [1972] ECR 1219.

Treaties concluded after the Community Treaties by the Member States on subjects within the competence of the Community are probably void, although in practice this is an unlikely eventuality because of the propensity of the Community to participate in all agreements which might conceivably relate to its affairs.

d) *Incorporation of treaties into European Community law*

The EC Treaty itself does not specify the status and effect of international agreements within the Community legal order, nor does it identify the means through which such obligations are incorporated into Community law. Although the practice of the Council is to enact a decision or a regulation to approve an agreement, it appears that the actual instrument of approval itself is not the source of authority for an agreement in Community law. Rather, an international agreement concluded by the Community, by its mere conclusion and approval by the Council, and subsequent publication in the Community Official Journal, is incorporated into Community law: see *Haegemann* v *Belgian State* [1973] ECR 125.

e) *Effect of treaties in Community law*

Treaties concluded by the Community exercising its express or implied treaty-making powers are 'binding on the institutions of the Community and the Member States' by virtue of Article 228(2) of the EC Treaty.

Community treaties form an integral element of Community law and have been given direct effect by the European Court. In other words, individuals may rely upon the terms of treaties negotiated by the Community. In order to have direct effect, a particular provision of a Treaty must satisfy two main criteria:

i) an individual may only rely on such a provision if it is 'capable of creating rights of which interested parties may avail themselves in a court of law': *International Fruit*, above; and

ii) in order to ascertain whether a Community agreement confers rights upon individuals, regard must be had to the 'purpose and nature of the agreement itself' to determine if the provision in question 'contains a clear and precise obligation which is not subject, in its implementation or effects, to the adoption of any subsequent measure': *Demirel* v *Stadt Schwabisch Gmund* [1989] 1 CMLR 421.

If these conditions are satisfied, then direct effect may be given to the terms of a Community agreement: see *Hauptzollamt Mainz* v *Kupferberg* [1983] 1 CMLR 1.

f) *The contents and effect of the Common Commercial Policy*

The Community Common Commercial Policy is founded on the uniform application of principles relating to tariff rates, the conclusion of tariff and trade agreements, the attainment of uniformity in measures of trade liberalisation, the formulation of a consistent export policy and the adoption of measures to protect against unfair trade practices: Article 113(1) of the EC Treaty.

The process for the formulation of the CCP is similar to the normal decision-making procedures within the Community. The European Commission drafts proposals after consultations with interested parties, or third states in the case of negotiating agreements. These proposals are submitted to the Council of Ministers, which must adopt proposals by a qualified majority: Article 148 EC Treaty. The Council has authority to enact regulations, directives and decisions in the pursuit of the Common Commercial Policy.

g) *European Community trade protection laws*

The Community has a number of powers to impose measures on imports from third countries in order to protect industry and commerce within the Community from unfair foreign trade practices. These measures may be classified into four categories: (i) anti-dumping measures; (ii) countervailing (or anti-subsidy) measures; (iii) safeguard measures; and (iv) measures under the New Commercial Policy Instrument.

i) Anti-dumping actions

The Community authorities are authorised to impose anti-dumping duties on foreign products which are deemed to have been 'dumped' within the Community and which have caused injury to a Community industry: Council Regulation 3283/94 (1994). A foreign product has been 'dumped' inside the Community if it has been introduced into the internal market at a price less than the comparable price for the identical product in the country of manufacture.

Protection against dumped products is the most common form of trade protection measure employed by the European Community.

ii) Countervailing duty (or anti-subsidy) actions

Countervailing duties are imposed by the Community on foreign products that have benefited from subsidies from foreign governments during their manufacture, distribution or export, if such products cause injury to Community industries producing similar goods. Such duties are infrequently imposed by the Community on foreign products. The authority under which the Community imposes countervailing duties is contained in Council Regulation 3284/94 (1994).

iii) Safeguard actions

Imports into the Community from third countries may also be subject to safeguard measures under the relevant provisions of Council Regulation 3285/94 (1994). If foreign products are being imported into the Community in such increased quantities as to cause, or threaten to cause, serious injury to a Community industry, safeguard measures may be imposed to protect the Community industry, regardless of the cause or source of the increase in the volume of imports.

If the existence of increased imports can be established, and if such imports cause serious injury, the Community may impose additional duties, tariffs or quotas on the importation of such products to protect the Community industry.

iv) The new Commercial Policy Instrument

The Community authorities are also empowered to adopt measures designed to combat the 'illicit commercial practices' of third countries under Council Regulation 3286/94 (1994). This measure is designed to protect the interests of Community industries and exports to foreign markets which are being obstructed by illicit practices on the part of the governments of the third state. The Policy Instrument allows individuals within the Community to complain to the Community authorities regarding foreign commercial practices and, after investigation, if these practices are found to be illicit, retaliatory measures may be adopted in order to coerce the foreign state into desisting in such practices.

14.3 Relevant cases

EC Commission v *EC Council (Re ERTA)* [1971] 1 CMLR 335: Development by the Court of the doctrine of the implied powers of the Community.

Hauptzollamt Mainz v *Kupferberg* [1983] 1 CMLR 1: A decision relating to the direct effect of treaties negotiated by the Community within the Community legal system

International Fruit Company v *Produktschap voor Groenten en Fruit* [1972] ECR 1219: The direct effect of treaties negotiated by the Member States prior to the adopting of the three founding Community Treaties.

Polydor v *Harlequin Record Shops* [1982] ECR 329: The effect of free trade agreements between the Community and third states in Community law.

Demirel v *Stadt Schwabisch Gmund* [1989] 1 CMLR 421: The direct effect of the EC-Turkey association agreement.

14.4 Relevant materials

P Pescatore, 'Treaty-making by the European Communities' in FG Jacobs & S Roberts (eds), *The Effect of Treaties in Domestic Law* (1987) 171–195.

D O'Keefe & HG Schermers (eds), *Mixed Agreements* (1983).

G Bebr, 'Agreements Concluded by the Community and Their Possible Direct Effect' (1983) 20 CML Rev 35.

M Hilf et al (eds), *The European Community and the GATT* (1986).

I Van Bael & J-F Bellis, *International Trade Law and Practice of the European Community* (Second edition, 1990).

EA Vermulst, *Anti-Dumping Law and Practice in the United States and the European Community* (1987).

J Cunnane & C Stanbrook, *Dumping and Subsidies in the European Community* (1983).

14.5 Analysis of questions

The subject of the external relations of the European Community is a specialist field which explains the relative scarcity of questions relating to this topic among examiners. However, the external relations of the Community has acquired a greater degree of significance in light of the Community participation in the Uruguay Round of GATT multilateral trade negotiations and the decisions of the European Court giving direct effect to terms of certain types of international agreements negotiated between the Community and third states. Not surprisingly, the following questions focus on these issues together with the matter of Community trade protection laws.

14.6 Questions

QUESTION ONE

What role has the Court of Justice played in defining the extent of the Community's powers in the external relations field?

University of Glasgow LLB Examination
1989 Q9

General Comment

A general question on the function of the European Court in determining the scope of the external competence of the Community.

Skeleton Solution

• Express powers of the Community to negotiate treaties.
• Implied powers imputed by the Court.
• Development of the doctrine through the jurisprudence of the Court.

Suggested Solution

The Community has capacity to enter international agreements between itself and third states without the participation of the Member States in the negotiating processes. Express treaty-making capacity is conferred in the EC Treaty for two particular forms of agreement.

Article 113 authorises the Community to conclude commercial agreements relating to tariff and trade matters for the purposes of achieving the objectives of the common commercial policy. This authority expressly extends to export aids, credit and finance, and matters relating to multilateral commodity agreements.

Article 238 of the EC Treaty also authorises the Community to negotiate with third states, unions of states or international organisations, association agreements creating reciprocal rights and obligations, and facilitating common action through special procedures. Association agreements perform two functions. In the case of certain European countries the purpose of this form of agreement is to act as a preliminary procedure prior to membership of the Community. Other association agreements establish free trade status between the products of the Community and the third state in each others markets.

Agreements under Article 238 are supplemented by a special form of association agreement under Articles 131 to 136 of the EC Treaty which provide for agreements between the Community and overseas countries and territories. These territories are listed in Annex IV to the Treaty and were originally dependencies of the Member States. The purpose of such agreements is to promote the economic and social development of these territories by establishing 'close economic relations' between the Community and the territory.

The exercise of power under Article 113 of the EC Treaty has a potentially greater application. Two developments have significantly expanded the powers of the Community under Article 113 to the exclusion of the participation of the Member States: the development of a broad interpretation by the Court of the concept of the common commercial policy; and the creation, also by the Court, of the 'theory of parallelism'.

The intention of the European Court to interpret the concept of the CCP in broad terms was made clear in the *International Agreement on Rubber Case* (1979), which was an advisory opinion from the European Court on a reference by the Commission under Article 228(1). The case concerned the participation of the Community in the negotiation of an international commodity agreement to regulate the supply of rubber. The Court stressed that a coherent common commercial policy would not be feasible if the Community was unable to exercise its treaty-making powers in relation to those international agreements which, alongside traditional commercial agreements, form an important element of the international economic environment. A broad interpretation of this provision was supported by the fact that the enumeration of the individual subjects covered by the article was conceived in a non-exhaustive fashion.

However, at the same time the Court believed that an important factor in deciding whether the Community had exclusive competence in this matter was the financial burden of participating in an agreement. In the case of a commodity agreement, if the burden of financing the agreement is placed on the Community budget, the Community has exclusive jurisdiction. Alternatively, if the charges are to be borne directly by the Member States, this factor implies the participation of the Member States in the negotiation of the agreement. The effect of this decision was in fact to expand the concept of the CCP itself, and also, in turn, the powers of the Community.

While the *Rubber Case* confirms that the Community has express authority to achieve those objectives specified for the achievement of the common commercial policy, the European Court has gone much further in developing the theory of implied powers, not only for the purposes of achieving a common commercial policy, but in fact to attain the objectives set out in Part 1 of the EC Treaty. This has been achieved by the development of the theory of parallelism by the Court which was originally elaborated *EC Commission v EC Council (Re ERTA)* (1971).

In 1967 the Member States entered into negotiations with other European states to establish a European Road Transport Agreement. During these negotiations, the Council enacted a regulation which covered substantially the same subject-matter, but the Member States, anxious to include third states within the scope of the agreement continued negotiations on the subject. In 1970 the Council decided that negotiations would continue on an individual Member State basis without the participation of the Commission in the process. The Commission objected to this situation and brought an action before the European Court to annul the Council resolution deciding to conduct the negotiations on a Member State basis.

The Court held that authority to enter international agreements not only arose from those provisions which granted express authority, but also from other provisions of the Treaty which require international agreement for their achievement. In particular, each time the Community adopts legislation for the purpose of implementing a common policy envisaged by the Treaty, the Member States no longer have the right, acting individually or even collectively, to undertake obligations with third countries which would affect those rules. The doctrine of parallelism therefore requires that if the Community exercises an internal power, it simultaneously acquires a parallel external power to government the subject-matter.

In other words, the exercise of the internal capacity of the Community over a particular subject-matter deprives the Member States of individual authority to regulate the matter by international agreement. The basis for this determination was the need for the Community to assume and carry out contractual obligations towards third states affecting the whole sphere of the application of the Community legal system. This rationale was later confirmed in *Hauptzollamt Mainz v Kupferberg* (1983).

One qualification was, in fact, made to the functioning of the theory of parallelism under the EC Treaty. The mere existence of internal legislative competence within the scheme of the Treaty was not ipso facto conclusive of the inability of the Member States to conclude international agreements bearing on such matters. Not only must legislative competence exist, but this power must be exercised by the Community. This restriction stems from the construction given by the Court to the rationale behind the theory – the desirability of avoiding conflicts between internal Community legislative and the international obligations of the Member States.

The Court has elaborated upon the doctrine of parallelism in a number of subsequent cases, one of the most significant being the *North-East Atlantic Fisheries Convention Case* (1975). Seven of the nine Member States entered into a convention to conserve fishing stocks in the North-East Atlantic and the Netherlands promulgated legislation implementing the provisions of the convention which provided inter alia for criminal prosecutions. A number of Dutch fishermen were prosecuted in a Dutch court for violating this statute. In their defence, the fishermen alleged that the Member States had no authority to enter international agreements on this subject since competence to regulate fishing policy had been passed to the Community. The Dutch legislation therefore infringed Community law.

The Community had in fact passed two regulations dealing with a common fishing policy but neither concerned the issue of conservation. Therefore, no Community legislation had been passed and no express authority to enter fishing conservation agreements had been conferred by the EC Treaty. The Court held that the Community had authority to enter international commitments for the conservation of the resources of the sea, even though the Community had not passed legislation in exercise of this internal capacity. However, since the Community had not yet exercised its powers for this purpose, concurrent authority over this matter existed between the Community and the Member States and the Dutch legislation was upheld.

The Court later abandoned these restrictions on the implied powers of the Community to enter international agreements in the *Inland Waterway Vessels Case* (1977). In this case, the Community had no express treaty-making power to regulate inland waterway administration, although it did have authority to pass internal legislation in pursuit of a common transport policy under Articles 74 and 75 of the EC Treaty. This internal legislative power had not been exercised.

Nevertheless, the European Court declared that the theory of parallelism extended not only to cases in which internal legislative power had been exercised by the Community but also to those cases which the Treaty creates an internal legislative capacity and the participation of the Community in the negotiation of an agreement 'is necessary for the attainment of one of the objectives of the Community'. In this decision, the Court conferred upon the Community authority to negotiate all agreements which fell within the competence of the Community by virtue of the EC Treaty.

The European Court has therefore played a significant role in the expansion of the powers of the Community in the field of external relations. This has, in turn, resulted in a restriction of the powers of the Member States to conduct international affairs. The Court has achieved this expansion primarily through the teleological interpretation of the terms of the EC Treaty.

QUESTION TWO

What criteria does the Court of Justice apply in deciding whether a provision of an international agreement has direct effects?

University of Glasgow LLB Examination 1988 Q1

General Comment

A difficult question requiring detailed knowledge of the recent jurisprudence of the European Court.

Skeleton Solution

• Legal effect of agreements within the Community.
• Rights of individuals.
• Criteria for establishing direct effect.
• Examples of the application of the principle.

Suggested Solution

Treaties concluded by the Community within the powers vested by the EC Treaty are 'binding on the institutions of the Community and the Member States' by virtue of Article 228(2) of the EC Treaty. The European Court has taken the view that treaties to which the Community is a party, either by succession or direct negotiation, are an 'integral element of community law': *Haegemann v Belgian State* (1973). The Court has taken this view to ensure that international obligations assumed by the Community are consistently respected by the Member States.

In *Hauptzollamt Mainz v Kupferberg* (1983), the Court held that in order to 'ensure respect for treaty obligations concluded by the Community institutions, the Member States fulfil an obligation not only in relation to the non-Member country concerned but also and above all in relation to the Community which has assumed responsibility for the due performance of the obligation'. However, naturally a Community Treaty may be binding on both the Community and the Member States without conferring rights on individuals.

While a Community treaty may form an integral element of Community law, the Court has not automatically granted directly enforceable rights to individuals to vindicate this aspect of community law in the national tribunals of the Member States. The jurisprudence of the Court establishes a number of conditions which must be satisfied before an individual may exercise rights created under a Community agreement.

First, an individual may only contest the validity of a Community Regulation or a national rule of law if the treaty provision is 'capable of creating rights of which interested parties may avail themselves in a court of law': *International Fruit Company v Produktschap voor Groenten en Fruit* (1972); *Schluter v Hauptzollamt Lorrach* (1973).

Second, in order to ascertain whether a Community agreement confers rights upon individuals, regard must be had to 'the purpose and nature of the agreement itself' to determine whether the provision in question 'contains a clear and precise obligation which is not subject, in its implementation or effects, to the adoption of any subsequent measure: *Demirel v Stadt Schwabisch Gmund* (1989). If these conditions are satisfied, then direct effect may be given to the terms of a Community agreement under Community law.

The Court has demonstrated a greater reluctance to construe treaties to which the Community has succeeded as conferring individual enforceable rights than under treaties which the Community has negotiated itself. In *Bresciani v Amministrazione Italiana delle Finanze* (1976), the Court was prepared to accept that certain provisions of the Yaounde Convention of 1963 were directly enforceable after ascertaining that the purpose and nature of the provisions being relied upon was the automatic abolition of charges having an equivalent effect. Also, in *Pabst & Richarz* v *Hauptzollamt Oldenberg* (1982), the Court was willing to give direct effect to certain provisions of the EC-Greece Association Agreement.

While the plaintiff in the *Kupferberg Case*, above, was unsuccessful in invoking the EC-Portugal Free Trade Agreement as a defence, nevertheless the Court made a number of important points in defining the direct enforcement of Community agreements. The Court elaborated on the nature of the obligations assumed by the Community under Community agreements. On the one hand, it was the Community which was internationally responsible for the execution of the international obligations, while on the other hand, the obligation extended to the third state. A refusal by a national court to implement an obligation assumed by the Community did not invariably constitute an infringement of a reciprocal obligation since such agreements did not always require incorporation into national law. The full performance of an obligation might leave a party free to determine the legal means necessary within its legal system to pursue the objectives agreed.

Since this distinction existed, it was impossible to allow individuals to enforce rights at the national level unless the Member State in question would be failing to conform to its international obligations assumed through the Community. This was the ultimate rationale for distinguishing between the enforceable and unenforceable exercise of rights by individuals under Community treaties. In *R* v *Secretary of State, ex parte Narin* (1990), the English High Court applied this rationale in rejecting the argument that provisions of the EC-Turkey association could be given direct effect in English law.

In an earlier case relating to the direct effect of the provisions of the EC Treaty, the European Court acknowledged that 'the vigilance of individuals concerned to protect their rights amounts to an effective supervision in addition to the supervision by other states or by international organs': *Van Gend en Loos* v *Netherlands* (1963). Where EC Treaty provisions were capable of clear, unqualified and unconditional application then they were capable of being directly effective as a source of Community law. The Court has not adopted a similar policy with regard to the enforceability of treaties in Community law.

This aims and purposes standard established for the direct enforceability of such agreements, while perhaps more rigorous than the test for the direct enforcement of EC Treaty provisions, is eminently sensible. First, the EC Treaties and the related founding agreements are the constitution of the Community and should enjoy a preferred status to agreements negotiated under authority of them. Second, a dramatic expansion of enforceable rights would arise if every Community treaty was capable of conferring directly enforceable rights. Third, direct enforcement of Community treaties as an element of Community law would represent a usurpation of those legal systems which maintain a dualist legal tradition such as the United Kingdom. Fourth, considerable opposition has been manifested by a number of Member States to this limited inroad into the direct enforceability of Community treaties by the Court.

QUESTION THREE

Describe the processes which are involved in the formulation and administration of the common commercial policy within the European Community and comment on the extent to which the scope of this policy is limited by international regulations.

Question prepared by the Author

General Comment

A narrative question requiring a descriptive answer.

Skeleton Solution

- The scope of Articles 110–116 EC Treaty.
- Procedure for the formulation of the CCP.
- An illustration of the tensions involved.
- The existence of international restraints and their effects.

Suggested Solution

The creation of a consistent trade policy among the Member States of the European Community has been achieved by the delegation of decision-making authority over this subject-matter to the centralised agencies of the Community. Both the EC Treaty and the ECSC Treaty reserve exclusive competence to the Community for the conduct of 'commercial policy': Articles 110–116 EC Treaty; Articles 71–75 ECSC Treaty. Individual Member States no longer retain competence to legislate or enter into international obligations relating to these matters, in the absence of specific authorisation from the Community: *Donckerwolke* v *Procureur de la Republique* (1975). While the exact scope of the right to formulate commercial policy has not been clearly defined, the European Commission has consistently adopted an aggressive interpretation of this authority and on the whole, this policy has been supported by the ECJ.

From an international trade policy perspective, the European Community is a customs territory which is erected on the establishment of a common customs tariff and the creation of a common commercial policy towards third countries. The common customs tariff has replaced individual national tariff schedules with a harmonised and comprehensive scheme to facilitate the levying of duties on goods and products entering the Community. The Community common commercial policy is founded on the uniform application of principles relating, inter alia, to tariff changes, the conclusion of tariff and trade agreements, the achievement of uniformity in measures of trade liberalisation, the formulation of a consistent export policy and the adoption of measures to protect against unfair trade practices.

The procedure for the formulation of the common commercial policy is similar to the normal decision-making processes within the Community. The European Commission drafts proposals after consultations with various foreign representatives and forwards these initial draft texts to working groups composed of national representatives which negotiate a minimum acceptable proposal for submission to the Council of Ministers. The final content of the policy is the product of a continuous process of negotiation between the Commission and the Council of Ministers on the one hand, and where international agreements are involved, between the Commission and third states on the other hand. Although ultimate authority for Community legislation rests with the Council of Ministers, the powers of that organ are circumscribed by the requirement that the Council may only act on the basis of a proposal from the Commission.

This separation of powers in the adoption of trade policy is a hallmark of the institutional structure of the Community legislative process. The Commission is the initiator of policy, both within the Community itself and in relation to agreements with foreign states. The Council is compelled to act upon a formal proposal from the Commission as the basis for its final policy position. A tension has developed between the Council and the Commission, since the Member States demonstrate a propensity to attempt to preserve national control over the conduct of foreign policy.

The final content of Community trade policy is the compromise reached between the Council and the Commission, tempered by the need to accommodate international obligations assumed by the Community in the exercise of its external affairs competence.

The tension between the interests of the Member States, as manifested in the Council of Ministers, and the objectives of the Community, as advocated by the Commission, surfaced during the Tokyo Round of Multilateral Tariff Negotiations held under the auspices of the GATT, and again during the European Community – United States steel dispute in the early 1980s. After the conclusion of the 1979 GATT Code on Non-Tariff Barriers to Trade, a number of Member States of the Community argued that the subject-matters of certain agreements fell within the jurisdiction of the Member States and outside that of the Community. During the steel dispute, a number of Member States pointed to the less rigorous Community provisions in the ECSC Treaty in contrast to the comparable provisions in the EC Treaty. The final resolution of this dispute required the negotiation of an extensive mandate between the Member States to allow the Commission to settle the issue with the United States government.

Despite the expiry of the transition periods for the completion of the objectives of the EC Treaty, and the renewed impetus towards the creation of an internal market by the Single European Act, Member States continue to express a reluctance to transfer complete authority to the Community to formulate a comprehensive and coherent common commercial policy. This reluctance may be attributed to two separate factors. First, the institutional structure established for the creation of a commercial policy is insufficient. Second, the objectives of the common commercial policy are fragmented and not comprehensively stated to a degree which would encourage transfer of competence to the Community.

Consistent commercial policy requires a centralised agency to express policy objectives. Within the Community, the Council of Ministers, which is the organ with ultimate responsibility for commercial policy, indulges in extensive internal debate and bargaining before a mandate is given to the Commission to present the policy at the global level. Since the final position within the Council is the embodiment of an internal political compromise, the final Community policy is rigid and inflexible. The internal decision-making processes, by allowing for the continued voicing of national concerns, are not suitable for consistent policy formulation.

Also the objectives of the common commercial policy are organically integrated with the success of other Community policies. The ineffective control of the Community over certain areas of the Community economy, such as agriculture, has undermined even this weak policy position. While the Community has failed to adopt legislation standardising technical requirements for intra-Community trade, it is unlikely that it will succeed in doing so for foreign goods. The failure of the Community at this level, ultimately exacerbates the problems at the international level. For example, the Member States of the Community continue to negotiate voluntary export restraints with foreign nations even though this matter is an issue for Community regulation.

The ultimate consequence of the fragmented approach to policy formulation is the reluctance of Member States to transfer regulatory authority to the Community.

Community external policy depends on the Common Customs Tariff (CCT) and the Common Commercial Policy (CCP). Each of these is subject to the international regulations established under the GATT and assumed by the Community on behalf of the individual Member States. Non-adherence or violation of such rules would therefore ex facie give rise to a presumption of protectionism. The existence of international rules negotiated in the GATT does limit the scope of the Community to formulate the CCP, but this effect is minimised by the fact that international rules regulating economic matters are generally vague and imprecise. As a result, the normative effect of such rules is strictly circumscribed. This is particularly true as regards the international legal restraints on the use of trade protection measures such as anti-dumping duties.

The European Community appears to have tightened its legislation in the field of trade protection laws in order to take advantage of the relative laxity of the international rules. A number of trade remedy provisions do in fact seem to violate the international rules. But greater concern must be raised by the volume of actions taken under the authority of trade protection laws. One disconcerting illustration of this problem is the adoption of anti-dumping measures by the Community. Before the accession to the Tokyo Round Agreement on Anti-Dumping in 1979, the European Community first enacted anti-dumping legislation in 1968. In the next 10 year intervening period, a total of 60 anti-dumping investigations were initiated. But, in the 10 year period between 1979 and 1989, this average has climbed dramatically: IV Bael & J-F Bellis, *International Trade Law and Practice of the European Community* (second edition, 1990).

Although a number of reasons have been offered to explain this phenomenon, at least one commentator is prepared to acknowledge that these trends may be attributed to two factors: the economic recession within the Community prompted an increase in the number of actions, coupled with the realisation that anti-dumping duty actions constituted an effective instrument of economic coercion: I Van Bael, 'EC Anti-Dumping Law and Practice Revisited' (1990) 24 JWT 5.

Despite recognition that the abuse of measures of contingent protection represents a serious threat to the stability of the global trading system – a fact acknowledged during the Tokyo Round of Multilateral Tariff Negotiations – the introduction of Community legislation to implement the 1979 Anti-Dumping Code has done nothing to stem the growth of anti-dumping duty actions. The conclusion must therefore be reached that the Code itself is ineffective.

At the same time, subsequent amendments to the 1979 legislation have attempted to close any loopholes in the law which may facilitate abuse. The general theme of this process has been a tightening of the regulations against the interests of foreign producers and importers. As the subject of dumping has been increasingly regulated, it has become progressively easier for a complainer to be successful in its action, or at least to harass the importer or foreign producer.

QUESTION FOUR

The Mitsubishi Corporation of Japan has been accused of dumping video cassette recorders in the European Community by the Government of France. This allegation is denied by Mitsubishi who seek advice from you in relation to the nature of the investigation by the Commission into the allegation of dumping. The French government has also alleged that Mitsubishi has established a manufacturing plant in Sunderland, England, in order to circumvent the payment of earlier anti-dumping duties by importing the component parts for final assembly in Sunderland.

Advise Mitsubishi of the nature of the investigation which will be carried out by the Commission and of the legitimacy its activities in Sunderland.

Question prepared by the Author

General Comment

A problem-type question requiring the student to apply Community anti-dumping procedure to a hypothetical factual situation.

Skeleton Solution

• The Anti-Dumping Regulation.
• The elements of a dumping action – procedure and substantive.
• Screwdriver Regulation.

Suggested Solution

Dumping is the practice by which goods are introduced into the Community at a price lower than the price of equivalent goods on the domestic market of the exporting country. It is deemed to be an unfair trade practice and most states, including the Community, have legislation which allows anti-dumping duties to be levied in order to prevent injury to domestic industries competing with the foreign products.

The European Commission has responsibility for investigating the facts surrounding an anti-dumping petition and determines whether or not there is sufficient evidence to justify an investigation: Council Regulation 3283/94 (1994). It is also empowered under certain conditions to impose provisional anti-dumping duties for a maximum period of six months and to accept undertakings by foreign exporters. However, the Council of Ministers has sole competence to order definitive anti-dumping duties.

A dumping complaint may be lodged by any legal person (an individual or company) or by an association not having legal personality, acting on behalf of a Community industry. According to the Council Regulation, investigations of anti-dumping must normally be completed within a period of not less than six months immediately prior to the initiation of the complaint.

The complaint itself must contain 'sufficient evidence' of the existence of both dumping and injury to a Community industry. In general, this requires information relating to: (a) the nature of the allegedly dumped product; (b) the origin of the exporting country; (c) the names of the country of origin, the producer and the exporter of the product in question; and (d) evidence of dumping and injury resulting therefrom from the industry which considers itself injured or threatened. Upon receipt of a complaint setting forth such facts, the Commission will begin its investigation.

The Commission investigates the question of dumping until its final determination. If this is negative, the investigation terminates, but where the finding is positive, definitive anti-dumping duties may be imposed. This is done by way of a report submitted to the Council of Ministers which has the discretion to accept, modify or reject the Commission's proposal. Where duties are imposed, this is achieved by the adoption of a Regulation (or a Decision) sanctioning the imposition of duties.

The basic substantive elements of an anti-dumping action are the existence of dumping, injury and 'Community interests' requiring intervention.

The procedure for determining the existence of dumping in the Community is deceptively simple. It involves four basic steps: (a) the determination of 'normal value'; (b) the determination of 'export price'; (c) a comparison of the normal value to export price; and (d) the calculation of the 'margin of dumping' (the normal price minus the export price). Each of these determinations allows considerable latitude for interpretation.

Normal value is the price of the goods in the country of origin, while the export price is the price of the goods inside the Community. The margin of dumping is the difference between these two figures and is also the quantum of the anti-dumping duty which will be levied to neutralise the unfair competitive advantage enjoyed by the foreign product.

In addition to establishing the existence of actual dumped products, it is also necessary to prove that these products have caused material injury to an industry within the Community. This involves proof of actual material injury, the threat of material injury or the material retardation of an industry. In addition, the investigation must reveal that the dumped products have caused the material injury. If it cannot be shown that the dumped products are the cause of the injury, no anti-dumping duties can be imposed.

Finally, before anti-dumping duties can be assessed, a third condition must be met; it must be decided that 'the interests of the Community call for intervention'. No list of definitive Community interests is provided in the Regulation concerning the imposition of dumping duties. However, the concept of Community interests will cover a wide range of factors, but the most important concern the interests of the consumer and processors of imported products and the need to have regard to the competitive equilibrium within the Community market.

If all these elements are established during the Commission investigation, Mitsubishi may be subject to anti-dumping duties in respect of its VCR products.

The Community has also adopted legislation to prevent foreign importers from circumventing the application of anti-dumping duties by breaking down their products into their component parts and then importing these for reassembly inside the Community. Anti-dumping duties may be imposed on the finished product even if assembled in a factory within the Community, at the rate applicable to the finished product but by reference to the CIF value of the parts imported for assembly in this manner. The relevant legislation which achieves this goal is known as the 'Screwdriver Regulation'.

Three conditions must be satisfied in order to attract this form of anti-dumping duty: (a) the assembly must be carried out by a person related to the exporter of the like products subject to the anti-dumping duties; (b) the assembly has started or substantially increased after the anti-dumping investigation leading to the imposition of duties had commenced; and (c) the value of the parts or materials used in the finished product which have come from the country concerned constitutes at least 60 per cent of the parts and materials used.

The Screwdriver Regulation has in fact been held to be unlawful by a recent GATT panel report and the Regulation itself will most likely be amended or repealed in the near future. Until then, it is likely that Mitsubishi may be subject to additional duties in respect of VCRs if the component parts for the finished product have entered the Community for assembly for the purpose of avoiding the imposition of duties.

15 UNIVERSITY OF LONDON LLB (EXTERNAL) 1994 QUESTIONS AND SUGGESTED SOLUTIONS

UNIVERSITY OF LONDON
LLB EXAMINATIONS 1994
for External Students
PARTS I and II EXAMINATION (Scheme A) and
THIRD AND FOURTH YEAR EXAMINATIONS (Scheme B)

EUROPEAN COMMUNITY LAW

Wednesday, 15 June: 10.00am to 1.00pm

Answer *FOUR* of the following EIGHT questions

1 'Arguably the greatest achievement of the European Court of Justice is the development of the doctrine of direct effect.'

Discuss with reference to application to different types of EC primary and secondary legislation and to case law.

2 How has the Treaty on European Union affected the relationship between the European institutions?

Discuss with particular reference to at least two of the institutions.

3 What are the legal implications for EC and for national law of the following cases:

Francovich & Boniface v *Italian Republic* – Joined Cases C–6/90 and C–9/90

European Parliament v *Council*, Case 70/88 ('Post-Chernobyl')

R v *Secretary of State for Transport, ex parte Factortame* (I) and (II), Cases C–213/89 and C–221/89

4 Explain how the European Court of Justice in the development of its case law has complied with Art. 164 of the Treaty on European Union.

5 Mr Jones has a small soft drinks importing firm in Cardiff. Wanting to expand his business, he is always looking for new products and discovers a herbal soft drink called Schwipps which is extremely popular in Germany because of its allegedly health-giving properties. He places an order for 10,000 bottles with Schmidt AG, the manufacturers.

Schmidt refuse to supply him and tell him to order the drinks from Smith Ltd in Birmingham, their distributors in the UK. Jones is very disappointed as Smith Ltd are direct competitors of his and charge much higher prices than Schwipps.

259

He is then approached by a distributor of Schwipps in Germany who offers him a good deal, proposing to send him a shipment in bulk containers which Jones can then bottle himself.

He accepts and the consignment arrives in Dover. It is stopped there by the customs because the drink contains 5% algiphit, a substance which is permitted in drinks under UK legislation in concentrations of up to 4.5% only but which is considered beneficial in Germany, where there is no such limit. Jones hires a specialist firm at considerable expense which analyses and then dilutes the concentration until it complies with the UK limit of 4.5%. The consignment is then admitted. Sales are going well. Smith Ltd hear of this and apply to the courts for an injunction to stop Jones selling the drink.

Advise Jones. Can he contest the application for an injunction? What aspects of Community law might be considered?

6 'The right to challenge the legality of acts of Community institutions extends to institutions and Member States, but also individuals.'

Discuss and compare these different rights.

7 A British engineering company with its headquarters in Guildford has decided to establish a branch in Greece. They are sending out an exploration team of engineers who intend to spend three months exploring suitable sites and looking at the available skilled labour.

If all goes well, the company will then open the branch and bring the managerial staff over from England.

Before embarking on this venture, they come to you for advice. They want to know:

a) Whether the 'exploration team' will encounter any difficulties with regard to residence and work permits;

b) once the branch is open, whether they can send any of their staff members out to work there, and, in particular

   i) Mary, deputy head of the accountancy department. She is British, but has been co-habiting with Jason, an Australian who is an engineer with the firm, for five years and the company intends to send them out together.

   ii) Malcolm, a computer specialist, whose wife Deirdre has a criminal conviction for possession of cannabis which she received three years ago.

Advise them.

8 'The Community legislation in the area of the free movement of persons is no longer sufficient given the strains imposed by the objective of the single market and external pressures.' (O'Keeffe)

Discuss.

QUESTION ONE

'Arguably the greatest achievement of the European Court of Justice is the development of the doctrine of direct effect.'

Discuss with reference to application to different types of EC primary and secondary legislation and to case law.

University of London LLB Examination
(for External Students) European Community Law June 1994 Q1

General Comment

This is a broad question requiring the application of a single principle to four separate sources of Community law. The answer is relatively long due to the sizeable volume of caselaw on this subject. However, in the final analysis, the question itself is relatively straightforward and involves one of the most basic concepts of Community law.

Skeleton Solution

- Direct effect of EC primary legislation: EC Treaty provisions and international treaties.
- Conditions required for application of the principle to primary legislation.
- Direct effect of EC secondary legislation: regulations and directives.
- Conditions required for application of the principle to secondary legislation.

Suggested Solution

When negotiating the EC Treaty the draftsmen envisaged Community law being created through the institutional framework created by the Treaty itself. The principal sources of law were to be regulations, directives and decisions according to Article 189. These laws were to be enacted by the Council of Ministers and the European Commission in accordance with the procedures laid down in the Treaty.

Had this remained the position, many of the fundamental principles of EC law would never have seen the light of day. For example, the principles of non-discrimination on the grounds of nationality or on the ground of gender were not enacted by Community institutions nor was the principle of the supremacy of Community law over national law. These concepts were created by the European Court through the direct application of the EC Treaty provisions.

In a deliberate act of judicial activism, the European Court created the doctrine of direct effect in order to expand the scope of the legal principles of Community law. Initially, this doctrine was applied to EC Treaty provisions to allow private individuals to rely on the terms of that agreement. Gradually, the doctrine was extended to encompass international agreements entered into by the Community with third states and to directives. So, while originally only Community regulations were intended to have the quality of direct effect, after the Court's interventions EC Treaty provisions, Community treaties with non-EC countries and directives are all capable of having direct effect if certain circumstances are satisfied.

261

The circumstances and conditions under which these measures have direct effect differ and therefore it is appropriate to consider each separately.

Direct effect of EC Treaty provisions

In *Van Gend en Loos* v *The Netherlands* (1963), the European Court held that where a provision of the EC Treaty imposes a clear and unconditional obligation on a Member State, unqualified by any reservation preserving the right of Member States to give effect to the provision in the form of a national law, such a provision may be capable of direct effect. The quality of direct effect creates private rights for individuals which can be enforced by bringing legal proceedings in national courts and tribunals.

Examining this decision in detail, three specific conditions are therefore required for a term of a Community treaty to have direct effect. First, the provision being relied on must be clear and precise: see *Gimenez Zaera* v *Instituto Nacional de la Seguridad Social* (1987). Second, the term must be unqualified and not subject to the actions of national authorities for its operation: see *Sociaal Fonds voor de Diamantarbeiders* v *Brachfeld & Chougol Diamond Co* (1969). Finally, the obligation established must not leave substantial discretion to Member States or the European Commission to effect its performance: see *Salgoil* v *Italian Ministry for Foreign Trade* (1968).

The application of the doctrine is not confined to the European Court. National courts are bound to give effect to this principle if the necessary conditions are satisfied and in fact the courts of the United Kingdom regularly give direct effect to EC Treaty provisions. For example, in *R* v *Secretary of State for Transport, ex parte Factortame (No 3)* (1989), the House of Lords gave direct effect, inter alia, to Article 6 (formerly Article 7 until the amendments made to the EC Treaty by the Treaty on European Union), and held the Merchant Shipping Act 1988 to be incompatible with that provision. In rendering his judgment, Lord Bridge of Harwich observed:

'Directly enforceable Community rights are part of the legal heritage of every citizen of a Member State of the EEC. They arise from the Treaty itself and not from any judgment of the ECJ declaring their existence.'

Among the articles which have been given direct effect by the European Court are Article 6 (non-discrimination on the grounds of nationality), Articles 9 and 12 (elimination of customs duties and charges having an equivalent effect), Article 30 (elimination of quantitative restrictions and measures having an equivalent effect), Articles 85 and 86 (European Community competition policy) and Article 119 (non-discrimination on the grounds of gender).

Direct effect of Community treaties

The second source of primary legislation, in addition to the Community treaties, is international agreements entered into by the Community with non-Community states. These agreements are also capable of providing a reservoir of directly applicable principles of Community law: see *Hauptzollamt Mainz* v *Kupferberg & Cie KG* (1982). Further, the European Court has also held that such agreements prevail over inconsistent provisions of national law.

The case of *Kupferberg* provides an interesting illustration of the application of the principle to agreements entered into by the Community. Kupferberg, a German importer, was charged duties on imports of Portuguese port. He believed these charges were contrary to the terms of the Association Agreement between the European Community and Portugal which prohibited, on a reciprocal basis, discriminatory internal taxation between imported and domestic products. The matter was referred by the German court to the European Court for a preliminary ruling.

The European Court held that, since international responsibility for breach of such treaties rested with the Community, the Court must recognise the need to ensure uniform application of these obligations within the Community. Hence, the terms of the agreement could be given direct effect if the provision being relied on was unconditional and precise and also capable of conferring individual rights which could be enforced in national courts or tribunals: see also *Demirel v Stadt Schwabisch Gmund* (1989).

It should be noted that the conditions required for the direct effect of international agreements entered into by the Community on the one hand, and those for direct effect of provisions of the EC Treaty on the other hand, differ in some respects. Hence, two separate tests have been established for giving direct effect to these different types of Community primary legislation.

Direct effect of regulations

Under Article 189 of the EC Treaty, regulations are 'binding in their entirety and directly applicable in all Member States'. Community regulations which have entered into force may be enforced by or against the subjects of the regulation and the application of such measures is independent of any supplementing measure of national law: *Bussone v Ministry of Agriculture and Forestry* (1978).

Direct effect of directives

'Vertical direct effect' may be given to directives which have remained unimplemented by Member States after the period provided for the adoption of the measure into national law. In other words, the Court has been prepared to refuse to allow the failure of a state to adopt a directive as a justification for denying private individuals their legitimate rights.

The right to rely on the terms of an unimplemented directive is not absolute. Three conditions must be satisfied before reliance can be placed on the measure. First, the terms of the directive must be sufficiently precise to allow the creation of directly enforceable legal obligations. Second, the provision must specify an obligation which is not subject to any qualification, exception or condition. Third, the provision must not require intervention on the part of a Community institution or a Member State.

There are, however, two major limitations placed on the application of the principle of direct effect to Community directives.

First, the principle applies only to directives which remain unimplemented after the date has passed for adoption. The entry into force of directives which have been adopted, but which have not yet entered into force, cannot be anticipated or pre-empted.

Second, and more importantly, the Court has only been prepared to apply this principle to the relationships between individuals and the national authorities as opposed to the relationships among private individuals themselves. In other words,

263

while an individual can invoke an unimplemented directive against national authorities, the rights conferred by the unimplemented directives cannot be enforced in private relationships.

The application of the principle of direct effect to private relationships is known as 'horizontal direct effect' as opposed to 'vertical direct effect', which refers to the relationship between individuals and the state. In *Marshall* v *Southampton and South-West Hampshire Area Health Authority* (1986), the European Court denied that unimplemented directives were capable of horizontal direct effect.

That is not, however, the end of the matter. The situation has been made more complex by decisions of the Court which, while continuing the general policy of refusing to give horizontal direct effect to directives, have nevertheless opened an alternative channel to allow relief to private individuals denied their rights against other individuals because a Member State has failed to implement a directive in time.

First, in *Von Colson* v *Land Nordrhein-Westfahlen* (1984), and more recently in *Marleasing SA* v *La Commercial Internacional De Alimentacion SA* (1992), the Court has given indirect effect to unimplemented directives via Article 5 of the EC Treaty. This article requires Member States to 'take all appropriate measures' to ensure the fulfilment of the obligations arising out of the Treaty.

In *Marleasing*, the plaintiffs alleged that a Spanish company had been wound up for the purpose of defrauding its creditors. The company was formed by a founders' contract which is an agreement among the participants in the company to establish the company. This is a legitimate means of incorporating a company under Spanish law. The plaintiffs were challenging the winding-up on the basis that the founders' contract was void for lack of consideration, also a concept recognised in Spanish company law. If the contract was void, the directors would be liable for its debt since there would have been no valid incorporation in the first place.

The grounds on which a company can be annulled are exhaustively listed in Council Directive 68/151. Lack of consideration is not one of the grounds listed in the directive but in any event the Spanish government had not implemented its terms at the time the dispute arose. The defendants relied on this directive to support the assertion that the company could not be wound up for lack of consideration because this was not a ground for declaring a company void under the directive. The Court was asked to rule on the effect of the unimplemented directive on the relationship between these two private parties.

While the Court rejected the notion of horizontal direct effect, it observed that Article 5 of the EC Treaty placed Member States under an obligation to give effect to Community obligations. Spanish law had to be interpreted in light of this obligation. Hence, Spanish company law was to be interpreted and applied in terms compatible with the directive. Since the directive exhaustively listed all the grounds for annulling a company, the Spanish company could not be annulled for lack of consideration. Hence the directors were not personally liable for the debts of the company.

It is difficult to avoid the conclusion that this decision was simply a means of permitting horizontal direct effect through interpretative sleight of hand. In other words, the Court is prepared to apply the terms of unimplemented directives to the relationships between individuals where this can be achieved by means of interpretative implication.

QUESTION TWO

How has the Treaty on European Union affected the relationship between the European institutions?

Discuss with particular reference to at least two of the institutions.

University of London LLB Examination
(for External Students) European Community Law June 1994 Q2

General Comment

This is a question focusing on the relationships between the Community institutions and requiring comment on the way in which these relationships have altered now the Treaty on European Union has come into effect. The main constitutional changes brought by the Treaty have involved the European Parliament and, therefore, the relationships between this institution and the Council of Ministers and the European Commission are most worthy of attention in this context.

Skeleton Solution

Relationship between the European Parliament and Council of Ministers:

• legislative functions;

• judicial review;

• power to approve new members.

Relationship between the European Parliament and the European Commission:

• broad maintenance of the status quo;

• existing powers;

• new power to propose iniatives under Article 138b(2).

Suggested Solution

The European Community, as established under the original EC Treaty, was founded on a constitution based on the doctrine of the separation of interests rather than the separation of powers. The Council of Ministers embodies the interests of the Member States while the European Commission represents the fundamental interests of the Community. The role of the European Parliament is to represent the interests of the peoples of the Community.

The Treaty on European Union made many structural changes to the relationships between the various institutions but did not significantly alter this basic constitutional philosophy. Its main impact was to confer greater authority on the European Parliament mainly at the expense of the Council of Ministers in order to rectify, at least in part, the 'democratic deficit' for which the European Community was being criticised. In the circumstances the new relationships between the European

265

Parliament and the Council of Ministers, on the one hand, and the European Parliament and the European Commission, on the other hand, therefore merit most attention.

Relationship between the European Parliament and the Council of Ministers

Until the amendments made by the Treaty on European Union, the relationship between the Parliament and the Council of Ministers can be characterised as a one-sided affair. The Parliament had little control over the activities of the Council and the Council acted with impunity towards the Parliament. This is clear if the legislative process within the Community is considered.

The original legislative role of the Parliament was primarily consultative. The Parliament commented on proposals put forward by the Commission before the Council. It had a right to be consulted on certain matters, ie under Articles 43, 54, 56 and 87 of the EC Treaty, and in practice the Commission frequently consulted the Parliament during the consultative phase of drafting legislation.

Nevertheless, this consultative role was circumscribed in two respects. First, the vast majority of measures did not strictly require the opinion of the Parliament and so the Council could generally ignore its views. Second, unlike the Member States and the Commission, the Parliament was not permitted to bring proceedings in the European Court against the Council under Article 173(1) of the EC Treaty. Hence, Parliament exercised little control over the activities of the Council.

The legislative relationship between these two organs was altered slightly by the introduction of the co-operation procedure by the Single European Act in 1986. The use of the co-operation procedure was required to enact legislation in specific subjects and especially the freedom of establishment, working conditions, and certain forms of harmonisation legislation. This procedure extended the authority of the Parliament over the Council insofar as the Parliament was permitted two opportunities to discuss proposed measures but, as always, ultimate authority to adopt or reject measures resided in the Council of Ministers.

This was the position prior to the Treaty on European Union. The Treaty again altered the relationship between the Council and the European Parliament in a number of respects, one of the most important being the introduction of the 'co-decision' procedure. Under the co-decision procedure, the Commission continues to formulate legislative proposals which are sent to both the Council and the Parliament. The Parliament compiles a report on the proposal which is considered by the Commission when redrafting the proposal after obtaining the views of the Council. The proposal is again submitted to the Council with the Parliament's report and the Council is required to adopt a common position on the measure and the common position is communicated to the Parliament.

After examining the common position of the Council, the Parliament has four options: first, to approve the common position – in which case the proposal returns to the Council for formal approval; second, to take no action – in which case, after a period of three months, the Council may adopt the proposal; third, to suggest amendments to the common position which must be by an absolute majority and these suggested amendments are returned to the Commission and amended before being resubmitted to the Council; fourth, to reject the common position, again by an absolute majority, in which case a Conciliation Committee may be established to resolve the impasse.

This procedure allows the Parliament to have a second reading of European legislation and applies to a considerable range of legislative proposals, although not to all. Nevertheless, its application is more extensive than the co-operation procedure which was previously the European Parliament's main influence in the legislative process.

Another significant power made by the amendments of the Treaty on European Union was the right to initiate proceedings against the Council of Ministers which is formally recognised in an amended Article 173(3) of the EC Treaty. Hence, the European Parliament will be more active in compelling judicial review of the actions of the Council when these trespass on its own areas of competence.

A number of powers were also consolidated. For example, the consent of the Parliament is required for the admission of new members into the Community and for the conclusion of association agreements between the Community and third states. The Parliament can technically veto the decision of the Council on admission and establishing association agreements, which is a significant limitation on the Council's authority in this respect.

However, in the final analysis, there has not been a sea change in the relationship caused by the successful conclusion of the Treaty on European Union. The European Parliament's powers remain limited, especially in comparison to those of the Council of Ministers.

Relationship between the European Parliament and the European Commission

The powers of the European Parliament in the institutional balance of the Community were traditionally aimed at countering the exercise of authority by the European Commission rather than the Council of Ministers. Hence, the Treaty on European Union has not significantly extended these powers and the relationship remains only slightly altered in favour of the Parliament.

Since its conception, Parliament's primary authority over the Commission lay in its power to collectively dismiss the Commission by a motion of censure carried by a two-thirds majority of votes cast if representing a majority of the members of the Parliament: Article 144 EC Treaty. On occasion, motions have been tabled in the Parliament for the censure of the Commission but, to date, none has been successfully carried. In practice this device is considerably less powerful than it might first appear. Individual Commissioners cannot be dismissed by a vote of the Parliament; all the Commissioners must resign. Therefore, such a motion would penalise Commissioners who have not committed any indiscretion.

Parliament members are also permitted to put questions to Commission officials which the Commission staff are obliged to answer: Article 140 EC Treaty. Questions may be submitted both orally and in writing. Commission officials may be subject to scrutiny in both the plenary session and committees of the Parliament. This power is part of the watchdog function carried out by the Parliament. In a similar vein, the Commission is also required to submit an annual general report to the Parliament on the subject of the affairs of the Community: Article 143 EC Treaty. This report forms the basis for the annual parliamentary debate on the affairs of the Community.

In addition to these powers, Article 138b(2) of the EC Treaty, as amended by the Treaty on European Union, now permits the European Parliament, acting by a majority of its members, to request the European Commission to submit any appropriate proposal on matters on which it considers Community legislation is required. This is a new power and permits the Parliament to initiate legislative proposals albeit in an indirect matter.

The other main change has been the creation of the Parliamentary Ombudsman to investigate complaints of maladministration. While the powers of this office extend over both the Council of Ministers and the European Commission, since it is the Commission which carries out most of the administrative tasks in the Community, it is likely that the Commission will be the subject of most investigations.

QUESTION THREEE

What are the legal implications for EC and for national law of the following cases:

Francovich & Boniface v *Italian Republic* – Joined Cases C–6/90 and C–9/90

European Parliament v *Council,* Case 70/88 ('Post-Chernobyl')

R v *Secretary of State for Transport, ex parte Factortame* (I) and (II), Cases C–213/89 and C–221/89

University of London LLB Examination
(for External Students) European Community Law June 1994 Q3

General Comment

Three of the most fundamental changes in Community law in recent years have occurred as a result of case law from the European Court and the English courts. These three cases are the source of these changes and students should be familiar with their content in light of their significance. Consequently, this question should not pose insurmountable problems to candidates.

Skeleton Solution

Francovich & Boniface v *Italian Republic,* Cases C6/90 & C9/90

- The facts of the case.
- The principle of state liability to individuals for breach of Community law.
- The conditions for liability.

European Parliament v *EC Council* ('Post-Chernobyl') Case 70/88

- Judicial review at the instance of the Parliament under the original EC Treaty.
- The decision of the Court.
- Confirmation of the decision in the Treaty on European Union amendments.

R v *Secretary of State for Transport, ex parte Factortame (Nos 1 and 2),* Cases C213/89 and C221/89

- Conflict between the Merchant Shipping Act and Community law.
- The issues raised in the two references.
- The decision of the ECJ in *Factortame (No 2).*
- The demise of the principle of absolute parliamentary sovereignty.

Suggested Solution

Francovich & Boniface v Italian Republic

The European Court's ruling in the *Francovich* case (1993) established the principle that Member States can be liable to private individuals for failing to comply with Community law if the failure causes injury or damage to those individuals.

The facts of this case may briefly be stated as follows. The plaintiff raised an action in an Italian court claiming damages for loss of salary caused by the failure of the Italian government to establish a fund to pay redundancy payments in the event that an employee is made redundant through the insolvency of his or her employer. The duty to establish such a fund was imposed by a Community directive which Italy had failed to implement.

The Italian court referred the question to the European Court for a preliminary ruling. The European Court replied that, under Community law, states are liable to private individuals for failing to comply with Community law if three conditions are satisfied. First, the purpose of the Community measure was to create private rights for individuals. Second, the nature and content of these rights must be identifiable from the terms of the measure. Third, there must exist a causal link between the failure by the Member State to comply with Community law and the injury sustained by the individual.

In the event that these conditions are fulfilled, the Member State is liable to remedy the consequence of any damage or injury suffered as a result of the denial of Community rights. While the European Court established this general principle in this decision, it provided little guidance on its application by national courts and tribunals. For example, each Member State is responsible for adopting procedures to allow for the vindication of this right. Hence, within the United Kingdom, the national courts are responsible for ensuring that a mechanism exists to bring such actions against the United Kingdom government. As yet, the legal basis for such a claim in English law is uncertain: see *Bourgoin SA v Ministry of Agriculture, Fisheries and Food* (1986).

In addition, there is no certainty as to the types of Community measures that may be relied on to establish such rights. In the *Francovich* case itself, the infringement of Community law was a failure to implement the terms of a directive. However, it is not clear from the decision whether violations of EC Treaty articles, regulations, decisions or general principles of Community law will also result in this form of liability. This is still to be resolved by the European Court.

Also, it is not apparent whether or not it is a prerequisite to a claim that the European Court has held a Member State in violation of Community law through a direct action under Article 169. In the *Francovich* case, the Court had already found Italy in breach of Community law in an earlier direct action brought by the Commission.

Notwithstanding these shortcomings, the Court's decision in this case is a landmark, establishing that Member States can be liable to private individuals for failing to comply with Community law. Prior to the ruling, this liability had not been definitively established: see *Asteris AE v Greece* (1990). The Court has still to elaborate on the exact scope of this right, but there is little doubt that the decision will encourage a rash of cases on this point, which will hopefully clarify the position.

In fact, the legal fraternity is awaiting the decision of the European Court on the application made by the plaintiffs in the *Factortame* series of cases which established that the Merchant Shipping Act 1988 infringed the terms of Community law. The same plaintiffs have raised an action for compensation from the United Kingdom government for violation of their Community rights and the injury sustained as a result. The Queen's Bench Division has made a preliminary reference to the European Court of Justice seeking assistance in implementing the *Francovich* doctrine and the decision of the Court is due in late November 1994. It is anticipated that this decision will go a long way towards clarifying the uncertainties which surround the initial decision.

European Parliament v *EC Council* ('Post-Chernobyl')

In the text of the original EC Treaty, Article 173 authorised Member States, the Council and the Commission to bring actions before the European Court of Justice for judicial review of the Council and Commission. No such competence was expressly conferred on the European Parliament. Nevertheless, the Parliament brought a series of actions in repeated attempts to have its rights to bring such actions recognised.

After a series of unsuccessful actions to have such a right recognised (see, for example, *European Parliament* v *European Council (Re Comitology)* (1988), the European Court eventually recognised such a power in *European Parliament* v *EC Council (Re Tchernobyl)* (1992). In what was a dramatic reversal of its earlier decisions, the Court held that the Parliament could competently bring an action where the complaint was brought to protect the rights of the Parliament under the Community treaties.

The case was in fact brought under Article 146 of the Euratom Treaty but this provision contains identical terms to Article 173 of the EC Treaty and therefore the judgment is equally applicable to actions brought under the authority of that provision.

This decision was seen to redress an imbalance in the constitutional position of the Parliament since Member States and other Community institutions were allowed to bring actions for judicial review of its acts. For example, in *Luxembourg* v *European Parliament* (1983), Luxembourg brought an action against the Parliament, challenging the Parliament's competence to decide the location of its secretariat. Equally, individuals were permitted to seek judicial review of the Parliament's actions: see *Partie Ecologiste 'Les Verts'* v *European Parliament* (1986).

The effect of the judgment was to provide the Parliament with the power to challenge decisions which it believed affected its constitutional powers. The decision also reaffirmed the European Court's policy of extending the powers and competence of the European Parliament.

The judgment was immediately followed by a second case, this time brought under the original terms of Article 173 itself. In *European Parliament* v *EC Council (Re Students' Rights)* (1992), the Court heard an application by the Parliament claiming that a directive relating to the residence rights of students on vocational courses had been adopted by the Council on an incorrect legal basis. The disputed measure had been adopted by the Council over the opposition of the Parliament.

Interestingly, the Parliament did not base its standing on Article 173 of the Treaty which permits Member States, the Council and the Commission to challenge acts of

Community institutions. Instead, it brought the action on the basis of its inherent power to protect its rights under the EC Treaty.

The Court accepted that the European Parliament had standing to bring actions to protect its interests as long as such challenges were brought for the purpose of safeguarding the prerogatives of the Parliament and were founded only on submissions alleging infringements of such rights. It did not expressly refer to Article 173(1) in establishing the right to challenge. The fact that the Council's actions deprived the European Parliament of an opportunity to review the terms of the draft measure was sufficient to satisfy both substantive requirements.

The effect of the first decision, taken in conjunction with the second, was to require the draughtsmen of the Treaty on European Union to amend the terms of Article 173 to incorporate the right of the European Parliament to challenge the validity of acts of other Community institutions 'for the purpose of protecting its prerogatives'. In other words, the decisions of the Court in these judgments became enshrined in the text of the EC Treaty. Now the European Parliament has capacity to initiate proceedings for judicial review against the actions of its sister institutions when no such power was originally intended.

R v Secretary of State for Transport, ex parte Factortame (Nos 1 and 2)

Parliament enacted the Merchant Shipping Act 1988 in an attempt to impose controls over the ownership of fishing vessels registered in the United Kingdom. The purpose of the legislation was to end 'quota hopping' which facilitated foreign nationals registering their vessels in the United Kingdom and becoming eligible for the British quotas of fishing stocks granted by the European Community.

One of the conditions of the Act was that the owner of the ship must possess British nationality in order to be eligible to register his vessel in the British register. The effect of this condition was to deprive a number of shipowners of the registration of their vessels. A group of Spanish nationals challenged this statute as being contrary to European Community law, and in particular the prohibition against discrimination on the grounds of nationality.

The matter came before the Divisional Court which referred the substantive question to the European Court for a preliminary ruling and, in the meantime, suspended the application of the statute pending the reference. This first reference, on the consistency of the United Kingdom law with the terms of the EC Treaty, became known as *R v Secretary of State for Transport, ex parte Factortame (No 2)*, Case C221/89 (1991) because the ECJ answered the question on interim suspension before the reference on the actual merits of the case was given out by the court.

In the interim, the United Kingdom government appealed the suspension order to the House of Lords, which was asked to determine whether a British court could suspend the application of a statute that was considered prima facie to violate Community law. The House of Lords refused to grant the order and instead also referred the question whether Community national courts were obliged to grant interim protection to Community nationals whose Community rights would be eroded if a statute was applied, to the European Court. This second reference became known as *R v Secretary of State for Transport, ex parte Factortame (No 1)*, Case C213/89 (1990).

The decision of the European Court in *Factortame (No 2)* was not especially controversial or of supreme constitutional significance. The Court held that the United Kingdom statute was tainted by unlawful discrimination between United Kingdom nationals and nationals of other EC countries. Hence, the statute was incompatible with Community law and could not be applied by the United Kingdom courts. This result was not surprising since the European Court had consistently held, since its decision in *Costa* v *ENEL* (1964), that Community law prevailed over inconsistent national laws. This doctrine applied whether the form of Community law was EC Treaty provisions, regulations or unimplemented directives.

Inside the United Kingdom, until this case arose, direct conflicts between United Kingdom statutes and Community law had been avoided by using two fictions. First, if the United Kingdom statute was pre-1972, then the Community measure could be given priority through the operation of the European Communities Act 1972 which gave effect to the EC Treaty in United Kingdom domestic law. In such a situation, the problem was considered as the simple application of a subsequent Act of Parliament over a prior statute. For conflicts involving post-1972 statutes, the problem was resolved by employing an interpretative presumption that Parliament did not intend to legislate in conflict with Community law. Hence, in the process of interpretation of statutes against Community law, an inconsistency was to be attributed to an oversight on the part of the parliamentary draftsmen: see *Shields* v *E Coomes (Holdings) Ltd* (1979).

The facts which arose in *Factortame* did not allow for such interpretative sleight of hand. There was an irresolvable confrontation between a United Kingdom statute and Community law. Hence, when the European Court confirmed that no effect could be given to post-1972 statutes which were incompatible with Community law, the United Kingdom courts had to face the inevitable demise of the principle of parliamentary sovereignty for the first time.

In fact, the English courts accepted the implications of the *Factortame (No 2)* decision gracefully. Lord Bridge of Harwich, once the reference to the European Court was returned to the House of Lords for implementation, made the following comment:

'Some public comments on the decision of the Court of Justice, affirming the jurisdiction of the courts of the Member States to override national legislation if necessary to enable interim relief to be granted for the protection of rights under Community law have suggested that this was a novel and dangerous invasion by a Community institution of the sovereignty of the United Kingdom Parliament.

But such comments are based on a misconception. If the supremacy within the European Community of Community law over the national law of Member States was not always inherent in the EEC Treaty it was certainly well established in the jurisprudence of the Court of Justice long before the United Kingdom joined the Community. Thus, whatever limitation of its sovereignty Parliament accepted when it enacted the European Communities Act 1972 was entirely voluntary.'

The *Factortame (No 1)* case was, however, of significant constitutional importance. In this decision, the European Court held that national courts were obliged to suspend the application of national laws infringing the Community rights of individuals. In the event that interim relief was appropriate to protect the Community rights of individuals, this must be granted notwithstanding any principle or rule of national law to the contrary.

Prior to the reference, no English court had jurisdiction to grant interim relief which would involve either overturning an English statute, in advance of any decision by the European Court of Justice that the statute infringed Community law, or granting an injunction against the Crown. The House of Lords considered that the decision in the second reference empowered it to grant such a remedy to an applicant for the first time.

The extent of this authority is contained in the judgment of the European Court which stated that national courts had jurisdiction to grant interim relief for the protection of directly enforceable rights under Community law and that no limitation on the power to do so could be imposed by any rule of national law.

The House of Lords then proceeded to grant the relief requested to the applicants and suspended the application of the 1988 Act. The historical significance of this decision is immense. Quite simply, it was recognition that the doctrine of parliamentary sovereignty was not absolute, which *was* considered to be the case before the European Court's decision. Parliament is no longer supreme when enacting statutes if these conflict with EC law and any statute which so conflicts will be denied effect by the courts.

QUESTION FOUR

Explain how the European Court of Justice in the development of its case law has complied with Article 164 of the Treaty on European Union.

University of London LLB Examination
(for External Students) European Community Law June 1994 Q4

General Comment

A rather vague question concerning the policy of judicial activism pursued by the Court. The question gives little guidance to the kind of answer that the examiner wishes and is therefore quite dangerous.

Skeleton Solution

- The policy of judicial activism pursued by the Court to protect the integrity of Community law.
- The twin principles of the supremacy of Community law and direct effect.
- The Court's decision in *Francovich*.
- The application of Community law against Member States.

Suggested Solution

The European Court is instructed under Article 164 of the EC Treaty to ensure that, in the interpretation and application of the Treaty, the law is observed. The Court has discharged this obligation by developing principles in its own jurisprudence to ensure that the rights and obligations contained in the EC Treaty are protected from encroachment by Member States.

The most obvious manifestation of this policy was the creation of the doctrine of the supremacy of Community law over inconsistent provisions of national law. No

273

provision of the EC Treaty expressly regulates the issue of supremacy between Community law and national law. The only implied reference to the issue of supremacy is Article 5 which imposes an obligation on all Member States to adopt all appropriate measures to ensure that the obligations of the Treaty are observed, together with an additional duty to abstain from acts which might jeopardise achievement of the objectives of the Treaty.

Despite this omission, the European Court had adopted an unequivocal position on the question of supremacy between Community law and national law. In *Costa* v *ENEL* (1964), the Court was asked to decide whether an Italian statute enacted after the creation of the Community could prevail over the terms of the EC Treaty. The Court resolved the issue of supremacy in favour of Community law, arguing that the objectives and purposes of the Community would be frustrated if national law was allowed to deviate from Community law.

The principle of supremacy has subsequently become a fundamental principle of Community law and must be given effect even by the courts and tribunals of Member States. This requirement has been acknowledged by the courts of all the Member States, even the English courts. For example, in *R* v *Secretary of State, ex parte Factortame (No 3)* (1989), the House of Lords acknowledged that the application of a United Kingdom statute must be suspended in the event of inconsistency with Community law.

The quality of supremacy extends also to secondary Community legislation such as regulations and directives.

By creating this principle, the European Court ensured that the rule of Community law could not be usurped by inconsistent national measures, thereby protecting the integrity of the Community legal system. Similarly, the extension of the doctrine to national courts was necessary to ensure the application of this principle at the grass roots of the Community legal order.

Another principle developed by the Court to guarantee that Community law was observed in all Member States at all levels is the principle of direct effect. Provisions of the EC Treaty may be relied on by private individuals in national courts to create rights and duties through this principle. By giving private individuals direct rights, the European Court ensured that Member States would have to apply the terms of Community law through their court structures.

Again, the Court has extended the principle of direct effect to secondary legislation. Of course, Community regulations were always intended to have immediate and automatic effect but directives were not conferred with this quality. Where a Member State has failed to adopt a directive within the specified period of time, the European Court has not permitted such oversights to prevent the exercise by private individuals of Community rights contained in the directive. If certain circumstances are present, the European Court has been prepared to ignore the fact of non-implementation and apply the rights granted in any event.

The European Court has also created fundamental principles of Community law which are of such significance that they are virtually constitutional tenets. For example, the principle of non-discrimination on the grounds of nationality contained in Article 6 of the EC Treaty, as amended, has been ensconced in Community law.

Similarly, Article 119 on gender discrimination has attained a similar stature. The aim of the Court in this process has been to confirm that the principles at the very heart of the Community order are immutable cornerstones of the legal order.

The sanctity of Community law has also been protected by the extension of the concept of liability for breaches of Community law by Member States. Since the Court's decision in *Francovich & Boniface* v *Italian Republic* (1993), Member States are now liable to private individuals in the event that they violate Community law and injury is suffered by private individuals as a result of this action. Since Member States will now be required to pay compensation for actions which are inconsistent with the terms of the EC Treaty, they will in the future be even more careful to ensure that their actions do not infringe the terms of the EC Treaty or the laws made on the basis of that agreement.

The assault of the Court on attempts by Member States to restrict the application of Community law has not been confined to the development of these fundamental principles. The Court has also aggressively pursued Member States failing to implement the terms of the EC Treaty when brought before the Court by the European Commission.

Even if a Member States has genuine constitutional difficulties in complying with Community law, no excuse for non-compliance will be accepted by the Court as justifying deviation. For example, in *EC Commission* v *Belgium (Management of Waste)* (1989), the Court refused to consider the constitutional difficulties of the Belgian government in implementing Community law as a defence to a violation of its Community obligations.

Similarly, in *EC Commission* v *Greece (Re Electronic Cash Registers)* (1992), the Court held that Member States were under a separate obligation to co-operate with the European Commission when that agency was investigating alleged infringements of Community law. This duty was owed over and above the duty to conform to the substantive principles of Community law which were considered to have been violated by the European Commission.

The Court has pursued a deliberate policy of judicial activism to secure the widespread recognition of these principles even though none was expressly stated in the EC Treaty. Each of these principles preserves the integrity of the Community order and has been developed by the Court in order to ensure that Community law is observed at all levels of the Community legal hierarchy.

QUESTION FIVE

Mr Jones has a small soft drinks importing firm in Cardiff. Wanting to expand his business, he is always looking for new products and discovers a herbal soft drink called Schwipps which is extremely popular in Germany because of its allegedly health-giving properties. He places an order for 10,000 bottles with Schmidt AG, the manufacturers.

Schmidt refuse to supply him and tell him to order the drinks from Smith Ltd in Birmingham, their distributors in the UK. Jones is very disappointed as Smith Ltd are direct competitors of his and charge much higher prices than Schwipps.

He is then approached by a distributor of Schwipps in Germany who offers him a good deal, proposing to send him a shipment in bulk containers which Jones can then bottle himself.

He accepts and the consignment arrives in Dover. It is stopped there by the customs because the drink contains 5% algiphit, a substance which is permitted in drinks under UK legislation in concentrations of up to 4.5% only but which is considered beneficial in Germany, where there is no such limit. Jones hires a specialist firm at considerable expense which analyses and then dilutes the concentration until it complies with the UK limit of 4.5%. The consignment is then admitted. Sales are going well. Smith Ltd hear of this and apply to the courts for an injunction to stop Jones selling the drink.

Advise Jones. Can he contest the application for an injunction? What aspects of Community law might be considered?

University of London LLB Examination
(for External Students) European Community Law June 1994 Q5

General Comment

Despite the reference in the facts of the case to national measures impeding the flow of goods into the United Kingdom, consideration of the application of the principle of the free movement of goods is excluded by the requirement that the answer concentrates on the grounds of law raised in the application for an injunction. In such an application, the sole ground which could be considered is Article 85 of the EC Treaty. Therefore, the following solution concentrates on that dimension.

Skeleton Solution

- Right of Jones to be heard at the application for the injunction.
- Direct effect of Article 85(1) and (2).
- The three criteria for the application of Article 85(1).
- The possibility of exemption under the block exemption or by individual exemption.
- The doctrine of severability.

Suggested Solution

The application by Smith Ltd for an injunction would be based on its rights under the distribution contract which provides the company with the exclusive right to sell the product in the United Kingdom. Smith Ltd will allege that the activities of Jones contravene the exclusive rights granted under that contract and the application for the injunction will claim that allowing Jones to continue to make such sales will irreparably damage its own commercial activities.

Jones will have the right to be heard during the application for the injunction and will be able to submit arguments contesting the allegations made by Smith Ltd. In terms of Community law, Jones will be able to rely on the protections made available to private individuals by Article 85 of the EC Treaty and these provisions can also be relied on to counter the arguments made by Smith Ltd in its application for the injunction.

Article 85(1) prohibits private commercial agreements, decisions and concerted practices which may affect trade between the Member States of the European Community and which have as their object or effect the prevention, restriction or distortion of competition within the Community. Agreements and decisions which are contrary to this provision are void and unenforceable.

Both Articles 85(1) and 85(2) have direct effect and are capable of creating rights which may be relied on by private individuals: *Garden Cottage* v *Milk Marketing Board* (1984). These may form the basis of an action for damages against a party infringing their terms at the instance of a plaintiff whose business activities have been injured as a consequence of the anti-competitive practices. Conversely, the same provisions may form a defence to an action including grounds to challenge an application for an injunction. Therefore Jones can rely on the terms of Articles 85(1) and 85(2) to counter the application.

The grounds on which Smith Ltd's application for injunction would be based would be the existence of an exclusive distribution contract between themselves and Schmidt for the supply of the product in the United Kingdom. In order to successfully contest the application for the injunction, Jones must show that the distribution contract violates the terms of Article 85(1) and is therefore void according to Article 85(2).

To ascertain whether or not the agreement between Schmidt and Smith Ltd infringes Article 85(1) three separate determinations must be made: (a) their activities must constitute an agreement, decision or concerted practice; (b) the agreement or practices must affect trade between Member States; and (c) the agreement or practices must prevent, restrict or distort competition.

Quite clearly, the first condition is satisfied. An exclusive distribution contract exists between Schmidt and Smith Ltd since Schmidt refused to supply Jones with the goods because they had appointed Smith Ltd as their exclusive supplier. Such a contract qualifies as an agreement for the purposes of Article 85(1).

To fall inside the scope of Article 85(1), an agreement such as an exclusive distribution contract must also affect trade between Member States. As a general principle, exclusive distribution agreements between parties situated in two different Member States are deemed to affect trade between Member States unless they can benefit from the de minimis principle. As the European Court stated in *Consten and Grundig* v *EC Commission* (1966), in deciding whether such an agreement affects trade between Member States:

'... what is particularly important is whether the agreement is capable of constituting a threat, either direct or indirect, actual or potential, to freedom of trade between Member States in a manner which might harm the attainment of the objectives of a single market between States.'

The anti-competitive nature of distribution agreements stems from the restrictions placed on Schmidt and the distributer, Smith Ltd, particularly when the contract is exclusive. By granting exclusive rights to the United Kingdom company to distribute the products exclusively in the United Kingdom, Schmidt is effectively impeding consumers from obtaining the products from other suppliers either in the United

Kingdom or other European Community countries. If the products are impeded from flowing freely throughout the European Community by the restrictions on the parties there will be an effect on trade between Member States.

Of course, the agreement will not affect trade between Member States if it can be shown to be de minimis. In the Notice Concerning Agreements, Decisions and Concerted Practices of Minor Importance 1986, the Commission indicated that agreements would fall outside the scope of Article 85(1) if two conditions can be established:

a) the goods which are the subject of the agreement or concerted practice and its immediate substitutes do not constitute more than 5 per cent of the total market for such goods in the area of the common market affected by the agreement; and

b) the aggregate annual turnover of the undertakings participating in the arrangement does not exceed 200 million ECU (approximately £130 million).

Taking the market share criterion first, to verify whether the parties have more than a 5 per cent share of the market, it is first necessary to identify the relevant product market and then the relevant geographical market.

The relevant product market consists of the market for the product under investigation together with the market for products which are identical or substantially equivalent to the product. Identical and substantially equivalent products must be interchangeable with the original product. Whether or not this requirement is satisfied is normally judged from the perspective of the consumer, taking into account the characteristics, price and intended use of the products. The relevant product markets will probably be soft drinks because the product in question is a part of that generic group.

The relevant geographical market is the area in the Community in which the agreement or concerted practice produces its effects: *Delimitis* v *Henninger Bräu AG* (1992). In the circumstances of the present case, the relevant market is the United Kingdom since that is the area where the agreement produces its effects.

No facts are provided to establish whether the parties can benefit from the de minimis doctrine and hence we shall proceed on the assumption that the agreement falls within the scope of Article 85(1) by having an appreciable effect on intra-Member State commerce.

Whether the terms of the distribution contract restrict, prevent or distort competition must be ascertained from an examination of its contents. Two terms of the contract, at least prima facie, appear to have anti-competitive implications. First, Jones cannot obtain his supplies directly from the manufacturer, Schmidt, and is required to purchase his supplies from the distributor. Second, Smith Ltd is actively preventing the supply of the product from the German distributor by making the application for injunction. This strongly implies that there is a term in the contract preventing other Community distributors of the product from supplying the United Kingdom market with the product. Both of these practices are generally accepted as anti-competitive.

However, even if the terms of a distribution contract fall within the scope of Article 85(1), the effects of Article 85(2) may be avoided if the agreement has the benefit either of an individual exemption or a group exemption. Individual exemptions are granted by the Commission after an application has been submitted to it for this purpose. The conditions for exemption are set out in Article 85(3). The Commission has also enacted a number of regulations in order to create block exemptions for particular types of agreements including exclusive distribution agreements (Commission Regulation 1983/83 (1983).

If an agreement falls within the scope of a group exemption under a Commission regulation, the parties to the agreement are not required to notify the agreement to the Commission and the parties cannot be fined for entering into such an agreement. Each block exemption contains specific and particular criteria which must be satisfied in order for an agreement to benefit from the protection provided.

In order to qualify under the terms of the block exemption created by Commission Regulation 1983/83 (1983), a distribution agreement must fulfil the following principal conditions: (a) the agreement must involve only two parties; (b) the products must be supplied for resale and not to be made into other products; (c) the sales area must be either a defined part of the European Community or the entire Community; (d) the only permitted restriction on the principal (supplier) is the obligation not to sell to other resellers in the sales area allocated to the exclusive distributor; and (e) the distributor must agree to purchase all his requirements from the principal.

On the other hand, specific clauses will deprive an agreement of the protection of the block exemption. These are most notably: (a) the agreement must not involve competing manufacturers since this might lead to market sharing; (b) there must be no effort by the parties to create absolute territorial protection for the distributor – in other words, parallel imports of the goods must remain possible.

In addition, there are a number of types of clauses which, although not expressly stated, will deprive an agreement of the protection of the block exemption because such practices are prohibited in general. Exemption will not be available under the block exemption where anti-competitive restrictions are imposed on the parties other than those expressly permitted. For example, export bans would not be permitted under the block exemption nor would clauses requiring the principal or distributor to impose restrictions, in terms of conditions of sale, on customers. Similarly, terms permitting the principal to dictate prices or terms to the distributor would not be permitted.

The terms of the contract are not stated in the question. However, the fact that the agreement contains provisions preventing the parallel importation of the goods into the United Kingdom strongly suggests that the agreement will not benefit from the terms of the block exemption. If the benefit of exemption is not available, the agreement is void and unenforceable and an application for an injunction will not be successful.

As a final point, it should be noted that if the contract falls within the scope of Article 85(1), then Article 85(2) provides that such agreements shall be automatically void. However, the European Court has applied the doctrine of severability to this provision. Only those terms which are contrary to the provision are void; the rest remain in force. The agreement itself is void only if those parts of it which are anti-competitive cannot be severed from the agreement itself: *Delimitis v Henninger Bräu GmbH.*

QUESTION SIX

'The right to challenge the legality of acts of Community institutions extends to institutions and Member States, but also individuals'.

Discuss and compare these different rights.

University of London LLB Examination
(for External Students) European Community Law June 1994 Q6

General Comment

This is a fairly common subject for examination and in this particular case the examiner is asking for a comparison of the different rights of Member States, Community institutions and private individuals to bring direct actions in the European Court. Questions in this area present an opportunity to score well during examinations.

Skeleton Solution

- The requirements of Article 173(1)–(4) as amended.
- Standing of Member States.
- Standing of Community institutions – differences between the Council, Commission and Parliament.
- The standing requirements of private individuals: (a) a decision; (b) direct and individual concern.

Suggested Solution

Community institutions must act within their scope of competencies as defined in the EC Treaty and failure to respect these limitations will render an institution liable to an action in the European Court of Justice for review of the legality of its actions. Exclusive jurisdiction to review the acts of Community institutions has been granted to the European Court. No such proceedings may be competently raised in a national court or tribunal: *Firma Foto-Frost* v *Hauptzollamt Lubeck-Ost* (1988).

Article 172(1) of the EC Treaty, as amended by the Treaty on European Union, authorises the judicial review of the legality of acts adopted jointly by the European Parliament and the Council as well as the acts of the Council, the Commission and the European Central Bank (when constituted), other than recommendations and opinions, together with those acts of the European Parliament intended to produce legal effects vis-à-vis third parties.

For the purposes of standing to bring such actions, a distinction is made between Member States and Community institutions, on the one hand, and private individuals on the other hand. This distinction is based on the separate locus standi requirements which must be satisfied before standing will be acknowledged by the European Court. Member States and Community institutions are considered privileged applicants for the purposes of initiating actions for judicial review of Community actions. In contrast, private individuals must establish that the measure being challenged is a decision of direct and individual concern to them.

Member States

Member States are entitled to initiate proceedings for the judicial review of the acts of the Council of Ministers, the European Commission and the European Parliament. The interest of a Member State in the actions of a Community institution is presumed and hence there is no need to establish standing in addition to a ground for review. In fact, even if a Member State challenges an act of a Community institution addressed to another Member State, interest and standing are still both presumed: *Italy* v *EC Commission (Re British Telecom)* (1985).

Member States frequently bring actions to protect their rights from the incursions of the European institutions. The European Commission is the most frequent target for such proceedings: see *United Kingdom* v *EC Commission* (1988) and *United Kingdom* v *EC Commission* (1989).

Proceedings are also brought against the Council of Ministers and the European Parliament by Member States but such cases are relatively rare. Actions against the Council of Ministers are infrequently initiated by states because that organ consists of national representatives. One rare instance of such proceedings occurred in *United Kingdom* v *EC Commission (Re Hormones)* (1988), when the United Kingdom challenged the competence of the Council to adopt Community legislation by simple majority instead of a qualified majority which was the voting requirement the United Kingdom believed applied. In this particular case, the European Court agreed with the United Kingdom and held that the measure was invalid.

Actions against the European Parliament are also not common, with one or two well-publicised exceptions: see, for example, *Luxembourg* v *European Parliament* (1983).

Community institutions

In the original Article 173(2), only the standing of the Council of Ministers and the European Commission was recognised and their standing to bring actions against other Community institutions was also presumed. No express reference was made to the power of the European Parliament to commence this type of proceedings.

In a series of cases, the European Parliament tried to persuade the European Court that it also has a similar capacity but this right was initially refused by the Court: see *European Parliament* v *EC Council (Re Comitology)* (1988). The Court subsequently reversed itself in *European Parliament* v *EC Council (Re Tchernobyl)* (1992), and permitted the European Parliament to contest the legal basis on which a Council regulation had been adopted. Having regard to the institutional balance within the Community, the Court held that the Parliament was able to proceed if two conditions were satisfied. First, the Parliament must demonstrate 'a specific interest in the proceedings'. Second, the action must seek to safeguard the powers of the Parliament and must be based exclusively on the infringement of those powers: see also *European Parliament* v *EC Council (Re Students' Rights)* (1992).

This formula, originally devised by the Court, has now been incorporated into the terms of Article 173 by the amendments made by the Treaty on European Union. Article 173(3) of the EC Treaty now reads:

'The Court shall have jurisdiction under the same conditions [outlined in Article 173(2)] in actions brought by the European Parliament and the ECB for the purpose of protecting their prerogatives'.

The standing of the European Parliament is not therefore unqualified as it is for the Council of Ministers and the European Commission. The Parliament must, as a prerequisite for standing, establish a specific interest in the proceedings and that the action is necessary to safeguard its prerogatives.

Private individuals

The final category of persons entitled to challenge the legality of acts of the Community institutions are private legal persons and individuals. Article 173(4) provides:

'Any natural or legal person may ... institute proceedings against a decision addressed to that person or against a decision which, although in the form of a regulation or a decision addressed to another person, is of direct and individual concern to the former.'

Private individuals are not privileged applicants for the purpose of reviewing the legality of the acts of Community institutions. To obtain standing, they must demonstrate that two pre-conditions are satisfied. First, the measure being challenged must be a decision. Second, the decision must be of direct and individual concern to them.

If the measure is a decision, as defined in Article 189 of the EC Treaty, the first condition will be satisfied. However, if the measure takes the form of a regulation, the applicant must show that, while the measure has the form of a regulation, it is in fact a series of individual decisions in the form of a regulation. The European Court has stated that even where a measure is generally applicable it may in fact amount to 'a conglomeration of individual decisions taken by the Commission' under the guise of a regulation: see *International Fruit Company* v *EC Commission* (1971).

Once this requirement has been settled, if the decision is not addressed to the applicant, then he or she must show that the decision is of 'direct and individual concern'. In the event that the decision is addressed to the applicant alone or as one of a limited group of individuals, the condition will be satisfied: see *Tokyo Electric Company plc* v *EC Council* (1989). The difficulties arise when the decision is addressed to another person or is a regulation which apparently has general application. In both these cases, the need to establish direct and individual concern poses a considerable handicap to private individuals seeking to obtain standing.

Direct concern means that the applicant must demonstrate that the measure applies without the intervention of any state authorities. If national authorities exercise a discretion as to the means of implementing a measure, or are involved in the administration of the measure, direct concern will not be established. Thus, for example, in *Bock* v *EC Commission* (1971), the European Court refused to allow the applicants standing because the implementation of the Community measure allocating quotas actually depended on the distribution of allowances by the individual states.

The test for individual concern requires the applicant to prove that the decision affects its legal position 'because of some factual situation which differentiates it individually in the same way to the person to whom it is addressed': *Sociedade Agro-Pecuaria* v *EC Council* (1990). Individual concern is difficult to establish when the applicant has not been specifically identified in the decision. If a measure applies to objectively determined situations and entails legal effects for categories of persons generally and in the abstract, it has general application and is incapable of having individual effect: *Cooperativa Veneta Allevatori Equini* v *EC Commission* (1989).

Conversely, individual concern has been held to exist where a regulation of general application named specific companies and firms and applied specific measures to them, and where a regulation had as its subject-matter the individual circumstances of the named importers. Similarly, individual concern has been established where a decision was issued by the Commission in response to the request of a particular group for relief even though the final decision itself was addressed to another person.

In practice, direct and individual concern is notoriously difficult to establish when general measures are involved, a situation which prevents private individuals obtaining access to the European Court to challenge the acts of Community institutions. This contrasts with the position of both Member States and Community institutions which do not have to cross this hurdle because both are considered privileged applicants.

QUESTION SEVEN

A British engineering company with its headquarters in Guildford has decided to establish a branch in Greece. They are sending out an exploration team of engineers who intend to spend three months exploring suitable sites and looking at the available skilled labour.

If all goes well, the company will then open the branch and bring the managerial staff over from England.

Before embarking on this venture, they come to you for advice. They want to know:

a) Whether the 'exploration team' will encounter any difficulties with regard to residence and work permits;

b) once the branch is open, whether they can send any of their staff members out to work there, and, in particular

   i) Mary, deputy head of the accountancy department. She is British, but has been co-habiting with Jason, an Australian who is an engineer with the firm, for five years and the company intends to send them out together.

   ii) Malcolm, a computer specialist, whose wife Deirdre has a criminal conviction for possession of cannabis which she received three years ago.

Advise them.

University of London LLB Examination
(for External Students) European Community Law June 1994 Q7

General Comment

This question combines two separate principles of Community law, namely the right of establishment and the freedom of movement of workers. The general principle behind both is the same – the elimination of discrimination based on nationality. There are no particularly difficult points raised and, in fact, the part concerning criminal convictions is a common theme for examination.

Skeleton Solution

• Right of establishment: Articles 52 and 53 EC Treaty.
• Direct effect and the principles behind *Francovich*.
• Article 48 EC Treaty and the concepts of 'worker', family rights and right to reside.
• Non-application of the principle to non-Community nationals who are not married to Community nationals
• Right to reside and the question of previous criminal convictions.

Suggested Solution

It is the intention of the British company to carry out two separate activities in Greece. First, it intends to investigate the feasibility of establishing a branch in Greece and, for that purpose, wishes to dispatch the exploration team to that country. Second, in the event that this project is successful, it will establish a permanent branch office. This distinction is important because two separate principles of Community law apply to these two particular activities.

Sending the team to investigate the possibilities of the market is covered by the right of freedom of establishment in Community law. Article 52 of the EC Treaty requires restrictions on the freedom of establishment of Community nationals to be progressively abolished. This progressive abolition also applies to the setting up of agencies, branches and subsidiaries by nationals of one Member State in the territory of another Member State. Article 53 prohibits the introduction of new restrictions on the exercise of this freedom.

The impact of these articles is to prohibit restrictions on the exercise of this freedom if based on discrimination on the grounds of nationality. In other words, companies exercising this freedom must be treated in the same way as nationals of that Member State.

In the event that the Greek authorities deny residence permits or work permits to the exploration team then prima facie they would be guilty of a violation of Articles 52 and 53 if, in identical circumstances, they would not have done so had the application been made by Greek nationals. Any refusal must be based on objective criteria unrelated to nationality.

Both Articles 52 and 53 have been held to have direct effect: see *Reyners* v *Belgian State* (1974); and *Costa* v *ENEL* (1964). The British company can therefore rely on these provisions to create directly enforceable private rights. Further, should the applications for residence and work permits be denied, the company can rely on the principles in *Francovich* v *Italian Republic* (1993) to make a claim against the Greek authorities for any injury sustained as a consequence of the denial to grant the necessary permissions.

If the company proceeds to open a branch office and wishes to send personnel from the United Kingdom to operate the office, another set of principles will be involved. Article 48 creates the right of free movement of workers and requires Member States to abolish any discrimination based on nationality between workers as regards employment, remuneration and other conditions of work and employment. Once again, the European Court has given direct effect to this provision of the EC Treaty: *Van Duyn* v *Home Office* (1974).

284

This freedom includes the rights to accept offers of employment, to move freely within the territory of the Member State for this purpose and to reside in a Member State for the purposes of employment in accordance with the laws of that Member State governing the employment of nationals.

The key to the operation of this provision is the term 'worker'. If a person qualifies as a worker, he or she is entitled to exercise this freedom and his or her family is also entitled to the protections granted to them as members of the family of a worker. As long as an individual is pursuing an effective and genuine activity which is not marginal or ancillary, he will be deemed a worker. Even part-time work qualifies a person as a worker for the purposes of applying this right: see *Levin* v *Staatsecretaris van Justitie* (1982).

Workers are entitled not only to the rights contained in Article 48(2) but also the rights conferred by the secondary legislation in this field, namely Council Regulation 1612/68 and Council Directive 64/221. According to the terms of the first measure, a worker has the right to take employment with the same priority as nationals of the United Kingdom and to exercise this right free from discrimination on the grounds of nationality.

Applying these provisions to the four individuals specified in the question, quite clearly Mary is entitled to exercise the right of free movement. She is a British (and hence Community) national travelling to another Member State for the purposes of taking up an employment position.

Jason, her partner, is not a Community national and therefore is not entitled to exercise this right. Had he been married to Mary, he would have been able to rely on the rights conferred on spouses of workers to remain with spouses exercising the freedom of movement. This right applies regardless of whether the unemployed spouse is a Community national or not: *R* v *Immigration Appeal Tribunal and Singh, ex parte Secretary of State for the Home Department* (1992). However, Mary and Jason are not married and Council Regulation 1612/68 is quite explicit in restricting the right to residence to 'spouses' of workers.

There is, nevertheless, a strong argument that the right of a long-term partner to reside with a worker is implied in Article 48. Society has evolved since 1957 when the original provision was conceived. Perhaps the European Court would now be prepared to recognise that the right to reside should be extended to cohabiting couples. However, as yet there is no precedent on this point from the European Court and Jason would have to be advised that, as the law presently stands, without the intervention of the European Court he has no right to reside in Greece as the partner of Mary.

The other couple is Malcolm and Deirdre. Like Mary, Malcolm is a British national and therefore entitled, without doubt, to exercise the right of free movement. His wife Deirdre, therefore, would prima facie be entitled to reside as the spouse of a Community worker. Unfortunately she has a previous conviction for possession of cannabis which she received three years ago. The question is whether this conviction would prevent her exercising the right to remain with Malcolm.

Council Directive 64/221 does confer on Member States certain rights to restrict the free movement of persons within their territories. This directive applies to all measures concerning the entry and expulsion of nationals from other Community countries. In certain circumstances, denial of entry and deportation may be justified on the grounds of public policy, public security or public health.

However, it is unlikely that the Greek authorities could rely on the terms of this directive to justify a refusal to admit Deirdre. At the outset, it can hardly be justifiably maintained that a conviction for possession of a drug constitutes a genuine threat to public policy, public security or public health. Further, in assessing whether a decision to expel a Community national from a Member State, the directive requires the government to take into account a number of factors. First, a decision to deny entry must be based exclusively on the personal conduct of the individual concerned. In addition, denial of entry for the purposes of deterring foreign nationals from acting in a similar manner is not permissible: see *Bonsignore* v *Oberstadt-Direktor of the City of Cologne* (1975).

Also, previous criminal convictions are not in themselves sufficient for taking such measures unless these indicate a propensity to act in a similar manner in the future: *R* v *Bouchereau* (1977). A single conviction for possession of cannabis would probably not provide such an indication. If Deirdre had only received a small fine and not imprisonment, this would also indicate that the offence was a minor one which did not justify the claim that her presence would be a danger to the general public welfare.

QUESTION EIGHT

'The Community legislation in the area of the free movement of persons is no longer sufficient given the strains imposed by the objective of the single market and external pressures.' (O'Keeffe)

Discuss.

University of London LLB Examination
(for External Students) European Community Law June 1994 Q8

General Comment

This is a rather vague question which gives little guidance as to the points which the examiner wishes answered. As a general principle, such questions are to be avoided unless the candidate is particularly knowledgeable in the field being considered.

Skeleton Solution

• The original concept of the customs union and the lack of progress towards its achievement.

• The 1985 White Paper and the Internal Market Programme introduced under Article 8A (now 7A).

• The emphasis of the programme on the freedom of movement of goods as opposed to persons.

• The existing legal regime for the free movement of persons.

• The relationship between the free movement of persons and the concept of European citizenship.

Suggested Solution

As one of the fundamental objectives of the EC Treaty, Article 2 identifies the creation of a common market among the Member States of the organisation. Originally, the achievement of this common market was to be attained through implementation of the four freedoms contained in the EC Treaty, namely the free movement of goods, persons, services and capital. Throughout the European Union, these elements were to move freely without national barriers such as duties, tariffs or quantitative restrictions. In economic theory, in the absence of barriers distorting trade, the collective prosperity of the Member States would rise as national measures interfering with the flow of the factors of production were eliminated or decreased.

The original six Member States completed the elimination of tariff and quantitative restrictions among them by July 1968, one and a half years in advance of the schedule laid down in the EC Treaty itself. With enlargement in 1973, the three new acceding states underwent a similar process and tariffs and quantitative restrictions were removed for the flow of these factors of production between the new states and the European Community. Greece, Spain and Portugal have all been required to comply in a similar fashion.

Although legal measures such as tariffs and quantitative restrictions have been removed from the flow of these factors of production among the 12 Member States, it was realised by the European Commission that, in reality, trade was impeded by national measures operating to restrict the free movement of goods, persons, services and capital. The European Community had failed to achieve one of its most fundamental objectives and to create a true common market. Recognition of this failure encouraged the European Commission to publish a White Paper in 1985 recommending the adoption of a programme designed to achieve a genuine common market by a specified date.

This proposal was eventually given form in Article 8A of the EC Treaty (now renumbered Article 7A after the amendments made by the Treaty on European Union), which required the Community to adopt measures with the aim of progressively establishing an internal market before 31 December 1992. The internal market was defined as:

'... an area without internal frontiers in which the free movement of goods, persons, services and capital is ensured in accordance with the provisions of the [EC Treaty].'

Quite clearly, the internal market programme was simply an attempt to rejuvenate the initiative towards creating a customs union. The creation of the internal market did not envisage any new policies or competencies for the European Community but merely the consolidation of objectives which had been expressed in the original terms of the EC Treaty.

The single market programme which was to achieve the internal market was a package of over 280 Community laws harmonising the laws of Member States relating to barriers preventing the free flow of goods, persons, services and capital. The programme entailed an extensive legislative agenda harmonising national legal provisions relating to customs procedures, taxation, public procurement, company law, intellectual property and investment. Community measures were required in these fields because the existing disparities between each of the Member States impeded the creation of a harmonious and consistent environment for the production and sale of goods and services and the conduct of commerce.

Of these measures, the vast majority relate to the liberalisation of restrictions preventing the free movement of goods. For example, measures were required to eliminate physical barriers to the flow of goods such as customs procedures, health inspections and checks, inspections to ensure compliance with transportation regulations and bureaucratic procedures conducted to collect information and statistics, all of which hamper the movement of goods.

Equally, technical barriers to trade in goods were also required to be eliminated or reduced. Technical barriers result from the diversity of national regulations and standards for the manufacture of products and, in particular, those necessary to ensure the protection and safety of the consumer. For example, if one Member State refused to certify a particular product as approved for distribution in its territory even though the product had been cleared by the authorities of another Member State, the marketing of the product in the territory of the first state would be impeded. However, if the standard was harmonised throughout the Community, certification in one Member State would allow the goods to move freely throughout the Community.

Since the bulk of these measures concerned the eradication of barriers to trade in goods, promotion of the other three freedoms – persons, services and capital – were given a lesser priority. Fewer measures were proposed in these fields relative to measures for securing the free movement of goods and now that the deadline for completion of the project has passed, this shortcoming has become noticeable. Hence, the Community is subject to the criticism that its laws in the area of the free movement of persons have failed to keep pace with the process of liberalisation undertaken, particularly in the area of trade in goods.

At present, the Community law concerning the free movement of persons consists of the basic EC Treaty provisions (Articles 48–58), the fundamental basic regulations and directives in this area and the various provisions which have been enacted for the purposes of securing the right of establishment for professionals.

Articles 48, 52 and 53 of the EC Treaty have been given direct effect in the past by the European Court: see *Van Duyn* v *Home Office* (1974) and *Reyners* v *Belgian State* (1974). However, none of these provisions is stated with a sufficient degree of precision to confer the detailed rights required to prevent Member States eroding the freedom of movement of persons and the right of establishment.

The legal regime regulating the freedom of movement of persons consists of three primary measures. First, Directive 64/221 states the grounds justifying the exclusion of persons from the scope of the freedom granted by Article 48. Second, Regulation 1612/68 eliminates the ability of a Member State to reserve positions of employment for its own nationals. Third, Directive 68/360 deals with the rights of workers to obtain residence permits. Finally, Regulation 1251/70 regulates the rights of a worker to remain in a Member State once the period of employment has expired.

These provisions have been the core of the freedom of movement of persons for almost 25 years without radical amendment. However, recognition of the frustration of the objective of achieving a common market was not confined to the free movement of goods but also extended to the movement of persons. Nevertheless, the single internal market programme contained few measures to reduce the powers of Member States to deny Community nationals the right of free movement.

The few measures contained in the programme concerning the movement of workers related to the mutual recognition of qualifications among the Member States. If a particular qualification is required before an individual can obtain a position, the denial of such a qualification to a non-national would effectively amount to the withdrawal of the right of free movement. Hence, a number of measures dealt with the mutual recognition of qualifications to facilitate the effective exercise of the right of establishment.

Where a profession has been the subject of harmonising legislation, Member States are prohibited from implementing these measures in a manner likely to prevent their proper functioning: see *EC Commission* v *Germany (Re Restrictions on the Legal Profession)* (1989). The position as regards professional qualifications that have not been the subject of harmonising legislation is that Member States are entitled to specify equivalent criteria or conditions required for appointment to a position, to ensure that appointees possess sufficient knowledge and qualifications, and subject to the proviso that there can be no discrimination on the grounds of nationality: *UNECTEF* v *George Heylens* (1989).

The conclusion is therefore that the Community legislation for the freedom of movement of workers and the freedom of establishment is no longer adequate in relation to the liberalisation which has occurred relative to the movement of goods and, to a lesser extent, services and capital. It is the most ill-defined of the four freedoms, notwithstanding the fact that the objective of the internal market programme was to advance this freedom as much as the other three freedoms.

At the same time, the whole freedom of movement of workers may, in the course of time, become redundant. Article 8 of the EC Treaty, as amended by the Treaty on European Union, establishes the concept of citizenship of the European Union. Every person holding the nationality of a Member State is to be considered as a citizen of the European Union and such citizens are entitled to enjoy the right to move and reside freely within the territory of all Member States. This right is subject only to the limitations and conditions laid down in the EC Treaty and by the measures adopted to give effect to this right.

HLT Publications

HLT books are specially planned and written to help you in every stage of your studies. Each of the wide range of textbooks is brought up-to-date annually, and the companion volumes of our Law Series are all designed to work together.

You can buy HLT books from your local bookshop, or in case of difficulty, order direct using this form.

The Law Series covers the following modules:

Administrative Law	Evidence
Commercial Law	Family Law
Company Law	Jurisprudence
Conflict of Laws	Land Law
Constitutional Law	Law of International Trade
Contract Law	Legal Skills and System
Criminal Law	Public International Law
Criminology	Revenue Law
English Legal System	Succession
Equity and Trusts	Tort
European Union Law	

The HLT Law Series:
A comprehensive range of books for your law course, and the legal aspects of business and commercial studies.

Each module is covered by a comprehensive six-part set of books

- ● Textbook
- ● Casebook
- ● Revision Workbook
- ● Suggested Solutions, for:
  - ● 1985-90
  - ● 1991-94
  - ● 1995

Module	Books required	Cost

To complete your order, please fill in the form overleaf

Postage	
TOTAL	

Prices (including postage and packing in the UK): Textbooks £19.00; Casebooks £19.00; Revision Workbooks £10.00; Suggested Solutions (1985-90) £9.00, Suggested Solutions (1991-94) £6.00, Suggested Solutions (1995) £3.00.

For Europe, add 15% postage and packing (£20 maximum). For the rest of the world, add 40% for airmail (£35 maximum).

ORDERING

By telephone to 01892 724371, with your credit card to hand

By fax to 01892 724206 (giving your credit card details).

By post to:

HLT Publications,
The Gatehouse, Ruck Lane, Horsmonden, Tonbridge, Kent TN12 8EA

When ordering by post, please enclose full payment by cheque or banker's draft, or complete the credit card details below.

We aim to dispatch your books within 3 working days of receiving your order.

Name

Address

Postcode

Telephone

Total value of order, including postage: £

I enclose a cheque/banker's draft for the above sum, or

charge my ☐ Access/Mastercard ☐ Visa ☐ American Express

Card number

Expiry date

Signature

Date

Publications from **The Old Bailey Press**

Cracknell's Statutes

A full understanding of statute law is vital for any student, and this series presents the original wording of legislation, together with any amendments and substitutions and the sources of these changes.

Cracknell's Companions

Recognised as invaluable study aids since their introduction in 1961, this series summarises all the most important court decisions and acts, and features a glossary of Latin words, as well as full indexing.

Please telephone our Order Hotline on 01892 724371, or write to our order department, for full details of these series.